Practical Oracle Cloud Infrastructure

Infrastructure as a Service, Autonomous Database, Managed Kubernetes, and Serverless

Michał Tomasz Jakóbczyk

Apress®

Practical Oracle Cloud Infrastructure: Infrastructure as a Service, Autonomous Database, Managed Kubernetes, and Serverless

Michał Tomasz Jakóbczyk
Warszawa, Poland

ISBN 978-1-4842-5505-6   ISBN 978-1-4842-5506-3 (eBook)
https://doi.org/10.1007/978-1-4842-5506-3

Managing Director, Apress Media LLC: Welmoed Spahr
Acquisitions Editor: Jonathan Gennick
Development Editor: Laura Berendson
Coordinating Editor: Jill Balzano

Cover image taken in Swiss mountains by Michał Jakóbczyk

Distributed to the book trade worldwide by Springer Science+Business Media New York, 233 Spring Street, 6th Floor, New York, NY 10013. Phone 1-800-SPRINGER, fax (201) 348-4505, e-mail orders-ny@springer-sbm.com, or visit www.springeronline.com. Apress Media, LLC is a California LLC and the sole member (owner) is Springer Science + Business Media Finance Inc (SSBM Finance Inc). SSBM Finance Inc is a **Delaware** corporation.

For information on translations, please e-mail rights@apress.com, or visit http://www.apress.com/rights-permissions.

Apress titles may be purchased in bulk for academic, corporate, or promotional use. eBook versions and licenses are also available for most titles. For more information, reference our Print and eBook Bulk Sales web page at http://www.apress.com/bulk-sales.

Any source code or other supplementary material referenced by the author in this book is available to readers on GitHub via the book's product page, located at www.apress.com/9781484255056. For more detailed information, please visit http://www.apress.com/source-code.

Printed on acid-free paper

To my family, friends, and colleagues

Table of Contents

About the Author

Michał Tomasz Jakóbczyk is a cloud integration architect at Oracle Corporation and works in Europe. He consults with and provides advice to clients on integration architecture and cloud infrastructure. He holds a bachelor of science in engineering in the field of decision support systems – computer science from the Warsaw University of Technology. He speaks Polish, English, and German.

About the Technical Reviewer

Michelle Malcher is a security architect for databases at Extreme Scale Solutions. Her deep technical expertise in areas from database to security as well as her senior-level contributions as a speaker, author, Oracle ACE director, and customer advisory board participant have aided many corporations in the areas of architecture and risk assessment, purchasing and installation, and ongoing systems oversight. She is on the board of directors for FUEL, the Palo Alto Networks user community, and she volunteers for the Independent Oracle Users Group (IOUG). Michelle has built out teams for database security and data services and enjoys sharing knowledge about data intelligence and providing secure and standardized database environments.

Acknowledgments

First and foremost, I would like to thank

- Michelle Malcher, Łukasz Antoniak, Tomasz Sawiński, Piotr Kusiak, and Igor Sawczuk for their feedback and technical reviews

- Wojciech Wcisło and his Oracle consulting team in Warsaw for creating an incredible atmosphere at work

- Ben Lackey at Oracle for his support

- Jill Balzano, Jonathan Gennick, Kim Wimpsett, and Laura Berendson at Apress for everything involved in making this book real

This book is a result of my dreams to unleash my creativity and share my valuable technical knowledge and experience with other technology enthusiasts in the structured form of a technology handbook. I am a great believer in the importance of a learning-oriented mind-set, and I would like to say to everyone who contributed to that throughout my entire life and career: thank you!

Introduction

Welcome to *Practical Oracle Cloud Infrastructure*. I have written this book to provide readers with a fast-paced, hands-on introduction to the most important aspects of Oracle Cloud Generation 2. This handbook is meant to guide you using a series of practical exercises that will give you the opportunity to learn by doing. After having read this book, you will have a broad understanding of various cloud infrastructure concepts. Moreover, you will be able to build cloud-based applications that leverage different types of cloud services available on Oracle Cloud. I am a great fan of automation applied to cloud infrastructure provisioning, system configuration, and the software development lifecycle. Throughout this book, you will learn to employ a large amount of automation and apply an infrastructure-as-code approach.

Who Is This Book For?

This book is meant for cloud architects, consultants, engineers, computer science, and technology students, as well as anyone who would like to learn about infrastructure as a service delivered on the Oracle public cloud. To fully benefit from the exercises described in this book, you should have a working knowledge of Linux or the macOS shell, a basic understanding of IP networking concepts, and some exposure to programming.

How to Work with This Book?

This book is code-driven. While reading this book, you will see I am assuming that you are using the code that accompanies this book. This is why you should clone the Git repository that holds all the code snippets, source code, and configuration file templates. You will find the relevant Git repository at these links:

```
https://github.com/mtjakobczyk/oci-book
www.apress.com/source-code
```

The code snippets are meant to be executed in macOS (Terminal), Linux (Shell), or Windows Subsystem for Linux. If you are on Windows, please use Windows Subsystem for Linux or launch a virtual machine with a Linux guest system. The Git repository is composed of a number of directories, one for every chapter. Inside each directory, you will find a chapter-specific `README.md` file. These `README.md` files use convenient Markdown notation and include all the code snippets needed to make it easier and faster to work with the code by copying it straight to your terminal. Furthermore, if something changes in Oracle Cloud, the code in the Git repository will be updated accordingly so that you will be able to work with an updated version of the code snippets. Just make sure you periodically check for updates and pull the latest versions. The majority of application code in this book is written in Python. If you do not know Python, you should still be fine, because the most important code pieces are explained.

I am aware that nowadays a small number of people read technical books from the beginning to the end. Yet, I strongly recommend you work through this book in an ordered manner, reading and more importantly doing hands-on exercises starting from Chapter 1 and continuing chapter after chapter. If you just want to get some basic understanding, read Chapter 1 and complete the exercises covered in Chapter 2. If you are interested in automation, continue to Chapter 3. To fully benefit from the hands-on exercises included in this book, it is recommended that you set up your environment as described in Chapters 3 and 4 before moving on to subsequent chapters. This is because the exercises from Chapters 5 to 9 assume that the environment configuration covered in Chapters 3 and 4 is still in place. All in all, my advice is to read and work through this book chapter after chapter.

Cloud Account

To perform the exercises included in this book, you will need an Oracle Cloud account. At the end of Chapter 1, you will learn how to subscribe to a new Trial cloud account that allows you to work with Oracle Cloud for 30 days at no cost. If you want, you can work using a paid account, but just be aware that some services will incur costs. I have created the exercises for this book using mainly my personal, paid cloud account.

Managing Change

Nowadays, cloud services are evolving at an incredible pace, sometimes introducing breaking changes. This is especially important for the relatively new services such as Oracle Kubernetes Engine and Oracle Functions that are covered in this book. If you experience that something works in a different way than described, make sure you pull the latest version from the GitHub repository associated with this book and read the README.md file for a particular chapter.

## CHAPTER 1

Introducing Oracle Cloud Infrastructure

Technology is constantly evolving and is now one of the foundations of our everyday lives. Computerization, digitalization, and the Internet have brought us to the *information age* we live in. Nowadays, nearly every kind of business requires information technology to exist and grow. Software is employed to serve a diverse range of business, technical, and industrial processes, while hardware is used to run the software, store data, and provide interconnectivity.

During this information age, the way we use technology has gone through a number of turning points. One of them was the emergence and spread of the *open source* movement that sparked communities around the globe to build new tools, platforms, and applications at a pace unseen before. The freedom in distribution and the transparence of the source code made it possible to deliver solutions faster by creating derivative works and reusing existing components. What was initially seen as part of the hacker culture and a niche market was eventually adopted by enterprises and large organizations.

The arrival of business-ready *cloud computing* was another turning point. This time, the subject of change was the perception of seeing and using hardware and software systems as a whole. This chapter will explain this statement step-by-step and be your guide through the most important concepts associated with cloud computing. Furthermore, it will introduce you to Oracle Cloud Infrastructure, which is Oracle's infrastructure-as-a-service (IaaS) public cloud platform that delivers compute, storage, and networking capabilities. It also hosts various platform-as-a-service (PaaS) capabilities such as a fully managed Oracle Autonomous Database, container orchestration engine, serverless computing, and others.

1

© Michał Tomasz Jakóbczyk 2020
M. T. Jakóbczyk, *Practical Oracle Cloud Infrastructure*, https://doi.org/10.1007/978-1-4842-5506-3_1

Cloud Computing Characteristics

Running a business nowadays involves process automation. A single business process can consist of scheduled activities, user interactions, data transformations, external system calls, and even machine control. It usually engages numerous computer programs we know as *software*. Software runs on hardware, at least in theory.

Hardware and Virtual Resources

Hardware, as opposed to software, takes physical space and requires proper cooling and a reliable power supply. In the traditional model, small businesses place their backend equipment in server rooms, usually on-site. For medium and larger companies, their local server rooms are used as network connection points to remote data centers where production backend systems operate. The organization still manages its own equipment but rents space for servers, power supply capacity, and network resources (like public IP addresses, network throughput, dedicated links) in a professional third-party data center that also serves other customers. This is called a data center *colocation* model. Alternatively, an organization can invest in a fully owned data center, which typically incurs the biggest cost. All in all, the traditional model entails relatively large *capital expenses* that include the money spent on purchasing and maintaining the fixed assets like equipment.

What actually matters is not the hardware itself but the compute power, storage, and networking *resources* that are available to applications. All in all, software needs to process its business logic in an efficient way; persist its data persisted to reliable, failsafe storage; and connect to any external systems it has to interact with. Usually, it does not matter if the software is running on virtualized or dedicated physical hardware. As a matter of fact, a number of unrelated computer programs can be executed on individual virtual machines that are launched on the same physical rack server.

From a management point of view, it is much more convenient to see the hardware entities such as CPUs, memory, or storage somehow decoupled from the physical hardware, represented as *virtual hardware resources* that are pooled together and made ready to be allocated to the compute instances used by a number of applications and systems that belong to a diverse range of projects and different tenants (cloud accounts). Figure 1-1 presents this concept using an illustration.

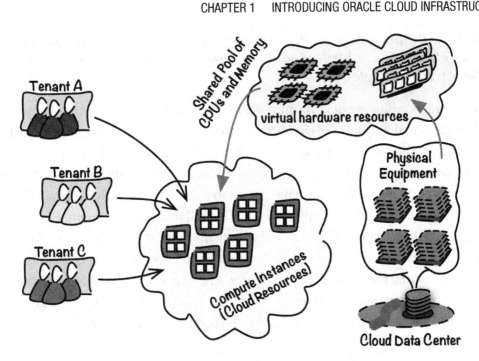

Figure 1-1. *Virtual resources and hardware*

Cloud Computing Definitions

Some people mistakenly assume cloud computing and the public cloud are the same. They are not. You can apply a *cloud computing approach* with your own hardware infrastructure. Let's take a look at the two definitions I like the most.

The National Institute of Standards and Technology (NIST) has coined a definition that, in my opinion, highlights the essence of cloud computing.

> *Cloud computing is a model for enabling ubiquitous, convenient, on-demand network access to **a shared pool of** configurable computing **resources** (e.g., networks, servers, storage, applications, and services) that can be **rapidly provisioned and released with minimal management effort or service provider interaction**. This cloud model is composed of five essential characteristics, three service models, and four deployment models.*[1]

Gartner, a well-known research and advisory company, has proposed another definition that points out two further characteristics (emphasis added).

*Gartner defines cloud computing as a style of computing in which **scalable and elastic IT-enabled capabilities are delivered as a service** using Internet technologies.*[2]

The rapid provisioning of IT resources that are available in a shared pool is one of the fundamental attributes of cloud computing. This *rapid provisioning* boosts the productivity by shortening any unwanted waiting time, eliminates possible errors through the repeatability of underlying automation, and eventually entails cost savings. Resources that are no longer in use may return to a *shared pool*, which allows other projects to reuse them, thereby optimizing the overall resource allocation. *Elasticity*, provided by resource scalability, is a key factor to optimize the resource use. Moreover, it can help to increase robustness by allowing computer systems to react to unexpected failures and varying the performance footprint. Resources of closely related types, such as compute, networking, different types of storage, and many more, are grouped together and made available as web services. Figure 1-2 illustrates the key characteristics of cloud computing.

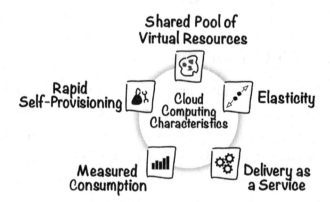

Figure 1-2. *Cloud computing key characteristics*

The next sections will describe these characteristics in more detail. But first let's take a closer look at what the word *provisioning* actually means.

Provisioning

The Oxford Dictionary defines the verb *to provision* as "the action of providing or supplying something for use." Well, the word *action* may sound a bit too granular. In the real world, providing a resource is always associated with a process of some kind.

Traditional Provisioning Process

For an existing data center site, an infrastructure provisioning process usually starts with a request that gets reviewed and approved, eventually becoming an order. This initial step is preceded by the relevant capacity planning effort to identify what equipment and software are really needed as part of the data center expansion. If we have all the requested hardware components and software licenses in stock, we are lucky. The order fulfillment can begin. We need to fetch the hardware components; register each of them, often including their associations in an assets catalog; and then install, configure, connect together, and enable them for use.

Things can get slightly more complicated if we still have to purchase the equipment. First, the buying itself may require a multilevel approval that takes even more time. Second, the provisioning process additionally involves procurement activities. Unless our company uses an automated procure-to-pay solution, all steps such as selecting the supplier, verifying the contract against policies, placing an order, submitting accounting invoices, and processing payments would involve a lot of lengthy human activities. All in all, it costs money and can take a lot of time.

Imagine now that we are responsible for resources in a small data center that is used by our company. What would happen if we were asked to launch a completely new environment for one of the development teams as soon as possible? If we follow the traditional approach, the long-lasting process would kick off. First, we kindly ask our colleagues to conduct the capacity planning to assess their needs and fill the request that would become subject to approval. As soon as the approvals have been collected, we check if the equipment is in stock and spawn a procurement subprocess for the missing components. Unless we are using a well-integrated procure-to-pay business software, the procurement subprocess itself may take a lot of time before the final purchase order gets fulfilled. Figure 1-3 uses a standard business process modeling notation (BPMN) to outline the traditional provisioning process.

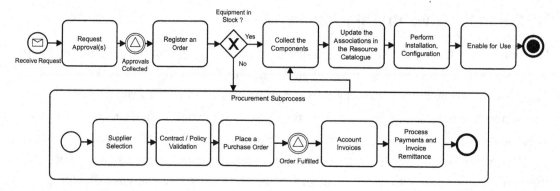

Figure 1-3. *Traditional provisioning process*

Rapid Self-Provisioning Process

In the world of cloud computing, the word *provisioning* is often encountered as the state of your virtual resource observed while your new resource instance is being launched. The definition from NIST emphasizes rapid provisioning with minimal service provider interaction. This is the key. Minimal service provider interaction means that there is no need to submit a ticket and wait until the resources are semimanually set up for you by a team of administrators. Instead, the process is fully automated, and as soon as you trigger an instance launch, the order will be validated against your permissions and quota, also known as *service limits*, and passed to the rapid provisioning engine. The engine will use various profiles and templates to launch and configure the resources. Figure 1-4 outlines the self-provisioning process.

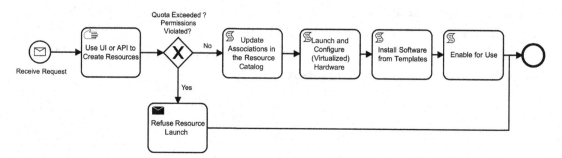

Figure 1-4. *Rapid self-provisioning*

Actually, we could say that a scripted configuration is nothing new. It has been standard for a few years now, gaining more popularity each year. For example, we can pick Ansible and use its playbook-based agentless automation to install a software stack on multiple servers parallelly. In this way, we are not only speeding things up but also allowing the automation to perform the same task on a number of machines, decreasing the risk of mistakes. This is how many administrators already achieve their daily tasks. The more you automate, the less time you spend on repeatable tasks. The vast majority of operators still limit the scope of their automation to their software stack rollouts. Hardware seems to be continually handled rather manually. Well, you still need to plug a cable into a switch or boot a new machine, don't you? Rapid self-provisioning, on the other hand, necessitates complete end-to-end automation for both the hardware and the software components. Yet, hardware provisioning automation doesn't seem easy. Even though it is absolutely possible to use a remote bare-metal machine boot using Preboot Execution Environment (PXE) booting, we rely nowadays more and more on virtualized pools of resources. Virtualization makes rapid resource provisioning much easier.

Elasticity and Scalability

An *elastic* object is able to return to its regular shape voluntarily, after it has been stretched (or squeezed). Such an object is thus highly adaptable to the impact of external circumstances. A web application can be considered highly adaptable or elastic if it is able to handle unexpected peaks of inbound traffic requests. A backend data warehousing extract-transform-load (ETL) engine is reckoned to be very elastic or adaptable if it is capable of staging sudden, extraordinarily large volumes of incoming data loads.

Computer system elasticity can be achieved through *scalability* of the underlying resources. For a modern, stateless web application, the number of containers that expose the API and encapsulate its request processing implementation logic could be increased, even by launching them on additional virtual machines. This action would enlarge the overall compute capacity of a cluster. In other words, we would have more application containers running on a larger set of host instances of the same size added to the cluster to increase the overall system throughput. This is called *horizontal scaling*. In the case of a backend ETL engine, the overall capacity of the attached block storage units for the staging area could be upsized. Put differently, we would add more hardware resources such as block volumes to each machine, keeping the number of machines unaltered. This is called *vertical scaling*. Figure 1-5 presents the two types of resource scaling.

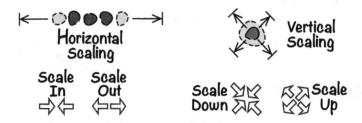

Figure 1-5. *Vertical and horizontal scalability*

If we consider only software architecture, *vertical scaling* may be often seen as easier and more appealing at first glance. If you move an application to a more powerful machine with a larger number of CPUs or simply extend the memory on the existing application host, the software would see new the hardware resources immediately or after a quick reboot. In most cases, there is no need to reconfigure the application. This approach has a major pain point, though. You cannot scale a single machine endlessly up. There will always be a limit in terms of the hardware availability because physical machines and even virtualized resource pools do have limits.

Horizontal scaling may indeed seem unlimited. In theory, we could expand a cluster by adding new machines virtually infinitely. This really crucial advantage of horizontal scaling comes at a cost of the required cluster management. Distributed computer systems have to be specifically designed in a way that it is possible to scale them out. They must be able to handle synchronization and replication across the machines that act as cluster nodes.

A computer system is truly elastic if the resources it uses are dynamically allocated and deallocated in response to the changing demand so that its performance always remains constant. In practice, such autoscaling is possible only with horizontal scaling.

Delivery as a Service

If you look at the definition from Gartner, you will see that the IT capabilities are said to be delivered as a service. To understand what that means and how it fits into the rapid provisioning of resources available in shared pools, let's start by looking at the concept of a shared pool.

Purchasing goods like computer hardware is related to capital expenses. If a project team requires a new server, they could buy one, in theory. Such an investment incurs an expense that has to be considered in the project budget and properly accounted for. This is not a flexible approach, however. By owning the asset, a project team has to maintain the lifecycle of the asset up to its decommissioning. A highly specialized task force team usually has neither people nor time to do this.

Sometimes, you need a set of additional machines just to perform a specific task that is limited in time. For example, you may have to carry out load-and-performance or acceptance tests in a dedicated environment for only a few weeks in every quarter. If you purchase the equipment, it might remain unused for the rest of the time, unless you are somehow able to return it to a resource pool available to other project teams. All resources in a *shared pool* could be used in a measured way only when really needed, thus minimizing their idle time. The project team would no longer own any hardware but rather have their cost centers charged based on the measured usage of the resources. From a project team perspective, this is nothing but a service that entails operational expenses. Furthermore, no hardware ownership results in no need for, or easier, asset management.

The hardware, which is used to back up a shared pool of virtual cloud resources, still incurs costs, usually for the one who is responsible for maintaining it. Such costs are eventually charged to the project teams that have used the virtual resources. To keep the cost split based on the real usage of each individual cloud consumer, the virtual resource consumption must be measured.

For a large organization, employing *self-service* as a core part of its processes can save a lot of effort and eliminate the unneeded waiting time. It boosts the productivity of project teams and individuals who are empowered to take matters into their own hands. A project team would be able to self-provision the required resources of various types (compute, storage, network, etc.) on their own, scale them out in an automated way up to the point in which the system performance meets the requirements, and eventually return them to the resource pool as soon as they are no longer in use. Self-service is possible only when the resource pool management system offers an interface to supervise the resources. The project teams, or *service consumers*, provision, manage, and monitor the resources through an application programming interface (API).

APIs

In the early days, an API was usually understood as a collection of programming language functions encapsulated for reuse in a library. Programmers would call these functions in the code using function headers. Computer program binaries would then link to a dynamic library (`.dll` or `.so`) to execute the implementations of the API functions. With computer systems becoming more and more distributed and interconnected, APIs gained another meaning, this time related to remote procedure calls and web services. Two production-grade API styles for web services are Simple Object Access Protocol (SOAP) and Representational State Transfer (REST). Let's briefly explore them.

SOAP APIs

The Simple Object Access Protocol is a mature standard that defines a role-based, multinode distributed processing model with an initial sender, optional intermediaries, and an ultimate receiver. Message exchange operations and their payload structure are defined in a contract. The payload is usually structured in a strict-schema XML format, ensuring that the format of a message is compliant with the contract. A SOAP-based web service contract is defined in a Web Services Description Language (WSDL) file.

The current version (SOAP 1.2) was standardized in 2007 by W3C in a document called a W3C Recommendation. An initial draft of the protocol was submitted in 2000 as SOAP 1.1 in a W3C Note for discussion. In SOAP, the focus is on custom-defined operations and strict-schema XML data interchange. APIs are designed using a well-defined WSDL format. SOAP is designed in a transport-agnostic way. Two most dominant transports are HTTP and Java Message Service (JMS). Listing 1-1 shows a simplified example of a SOAP request sent over HTTP transport.

Listing 1-1. Sample SOAP Request in HTTP

```
POST /crm/shipmentService HTTP/1.1
Host: 192.168.10.15:8081
Content-Type: text/xml;charset=UTF-8
SOAPAction: "http://example.com/crm/shipments/search"

<?xml version='1.0' ?>
<env:Envelope xmlns:env="http://www.w3.org/2003/05/soap-envelope">
 <env:Header />
<env:Body>
  <p:SearchShipments xmlns:p="http://example.com/crm/shipments">
    <p:shipmentOrigin>WAW</p:shipmentOrigin>
    <p:shipmentDestination>FRA</p:shipmentDestination>
    <p:postingDateFrom>2018-06-25</p:postingDateFrom>
    <p:postingDateTo>2018-06-28</p:postingDateTo>
  </p:SearchShipments>
 </env:Body>
</env:Envelope>
```

REST APIs

REST stands for Representational State Transfer and has been present as a computer science term since 2000. It was introduced by Roy Fiedling in his PhD dissertation on network-based software architectures. Roy writes the following:

> *The key abstraction of information in REST is a **resource**. Any information that can be named can be a resource: a document or image, a temporal service (e.g. "today's weather in Los Angeles"), a collection of other resources, a non-virtual object (e.g. a person), and so on.*[4]

Contemporary RESTful services focus on resource lifecycle events (creation, update, deletion, and read access) represented by the corresponding HTTP methods (PUT, POST, DELETE, GET). The most natural resources are business entities such as shipment, invoice, or sales leads. Yet, business processes without any entity-like meaning, such as order fulfillment or timesheet submission or even nonfunctional processes like an advanced search, can also be represented as REST resources. In this way, we can trigger (usually with HTTP POST) and track (usually with HTTP GET) these processes. An interesting thing is that with REST, we usually avoid the word *contract* and simply talk about *API design*. Contrary to SOAP and its WSDL contract, there has been more than one way to define a REST API. The initial lack of an official standard has encouraged a kind of free-market competition to find the most popular way to design an API. One of the first, somehow indirect, attempts to introduce a standard for REST API design was Web Application Description Language (WADL), with a specification[5] being submitted to the W3C in 2009 by Sun Microsystems. Two years later, the Swagger suite was born and together with RAML and API Blueprint dominated the API design scene. In 2015, the OpenAPI Initiative was born at the Linux Foundation with a goal to create and maintain the ultimate API design standard. This standard is known as OpenAPI[6] and is based on Swagger.

The most popular payload format used for REST APIs is JavaScript Object Notation (JSON), but there is nothing against using XML or plain text in the body of either a request or a response. For some resource lifecycle events, it is reasonable to rely on HTTP status codes with no payload at all. Listing 1-2 presents an example of a call to a nonfunctional process resource responsible for an advanced search. The payload carries search criteria serialized in JSON format. The URL defines the resource over which the search operation is performed.

Listing 1-2. Sample REST Call

```
POST /crm/search/shipments HTTP/1.1
Host: 192.168.10.15:8081
Content-Type: application/json;charset=UTF-8
Accept: application/json

{
    "route": {
        "origin":"WAW",
        "destination":"FRA"
    },
```

```
"postingPeriod": {
   "from": "2018-06-25",
   "to": "2018-06-28"
  }
}
```

Well-structured, contract-driven, enterprise-oriented, but somehow overweight SOAP APIs have been gradually replaced by lightweight and pretty natural REST APIs. It is true that the majority of use cases can be fulfilled with REST APIs at a much lower cost than SOAP. Furthermore, REST is definitely preferred by new projects for small and medium companies, software-as-a-service APIs, IoT edge, and large-scale container-driven backend systems. Various API gateways as well as API management platforms position REST as the default style in the context of API management. These suites usually still support SOAP, simply because it is widely deployed and will stay in use across enterprises for some time, especially in the traditional service-oriented architecture deployments with Enterprise Service Bus (ESB) in the backend. The future of API evolution doesn't stop with REST APIs, however. It is worth observing GraphQL, which, you could say, builds on REST and brings into life the concept of a query-oriented API that combines flexibility with a light footprint. Figure 1-6 presents the evolution of APIs.

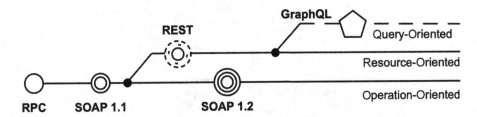

Figure 1-6. *The evolution of APIs*

A slightly different evolutionary direction is taken by gRPC. By design, this remote procedure call (RPC) framework is meant to be machine-readable and programming-language neutral. You define APIs typically using protocol buffers that allow you to specify both services and data structures in a more compact way than using WSDL/XSD in SOAP. There are many code generators that take these definitions and generate code stubs for clients and servers in various programming languages. gRPC is a good fit for high-performance messaging, thanks to a compact binary format used on the wire and the HTTP/2 feature set. The adoption is still in a relatively early phase and focuses on internal APIs, but we may get to the point where selected public-facing APIs are gradually moved to gRPC. This may begin with the APIs involved with streaming or low-power IoT devices.

Cloud Management Plane

Why do APIs matter? If we want to apply cloud computing to our own hardware, we need a system that manages pools of resources, enables rapid self-provisioning, and permits virtual machines to scale horizontally. Such a system, let's call it a *cloud management plane*, must offer an API that can be used by the project teams on a self-service basis. The REST style is a perfect fit for cloud computing because the cloud capabilities, which we will discuss in the next section, can be easily seen as first-class REST resources. When you manage cloud resources, direct API calls are rarely done. Usually, the API is used through a web console, software development kits (SDKs) for various languages, a command-line interface, or an infrastructure-as-code software such as Terraform. In all these cases, API calls are constructed and sent in the background. You only provide the required input. Figure 1-7 presents an overview of the various ways to consume the Oracle Cloud Infrastructure (OCI) API. You will learn more about this in Chapter 3.

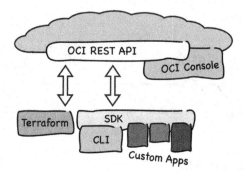

Figure 1-7. *Cloud management plane API ecosystem*

Until now, looking at my two favorite cloud computing definitions, we've explored the key cloud computing characteristics. We analyzed how rapid self-provisioning differs from the traditional provisioning model. Then, we briefly discussed how elasticity can be delivered through scalability. Finally, we learned about the vital role the contemporary APIs have in delivering cloud resources as services. Let's explore now the four core IT capabilities every infrastructure cloud has to deliver.

Core Cloud Capabilities

In the cloud, you build solutions using virtual *cloud resources* that resemble the hardware equipment that provides a physical platform for the software to run. There are different types of cloud resources. Some cloud resource types are intended to be used strictly together with other types of cloud resources. For example, a *routing rules table* is a cloud resource type that always exists within a *virtual cloud network* cloud resource. Together with a few other cloud resource types, they are collectively seen as part of the same *cloud capability*, which is a term you would more often see referenced as an individual *cloud service*. The way individual cloud resource types are grouped together depends on choices made by a particular cloud provider. Usually, you will see four core cloud capabilities typically referenced as cloud services, no matter how global or niche a cloud provider is.

- Compute

- Networking

- Storage

- Identity and access management

These four core cloud computing capabilities provide resources that are often used, in the background, as building blocks to deliver further infrastructure and platform capabilities such as the following:

- Container orchestration

- Managed databases

- Serverless computing

We will now get a glimpse of the four core cloud computing capabilities.

Compute

Executing programs and processing information are often seen as computational activities and considered two of the most important tasks for the solutions running on contemporary cloud computing platforms. One way to perform these activities is to run software on virtual hosts, also known as *compute instances*. You can think of these instances as if they were computer machines running in data centers that are managed by a particular cloud provider. You provision the instances either individually or grouped together using instance pools. You are able to establish a Secure Shell (SSH) or a Remote Desktop (RDP) connection to manage them or the software that they host remotely.

The vast majority of compute instances in the cloud are *virtual machines* (VMs). Multiple VMs that belong to different cloud tenancies (accounts) may be running on the same physical server. This is called *multitenancy*. Multiple tenants eventually share the same physical equipment, even not being aware of that, to leverage sharing economy principles. Using virtual machines makes it much easier for cloud providers to offer more granular compute resources managed in shared pools to their customers. More demanding customers who need to perform high-performance computing (HPC) or use systems that work better with no virtualization usually prefer to deploy their solutions on dedicated hosts with no multitenancy and no hypervisor involved. They then opt for *bare-metal* (BM) compute instances that do not use any hypervisor and are dedicated to a single cloud account at the time. What needs to be said at this stage is that not every cloud provider supports bare-metal machines. Oracle Cloud Infrastructure does. Figure 1-8 illustrates the differences between virtual machines and bare-metal machines.

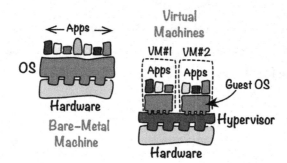

Figure 1-8. *Bare-metal machine vs. virtual machines*

Before provisioning an instance, no matter if it is going to be a virtual or a bare-metal machine, there are two fundamental choices you need to make. The initial configuration of a compute instance is typically done through the selection of the following:

- Hardware profile

- Preinstalled software

A *hardware configuration profile* defines elements that are available for the newly provisioned compute instance such as the number of CPU cores, the memory size, or the disk space on the primary block storage device where the base software gets installed. The choice of a profile will decide whether the instance is going to run on a virtual machine or a dedicated bare-metal host. Every cloud provider usually offers a broad range of hardware profiles you can choose from for the instances you are planning to launch. Depending on the cloud provider, you can encounter different names for the hardware configuration profiles. Some of them are as follows:

- Shape

- Flavor

- Instance type

- Size

Oracle Cloud Infrastructure compute uses *shape* as the name of a hardware profile for a compute instance.

The *preinstalled software stack* is generally called an *image*. First, it must include an operating system. Cloud providers tend to offer just a few operating system distributions, but these options are usually enough to satisfy your needs. Some large-scale cloud providers may even offer their own, branded versions of Linux based on one of the popular distributions. Deploying your cloud solutions on compute instances that work on a branded, vendor-provided operating system distribution will often let you benefit from professional support for operating system questions and issues. To apply the reuse principle to your architecture and infrastructure scripts, you will probably work with the images that ship with some additional preinstalled software on top of an operating system. For example, you may launch your instance using an image that already contains a preinstalled HTTP server, CI/CD tooling, an application runtime of your choice, or even a ready-to-launch application node. Where can you get these kinds of images from? One option is to obtain them directly from your cloud provider or the partner companies that build and maintain such images. Typically, some of the images that originate from the two sources I've just mentioned are offered in a location called a cloud *marketplace* that is maintained by your provider. Another option is to build *custom images* completely on your own. This approach gives you control over how an image is built. You can create a custom image by doing it manually, as a one-time activity, or by automating the entire process. To do the latter, you would write a script that launches an interim compute instance using a particular operating system image, installs the software of your choice, creates a new custom image based on the compute instance, and finally terminates the interim instance. This task can be performed using an open source tool called HashiCorp Packer using its Oracle Builder (oracle-oci) component. This initial effort will pay off, especially if you follow the strategy that assumes to always reprovision compute instances using the newest software versions instead of incrementally applying patches on the instances that have been initially built using an older version of the software.

In the context of compute capability, horizontal scaling typically means changing the number of compute instances as the demand for computing power grows or shrinks. To be more precise, the entire scaling process is more focused on the application nodes that are hosted on these instances. Because of the similarities between the application nodes, the compute instances will often be based on the same custom image with the preinstalled software and the same set of the startup scripts. The combination of an image and startup scripts followed with a few other provisioning choices over the instance shape (hardware profile) or the SSH keys can be materialized in the form of another cloud resource called an *instance configuration*. This type of a resource can be then used to launch and manage scalable groups of instances called *instance pools*.

As you can see, the compute capability is meant to provide the resources that would let you run your software in a similar way to how you do it using physical computers. An aspect that is closely related to data processing is storing that data. We are now going to discuss it.

Storage

Without the possibility to persist both the inputs and the results, any computational processing would make little sense. Various types of data follow different lifecycles that eventually result in nonidentical requirements. What follows is the variety of different cloud resource types that are used to fulfill diverse storage goals. If we skip the higher-level database storage for the moment, we can talk about *storage capability*. We usually break apart this capability into three groups of storage resource types.

- Object storage
- Block storage
- File storage

Object storage is meant to store any amount of data of any type providing redundancy, integrity, data encryption, and various types of access. Data entities such as files are seen as individual *objects* grouped together in a folder-like hierarchy that are called *buckets*. Access policies guard the stored objects and decide who can access them and what actions are allowed. Data is encrypted at rest, and redundant copies are distributed across data centers within a selected region. We often differentiate two types of object storage based on the access frequency.

- Standard *object storage* that offers an immediate, fast access to the data

- *Archive storage* that offers much cheaper way to preserve data at the cost of having to wait a few hours or more to be able to retrieve the data

Some lifecycle aspects such as moving these objects that are rarely accessed to the archive storage can be automated through the use of lifecycle policies. What kind of data do you typically persist in object storage buckets? This type of data can range from application logs, through database backups or data that is stored as part of your content delivery network, to large archives of business data that must be safely stored for a longer period of time to comply with the regulations.

Block storage, contrary to the object storage, plays a supplementary role in the context of the compute capability, even though we classify the resources such as block volumes, volume groups, or backup polices as belonging to the storage capability. The primary type of a cloud resource here is a *block volume*. You can think of it as a nonvolatile memory disk that is a subject of its own lifecycle, but it makes sense to use it only with compute instances such as virtual or bare-metal machines. Actually, nothing spectacular takes place while provisioning a new block volume. The life of a new block volume begins as soon as you attach it to a compute instance, create a filesystem, and mount it. From this moment, you can use the volume as an additional disk for your compute instance. As a matter of fact, depending on the applications you host on the instance, you may store all your application data on this volume instead of using the boot volume that every compute instance has from the beginning. Of course, if you architect a new cloud solution, you will probably choose another type of cloud resources such as object storage or managed database for storing the application data. Yet, you will still discover a lot of different types of applications, especially traditional ones, that will benefit more from using an attachable block volume.

Going further, we can distinguish two ways a block storage volume can be attached to a compute instance.

- Remote attachment over an IP network

- Direct attachment to the physical machine

The interconnectivity between servers and remotely attached volumes is often handled with the use of the *Internet Small Computer Systems Interface (iSCSI) protocol* standardized in RFC7143.

> *The Small Computer System Interface (SCSI) is a popular family of proto-cols for communicating with I/O devices, especially storage devices. (...) The iSCSI protocol (...) describes a means of transporting SCSI packets over TCP/IP.*[7]

The storage volumes that are directly attached to physical machines benefit immensely from the fact that disk operations do not involve any network communication. In combination with flash-based solid-state drive (SSD) devices and the Nonvolatile Memory Express (NVMe) protocol, which enhances block access concurrency with multiple I/O command queues, we receive amazing performance measured in input/output operations per second (IOPS). Nonetheless, this setup imposes a limit on how many storage volumes can be attached to an instance.

Based on the usage pattern, some block volumes, especially those used as persistent data stores, should be regularly backed up. Point-in-time backups are often called *snapshots*. These intermediate states can be either full or incremental. The latter tracks changes from the last backup or volume creation. Policies can be used to drive an automated, scheduled creation of volume backups. Snapshots taken on unmounted volumes are called *cold backups*. In this case, the volume cannot be used during an ongoing backup operation. Taking a snapshot of a volume that remains in use is called a *warm backup*. In most cases, block volume backups are persisted to highly available object storage. What can you do with an archived snapshot? Most often, there are a few options such as restoring the volume and cloning to or moving to a different cloud region.

Earlier in this chapter, we touched upon the meaning and the role of vertical and horizontal scaling. If you consider *vertical scaling*, you will discover two patterns that apply to block volumes. First, you should be able to scale a block volume up vertically by increasing its size. Second, storing all application data on remotely attached block volumes makes it relatively easy to replace the compute instance with a new one that uses a more powerful shape that has more CPUs or memory, because you just need to reattach the volume to the new instance. This operation can be thought of as scaling a compute instance vertically.

Finally, I would like to touch on the fact that a block volume can be optionally attached as read-only. This possibility is pretty handy if you would like to attach a volume just to browse through the filesystem, making sure that nothing gets accidentally written.

While a block storage device is typically meant to be attached to a single compute instance at a time, *file storage* is designed to enable file-oriented data exchange between multiple compute instances. It may be especially useful when these traditional systems leverage active-passive high availability that is built upon a file-based shared state. The shared file storage capability can be implemented using the Network File System (NFS) protocol that was introduced by Sun Microsystems in 1989 in RFC1094.

> *The Sun Network Filesystem (NFS) protocol provides transparent remote access to shared files across networks. The NFS protocol is designed to be portable across different machines, operating systems, network architectures, and transport protocols. (…) NFS assumes a file system that is hierarchical, with directories as all but the bottom level of files.*[8]

Since its introduction, the protocol has evolved from version 3 (RFC1813 in 1995) to version 4 (RFC7530 in 2015). Alternatively, some providers use the Common Internet File Service (CIFS) successor, namely, the Server Message Block (SMB) protocol, to deliver the same shared file storage capability.

From the user's point of view, a shared filesystem is mounted in a similar way as a filesystem present on a block volume. Things are completely different under the hood, and, depending on the chosen protocol, we may encounter some limitations or experience an increased complexity. Designing solutions based on shared filesystems often raises concerns about correct permission checking and concurrent file access. A lot depends on the operating system and network protocol that are in use. For example, Network File System 4 (NFS4) introduces native file locking, while an NFS3-based solution has to rely on an additional network lock manager.

While designing new cloud-based solutions or planning lift-and-shift migrations of the existing traditional systems from their on-premise environments to the cloud, you will probably employ a mixture of the three storage types we've outlined in this section. After having discussed compute and storage capabilities, we'll move to the third core cloud computing capability, which provides the virtual networking resources.

Networking

In a multitier or distributed architecture, the software solutions are often composed of multiple application nodes of different kinds that collaborate with the other nodes in a variety of ways such as the following:

- Exposing their services through web interfaces also known as APIs

- Remotely consuming the functionalities provided by other services

- Maintaining connections to other nodes that compose the cluster

- Accessing external dependencies such as the database or message broker

Cloud resources used to deliver *virtual networking* such as networks, subnets, route tables, security rules, or different types of gateways may seem conceptually similar to the building blocks of traditional, hardware-based networks. Yet, they are radically simplified in the way you configure them. Software-defined networking (SDN) plays a significant role in cloud computing. Cloud infrastructure can be seen as an SDN-enabled infrastructure that lets you create and terminate your isolated virtual overlay networks called *virtual cloud networks* (VCNs), subdivide them into subnets, and use them to roll out various networking patterns applied for your compute instances and other cloud resources. These are the cloud resources seen as part of the networking capability:

- *Virtual cloud networks and their subnets*

- *Reserved public IP addresses*

- *Security lists and security rules*

- *Various types of gateways*

- *Route tables and route rules*

- *Load balancers*

- *Virtual devices used to deliver VPN capabilities*

- *DNS zones*

- *Web Application Firewall (WAF) policies*

Carefully planning your virtual networking is a crucial part of delivering a robust security model for your cloud infrastructure and, likewise, securing your cloud-based solutions. Usually, the design process begins with creating a virtual cloud network and assigning a range of private IP addresses to be used within that network. Typically, a single cloud account may contain multiple VCNs, some of them fully isolated, while the others are interconnected with each other. To keep your infrastructure well-organized, you will provision the compute instances inside another type of cloud resource called VCN *subnets*. VCN subnets are basically a product of a logical subdivision done on a particular virtual cloud network. Every compute instance you provision has to be assigned to one or more subnets through a cloud resource called a *virtual network interface card* (vNIC). A vNIC attached to a public subnet can have a public IP address assigned and, in this way, be reachable from the Internet. Cloud providers own pools of public IP addresses. Typically, the compute instances in public subnets can use the public IP addresses that are dynamically assigned from these pools. When a compute instance terminates, the public IP address used by that instance will be returned to the pool and can be later attached to a completely different compute instance, even one owned by another cloud customer. If you need more control over the public IP addresses, you may benefit from a cloud resource called a *reserved public IP address*. A reserved address always remains allocated for your cloud account, no matter if it is assigned to an instance or not, and you are allowed to reassign it between your instances. A subnet designated as a private subnet prohibits the instances within from having public IP addresses attached. *Security lists* store security rules that add a layer of a software-defined firewall that is enforced before the packets reach compute instances. What these security rules basically do is verify whether the traffic for given IP addresses and ports is indeed allowed to pass through. *Route rules*, on the other hand, are used to properly direct the VCN outbound traffic and allow the packets to reach their next hop, which usually is some kind of *gateway* such as Internet, service, or peering gateway. The right combination of various gateways, route rules, security rules, and private subnets will let you tightly supervise the network and allow only the expected traffic from and to these subnets. *Load balancers* are used to evenly distribute the incoming traffic to the instances grouped in the so-called backend sets. They let you introduce high availability for fault tolerance to your infrastructure or scale the application cluster out to achieve an increased request processing throughput. Some cloud solutions may require access to the systems and data available in your traditional on-premise network. To connect your virtual cloud network with a private network inside your data center, you can either use a IPSec VPN, which tunnels the traffic over public Internet, or leverage a dedicated private connection, which in Oracle Cloud is called FastConnect. In the latter case, your on-premise data center will be either connected to a particular Oracle Cloud data center directly or connected via one of the nearest FastConnect Connectivity Partners that maintains a physical connection to the Oracle Cloud data centers. In both cases, whether IPSec VPN or FastConnect, you will have to create a cloud resource called a *dynamic routing gateway* (DRG), attach it to a VCN of your choice, and alter the VCN route table by creating a new route. The route rule will set the DRG as the destination for the outbound traffic which is addressed to the IP range used in your on-premise network segment. *DNS zones* let you maintain the web domains you own in Oracle Cloud DNS servers and manage the domain zones in detail, for example, by creating custom DNS records. To complete your cloud networking toolkit, Web Application Firewall (WAF) can be leveraged to protect your Internet-facing application endpoints from malicious and unwanted inbound traffic. WAF has more than 200 predefined rules that just need to be optionally configured and enabled. You redirect the domain record you manage in DNS to the WAF endpoint. If the traffic is compliant with the WAF policies that are enabled for the particular endpoint, the traffic is let through to reach the application endpoint.

Cloud resources are the subject of various management actions that should be performed only by authenticated and authorized users. This leads us to the next section to learn about the security topics collectively addressed by the fourth cloud computing capability.

Identity and Access Management

Identity and access management refers to a set of tools and principles that let you define and govern who can access and manage your cloud tenancy mainly by provisioning, changing, and terminating the cloud resources. Issuing a cloud management plane API call or using a management console can be done only by a successfully authenticated *user*. Usually, cloud providers implement two types of cloud users.

- Locally defined

- Retrieved from an external identity provider

Smaller organizations and startups will probably use locally defined users, while large organizations that already maintain their user hierarchy in an identity provider of some kind would rather federate their tenancy with this provider. What is an *identity provider* (IdP)? It is a system that stores and manages the lifecycle of human users, system users, and groups of users. Furthermore, an IdP usually offers authentication services that can be consumed by other systems and their IAM services. Federating your cloud tenancy with an external identity provider means that you are going to reuse the identity data that is already present in the IdP. To keep it simple, the users defined in the IdP will be recognized by your cloud tenancy IAM. Users alone can actually do very little, unless they are assigned to the proper *groups*. Authorization, which is the function that verifies what kind of actions a particular user is allowed to conduct over certain cloud resources, is enforced through *policies*. A policy decides which group is allowed to perform which kind of actions over a set of cloud resources either in the entire tenancy or in an individual *compartment*. Compartments are unique to Oracle Cloud Infrastructure and let you isolate different cloud resources that exist in your cloud tenancy. In this way, a single cloud account can be used to host a number of completely independent and unrelated projects. OCI lets you create hierarchies of compartments. Chapter 4 will cover the compartments in more detail.

When you design a new cloud-based solution or rearchitect an existing system before moving it to the cloud, you may decide that some applications hosted on selected compute instances must be allowed to issue API calls to perform particular tasks over other cloud resources as well. This can be achieved by creating policies for the *dynamic groups* that gather together dynamically included *instance principals* based on matching rules. An instance principal is basically an identity of a compute instance.

In this section, we discussed the four core cloud computing capabilities and the cloud resources they usually incorporate. If you recall the first cloud computing definition I've referenced at the beginning of this chapter, you may wonder what the four deployment models are. We are going to look at them in the next section.

Deployment Models

I've already said that some people mistakenly assume that cloud computing and public cloud are the same. Yet, it is the *public cloud* that the general public, press, and IT professionals most often refer to in their discussions about cloud computing. What does the term actually mean? Well, let's take a look at the three leading deployment models.

- Private cloud

- Public cloud

- Hybrid cloud

The first one is pretty straightforward. If you and your fellow admins reorganize and fully automate the way you serve the virtualized hardware resources that are maintained in shared pools and available as self-service services to different project teams within your organization, then you've built a *private cloud* and probably transformed the IT culture of your organization as well. Congratulations. This is a cumbersome and expensive task, though, because you need to rearchitect your hardware and virtualization layer, purchase or build your own cloud control plane, and hire even more admins to keep an eye on all these resources and services that have become your private cloud. Another major drawback is that your organization still owns all this equipment, which results in increased capital expenses. Well, not everyone is eager to accept these significant expenses that are related to the lifecycle of the hardware equipment, especially in a nontechnology business. Investing money and maintaining a private cloud could be satisfactory for a sizable, mature, and technology-focused enterprise or a public-sector organization. The great majority of organizations prefer to avoid owning too much, if any, hardware. Instead, they opt for outsourcing all costs related to any kind of data center maintenance, if possible.

A *public cloud* delivers various computing capabilities as services much in the same fashion as a private cloud does inside an organization's business network. The difference is in the audience or, to put it properly, in who are the consumers of the cloud service a public cloud offers. A typical *public cloud* provider maintains data centers, either own or collocated, in one or more geographical locations across the globe; owns the hardware; and is responsible for the overall maintenance, operations, security, and service availability. The service consumers, which could be as diverse as individuals, companies, nonprofit organizations, startups, or even government agencies, use secure APIs to rapidly self-provision, scale, and manage the cloud resources that eventually use hardware located in one or more data centers owned by the given public cloud provider.

Providing an accurate definition of *hybrid cloud* won't be as easy as it was with the previous two deployment models. To keep things simple, the most dominant understanding of a hybrid cloud is the use of one or more public cloud providers that are well-integrated and interconnected with a private cloud run on-premise. I am not going to elaborate on hybrid cloud architectures in this book because the topic itself is still somehow fluid in the way it is seen by the industry and much more complex than it may look at first glance.

Large-footprint public cloud consumption raises important questions about the risk of a costly vendor-lock with just one public cloud provider. If all our solutions are exclusively architected and based on a single public cloud, we are susceptible to a potential increase in service fees with no contingency plan. There are other perils to consider in the context of vendor-lock such as the theoretical scenario of a sudden, short-notice service deprecation that may force a rapid and expensive migration project. These concerns lead to the idea of a *multicloud* pattern applied to public cloud consumption. This pattern assumes that we subscribe to infrastructure and platform services provided by more than one public cloud provider. Furthermore, we design applications and workloads in such a way that they can be run in any of our cloud tenancies. Modern container platforms such as Kubernetes help us make this approach a reality. We will discuss Oracle Kubernetes Engine in Chapter 8.

The cloud computing characteristics outlined at the beginning of this chapter and the core capabilities briefly discussed a few sections earlier apply to every kind of cloud no matter what the deployment model and the service model are. Let's take a look at the three service models available.

Service Models

The responsibility is split between a cloud provider and a cloud service consumer. In other words, a cloud account owner's responsibilities depend on the type of service. In this context, we classify the cloud services using three commonly known cloud computing *service models*.

- Infrastructure as a service (IaaS)

- Platform as a service (PaaS)

- Software as a service (SaaS)

The four core cloud computing capabilities (compute, storage, networking, and IAM) are considered part of the most fundamental service model called *infrastructure as a service*. This service model gives you the greatest control over the individual, often low-level, elements such as virtual machines that host your cloud solution. Using cloud resources that, from an architecture point of view, can be easily conceptually mapped to the hardware infrastructure we are used to working with allows you to plan the cloud infrastructure in a similar way to what you would do if you were working with physical hardware. You just do not need to worry about things like power supply, cooling, or physical security enforced in on-premise data centers. Yet, you continue to be responsible for the networking configuration (virtual firewall security rules, routing, VPN setup, etc.), operating systems management (especially updates), and some aspects of the storage capability (logically attaching new block volumes, creating file systems, mounting shared filesystems, etc.). Greater flexibility comes at the cost of more responsibility.

If you would like to focus on designing and implementing cloud software and skip all the facets related to the runtime management, you will probably choose cloud resources such as a managed database or a managed container engine. That kind of cloud resource belongs to the service model called *platform as a service* because it provides you with a managed platform where all platform management tasks such as patching or managing the underlying hardware resources are done by the cloud provider. Your task is to deploy the solutions you've built and scale your platform instance to meet your expectations related to performance. You may encounter many types of PaaS services such as the following:

- Application runtime engines

- Container orchestration engines

- Data and application integration platforms

- API management platforms

- Relational and NoSQL databases

- Messaging solutions

- Big data analytics and business intelligence platforms

Various IaaS and PaaS cloud resources are, on numerous occasions, complementary to each other. You can imagine building your cloud solutions using a combination of virtual machines that host applications that use not only the object storage but a managed database and some kind of messaging cloud service as well.

The third service model, *software as a service*, is all about using the software. In this model, there is little, if nearly any, responsibility to build things. SaaS applications are meant to support your business processes, store process-related data such as customer master data, and let you automate all kinds of data imports and exports the business context requires. Multiple tenants (cloud consumers) usually work with the same cloud application cluster and physical data store, but their data and access are isolated from other cloud accounts. As a SaaS consumer, you do not need to install anything. You usually begin by setting up a tenancy, creating or federating users, assigning proper access rights, performing some startup configuration, and uploading the initial data sets such as your master data along with the historical transactions you would like to see in the new system. As a matter of fact, the list of SaaS application types may seem endless. Here are a few examples:

- E-mail service or an office suite available to the general public

- Customer relationship management used by different companies

- Large-scale enterprise performance management integrated with a cloud suite of enterprise resource planning services

As your company moves more business processes to the cloud, you will probably end up with a diverse set of cloud applications from different cloud providers. As a consequence, you will have to integrate these applications to make smooth data exchange between them possible. Otherwise, your processes won't work. This is the reason why, quite often, cloud architectures that include SaaS applications also encompass one or more PaaS platforms.

At the beginning of this section, I pointed out that different types of cloud services entail differing responsibilities split between cloud consumer and cloud provider. Next, I briefly explained how the three service models vary. Figure 1-9 presents these differences in the form of a single, tabular overview.

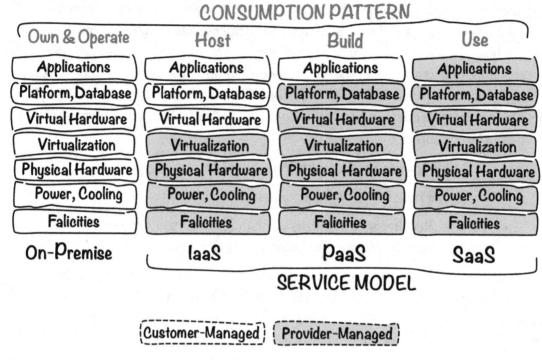

Figure 1-9. *Service models and consumption patterns*

In the next section, we will talk about cost-related matters.

Costs

A wise man once said that there is no such thing as a free lunch. Regardless of whether you are running a private cloud exclusively for your organization or, more likely, consuming public cloud services, someone still has to pay for the underlying equipment, maintenance, powering, cooling, and data center facilities.

From the cloud provider point of view, it is crucial to accurately measure the consumption of cloud services and charge the project teams and the cloud account owners according to what they have really used. What kind of *metrics* are used to track the consumption of cloud services usually depends on the type of cloud resources. For example, the overall compute instance consumption may be measured using the total number of CPU hours that have been used by the running instances within a chosen billing interval such as a calendar month. The usage metrics for the networking capability may be based on gigabytes of the outbound data traffic beyond some threshold.

Object storage utilization may be calculated based on the gigabytes of the stored data and the number of requests sent to the object storage API.

Now, let's take a quick look at the two most common pricing options available from public cloud providers. In the early stage of a software project, your teams are usually working with a number of development and test environments. These kinds of environments tend to constantly change by expanding and contracting the number and the size of the cloud resources. The usage of cloud services can largely differ each month, and, as a result, it may be difficult to predict any future consumption. *Pay as you go* is the pricing option that will work well in this case. On the grounds of metrics-based measurements, you and your cloud provider know precisely the level of consumption and the cost you are going to bear at the end of the billing interval. This pricing option allows one more thing that is especially important for some proof-of-concept or research-and-development activities. Specifically, not every attempt to innovate or simply build a new cloud solution succeeds or finds the reasonable audience to pay its bill in the long term. The pay-as-you-go pricing does not entail any commitment. If you want, you can terminate all your cloud resources at any time, effectively stopping any further charges.

The second pricing model is based on a yearly or even longer *commitment*. You commit yourself that you are going to spend an agreed amount of money on cloud services each month. If you spend less than what you have declared, it is your loss. If you spend more, the *overcharges* would kick in and probably result in additional charges based on the pay-as-you-go pricing model. At first glance, this model makes no sense because it lacks the flexibility of the first one. Yet, the fact that you commit yourself (or rather your organization) to spend a set amount of money on the cloud services each month makes you eligible to benefit from, usually significantly, *discounted prices*. This pricing option seems to be a perfect fit for a stable production environment, where you already know the average monthly consumption. Alternatively, you can decide to switch to the commitment-based pricing from the pay-as-you-go pricing for your development and test environments, as soon as you are able to say that the risk of a sudden project closure is low and it is possible to predict the future consumption. Figure 1-10 presents a cost comparison between a pay-as-you-go (PAYG) option and a commitment-based option with a 20 percent discount.

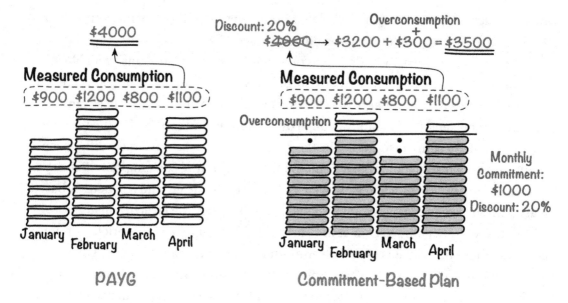

Figure 1-10. *PAYG vs. commitment-based plan*

You should now have a pretty consistent, high-level understanding of cloud computing. It is time to introduce you to the main subject of this book: Oracle Cloud Infrastructure.

Oracle Cloud Infrastructure

Oracle Cloud Infrastructure (OCI) is a suite of infrastructure-as-a-service public cloud services Oracle has made available for the general public, small businesses, nonprofit organizations, government agencies, and large enterprises. OCI delivers a broad range of cloud resources that fulfill core cloud capabilities such as compute, networking, different kinds of storage, and identity and access management. Furthermore, OCI features a number of integrated platform-as-a-service cloud services built on top of the OCI IaaS layer. These include, but are not limited to, two types of fully managed Oracle Database known as Autonomous Transaction Processing (ATP) and Autonomous Data Warehouse (ADW), managed container orchestration using the open source Kubernetes engine, and an integrated Docker container registry. Furthermore, the OCI ecosystem includes a rich choice of diverse templates that use the open source provisioning tool called Terraform to deploy systems such as different NoSQL databases, data integration platforms, and data science workbenches.

Oracle Cloud Infrastructure evolved from the smaller-in-scope Oracle Bare Metal Cloud Service (BMCS) built by a Seattle-based Oracle team of experienced cloud professionals coming from diverse backgrounds such as other public cloud providers, independent software vendors, and the open source ecosystem.

Regions

Oracle has been a global leader in database systems and business applications for decades. Moreover, nowadays, its portfolio of information technology solutions includes middleware platforms, integration tools, business intelligence, analytics products, and more. Since the acquisition of Sun Microsystems, Oracle has additionally become the custodian of the Java ecosystem. Currently, Oracle is on its way to complete the company's transformation to the cloud by adding more advanced features to Oracle Cloud Infrastructure, which is sometimes referenced as the Gen2 cloud infrastructure, moving its PaaS services to OCI and geographically expanding its global footprint by adding new data center regions, as shown in Figure 1-11. You can always find an updated map at `https://cloud.oracle.com/regions`.

Figure 1-11. *Oracle Cloud Infrastructure regions*[9]

Each Oracle Cloud Infrastructure *region* consists of one or more *availability domains* located in a geographical proximity and composed of one or more data centers. The availability domains within a single region are interconnected using low-latency and high-bandwidth links but still physically isolated to help survive sudden natural disasters or, more often, a cascade of equipment failure. The likelihood of two availability domains failing at the same time is rather small, so it should be enough to design your cloud solutions in a way that the cloud resources are replicated across two or even three availability domains in order to achieve truly highly available architecture.

Note   Newly introduced regions may offer a single availability domain either permanently or just for some initial period of time.

Less critical systems can be distributed across two or three *fault domains* within a single availability domain. What does this mean? Hardware inside a single availability domain can be split into physically isolated units of equipment called *fault domains*. In this way, a power unit failure or a cascade of equipment failures within a single hardware unit may be separated from impacting other units. Instances provisioned in one fault domain are less likely to be impacted by the technical problems originating in a different fault domain. Still, if possible, it is recommended to rely on the availability domains if your cloud solutions are meant to survive and remain in operation under unexpected conditions. Figure 1-12 presents the relationships between region, availability domains, and fault domains.

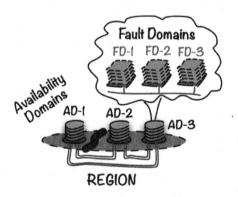

Figure 1-12. *Regions, availability domains, and fault domains*

What kind of workloads are we able to execute on Oracle Cloud Infrastructure? Let's move to the next section to answer this question.

Workloads

When you consider moving an existing solution or building a completely new service in the cloud, you should always begin by looking at the data you are going to process and store in the cloud. Depending on the geographical region and the legal jurisdiction you fall within, you will be often legally obliged to comply with various data protection acts. This is the aspect to which you should actually pay more attention in the beginning than the application architecture planned for your cloud-based solution.

From a purely technical point of view, as long as it is possible to successfully compose a sufficient set of cloud infrastructure resources that collectively serves as a backbone to the cloud solution you are working on, we can say that this kind of application or *workload* is indeed supported by Oracle Cloud Infrastructure. If we were asked to list a few typical types of systems you could run on OCI, we could come up with applications such as the following:

- **Multitier web applications** provisioned using virtual machines or powerful, dedicated bare-metal hosts launched in public and private virtual cloud network subnets. Using a proper mix of public and private subnets allows you to keep an accurate isolation for each application tier.

- Distributed, microservices-oriented, **container-based systems** running on a managed Kubernetes container engine, called Oracle Kubernetes Engine.

- **Database-contained workflows**, transactional or analytical, backed up by a feature-complete, market-leading, fully managed relational database management system, called Oracle Autonomous Database.

- **High-performance computing** (HPC) that supports things like rendering, engineering simulations, or big data workloads.

- Various **traditional applications** lift-and-shifted from their earlier on-premise environment and deployed in the cloud infrastructure that design mirrors the on-premise hardware setup.

- **Serverless** workloads using Oracle Functions that relies on the open source Fn Project.

- Or anything else that requires **additional, peak-time processing capacity** beyond what you are able to deliver with your current infrastructure.

Last but not least, independent professionals could also benefit from subscribing to their own cloud tenancies. Instead of using a dozen VMs, individual developers could consider performing some of their work using cloud-based compute instances in place of heavy-footprint, locally hosted virtual machines. As another example, it is faster to provision a managed Kubernetes engine that consists of multiple worker nodes in the cloud than doing it on a set of virtual machines hosted locally on your laptop.

Services

Each of the core cloud capabilities we've discussed so far in this chapter is a logical grouping of related cloud resource types. For example, the compute capability can be delivered with the cloud resources such as a compute instance, an instance pool, or a compute image. From the naming point of view, Oracle Cloud Infrastructure organizes cloud resource types into *services*. In this section, we will briefly outline and characterize these services and their most common cloud resource types. I've collected them in Table 1-1.

Table 1-1. *Oracle Cloud Infrastructure Services*

Service	Selected Cloud Resource Types
Compute	*Compute instances* provide computational power to run software in the cloud. They are based on *images*, which specify a preinstalled software stack for an instance. They use *shapes* to determine the allocated virtual hardware profile. The instances can be provisioned stand-alone or pooled using *node pools*. A node pool is created based on an *instance configuration* that can be seen as an extended instance definition. A *vNIC attachment* cloud resource attaches a particular compute instance to a virtual network interface card. A vNIC gets created in a selected virtual cloud network subnet and connects the instance to a virtual cloud network.

(*continued*)

Table 1-1. (*continued*)

Service	Selected Cloud Resource Types
Networking	A *virtual cloud network* is a software-defined private network created within an Oracle Cloud Infrastructure region. It can span multiple availability domains. You subdivide it into one or more *subnets*. Traffic is routed based on the route rules created in a *route table* that gets referenced by one or more subnets. Access to the Internet is enabled by an *Internet gateway* you point to as a route rule target. *NAT gateways* let instances in private subnets establish outbound connections to the Internet. A subnet can reference one or more security lists that consist of stateful and stateless *security rules*. The rules effectively furnish a particular subnet with an additional layer of a virtual firewall. An instance that attaches to a *public IP* cloud resource is directly reachable from the Internet as long as the particular traffic is allowed by the security rules that are being enforced.
Block volume	A *boot volume* holds a compute image, provides a root filesystem, and is used to fire up a compute instance. An instance can get additional *block volumes* attached to increase the available total block storage. It is possible to create point-in-time *volume backups* of both types of volumes. The backups can be either incremental or full and optionally driven by automated *volume backup policies.*
Object storage	Data entities of any type are stored as *objects* inside virtual containers called *buckets* that are usually used to group related objects. The objects can be accessed by authenticated and authorized OCI users or with the use of short-living *pre-authenticated requests*. A bucket can be created as an *archive* only, which would decrease the cost of storage but add some time before an object is available for a download. Moreover, it is possible to employ *lifecycle policy rules* to either delete or archive an object after a given period of time has elapsed.
File storage	A shared file storage *file system* can be created in a selected subnet. You attach your compute instance to a particular file system using details provided by a *mount target* cloud resource, which exists within the file system cloud resource. You can use point-in-time views called *snapshots* to implement a backup mechanism for your shared file system.

(*continued*)

Table 1-1. (*continued*)

Service	Selected Cloud Resource Types
IAM	*Compartments* are used to isolate cloud resources that usually belong to different projects hosted under a single cloud tenancy. You define cloud *users* locally or federate the tenancy with an external identity provider. A *policy* consists of policy statements that grant various types of access over cloud resources to *groups* of users. *Dynamic groups* allow matching compute instances to issue API calls permitted for that group.
Load balancing	A *load balancer* distributes the incoming traffic to the instances registered in *backend sets* based on the chosen distribution algorithm.
Database	OLTP applications, which have to support write-intensive, high-throughput, and transaction-intensive operations, can leverage *autonomous transaction processing*. OLAP workloads, which reinforce data warehousing and business intelligence systems, are meant to use *autonomous data warehouse*. The instances of both cloud resource types give you a fully managed Oracle database experience.
Container registry	Each cloud account comes with an associated container image registry where you can store Docker images using public and private *repositories*.
Container engine	The container engine for Kubernetes lets you launch fully managed Kubernetes *clusters* with associated *node pools* for worker nodes that are provisioned as compute instances.
Serverless	Open source Fn Project *functions* can be deployed to the managed Oracle Functions service for serverless computing.
DNS	The domains you own can be redirected to a DNS *zone* where custom DNS *records* can be created.
Web Application Firewall (WAF)	Internet-facing application endpoints can be protected against potentially malicious and unwanted inbound traffic using a set of predefined *WAF policies* ranging from simple captcha or geolocation filters to more sophisticated traffic patterns.

Table 1-1 is meant to give you a high-level overview by describing the selected cloud resources types grouped into Oracle Cloud Infrastructure services. Still, there are more cloud resource types available already, and we should expect even more arriving in the future.

Some cloud resources such as virtual cloud networks or IAM users are free of charge. Others, for example, compute instances, database instances, or load balancers, will incur consumption-related costs. Let's take a closer look at the billings.

Billings

In the "Costs" section earlier in this chapter, I mentioned how the cloud resource consumption is usually measured and what the two pricing options typically encountered are while working with any public cloud provider.

- Pay-as-you-go pricing

- Commitment-based pricing

Oracle Cloud Infrastructure indeed offers a pay-as-you-go pricing option. This is the default pricing option for a new cloud tenancy you create on your own. The consumption is measured based on different kinds of metrics, depending on a particular cloud resource type. At the end of each month, your credit card is charged, and you eventually receive an invoice. It's as simple as that. This option is a good choice for an evaluation phase, for prototyping, or when you are simply unable or do not want to make any estimate of the regular service consumption in future months. No commitment gives you full flexibility to scale your consumption down or up, any time you want, with no need to pay for unused credits.

I've just mentioned the word *credits*. We will learn why by discussing how Oracle offers commitment-based pricing. In 2018, Oracle announced *universal credits* as the term associated with its purchasing model for this kind of consumption. A customer who feels confident about their regular cloud services consumption can enter into an agreement with Oracle and consequently purchase a number of universal credits for a discounted price. At the time of writing, the shortest commitment possible is 12 months. The discount can be significant, but it may depend on the commitment period and the number of purchased credits. Universal credits can be spent on any type of Oracle Cloud Infrastructure setup and a large number of various PaaS services. At the time of writing, this model makes it possible to completely change the consumption pattern under the same agreement. For example, you could move your application from a multitier architecture built on a large number of virtual machines to a microservices-based system running on Oracle Kubernetes Engine whose worker nodes are backed by fewer but more powerful bare-metal hosts. After this change, your credits would be simply consumed by resources related to your new setup.

Note   As with every kind of business, pricing models can change rapidly; therefore, please refer to the official documents or sales representatives to get the most up-to-date pricing options. You can find more details at `https://cloud.oracle.com/pricing/options`

Companies and organizations that are already using Oracle Database may be eligible to decrease their cloud-based Oracle Database costs even further by choosing the *bring-your-own-license* (BYOL) option. First, you have to make sure that your current on-premise license is compliant with this option. If confirmed, to leverage lower charges, you just need to check the appropriate box or pass the required API request parameter while provisioning a new instance of any Oracle Database type that is available on Oracle Cloud Infrastructure.

The most convenient way to visualize the costs incurred by various types of cloud resources is to use the billings view in the OCI Console, as shown in Figure 1-13. You can use filters to see the charges for a selected period of time.

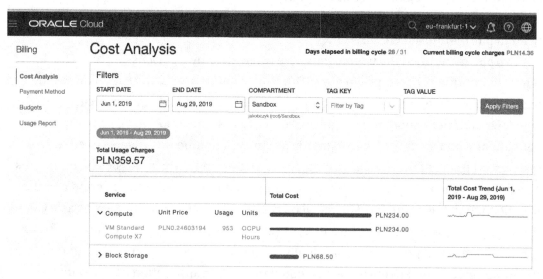

Figure 1-13. *Viewing billings in the OCI Console*

No matter which pricing option your cloud account is subject to, you or your tenancy administrators will probably want to see the *aggregated cost split* of the consumed cloud resources between each business unit or project. Oracle Cloud Infrastructure provides two tools that can help you make the cost split visible: compartments and cost-tracking tags. You will learn about compartments in Chapter 4 where we take a closer look at how to organize a project hierarchy. Using multiple compartments and attaching cost-tracking tags to cloud resources will result in additional filters you can apply in the billings view in the OCI Console.

Support

At some point in time, it is inevitable that you will find yourself in need of some assistance. First, you may have questions related to cloud services to which you cannot find straightforward answers in the documentation. You may even spot some cloud service issues that have to be explained and, if confirmed, solved. In all likelihood, however, your first service requests will be associated with *increasing service limits*.

What is a service limit? I would say it is an aid used by the cloud provider to supervise the greatest possible consumption of various types of cloud resources and avoid any potentially hazardous oversubscription. If this sounds a bit vague, let me give an example that should shed some light on the practical implications for cloud consumers. Imagine a hypothetical situation in which there are exactly 1,000 bare-metal machines with 52 CPUs each in the first availability domain of a particular region. What would happen if all of them were in use, with some running virtual machines and others being dedicated to a single tenant, while a new customer is trying to provision another compute instance? Well, the provisioning process would most likely fail, due to a missing physical CPU in a pool. To avoid such situations, the cloud provider keeps track of the granted service limits on each customer for each cloud resource. For example, your cloud account may have service limits set in a way that you are allowed to provision no more than 30 VMs with 1 CPU each, 10 VMs with 2 CPUs, and 1 bare-metal machine with 52 CPUs, all in a particular availability domain (AD). In this way, the cloud provider would be aware that you can self-provision up to 40 VMs that would consume 50 CPUs in total and one additional bare-metal machine that requires 52 CPUs. Adding up service limits from all cloud accounts, the cloud provider is able to see whether the physical resources in a particular AD are able to serve all virtual cloud resources that may get provisioned and react properly.

Before you provision your target architecture, you need to make sure your service limits will let you create the cloud resources you want to use. The standard service limits you start with using a trial account are set to really low values, so you may find yourself needing to get some of them increased almost immediately. Although the task itself is done by the support team, your responsibility is to create a new service request and provide the details of what exactly has to be increased. You can do this in the OCI Console, as shown in Figure 1-14.

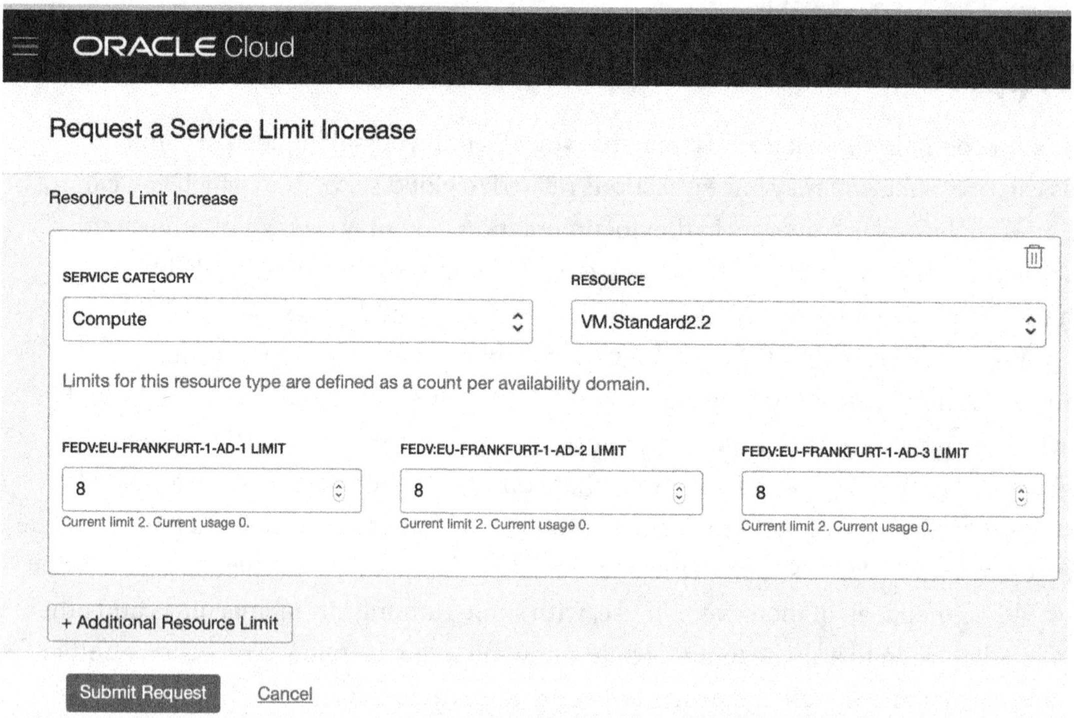

Figure 1-14. *Increasing service limits in the OCI Console*

Other types of service requests have to be submitted through the Oracle Cloud support portal. You can find it at https://support.oracle.com. Remember to select the Cloud Support portal option before or after you sign in.

SLA

Both software and hardware can break at the least expected moment. It is no different in the cloud computing world. The failure of software or hardware in a data center that backs a public cloud platform can result in immense problems with the deployed cloud solutions, including service unavailability, interrupted transactions, business processes put on hold, and data corruption. Cloud providers make their best effort to eliminate the risk or mitigate the potential consequences of cloud service failures. Some of them use *service-level agreements* (SLAs) to make a written, official promise about the availability, manageability, or performance of the various cloud resources they host. For example, at the time of writing, Oracle guarantees that a compute region will be available for at least 99.99 percent of time and an availability domain for at least 99.95 percent of time. If these thresholds are not met, Oracle would issue some amount of service credits as compensation. The number of service credits depends on multiple factors such as your cloud consumption in the given month in which a particular SLA was unmet, the type of unsatisfied SLA, and the extent to which the SLA hasn't been met expressed as a percentage. Service credits can be used in one of the future billing periods as additional credits to pay for cloud resource consumption and, in this way, effectively decrease either your PAYG charges or any potential overcharges on a commitment-based plan.

Note   SLAs and their rules can change in an instant; therefore, please refer to the official documents or contact sales representatives. You can find more details at `https://www.oracle.com/cloud/iaas/sla.html`.

Let's take a look at a simplified example. Please note that, at the time you are reading this, the rules or even the entire process might have changed, so treat this as an introduction to the topic of cloud SLAs. Figure 1-15 illustrates the scenario we will discuss.

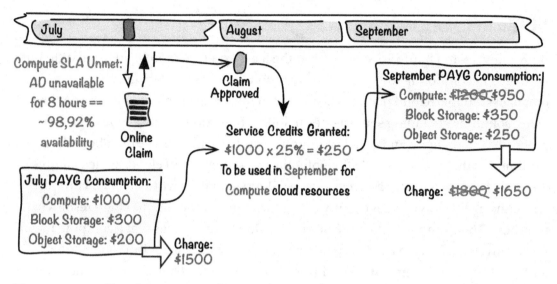

Figure 1-15. *Cloud SLA example*

You are running an application in your pay-as-you-go cloud tenancy. The application nodes are operating on multiple virtual machines deployed in a fault-tolerant way and spread across two different fault domains within one availability domain. The compute instances are using block storage for their boot volumes. In addition, the application is persisting business-related data in object storage buckets. Suppose there is an SLA that guarantees that an availability domain (AD) is available at least 99.95 percent of time in each calendar month. If this threshold is not met, Table 1-2 presents the service credits that apply.

Table 1-2. *Service Credit Levels*

AD Availability	Service Credits
99.00%–99.95%	10%
Less than 99.00%	25%

What does "an availability of an AD" actually mean? At the time of writing, an AD is considered unavailable if you experience no external connectivity to the compute instances that are running in at least two fault domains within that particular availability domain. Returning to our example, let's assume you were not able to connect to your application instances for eight hours in July. You collect logs as proof, attach them to an online claim, and submit the claim for approval. Oracle approves the claim at the beginning of August and grants you $250 in the form of service credits based on these two facts:

- Your compute-related consumption in July incurred the cost of $1,000.

- The AD was available less than 99.00 percent of the time in July.

Now, you should be able to decrease the cost of compute cloud resources in September by $250. Again, please remember that this was just an example to illustrate the way some SLAs work. At the time of writing, the rules and SLA thresholds might be completely different, so please refer to the official SLA documentation.

This chapter has equipped you with a lot of introductory information. Now, it is time to sign up for a trial cloud account if you haven't done it already.

Trial

The best way to begin your journey with Oracle Cloud is to sign up for a new *trial cloud account*. At the time of writing, the trial account comes with $300 worth of credits for 30 days. To sign up for an Oracle Cloud trial, go to `https://oracle.com/cloud` and click the Try Oracle Cloud Free Tier button and then click Start for Free. The screen shown in Figure 1-16 will be displayed.

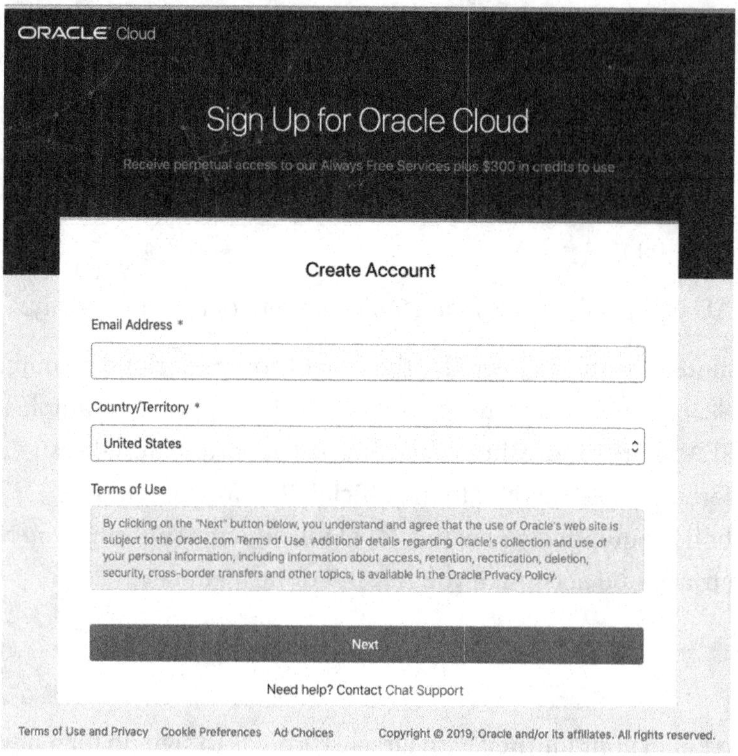

Figure 1-16. *Signing up for Oracle Cloud*

It usually takes a few minutes to fill in the form and validate your identity through a verification code sent to your mobile number. You will also need to provide your credit card details. This will let you smoothly upgrade your trial account, at the end of the evaluation period of 30 days, to a standard pay-as-you-go account, if you decide to, of course. Furthermore, you can try contacting your regional Oracle sales representative to negotiate more credits and a longer evaluation time for your trial.

The easiest way to recognize whether you are working with a trial or a regular paid account is to look at the top bar in the OCI Console. There will be a narrow purple-white bar with relevant information displayed at the top of the OCI Console. It takes a couple of minutes to fully initialize your new cloud account. During that time, you will see an orange bar informing you about that, as shown in Figure 1-17.

Figure 1-17. *Trial account information bar in the OCI Console*

To keep an eye on your ongoing service consumption, you can observe the Billing widget in the OCI Console. The trial tenancy will display something like what is shown in Figure 1-18. Information in the Billing widget is updated once a day.

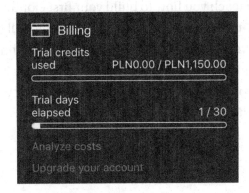

Figure 1-18. *Viewing the trial cloud account billing summary in the OCI Console*

Remember that selected services are additionally discounted during the trial period. This gives you more time to test the services that are a bit more expensive than the rest.

Summary

In this introductory chapter, you started your cloud computing journey by looking at hardware and virtual resources. Immediately afterward, I shared with you my two favorite cloud computing definitions, and we briefly discussed cloud computing characteristics. Next, we talked about each of them in more detail. Then, we covered the difference between the traditional and rapid self-provisioning of hardware resources, elasticity and scalability, and the implications of delivery as a service. As a next step, we took a quick look at the importance and types of APIs. Subsequently, the four core cloud computing capabilities (compute, storage, networking, IAM) were covered.

After that, you were able to read about cloud deployment models and cloud service models. Following that, we spent some time talking about cost-related matters such as metrics, consumption measurement, and two pricing options: pay-as-you-go and commitment-based plans. In the second part of this introductory chapter, I introduced you to Oracle Cloud Infrastructure. You learned about regions, availability domains, and fault domains. Afterward, we listed a few illustrative types of workloads you may run on OCI. The next section was devoted to OCI services and the types of cloud resources they include. Subsequently, I talked about pricing options available on OCI, billing, the role of support, and service-level agreements. Finally, I outlined the way you can sign up for a trial so you can test OCI for 30 days at no cost.

The next chapter will teach you how to build your first cloud-based solution using the Oracle Cloud Infrastructure Console. The basic concepts will be explained on the fly. To learn them properly, we are going to take the long way, avoiding OCI Console wizards that could speed things up. Do not worry; starting from Chapter 3, you will be using automation just as you would do in your daily work with OCI. If you are using a trial account, no costs will be incurred.

Notes

1. https://csrc.nist.gov/publications/detail/sp/800-145/final

2. Gartner, IT Glossary, Cloud Computing. https://www.gartner.com/it-glossary/cloud-computing

3. www.ics.uci.edu/~fielding/pubs/dissertation/rest_arch_style.htm

4. www.w3.org/Submission/wadl

5. https://github.com/OAI/OpenAPI-Specification/blob/master/versions/3.0.0.md

6. https://tools.ietf.org/html/rfc7143

7. https://tools.ietf.org/html/rfc1094

8. https://cloud.oracle.com/regions

CHAPTER 2

Building Your First Cloud Application

This chapter shows how to create a simple cloud infrastructure and run two instances of a custom REST API behind a load balancer. The API implementation presented in this chapter will serve as an example. The main goal is to guide you through the process of building your first cloud-based solution from scratch. Later, in the course of the book, you will also learn how to provision autoscaled instance pools, deploy your apps in Docker containers to Oracle Kubernetes Engine, and execute serverless functions on Oracle Functions. At this stage, however, let's focus on the foundations and use standard virtual machines.

There are multiple ways you can talk to an Oracle Cloud Infrastructure cloud management plane. In this chapter, we use the Oracle Cloud Infrastructure Console, which is a web browser interface for managing Oracle Cloud Infrastructure resources. This approach is appropriate only when you want to demonstrate selected capabilities or experiment with the features that are new for you. In the real world, you either automate the entire provisioning process with a dynamic, procedural command-line interface (CLI) or manage the infrastructure as code using declarative Terraform-driven infrastructure descriptors. The automation is the main subject of the third chapter. Moreover, the vast majority of walk-throughs in all the remaining chapters of this book present the cloud automation in action.

© Michał Tomasz Jakóbczyk 2020
M. T. Jakóbczyk, *Practical Oracle Cloud Infrastructure*, https://doi.org/10.1007/978-1-4842-5506-3_2

Planning the Infrastructure

In this section, we will take a look at the cloud application we are about to deliver and plan the cloud resources we will require for it.

Cloud Account

Before you proceed, you need to have a cloud account at your disposal. You will probably use either a trial account or a standard pay-as-you-go account. A trial account will let you complete all the walk-throughs from this book at no cost. If you have a paid account, you just need to remember to terminate (in other words, delete) every resource you build as part of the learning process so you won't be charged.

Tip   How is a new trial account created? See the "Trial" section of the previous chapter.

For some of you, there may be one more option. If the company you work for has an active Oracle Cloud Infrastructure subscription, you may consider asking your colleagues, the cloud admins, to create a dedicated *compartment* (e.g., called Sandbox) where you can complete the exercises from this book. Yet, some cloud resources described in this book and created as part of the hands-on exercises do require tenancy-owner access level; therefore, it is highly recommended you sign up for your own trial account.

Project Compartment

It is not unusual for an organization to use a single cloud account (also called a *cloud tenancy*) to host multiple, sometimes unrelated and isolated, projects. Different cloud providers provide various means to keep unrelated resources apart. Oracle Cloud Infrastructure does that with *compartments* and *tags*. Being aware of this helps you plan because you can easily divide the entire solution landscape into smaller, more granular, separately managed pieces of architecture with fewer components in each piece. In this way, the same cloud account can be used to host multiple development, test, and production environments for numerous projects. Figure 2-1 briefly illustrates that concept.

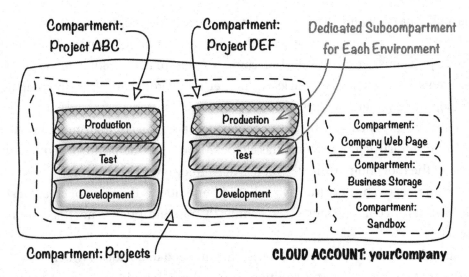

Figure 2-1. *Isolating projects using OCI compartments*

As you can see in Figure 2-1, compartments can reside inside other compartments, putting in place an entire hierarchy. The topmost compartment is called a *root compartment*, and all compartments you create or exist by default are its descendants. This is shown in Figure 2-2.

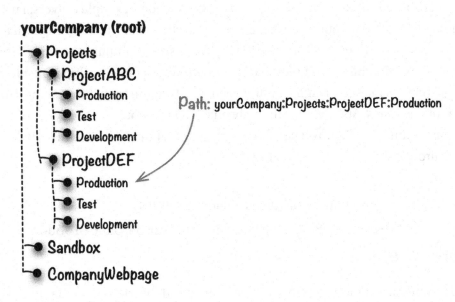

Figure 2-2. *A hierarchy of compartments*

The traditional split into three standard environments (development, test, and production) for each project is not necessarily the best one. I would even say it may lead to governance problems because production compartments remain children to the project compartments. In Chapter 4, you will learn another, more production-friendly compartment composition strategy that separates top-level projects and system compartments.

Well, technically speaking, the root compartment is not a compartment. Every Oracle Cloud Infrastructure resource has a type. All compartments are of *compartment* type, except the root compartment, which is of *tenancy* type. Do not worry if this is unclear at this stage. The only thing you should remember is this: do not create resources directly in your root compartment. It is technically possible, but it is not necessarily a good practice.

It is time for the first architectural decision. You need to decide in which compartment to place the sample solution we are about to build in this chapter. If you do not know, I will help you. Let it be a new Sandbox compartment. We will create it in a few minutes. Now read on.

Application Design

The cloud-based solution we are about to create provides a simple universal unique identifier (UUID) generation service. Each time a client calls the API, they will receive a new unique identifier. In short, a UUID is a fixed-size, immutable identifier created with an algorithm that guarantees that the probability of creating duplicate identifiers is negligible, no matter if run by multiple generators at the same time on the same or different machines. Applications that rely on UUIDs do not require any central identifier administration by design. You can find more details about UUIDs in RFC4122.

Figure 2-3 shows an example of a UUID.

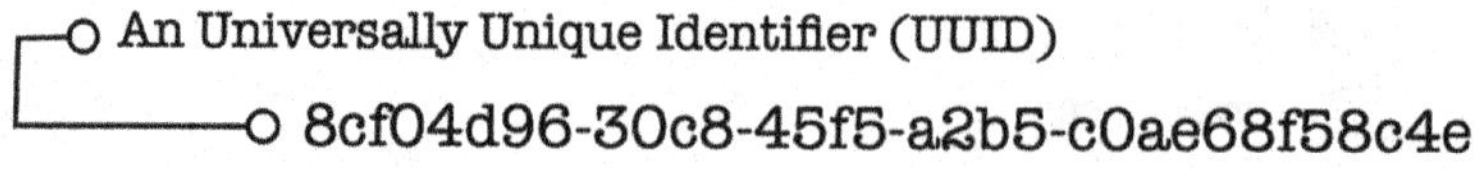

Figure 2-3. *UUID*

The implementation will consist of two independent compute nodes that host the same, stateless UUID generation logic in the backend, expose a simple REST API, and, on every request, return a newly generated UUID (uuid object) and compute node name (generator object) in JSON format, as shown in Listing 2-1.

Listing 2-1. API Response

```
{
"uuid": "8cf04d96-30c8-45f5-a2b5-c0ae68f58c4e",
"generator":"web1"
}
```

The requests are evenly distributed to the endpoints on both API nodes because we place a load balancer in front of them and rely on a simple round-robin policy. Even though this is a trivial demonstration scenario, we are still going to deploy each node in a different availability domain to create a highly available solution. Such a design increases the chances that our cloud service survives a disaster of a single data center. To recap, an *availability domain* can be thought of as a single data center interconnected with the remaining availability domains in the same region using a high-bandwidth link that provides low latency. The likelihood that more than one availability domain fails or gets destroyed at the same time is very low. Figure 2-4 shows a sketch of the solution components and how they map to physical data centers.

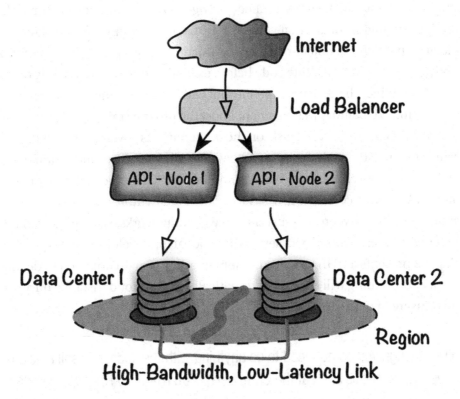

Figure 2-4. *Application components*

Tip   If your home region comes with a single availability domain, you can still perform all the hands-on exercises in this and all subsequent chapters by subscribing to another region that offers multiple ADs. You can perform this action in the OCI Console. Just go to Menu ➤ Administration ➤ Region Management and click the Subscribe button next to one of the regions that comes with three ADs. Subscribing to a new region can take a few moments. You will then need to choose the active region in the top-right corner of the OCI Console.

The time has come to take a closer look at the implementation. I have chosen to implement the API server in Flask, a web-oriented Python microframework. I am pretty sure you have already heard about the Python programming language. Introduced in the early 1990s, it has experienced a rapid growth in popularity, especially in the last decade. Python is considered a general-purpose language used across various domains such as web development, data science, machine learning, cloud ecosystem, and even the IoT. It is categorized as a multiparadigm, interpreted language with dynamic types and automatic memory management called *garbage collection*. Supporting multiple programming paradigms means that you are able to choose your preferred way of coding, let it be procedural, object-oriented, or functional. Interpreted languages do not need to be precompiled to machine code before execution but are run directly on an interpreter. It simplifies the delivery pipeline, but with a performance drop. Dynamic types and automated memory management boost the programming efficiency, making the language easier to work with. Flask, on the other hand, is a web development microframework with the main focus on processing HTTP requests and sending properly rendered HTTP responses. It is fully WSGI-compliant. WSGI has been defined in PEP3333 and stands for Web Service Gateway Interface, which is a Python-ecosystem standard that specifies an interface between web servers and web frameworks. For our convenience, Flask comes with an embedded web server that is ideal for development purposes.

Listing 2-2 presents a UUID service implementation. You do not need to do anything with the code. Everything will happen automatically on the cloud instance during its first boot. How? Just read on.

Tip   Even though you do not need to do anything with the code, it is still available in the Git repository for this book at the `chapter02/uuid-service/app.py` path.

Listing 2-2. UUID Service Implementation

```
import flask
import uuid
import os
import socket
import logging

app = flask.Flask(__name__)

@app.route('/identifiers', methods=['GET'])
def identifiers():
    generator_name = os.getenv('UUID_GENERATOR_NAME', socket.gethostname())
    generator_uuid = uuid.uuid4()
    app.logger.info('Generator: [%s] UUID: [%s]', generator_name,
    generator_uuid)
    rsp = flask.jsonify(uuid=generator_uuid, generator=generator_name)
    rsp.status_code = 200
    rsp.headers['Content-Type'] = 'application/json'
    return rsp

@app.before_first_request
def setup_logging():
    logging.getLogger('werkzeug').disabled = True
    app.logger.removeHandler(flask.logging.default_handler)
    handler = logging.StreamHandler()
    handler.setFormatter(logging.Formatter('%(asctime)s - %(levelname)s -
    %(message)s'))
    app.logger.addHandler(handler)
    app.logger.setLevel(logging.INFO)
```

To keep the focus on the main subject of this book, I will avoid explaining the line-by-line implementation details. What you should understand is that this application routes all GET requests sent via the /identifiers URL to the identifiers() handler function. The function prepares a response by combining a newly generated UUID with the name of generator. The latter is set to the hostname, unless the UUID_GENERATOR_ NAME environment variable exists. The response is sent in JSON format, as shown here:

```
{
  "generator":"uuid1",
  "uuid":"e22b5858-e70f-46ab-bd16-0da3d55aca73"
}
```

Now, let's get back on track and start defining the required Oracle Cloud Infrastructure resources so that we can create them.

Cloud Infrastructure

Based on the conceptual design that we briefly discussed in the previous section, we know we will need two compute instances in two different availability domains behind a highly available load balancer. The load balancer will use a public IP so that it can be reached from the Internet. There are a few other supplementary infrastructure resources we will create to make sure that the cloud design is complete.

First things first, however. We begin with designing the layout of the virtual network where our resources exist. A *virtual cloud network* (VCN) can be thought of as a virtual, private network that provides a contiguous block of IPv4 addresses. It is advisable to choose an IPv4 address block that is commonly considered as private. RFC1918 defines these addresses. If you want to adhere to this guideline, select any subset of the following address ranges:

- 192.168.0.0/16
- 172.16.0.0/12
- 10.0.0.0/8

For our cloud solution, we will use this range: 192.168.1.0/24.

A VCN is subdivided into one or more *subnets*. The IP address ranges of the subnets that belong to the same VCN have to be within the IP address range of the parent VCN and mustn't overlap with other subnets. Each compute instance you run in Oracle Cloud Infrastructure will be attached to a particular VCN subnet. This is done through a virtual network interface card called a vNIC.

Let's decide on the layout of our cloud networking. Figure 2-5 shows the VCN address space for our cloud solution and the address range split into subnets.

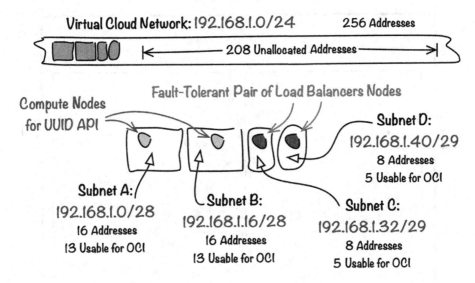

Figure 2-5. *Virtual cloud network address range layout*

As you can see in Figure 2-5, we will use four subnets.

- Subnet A for the first compute node hosting the UUID API

- Subnet B for the second compute node hosting the UUID API

- Subnet C for the first load balancer node

- Subnet D for the second load balancer node

In other words, we are going to run the UUID API application on two compute instances launched in subnets A and B. The pair of the load balancer nodes will run in subnets C and D. To achieve fault tolerance,

- Subnets A and C will be created in the first availability domain.

- Subnets B and D will be created in the second availability domain.

If you check the official OCI documents, white papers, or project architecture documents, you will find that OCI resources (compute instances, load balancers, networking resources, and others) are often presented using diagrams that follow the same style and reuse a set of standard icons. I will now use Oracle Cloud Infrastructure topology notation for the first time. Figure 2-6 illustrates the cloud infrastructure topology we are going to build in this chapter.

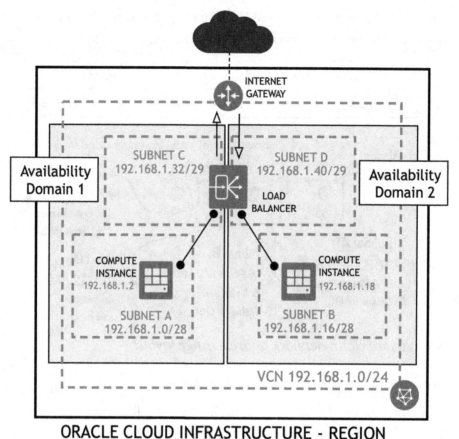

Figure 2-6. *Cloud infrastructure architecture*

Tip   Oracle has released a set of reusable graphical assets that everyone can use in their architecture documentation. You can find them at `https://bit.ly/2rfLk3V`.

At this stage, we have a pretty clear vision of the cloud networking layout. Now, let's make a few choices about the compute instances.

The shape is a profile of hardware resources (CPU cores, available memory) offered by a compute instance that is based on a given shape. Oracle Cloud Infrastructure features two families of compute instance shapes.

- **Bare-metal hosts**: Dedicated, single-tenant hardware, no hypervisor

- **Virtual machines**: General purpose, multitenant hardware, hypervisor

Some software such as messaging platforms, enterprise application servers, or database engines are reported to be more stable and efficient on dedicated, physical hardware with no hypervisor-managed virtualization involved. You can host them on fewer, more powerful bare-metal hosts. In all other general-purpose use cases, you will probably use more virtual machines to leverage horizontal scaling.

Note   The bare-metal compute shapes family is deeply rooted in the origins of Oracle Cloud Infrastructure. OCI actually evolved from a bare-metal-oriented cloud offering called Oracle Bare Metal Cloud Service.

Let me list just a few arbitrarily selected shapes that are offered at the time of writing.

- **VM.Standard2.1** is the smallest standard virtual machine shape that comes with 1 OCPU and 15GB of memory. It is powered by the X7 platform, which basically means that it is using Intel Xeon Skylake processors.

- **VM.Standard2.8** is another example of a standard virtual machine shape that offers 8 OCPUs and 120GB of memory.

- **BM.Standard2.52** is a standard bare-metal shape that leverages 52 OCPUs and 768GB of memory.

- **BM.Standard.E2.64** is a bare-metal shape that uses AMD EPYC processors with 64 OCPUs and 512GB of memory.

- **BM.DenseIO2.52** is a bare-metal shape dedicated to I/O-intensive workloads that are present in big data projects. It is backed with locally attached SSD NVMe drives that offer 51.2TB of storage capacity.

- **BM.GPU3.8** is a bare-metal shape intended to power machine learning processes and high-performance computing (HPC) software. In addition to 52 OCPUs and 768GB of memory, its real capacity comes from eight Nvidia Tesla V100 GPUs.

In the preceding list, I used a new abbreviation. An *Oracle compute unit* (OCPU) is a logical term and the most important metric for compute-related billings. You usually pay for 1 OCPU/hour. In other words, one hour of a running instance with 8 OCPUs will generate the same compute-related cost as an instance with just 1 OCPU running for eight hours.

In the case of Intel-based shapes, a single OCPU corresponds to a single, physical Intel Xeon core. The operating system actually sees two virtual cores for each physical CPU core because of hyperthreading technology. To sum up, one Intel-based OCPU means one physical CPU core and the capability of two nearly parallel execution threads, sometimes called vCPUs.

You can easily guess that our first choice related to compute instances is the selection of a shape for the nodes that will host the UUID service application. We are going to use the smallest virtual machine available: VM.Standard2.1.

An *image* is a template that specifies the operating system and any additional software that has to be preinstalled during the instance launch. An image is used to initiate a new boot volume that a compute instance uses. A boot volume remains associated with its compute instance until termination. A boot volume can be seen as the primary storage that an instance uses, mainly for its operating system and software.

Oracle-provided images are periodically updated and receive new versions. Yet, as soon as you launch an instance, it becomes your responsibility to schedule regular system updates.

At the time of writing, Oracle Cloud Infrastructure provides four types of base operating system images with the following operating systems:

- Oracle Linux

- CentOS

- Ubuntu

- Windows Server

In your daily work, you may end up creating a lot of custom images that add the required software, services, or scheduled scripts to the base image of your choice. It is also possible to import custom images that are not built on the available base images. In this case, you would use either paravirtualization or emulation on a virtual machine shape. Yet, the easiest way to create custom images is to rely on the base images provided by Oracle.

What about making another decision? We will use the newest Oracle Linux base image: Oracle Linux 7.6. You will probably use newer minor versions of Oracle Linux 7 as they appear in the future.

Note   Although the screenshots will show Oracle Linux 7.6, the exercises in this chapter were additionally tested with an Oracle Linux 7.7 image.

We will now move to the last step in our planning process.

Service Limits

You might wonder what would happen if too many tenants (cloud customers) launched a large number of the most powerful bare-metal shapes in the same region at once. The number of these machines is surely limited even in the largest data center, isn't it? Well, sure, it is. This is where the smart idea of service limits (also known as *quotas*) comes into play.

Every cloud account has a set of service limits that define how many resources of which type are allowed to be running at the same time. If you see that your current limits are insufficient for your needs, you can request them to be increased simply by raising a service request. This helps Oracle to plan and optimize data center capacity. Simple and wise, isn't it?

Tip   You can always verify your usage against the current service limits for your cloud account in the OCI Console. Just go to Menu ➤ Governance ➤ Limits, Quotas and Usage.

Verifying and optionally increasing the service limits before launching a new cloud project should be included in your checklist for the planning phase.

The sample cloud solution we are working on in this chapter will include the following OCI resources:

- One VCN

- Two VM.Standard2.1 compute instances

- One load balancer (100Mbps)

- One custom image

- Negligibly small size of block storage

If you are using a new trial account and haven't created any resources yet, you can be pretty sure that your default trial account service limits won't be violated.

If you are using a paid account that already contains some OCI resources, please go to Menu ➤ Governance ➤ Limits, Quotas and Usage in the OCI Console and check if you can add the ones I've just listed. You may also need to ask your cloud administrator to give you the numbers, if your OCI IAM user is not entitled to see the service limits.

What we've been doing until now was pure planning that was backed with some elementary Oracle Cloud Infrastructure concepts discussion. We began with looking at the application and mapped it to the cloud resources we would need. We are ready to provision these resources.

Provisioning the Infrastructure

We are now going to provision the cloud resources required to run the application, which we've talked about in the previous section. I will simplify this example as much as possible. This is why I am going to present how to deploy the UUID service on a single node first. Later, we will add load balancing and fault tolerance. Here and now, I am going to show you the manual way. What do I mean by that? We will manage all resources using the Oracle Cloud Infrastructure Console. You may recall that I mentioned this approach as appropriate only when you want to demonstrate selected capabilities or experiment with the features that are new for you. The proper production-ready automation will arrive in Chapter 3. For the time being, let's start!

Please log into the Oracle Cloud Infrastructure (OCI) Console. Figure 2-7 presents the main landing page in the OCI Console.

Figure 2-7. *Oracle Cloud Infrastructure Console*

In the top-right corner of the OCI Console, you will see your active region. In my case, as shown in Figure 2-7, it is the Germany Central region (eu-frankfurt-1). As I mentioned earlier, some regions may consist of only one availability domain. The exercises in this book have been tested in the Germany Central (eu-frankfurt-1) region, and it is assumed that there are three availability domains present in the region you are working with. At the time of writing, these are the following:

- Germany Central (eu-frankfurt-1)

- UK South (uk-london-1)

- US East (us-ashburn-1)

- US West (us-phoenix-1)

A single cloud account can own and manage resources in more than one region. You just need to activate the additional region(s). To do so, follow these steps:

1. Go to Menu ➤ Administration ➤ Region Management.

2. Click Infrastructure Regions in the Resources menu.

3. Click Subscribe To This Region next to the region name.

Subscribing to a new region is an asynchronous operation that can take a few minutes. At some point in time, after having refreshed the OCI Console, you should be able to choose between regions in the top-right corner of the OCI Console.

Note   Before proceeding with the exercises this book contains, please make sure you are working in a region that comes with three availability domains. Do not hesitate to subscribe to an additional region if needed.

You may be wondering how we achieve fault tolerance in single-AD regions such as the following:

- Australia East (ap-sydney-1)

- Brazil East (sa-saopaulo-1)

- Canada Southeast (ca-toronto-1)

- India West (ap-mumbai-1)

- Japan East (ap-tokyo-1)

- South Korea Central (ap-seoul-1)

- Switzerland North (eu-zurich-1)

There are two options that can be employed at the same time. First, you may remember that each AD comes with three fault domains, as described in the previous chapter. Fault domains are physically isolated units of equipment with separate powering and cooling. In this way, it is less likely that two fault domains fail at the same point in time. More critical systems can be spread across multiple regions. As an example, while running an active system site in Tokyo, you could maintain a passive system site in Seoul to enable disaster recovery (DR).

Compartment

We need to choose a compartment in which our first cloud application will run. Compartments serve as the primary mean to isolate unrelated OCI resources. In this way, they can be used to separate different projects. From a formal point of view, they belong to the IAM service. Unless you already have an existing compartment for learning, it is advised that you create a new compartment to keep the artifacts you provision as part of our Chapter 2 exercise isolated. Follow these steps:

1. Go to Menu ➤ Identity ➤ Compartments.

2. Click Create Compartment.

3. Enter **Sandbox** for the name.

4. Provide some description.

5. Click Create Compartment.

The new compartment should get created nearly immediately. You may need to refresh the page, unless you can see a new record for the newly created compartment, as shown in Figure 2-8.

Figure 2-8. *Viewing a compartment in the OCI Console*

From now on, every time you create a new OCI resource in the console, you will need to make sure that the appropriate compartment is selected in the Compartment combo box, as shown in Figure 2-9.

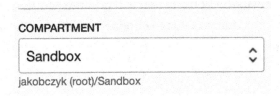

Figure 2-9. *Choosing an active compartment in the OCI Console*

As we move closer to automating Oracle Cloud Infrastructure with the CLI and Terraform, you will see that we are referencing the target compartment not by its name but by using its Oracle cloud identifier (OCID).

Every OCI resource, including your tenancy, is uniquely identified by an immutable, multipart, Oracle-assigned, strict-syntax key called an *Oracle cloud identifier*, abbreviated as OCID. The resource identifier structure is strict. For the time being, it always starts with ocid1, which indicates the current and only OCID version. The second element is more important because it shows a resource type. At the time of writing, the third element is always set to oc1. The fourth element denotes the region. Finally, the last element is unique for every OCI resource. Figure 2-10 illustrates the OCID structure.

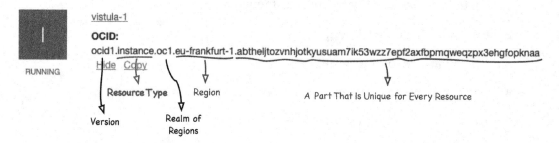

Figure 2-10. *OCID*

Virtual Cloud Network

As the name says, a *virtual cloud network* (VCN) is a virtual network that is private to your cloud tenancy. Yet, in the way you design and manage a VCN, it feels somehow similar to well-known, traditional, physical IP networks you may have worked with or learned about.

This is how you create a new VCN using the OCI Console:

1. Go to Menu ➤ Networking ➤ Virtual Cloud Networks.

2. Make sure that the Sandbox compartment is selected. On the left side, slightly to the bottom, you will find the Scope section with a combo box that you use to choose the name of the active compartment.

3. Click Create Virtual Cloud Network.

4. Provide an optional display name for the new VCN (uuid-vcn).

5. Select Create Virtual Cloud Network Only.

6. Provide the CIDR block (192.168.1.0/24).

7. Select the DNS Resolution box and leave the default of DNS label.

8. Click Create Virtual Cloud Network to provision the VCN.

Figure 2-11 shows the OCI Console VCN creation wizard.

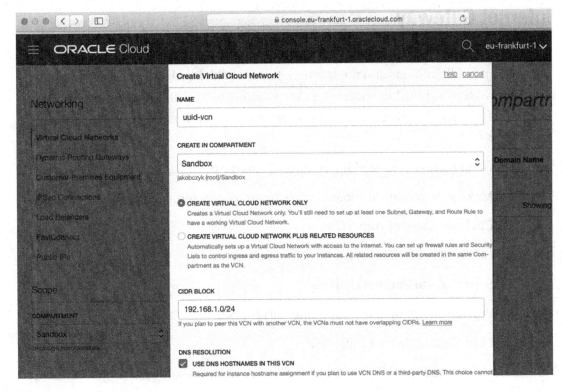

Figure 2-11. *Creating a new virtual cloud network*

At the bottom of the wizard, you may have spotted some fields related to tags. You will learn about tagging in Chapter 5.

We have decided to create a VCN because I am going to show you how to create all the (or adapt the existing) required child resources such as the Internet gateway, route rule, security rules, and subnets. In this way, you will understand how these components work together.

Tip   If you need to prototype a simple cloud setup, you can use the Networking Quickstart wizard. The OCI Console will not only create a VCN but also add the most common child resources such as the Internet gateway, route rule, and subnets. This can be helpful when you want to test something quick and do not need any special VCN setup.

Internet Gateway

An *Internet gateway* is a virtual router that provides connectivity between compute instances in public subnets and the Internet. It must be defined as a target in the route rule; otherwise, compute instances won't know where to send their outbound packets to. Let's start by provisioning a new Internet gateway. This is how you do it using the OCI Console:

1. Go to Menu ➤ Networking ➤ Virtual Cloud Networks.

2. Make sure that the Sandbox compartment is selected.

3. Click the name of your VCN.

4. Click Internet Gateways in the Resources menu.

5. Select Create Internet Gateway.

6. Provide an optional display name (uuid-igw).

7. Click Create Internet Gateway.

Figure 2-12 shows the OCI Console Internet gateway creation wizard.

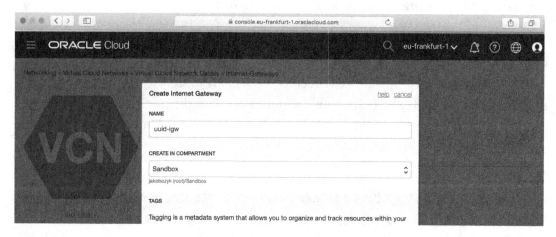

Figure 2-12. *Creating a new Internet gateway*

Route Table

It won't be a big surprise if I say that a *route table* stores route rules for a VCN. A route rule defines how to direct the outbound traffic that is destined to travel outside the VCN. In our case, we must define a rule that properly directs all packets sent to the IP addresses that do not belong to the VCN address range. In IPv4 language, 0.0.0.0/0 means all addresses, and this is the value we are going to use in the destination CIDR block of a route rule. We will also set the Internet gateway we've just provisioned as the target for this rule.

A VCN comes with a default but empty route table resource. This is how you add a new route rule to the existing default route table using the OCI Console:

1. Go to Menu ➤ Networking ➤ Virtual Cloud Networks.

2. Make sure that the Sandbox compartment is selected.

3. Click the name of your VCN.

4. Click Route Tables in the Resources menu.

5. Click the name of the default route table.

6. Click Add Route Rules.

7. Choose Internet Gateway in the Target Type selection box.

8. Place **0.0.0.0/0** in Destination CIDR Block.

9. Choose uuid-igw in Target Internet Gateway.

10. Click Add Route Rules.

Figure 2-13 shows the Add Route Rules screen in the OCI Console.

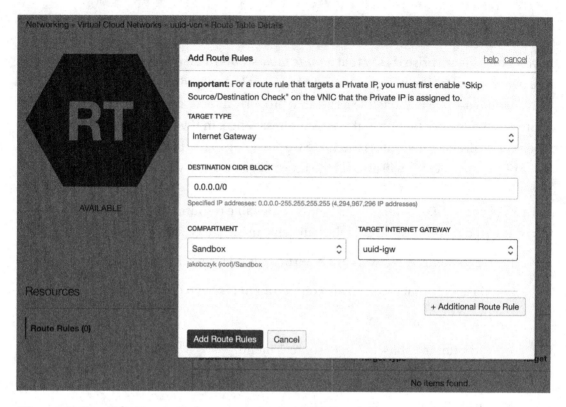

Figure 2-13.   Edit Route Rules screen in the OCI Console

Security List

We've already dealt with a virtual network, virtual router, and virtual route table. Now, it is time to add some security. Every VCN subnet is required to have at least one *security list*, which is a collection of security rules. You can think of these rules as an additional layer of a virtual firewall, independent from the operating system firewall you control on each individual compute instance. Before a request reaches a compute instance's virtual network interface, security rules are enforced.

There are two types of security rules based on traffic direction.

- **Ingress**, which means they validate the inbound traffic to VCN

- **Egress**, which means they validate the outbound traffic from VCN

A VCN comes with a default security list resource with some basic rules that allow ingress SSH and basic ICMP traffic as well as all egress traffic. We still need to add a rule that allows ingress traffic on the UUID service port (5000). This is how you add a new security rule to an existing security list using the OCI Console:

1. Go to Menu ➤ Networking ➤ Virtual Cloud Networks.

2. Make sure that the Sandbox compartment is selected.

3. Click the name of your VCN.

4. Click Security Lists in the Resources menu.

5. Click the name of the default security list.

6. Select Ingress Rules in the Resources menu.

7. Click Add Ingress Rule.

8. Provide the required values:

   a. Place **0.0.0.0/0** in Source CIDR.

   b. Place **5000** in Destination Port Range.

9. Click Add Ingress Rules.

Figure 2-14 shows a new ingress security rule we are adding.

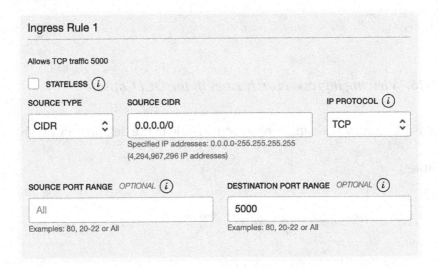

Figure 2-14. *An ingress security rule in the OCI Console*

You may wonder what a small checkbox next to the Stateless label actually means. We've left this checkbox empty. As a result, the new ingress rule we've added is a *stateful rule*. Every time an inbound traffic (a request) on port 5000 is accepted by this stateful ingress rule, the corresponding outbound traffic (a reply) will be automatically let through with no other egress rule enforced. If you decide to use a *stateless rule*, you will also need to create another stateless rule in the opposite direction that validates the related traffic.

Stateful rules may sound like a perfect solution. Then why would we still use stateless rules? Well, stateful rules require connection tracking that consumes resources and introduces some latency. Furthermore, each compute instance has a limit of how many connections can be tracked at a single moment. This is why the golden rule says that if you are able to design your security rules as stateless rules, do it.

Figure 2-15 shows existing ingress security rules in the amended default security list.

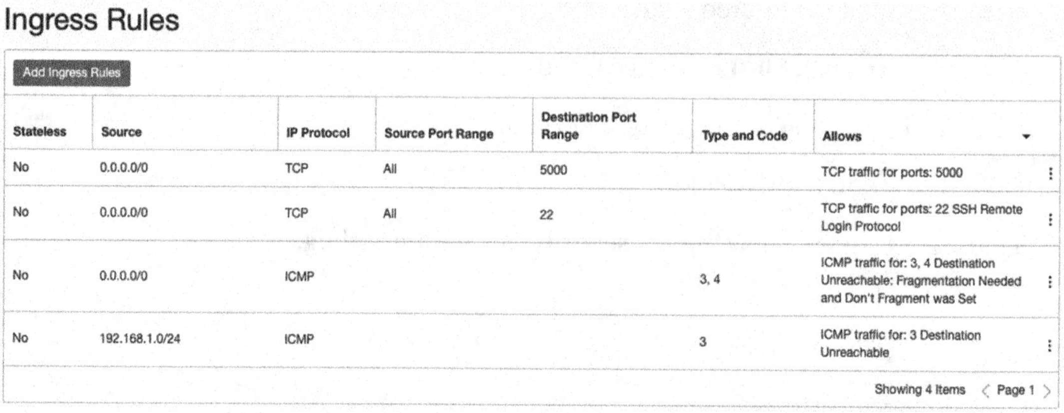

Ingress Rules

Stateless	Source	IP Protocol	Source Port Range	Destination Port Range	Type and Code	Allows	
No	0.0.0.0/0	TCP	All	5000		TCP traffic for ports: 5000	⋮
No	0.0.0.0/0	TCP	All	22		TCP traffic for ports: 22 SSH Remote Login Protocol	⋮
No	0.0.0.0/0	ICMP			3, 4	ICMP traffic for: 3, 4 Destination Unreachable: Fragmentation Needed and Don't Fragment was Set	⋮
No	192.168.1.0/24	ICMP			3	ICMP traffic for: 3 Destination Unreachable	⋮

Showing 4 Items   ⟨ Page 1 ⟩

Figure 2-15. *Viewing ingress security rules in the OCI Console*

Figure 2-16 shows an existing egress security rule in the default security list.

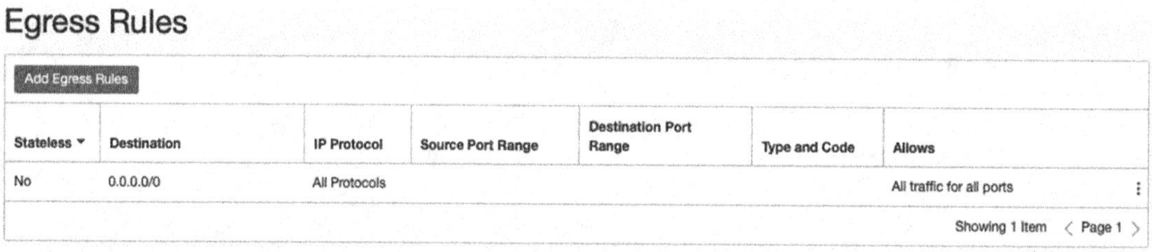

Egress Rules

Stateless ▾	Destination	IP Protocol	Source Port Range	Destination Port Range	Type and Code	Allows	
No	0.0.0.0/0	All Protocols				All traffic for all ports	⋮

Showing 1 Item   ⟨ Page 1 ⟩

Figure 2-16. *Viewing egress security rules in the OCI Console*

So far, we've provisioned a new VCN, launched an Internet gateway, added a new route rule to direct the outbound traffic via the Internet gateway, and created a stateful ingress security rule to allow all incoming TCP connections on port 5000. Next, we will create a new subnet and provision a new virtual machine.

Subnet

A VCN is divided into one or more *subnets*. We attach compute instances, or more precisely their vNICs, to the subnets. You may recall that as we were defining a new VCN, we did not make any choices about availability domains. It is a subnet that you can explicitly create in exactly one availability domain of your choice. All compute instances that are created in a particular subnet will eventually have to run in the availability domain the subnet was created in. Alternatively, it is possible to create subnets that span all availability domains in a given region. That kind of subnets lets you launch instances in a more flexible way, deterring the choice of an availability domain for an instance. You'll learn more about that in Chapter 6. For now, we are going to stick to subnets bound to single availability domains. This is how you create a new VCN subnet using the OCI Console:

1. Go to Menu ➤ Networking ➤ Virtual Cloud Networks.

2. Make sure that the Sandbox compartment is selected.

3. Click the name of your VCN.

4. Click Subnets in the Resources menu.

5. Click Create Subnet.

6. Provide the required values:

    a. Place **a-net** as a display name.

    b. Choose Availability Domain-specific Subnet Type.

    c. Select the first availability domain (suffixed AD-1) in your region.

    d. Place **192.168.1.0/28** as the CIDR block.

    e. Make sure that the default route table is chosen.

    f. Select the Public Subnet option.

    g. Mark Use DNS Hostnames in this subnet.

    h. Use the short, one-character label **a** as the subnet's DNS label.

    i. Make sure that the default DHCP Options setting is chosen.

    j. Make sure that the default security list is chosen.

7. Click Create Subnet.

Figure 2-17 shows the OCI Console VCN subnet creation wizard.

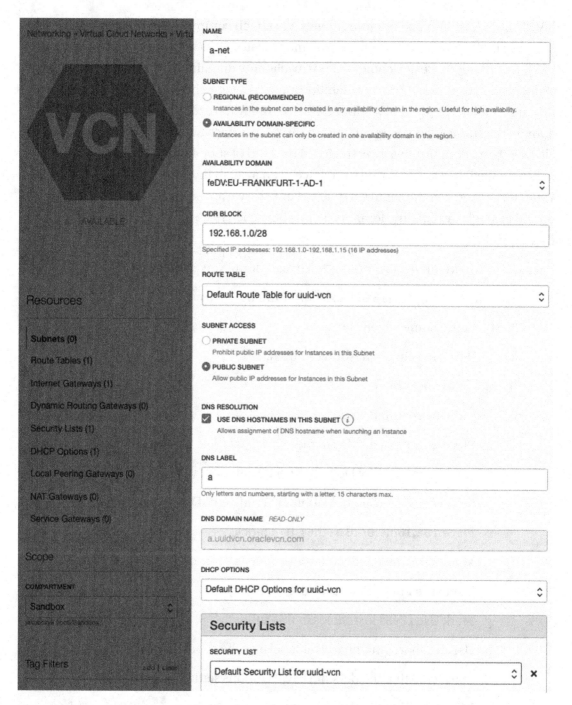

Figure 2-17. *Creating VCN subnet creation wizard in the OCI Console*

There are two types of subnets.

- **A public subnet** lets you assign public IP addresses to compute instances that have been provisioned in this subnet. You can still create compute instances with no public IP address in a public subnet.

- **A private subnet** does not allow you to you assign public IP addresses to compute instances that have been provisioned in this subnet. These instances can use different means to communicate with the Internet and other networks. You'll learn more about that in Chapter 6.

Compute Instance

The time has come to provision our first compute instance in Oracle Cloud Infrastructure. During the planning phase, which was described earlier in this chapter, we decided to use the smallest virtual machine shape, which is VM.Standard2.1. We also chose to use the newest available version of Oracle Linux 7. At the time of writing, this is Oracle Linux 7.6, but you may see newer minor versions as well. At the moment, there should be no compute instances in your learning compartment. Figure 2-18 shows an empty list in the Instances view in the OCI Console.

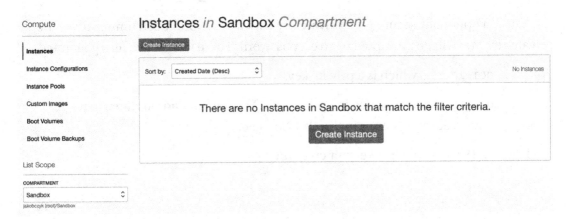

Figure 2-18. *Viewing OCI Console instances*

Even if you automate the entire startup procedure of a particular cloud-based virtual machine, you may still want to have the option to connect to the command line on that host remotely. In the case of Linux-based machines, like Oracle Linux, we are going to use SSH public key authentication. If you have worked primarily with Windows-based hosts, it might be the first time you hear about SSH. The principle is pretty simple. You generate a pair of related files, so-called keys. One is called a *private key*, and the other is called a *public key*. You upload the public key to one or more Linux machines in the cloud. To authenticate your remote terminal connection, you need the private key. The compute instance creation wizard in the OCI Console gives us an opportunity to upload a public key.

Note   The code snippets from this book have been tested on macOS and Windows Subsystem for Linux. Moreover, all commands should work on major Linux distributions. If you are using Windows and do not want to use Windows Subsystem for Linux, you can always run Linux on a VM. Furthermore, the majority of code snippets may also work in Git Bash on Windows.

If you would like to create a new SSH keypair by employing the RSA algorithm, just execute this command:

```
$ ssh-keygen -t rsa -b 2048 -C michal@vm -f ~/oci_id_rsa
```

You can optionally secure your private key with a password. Each time you use the private key, you will be prompted to give a password. There will be two files generated.

- `oci_id_rsa`, which is a private key.

- `oci_id_rsa.pub`, which is a public key. You will upload this file when you create an instance in the OCI Console.

Figure 2-19 shows an SSH keypair creation.

```
● ● ●                           ⌂ mjk — -bash — 104×29
mjk@Michals-MacBook-Pro:~$ ssh-keygen -t rsa -b 2048 -C michal@vm -f ~/oci_id_rsa
Generating public/private rsa key pair.
Enter passphrase (empty for no passphrase):
Enter same passphrase again:
Your identification has been saved in /Users/mjk/oci_id_rsa.
Your public key has been saved in /Users/mjk/oci_id_rsa.pub.
The key fingerprint is:
SHA256:N+cz9M/EKQRbI//wZPvylfAUZ8iTpV+54UiqRuDYvUk michal@vm
The key's randomart image is:
+---[RSA 2048]----+
|               .|
|           . =.|
|        .   o +*++|
|      + o   O ++*|
|     . oSEooo* *.|
|       o.+=..X.+|
|        = +..B+|
|       .   oo+o|
|               o=|
+----[SHA256]-----+
mjk@Michals-MacBook-Pro:~$ ls -l oci_id_rsa*
-rw-------  1 mjk  staff  1.8K Nov 26 14:20 oci_id_rsa
-rw-r--r--  1 mjk  staff  391B Nov 26 14:20 oci_id_rsa.pub
mjk@Michals-MacBook-Pro:~$ cat oci_id_rsa.pub
ssh-rsa AAAAB3NzaC1yc2EAAAADAQABAAABAQCydtfkTDIfRWaHz/CoRFE2v+CxJTs2x3EL2L9G6J/krt/cpQQRcs
cUx2Z9oWy76ZWyvOnIhraEM3RPfjrb310US3hJXZyrY1Ke6Vb0zHEgcm58s9Re4gjwVMJ5jYwLLkNO+3x/36oscp9k
Rr9JRJiw7uAC9d7S5GovyHyI7s+MQ0ap3+1z25bRAKgMdS05pl5Fph2l6oXp/XUywRHcp25Iu+Tq+6qgG+YMyKUbk7
x+znP8NUHGITUcoDy0BaVwwxgvEqN9+N8JGXT2zZbT/npbjh7jHd1UdKExPiS+VYdV4L michal@vm
mjk@Michals-MacBook-Pro:~$ █
```

***Figure 2-19.** Creating an SSH keypair*

We would like our Oracle Linux compute instance to be able to serve UUID service clients as soon as the machine is up and running. We do not want to perform neither manual installations nor configurations. We are going to leverage the *cloud-init* package that is preinstalled on our compute instance already with the base operating system image. The role of cloud-init is to perform an early initialization of a cloud instance during its first boot. Your role is to upload a *user data* file in one of the supported formats during instance creation. Listing 2-3 shows cloud-init user data in *cloud-config* YAML format. You will find the cloud-config file in the `git/chapter02/cloud-init` directory.

***Listing 2-3.** vm.config.yaml*

```
#cloud-config
yum_repos:
    ol7_developer_EPEL:
        name: Oracle Linux $releasever Developement Packages ($basearch)
        baseurl: http://yum.oracle.com/repo/OracleLinux/OL7/developer_
        EPEL/$basearch/
```

```yaml
        enabled: true
        gpgcheck: true
        gpgkey: file:///etc/pki/rpm-gpg/RPM-GPG-KEY-oracle
package_upgrade: true
packages:
 - tree
 - wget
 - python36
 - python36-pip
write_files:
-   content: |
      [Unit]
      Description = Launching UUID Service API
      After = network.target
      [Service]
      Environment=FLASK_APP=/home/opc/uuidservice/app.py
      Environment=LC_ALL=en_US.utf8
      Environment=LANG=en_US.utf8
      ExecStart = /home/opc/uuidservice/venv/bin/flask run --host=0.0.0.0
      User = opc
      [Install]
      WantedBy = multi-user.target
    path: /etc/systemd/system/uuidservice.service
runcmd:
  - [ "mkdir", "-p", "/home/opc/uuidservice/venv" ]
  - [ "chown", "opc:opc", "/home/opc/uuidservice" ]
  - [ "python3", "-m", "venv", "/home/opc/uuidservice/venv" ]
  - [ "/home/opc/uuidservice/venv/bin/python3", "-m", "pip", "install",
    "--upgrade", "pip" ]
  - [ "/home/opc/uuidservice/venv/bin/python3", "-m", "pip", "install",
    "flask" ]
  - [ "wget", "-qO", "/home/opc/uuidservice/app.py", "https://raw.
    githubusercontent.com/mtjakobczyk/oci-book/master/chapter02/
    uuid-service/app.py " ]
  - [ "firewall-offline-cmd", "--add-port=5000/tcp" ]
  - [ "systemctl", "restart", "firewalld" ]
```

```
  - [ "ln", "-s", "/etc/systemd/system/uuidservice.service", "/etc/systemd/
    system/multi-user.target.wants/uuidservice.service" ]
  - [ "systemctl", "enable", "uuidservice.service" ]
  - [ "systemctl", "start", "uuidservice.service" ]
final_message: "UUID Service API node is running, after $UPTIME seconds"
```

You will upload this file to the OCI Console instance creation wizard in a few moments. First, let's understand what it does. If you look closer at Listing 2-3, you will discover that it consists of six named sections.

- yum_repos defines a new repository that will be added to Yum.

- package_upgrade triggers a system-wide package update.

- packages lists new packages that will be installed on the machine.

- write_files creates a new file using provided content at the given path.

- runcmd executes commands in a provided sequence.

- final_message prints a message when the processing finishes.

But what does our cloud configuration actually do in more detail? First, it adds the Oracle Linux EPEL repository to Yum. This repository contains Python 3, which we need to run our Python-based UUID service. Cloud-init will perform a system-wide package upgrade and install not only Python 3 but also the wget and tree utilities. Another interesting thing is the write_files section, which, in our case, creates a new systemd unit file. The file content is created in such way to run the UUID service as a systemd service. In this way, we are able to follow a standardized approach to running applications as operating system services in Linux. Last but not least, the runcmd section runs a series of commands. First directories for a new Python virtual environment are created, and the virtual environment alone is generated using the Python 3 venv module. Next, already inside the virtual environment, we upgrade Package Installer for Python (pip) and use it to install Flask. The subsequent steps use the wget utility to download the UUID service code from the GitHub repository related to this book and open port 5000 in the operating system firewall. The final three commands effectively link, enable, and start the systemd service. In this way, the UUID service operates as an operating system service and is started on each restart.

You may wonder why are the commands are specified as arrays. There are two ways commands are run by cloud-init. The command will be executed as a new process, directly using an operating system call, if wrapped into an array like this:

runcmd:
```
- [ "mkdir", "-p", "/home/opc/uuidservice/venv" ]
```

The command will be written to a file first and then passed to the operating system shell for processing, if simply written as a string like this:

runcmd:
```
- mkdir -p /home/opc/uuidservice/venv
```

While the first way may be considered a bit faster from a performance point of view, only the latter will allow you to combine multiple commands by using piping like this:

runcmd:
```
- 'echo $(date) | tee /home/opc/datemarker'
```

It is fine to mix both styles in the same runcmd section.

Tip   Instead of copying the user data file straight from Listing 2-3, I recommend that you clone the Git repository associated with this book from my GitHub account and use the cloud-config user data file you will find at oci-book/chapter02/ cloud-init. In this way, you will be able to enjoy the code that is always up-to-date, in case something changes in the future.

Now, please prepare the two files we've just discussed.

- Public SSH key

- User data file for the UUID service

We are ready to launch the instance. This is how you create a new compute instance using the OCI Console:

1. Go to Menu ➤ Compute ➤ Instances.

2. Make sure that the Sandbox compartment is selected.

3. Click Create Instance.

4. Name your instance as **uuid-1**.

5. Click Show Shape, Network and Storage Options.

6. Set the image source to the newest Oracle Linux base image, such as Oracle Linux 7.6 or newer.

7. Provide the required details:

    a. Select the first availability domain in your region.

    b. Set the instance type to Virtual Machine.

    c. Select VM.Standard2.1 as your instance shape.

8. In the Configure Networking section, as shown in Figure 2-22:

    a. Make sure your new a-net subnet is selected.

    b. Check Assign a Public IP Address.

9. In the Add SSH Key section:

    a. Choose the newly generated public key (oci_id_rsa.pub), as shown in Figure 2-21.

10. Click Show Advanced Options.

11. On the Management tab under Advanced Options, as shown in Figure 2-23:

    a. Choose the user data file shown in Listing 2-3. You will always find the latest version of the user data file on my GitHub account at `https://raw.githubusercontent.com/mtjakobczyk/oci-book/master/chapter02/cloud-init/vm.config.yaml`.

12. On the Networking tab under Advanced Options, as shown in Figure 2-24:

    a. Set Private IP Address to **192.168.1.2**.

    b. Set Hostname to **uuid1**.

13. Click Create.

Figure 2-20 shows the instance creation view in the OCI Console.

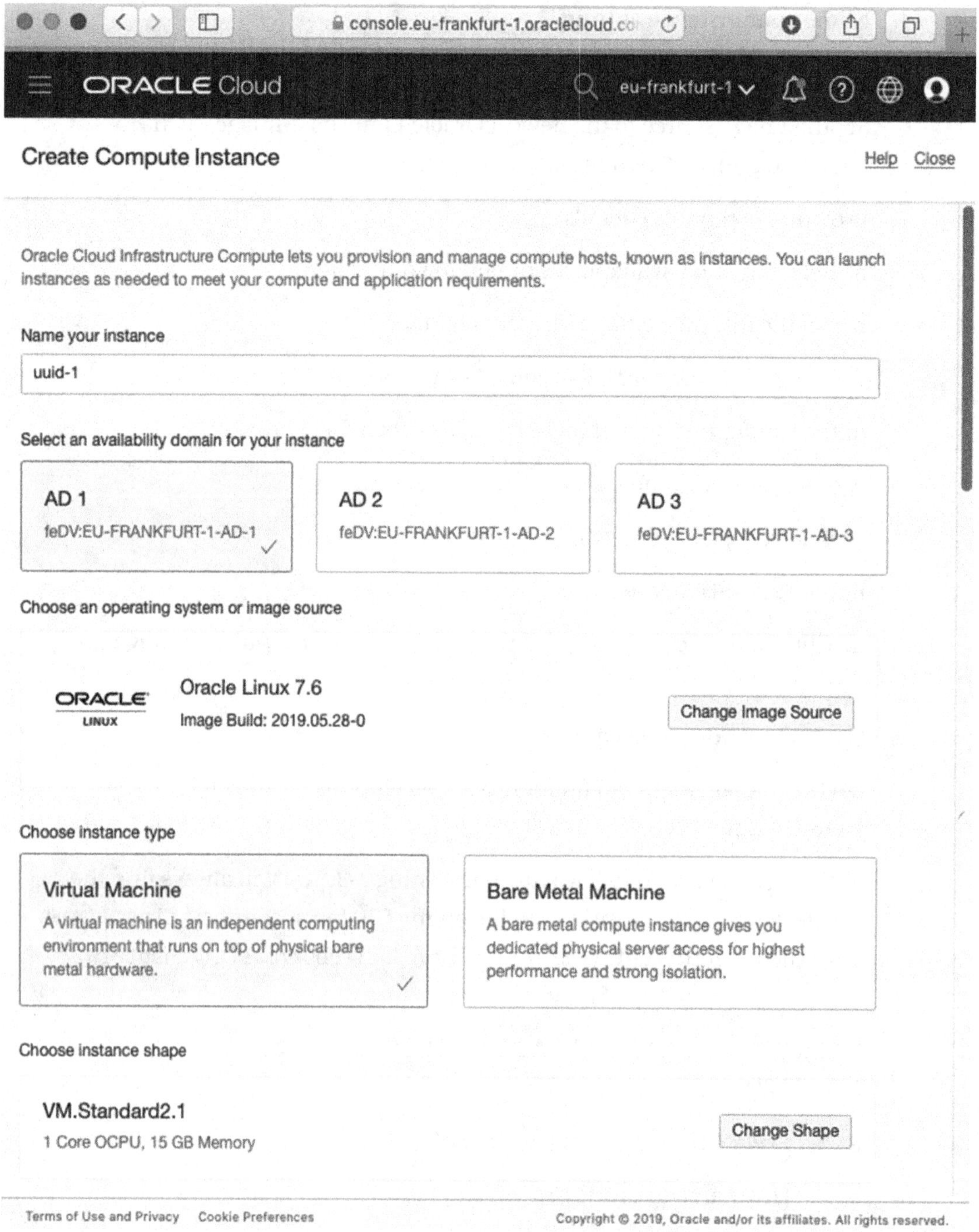

Figure 2-20. *Creating a new compute instance in the OCI Console*

Figure 2-21 shows the SSH key upload section in the OCI Console instance creation wizard.

Add SSH key ⓘ

⦿ Choose SSH key file   ◯ Paste SSH keys

Choose SSH key file (.pub) from your computer

oci_id_rsa.pub

Choose Files

Figure 2-21. *Uploading an SSH public key in the instance creation wizard*

Figure 2-22 shows the networking section in the OCI Console instance creation wizard.

Configure networking

Virtual cloud network compartment

Sandbox

jakobczyk (root)/Sandbox

Virtual cloud network

uuid-vcn

Subnet compartment

Sandbox

jakobczyk (root)/Sandbox

Subnet ⓘ

a-net

☐ Use network security groups to control traffic ⓘ

◯ Do not assign a public IP address   ⦿ Assign a public IP address

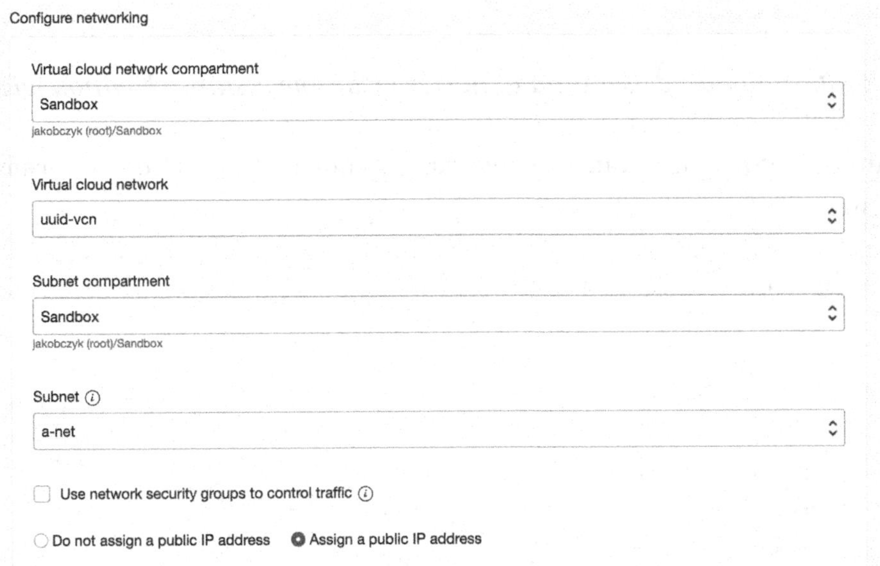

Figure 2-22. *Configuring networking in the instance creation wizard*

83

Figure 2-23 shows the user data upload section in the OCI Console instance creation wizard.

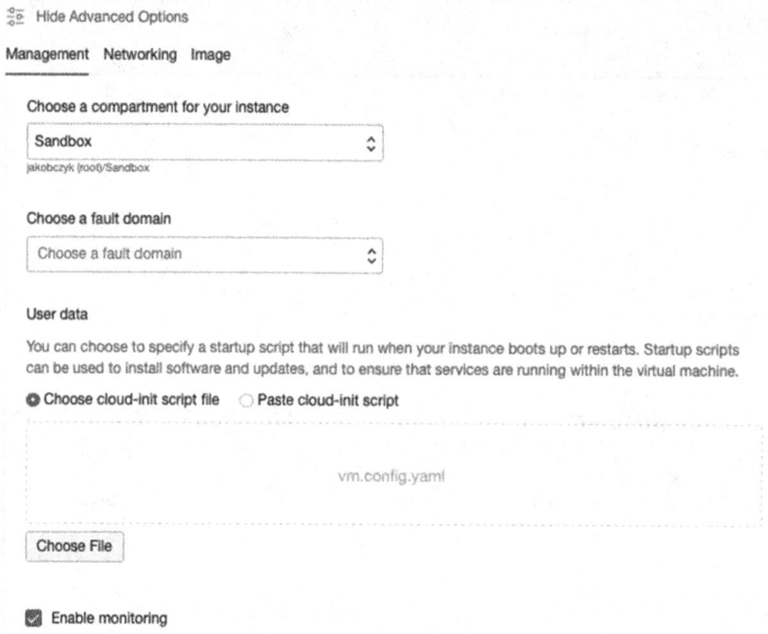

Figure 2-23. *Uploading user data in the OCI Console instance creation wizard*

Figure 2-24 shows the advanced networking section in the OCI Console instance creation wizard.

Figure 2-24. *Configuring advanced networking in the instance creation wizard*

It usually takes about one minute to provision this shape and the base image of a compute instance. We've selected the Assign Public IP Address checkbox; therefore, the primary vNIC attached to your instance will get a public IP address assigned from the Oracle Cloud pool of public IPv4 addresses. You will be able to connect to the instance using this IP address as long as the subnet's security list rules allow the particular traffic. Private IP addresses are used within the VCN to enable local communication between compute instances.

Figure 2-25 shows compute instance provisioning in the OCI Console.

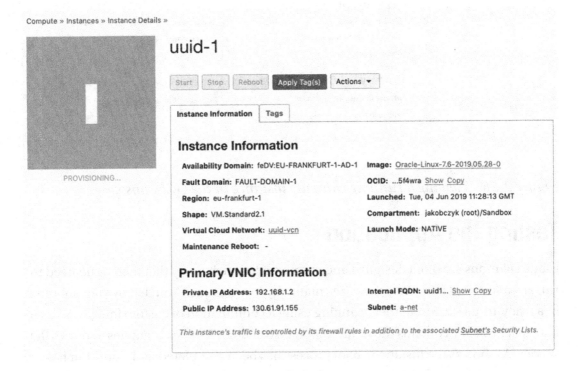

Figure 2-25. *Provisioning of a compute instance in the OCI Console*

Figure 2-26 shows a running compute instance in the OCI Console.

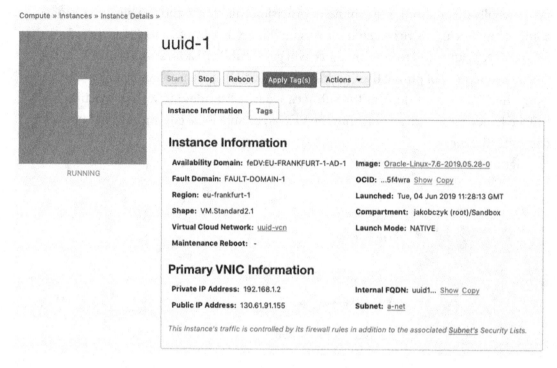

Compute » Instances » Instance Details »

Figure 2-26. *Viewing a running compute instance in the OCI Console*

Testing the Application

Cloud solutions are often designed and automated in such a way that there is no need to run any additional initialization scripts manually in a terminal. You deploy your solution in a ready-to-go state from the beginning using a combination of custom image and user data that basically contains the initialization instructions. The same applies to our UUID service. As soon as the instance's boot process has been completed and cloud-init has executed all the user data instructions, the API is up and running.

SSH Connection

Yet, let me make an exception here. I would like to show you around the instance, and there is no better way than using the operating system shell. Let's use SSH to connect to the uuid-1 compute instance remotely. You will find the instance's public IP in Instance Details, as shown in Figure 2-26. In my case, it is 130.61.91.155. Even though you will be using key-based authentication, a username for which you are establishing the connection is still expected. For Oracle Linux and CentOS, please use the `opc` username. For Ubuntu, please use the `ubuntu` username.

```
$ UUID1_INSTANCE=130.61.91.155
$ ssh -i ~/oci_id_rsa opc@$UUID1_INSTANCE
```

One more thing, do not be surprised if you are not able to connect to the terminal immediately after seeing the instance state moving from "provisioning" to "running." It can still take a few more seconds to start the SSH daemon, although an instance is said to be "running."

Tip If you are on Windows, I recommend using Windows Subsystem for Linux, Linux guest VM, or Git Bash to get the same `ssh` experience as if you were using a UNIX-based platform.

Figure 2-27 shows how to connect to a remote compute instance.

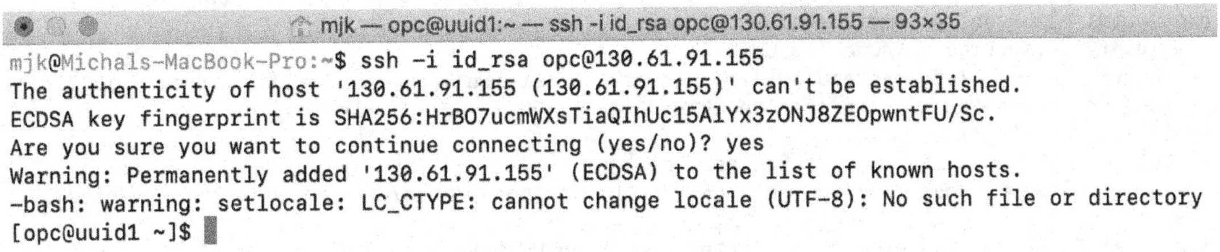

```
mjk@Michals-MacBook-Pro:~$ ssh -i id_rsa opc@130.61.91.155
The authenticity of host '130.61.91.155 (130.61.91.155)' can't be established.
ECDSA key fingerprint is SHA256:HrBO7ucmWXsTiaQIhUc15AlYx3zONJ8ZEOpwntFU/Sc.
Are you sure you want to continue connecting (yes/no)? yes
Warning: Permanently added '130.61.91.155' (ECDSA) to the list of known hosts.
-bash: warning: setlocale: LC_CTYPE: cannot change locale (UTF-8): No such file or directory
[opc@uuid1 ~]$
```

Figure 2-27. *Connecting to a compute instance over SSH*

Congratulations, you've just entered the cloud space.

Waiting for cloud-init

Before you take any action, we are going to find out whether the user data instructions have been completed. At the bottom of Listing 2-3, you will find `final message`. As the name says, this is the last instruction that is processed by cloud-init. Figure 2-28 shows the easiest way to find the message ("UUID Service API node is running") in the log (`/var/log/cloud-init.log`). Some cloud-init instructions can last a while, especially if they download or update software from remote repositories. In our case, it took four minutes to finish all the initialization steps. What does this mean? If you cannot see this message, you need to wait a bit. You can use the `tail -f` command and watch the progress by observing the /var/log/cloud-init.log file. Depending on the number of packages that are being updated, this operation can last a few minutes. Do not continue until you see this message in the log, as presented in Figure 2-28.

[opc@uuid1]$ **sudo cat /var/log/cloud-init.log | grep "node is running"**

```
●  ●  ●                  mjk — opc@uuid1:~ — ssh -i id_rsa opc@130.61.91.155 — 97×35
[[opc@uuid1 ~]$ sudo cat /var/log/cloud-init.log | grep "node is running"
2019-06-04 11:33:21,691 - util.py[DEBUG]: UUID Service API node is running, after 242.26 seconds
[opc@uuid1 ~]$ █
```

Figure 2-28. *Connecting to a compute instance over SSH*

Is our service really running? Seeing is believing. You can run this command to double-check the systemd service status:

[opc@uuid1]$ **sudo systemctl status uuidservice.service**

Figure 2-29 shows the expected output.

```
●  ●  ●                  mjk — opc@uuid1:~ — ssh -i id_rsa opc@130.61.91.155 — 94×35
[[opc@uuid1 ~]$ sudo systemctl status uuidservice.service
● uuidservice.service – Launching UUID Service API
   Loaded: loaded (/etc/systemd/system/uuidservice.service; enabled; vendor preset: disabled)
   Active: active (running) since Tue 2019-06-04 11:33:21 GMT; 14min ago
 Main PID: 12003 (flask)
   CGroup: /system.slice/uuidservice.service
           └─12003 /home/opc/uuidservice/venv/bin/python3 /home/opc/uuidservice/venv/bin/fl...

Jun 04 11:33:21 uuid1 systemd[1]: Started Launching UUID Service API.
Jun 04 11:33:21 uuid1 flask[12003]: * Serving Flask app "/home/opc/uuidservice/app.py"
```

Figure 2-29. *Expected systemd service status for the UUID service*

Is the service really listening on port 5000? Check it with this command:

[opc@uuid1]$ **ss -nltp**

Figure 2-30 shows the expected output.

```
●  ●  ●                  mjk — opc@uuid1:~ — ssh -i id_rsa opc@130.61.91.155 — 94×35
[opc@uuid1 ~]$ ss -nltp
State Recv-Q Send-Q  Local Address:Port   Peer Address:Port
LISTEN0    128         0.0.0.0:5000         0.0.0.0:*       users:(("flask",pid=12003,fd=3))
LISTEN0    128         0.0.0.0:111          0.0.0.0:*
LISTEN0    128         0.0.0.0:22           0.0.0.0:*
LISTEN0    128           [::]:111             [::]:*
LISTEN0    128           [::]:22              [::]:*
```

Figure 2-30. *Viewing the port on which the UUID service is listening for connections*

It seems our first cloud application is indeed running.

Open Ports

Typical problems you may need to troubleshoot on your future cloud projects are related to VCN security rules and operating system firewall rules. It is not enough to add a VCN security rule to the security list that is used by a subnet to which a particular compute instance is attached. You also need to open a required port in the operating system firewall. If you look at the user data we've uploaded to the uuid-1 instance, you will clearly see that we add a rule that opens port 5000. You can run this command in the instance's shell to confirm the rule has been created:

```
[opc@uuid1]$ sudo firewall-cmd --list-ports
```

Figure 2-31 shows the expected output.

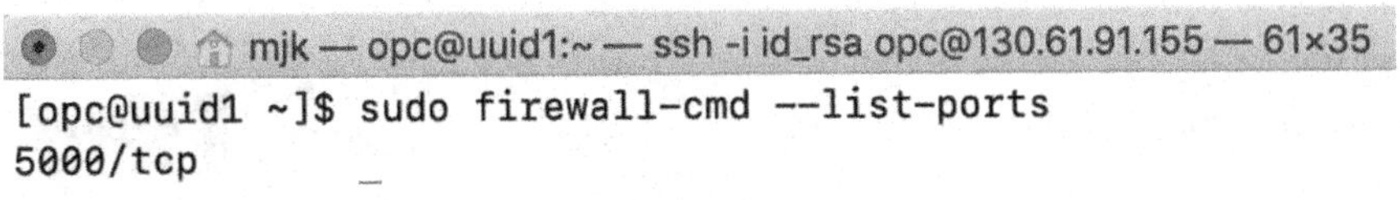

```
mjk — opc@uuid1:~ — ssh -i id_rsa opc@130.61.91.155 — 61×35
[opc@uuid1 ~]$ sudo firewall-cmd --list-ports
5000/tcp
```

Figure 2-31. *Listing open ports on uuid-1*

You can now disconnect from the instance by issuing the exit command.

API Test

Finally! It is time to perform a simple smoke test to see whether the UUID service is truly available in the cloud. We are dealing with a REST API that contains only one resource, identifiers, and supports only one method, GET. It cannot be easier. In our first attempt, we are going to use the curl command. It is available on the Mac/Linux console, Windows Subsystem for Linux, and GitBash on Windows. Please disconnect from the cloud instance and issue the following command, adapting it to include the public IP your instance has been attached to:

```
$ curl -is $UUID1_INSTANCE:5000/identifiers
```

You should see something like in Figure 2-32. In addition to the IP address, the uuid element will be different because it is by definition unique, isn't it?

```
● ● ●                    🏠 mjk — opc@uuid1:~ — -bash — 73×35
[mjk@Michals-MacBook-Pro:~$ curl -is 130.61.91.155:5000/identifiers
HTTP/1.0 200 OK
Content-Type: application/json
Content-Length: 68
Server: Werkzeug/0.15.4 Python/3.6.8
Date: Tue, 04 Jun 2019 12:09:29 GMT

{"generator":"uuid1","uuid":"52e0cf52-1b24-416c-bb2e-648f14afb0d1"}
```

Figure 2-32. *Testing the UUID service API using curl*

If you prefer graphical tools like Postman, you will see something like in Figure 2-33.

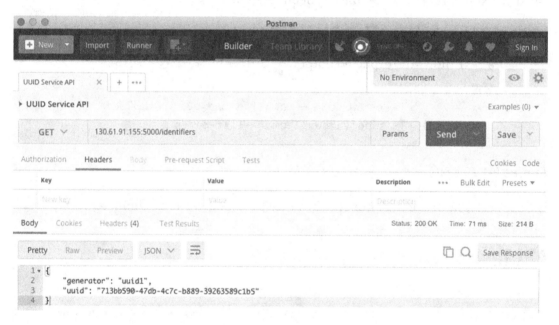

Figure 2-33. *Testing the UUID API using Postman*

Well done! You've reached the point in which the application is running and has been successfully tested. To sum up, we've managed to provision a new VCN with an Internet gateway, create a new public subnet, and add a new route rule to direct the outbound traffic via the Internet gateway and security rule to allow incoming TCP traffic to port 5000 on any compute instance to which this rule applies. On its first boot, the compute instance downloaded all the required packages, created the Python virtual environment, downloaded the UUID service code from GitHub, and installed a new systemd service for the application. Figure 2-34 shows an infrastructure diagram of what we've built.

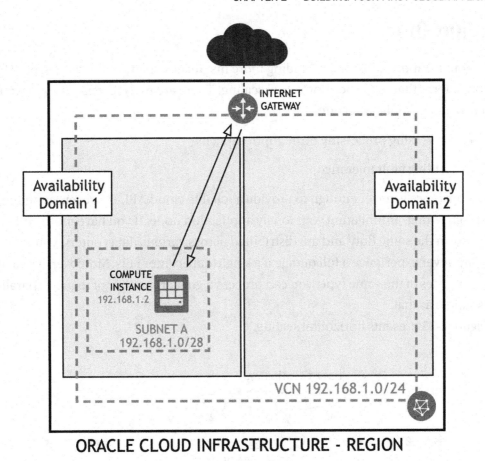

Figure 2-34. Single UUID service API node infrastructure diagram

In the next section, you will manually scale out the API. What does this mean? You will create a second instance in another availability domain and create a load balancer on top of the two instances. In this way, the setup will feature fault tolerance.

Scaling Out

Scaling out an application means adding more instances usually of the same type. This is another term that describes horizontal scaling. There are two reasons why you would want to scale an application out.

- Increasing processing throughput capacity

- Adding fault tolerance

One instance is never enough to provide a reliable cloud API. However, something can still go wrong, annihilating your lonely application node. If you have more nodes that perform the same duty and are distributed across various data centers, you will probably never experience a full outage if a single data center fails. Moreover, if you have more instances of the same type, you can process a greater number of requests parallelly. It's as simple as that.

Figure 2-35 presents horizontal scaling.

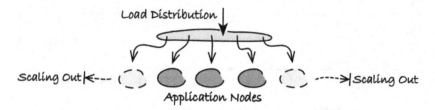

Figure 2-35. *Horizontally scaling an application*

One of the fundamental cloud concepts is autoscaling. *Autoscaling* takes place when the cloud control plane dynamically scales an application horizontally by adding or removing instance nodes based on changing metrics such as request count or CPU utilization. We will discuss autoscaling in more detail later in the book. In this section, I will show you how to manually scale an application out by using custom images.

Custom Image

An *image* is a template that specifies the operating system and any additional software that has to be preinstalled during the instance launch. Oracle Cloud Infrastructure comes with a few base images with various operating systems. You can provision an instance based on a selected operating system image, install the software of your choice, perform some additional configuration, and create a new *custom image* based on this instance. In this way, you will be able to reuse your custom software stack configuration to launch other compute instances.

If you have a running compute instance, you are able to create a new custom image based on that instance. Figure 2-36 shows operations you can issue on a compute instance. One of them is Create Custom Image.

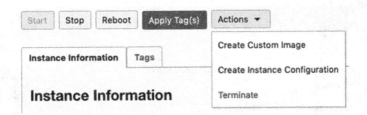

Figure 2-36. *Available compute instance operations*

This is how you create a new custom image based on an existing compute instance:

1. Go to Menu ➤ Compute ➤ Instances.

2. Make sure that the Sandbox compartment is selected.

3. Click the name of our compute instance.

4. Click Actions ➤ Create Custom Image to open a custom image wizard.

5. Provide a name for your new custom image.

6. Click Create Custom Image.

Tip   Consider suffixing your custom image name with the name of the original image used to create the custom image.

Figure 2-37 shows the custom image creation wizard in the OCI Console.

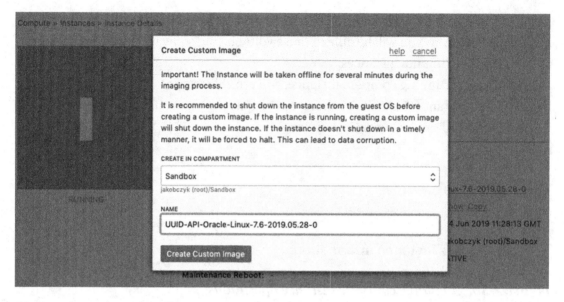

Figure 2-37. *Viewing the custom image creation wizard in the OCI Console*

If you decide to create a custom image based on a particular compute instance, this instance will be taken offline for the time it takes to build the image. As soon as the image has been created, the compute instance will be started again.

Figure 2-38 shows the compute instance that serves as a base for a new custom image while the image is created.

Figure 2-38. *Creating a custom image in the OCI Console instances list*

Figure 2-39 shows a new custom image while it is being created.

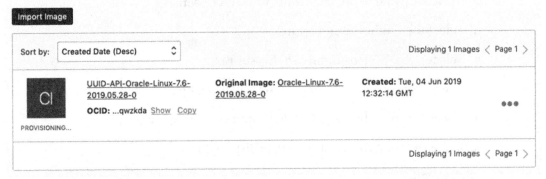

Figure 2-39. *Creating a custom image in the OCI Console images list*

We are going to use the newly created custom image to launch a second instance that runs the UUID service API. To achieve fault tolerance, we will deploy the second node in a different availability domain. Let's create a new subnet in the second availability domain exactly as we planned.

Subnet in a Different AD

We will follow the same sequence of steps we did a few sections earlier when we created the first subnet. To keep things simple, we will reuse the same route table and security list that are in use by the first subnet.

This is how you create a new VCN subnet using the OCI Console:

1. Go to Menu ➤ Networking ➤ Virtual Cloud Networks.

2. Make sure that the Sandbox compartment is selected.

3. Click the name of your VCN.

4. Click Subnets in the Resources menu.

5. Click Create Subnet.

6. Provide the required values:

    a. Enter **b-net** as a display name.

    b. Choose Availability Domain-specific Subnet Type.

    c. Select the second availability domain (suffixed AD-2) in your region.

    d. Place `192.168.1.16/28` as the CIDR block.

    e. Make sure that the default route table is chosen.

    f. Select the Public Subnet option.

    g. Select Use DNS Hostnames in this subnet.

    h. Use a short one-character label **b** as a DNS label.

    i. Make sure that the default DHCP Options setting is chosen.

    j. Make sure that the default security list is chosen.

7. Click Create.

At this stage, you should be able to see two subnets in two different availability domains, as shown in Figure 2-40. Please note that each subnet resides in a different availability domain.

Name		State	CIDR Block	Subnet Access	Created	
a-net	▲	● Available	192.168.1.0/28	Public (feDV:EU-FRANKFURT-1-AD-1)	Mon, Jun 3, 2019, 4:03:09 PM UTC	⋮
b-net		● Available	192.168.1.16/28	Public (feDV:EU-FRANKFURT-1-AD-2)	Tue, Jun 4, 2019, 12:47:26 PM UTC	⋮

Figure 2-40. *Two subnets in two different ADs shown in the OCI Console*

Now, we will create a second UUID service API instance in this newly created subnet.

Second Compute Instance

The second compute instance will run the same systemd service that runs on the first compute instance. This time, we won't upload any user data because everything has already been set up in the image we created from the first compute instance. Figure 2-41 shows the image selection screen and the choice you have to make this time.

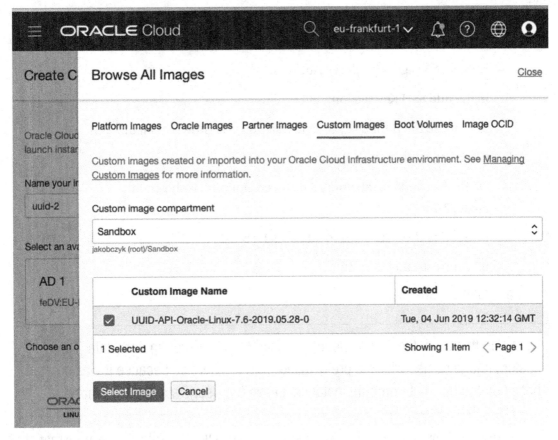

Figure 2-41. *Choosing a custom image in the OCI Console*

This is how you create the second compute instance using the OCI Console:

1. Go to Menu ➤ Compute ➤ Instances.

2. Make sure that the Sandbox compartment is selected.

3. Click Create Instance.

4. Provide the required details:

    a. Name your instance **uuid-2**.

    b. Select the second availability domain in your region.

    c. Set the image source to the newly created custom image; in my case, its name starts with UUID-API-Oracle-Linux-.

    d. Set the instance type to Virtual Machine.

    e. Select VM.Standard2.1 as your instance shape.

5. In the Configure Networking section:

   a. Make sure your new b-net subnet is selected.

   b. Select Assign a Public IP Address.

6. In the Add SSH Key section:

   a. Choose the public key (oci_id_rsa.pub), as shown in Figure 2-21.

7. Click Show Advanced Options.

8. On the Networking tab under Advanced Options, as shown in Figure 2-24:

   a. Set Private IP Address to **192.168.1.18**.

   b. Set Hostname to **uuid2**.

9. Click Create.

Note   In this case, there is no need to upload the cloud-config user data. The custom image comes with the preinstalled UUID API service because it was created based on the uuid-1 compute instance. Leave the User Data section empty.

Figure 2-42 shows the instance creation view in the OCI Console. Please note that this time we are using the second availability domain and custom image.

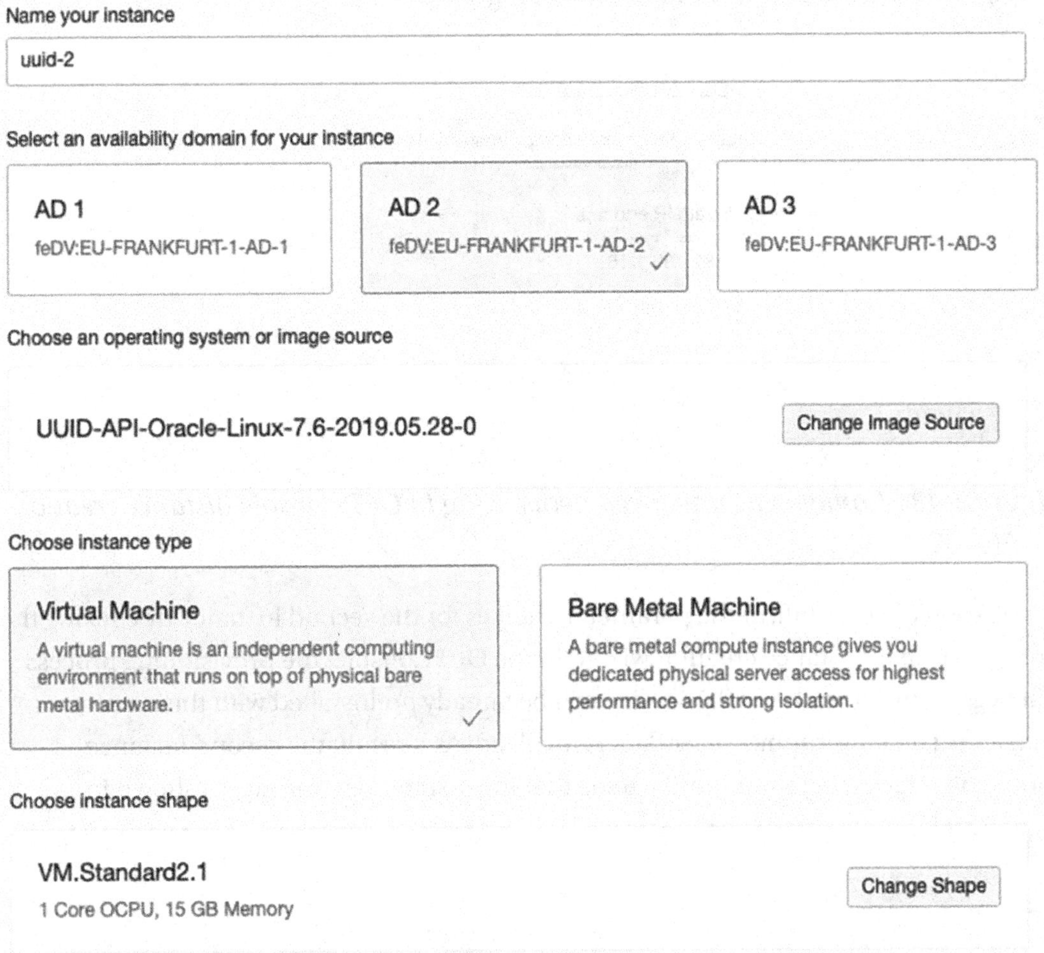

Name your instance

uuid-2

Select an availability domain for your instance

AD 1	AD 2	AD 3
feDV:EU-FRANKFURT-1-AD-1	feDV:EU-FRANKFURT-1-AD-2 ✓	feDV:EU-FRANKFURT-1-AD-3

Choose an operating system or image source

UUID-API-Oracle-Linux-7.6-2019.05.28-0   Change Image Source

Choose instance type

Virtual Machine

A virtual machine is an independent computing
environment that runs on top of physical bare
metal hardware.   ✓

Bare Metal Machine

A bare metal compute instance gives you
dedicated physical server access for highest
performance and strong isolation.

Choose instance shape

VM.Standard2.1

1 Core OCPU, 15 GB Memory   Change Shape

Figure 2-42. Creating the second compute instance in the OCI Console

Figure 2-43 shows the advanced networking section.

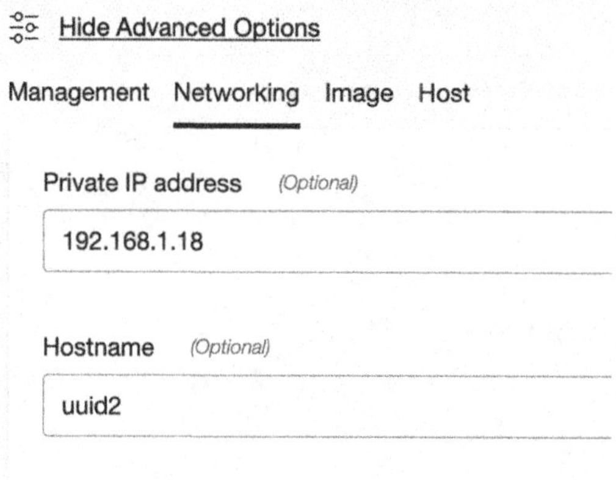

⸬ Hide Advanced Options

Management   Networking   Image   Host

Private IP address   *(Optional)*

192.168.1.18

Hostname   *(Optional)*

uuid2

Figure 2-43. *Configuring advanced networking in OCI Console instance creation wizard*

As soon as you confirm the parameter choices for the second instance by clicking the Create button in instance creation wizard in the OCI Console, the provisioning process will begin. This time, the UUID service will be already preinstalled with the custom image, and no long-running user data is involved. As a result, the second instance should boot faster. Let's wait until we see that the instance is running, as shown in Figure 2-44.

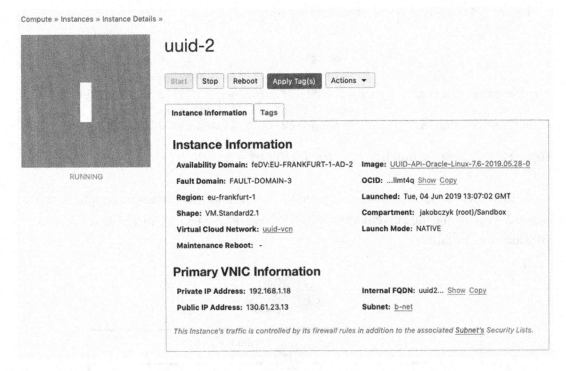

Figure 2-44. *Viewing the second running compute instance in the OCI Console*

You can now test the API on both nodes. Please remember to replace the public IP addresses and use the ones that have been assigned to your instances in both cases.

```
$ UUID2_INSTANCE=130.61.23.13
$ curl $UUID1_INSTANCE:5000/identifiers
{
  "generator":"uuid1",
  "uuid":"bc85b59f-cf0f-4035-a730-c25111db00ec"
}
$ curl $UUID2_INSTANCE:5000/identifiers
{
  "generator":"uuid2",
  "uuid":"6eca06e0-65f2-444b-acb8-b9c46741dc72"
}
```

Figure 2-45 shows that two instances are operative.

```
● ● ●                 🏠 mjk — opc@uuid1:~ — -bash — 73×35
[mjk@Michals-MacBook-Pro:~$ curl 130.61.91.155:5000/identifiers
{"generator":"uuid1","uuid":"bc85b59f-cf0f-4035-a730-c25111db00ec"}
[mjk@Michals-MacBook-Pro:~$ curl 130.61.23.13:5000/identifiers
{"generator":"uuid2","uuid":"6eca06e0-65f2-444b-acb8-b9c46741dc72"}
```

Figure 2-45. *Testing two nodes of the UUID service API*

In this section, we deployed and tested the second node that runs our application. Figure 2-46 presents the current application infrastructure using Oracle Cloud Infrastructure notation.

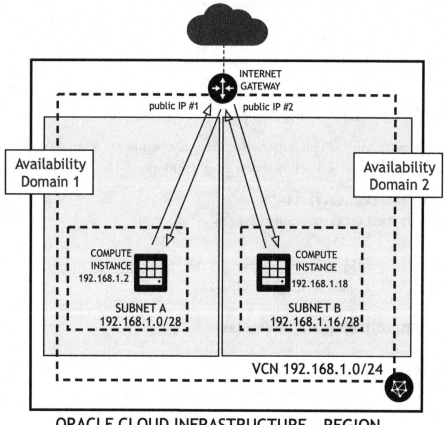

Figure 2-46. *Two nodes of the UUID API on the infrastructure diagram*

The current setup has one major pain point. The API consumers (in other words, applications that invoke the API) have to explicitly specify the public IP address of a particular virtual machine. With this approach, the more you scale the API out, the more unrelated endpoints with different public IP addresses you produce. This is not the best way to design a highly available solution. Luckily, we can change it by adding a load balancer.

Load Balancer

A load balancer provides a single point of entry and traffic distribution to the active servers or worker nodes. We are going to use an Internet-facing, so-called public load balancer that uses a public floating IP to support the failover mechanism. This means that you launch a pair of load balancer (LB) nodes, each in a different availability domain. At any given time, only one LB node is active and forwards traffic to the UUID service API nodes. The second LB node remains in Standby mode. If the active LB node fails, the standby LB node will detect this situation and announce itself as the active node and the current IP address holder.

Figure 2-47 shows how a fault-tolerant public load balancer works.

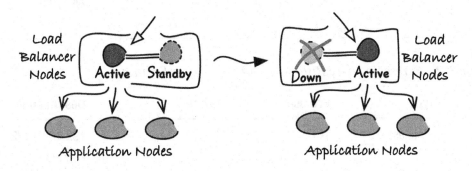

Figure 2-47. *Fault-tolerant public IP load balancer*

A public load balancer requires two dedicated public subnets. We are going to create them in the same VCN in which we host UUID service API nodes. This time, we will use a new security list because the rules will differ from the default security list that we use for our application node subnets.

Please create a new security list called lb-sl. This is how you create a new security using the OCI Console:

1. Go to Menu ➤ Networking ➤ Virtual Cloud Networks.

2. Make sure that the Sandbox compartment is selected.

3. Click the name of your VCN.

4. Click Security Lists in the Resources menu.

5. Click Create Security List.

6. Give it a name: **lb-sl**.

7. Create ingress rules as defined in Table 2-1. One rule has to be stateless.

8. Create egress rules as defined in Table 2-2. The rule has to be stateless.

9. Click Create Security List.

Table 2-1. *Ingress Security Rules for Load Balancer Subnet*

	Type	Protocol	Source	Destination
1	Stateful	TCP	0.0.0.0/0 All ports	Port 80
2	Stateless	TCP	192.168.1.0/24 Port 5000	All ports

Table 2-2. *Egress Security Rules for Load Balancer Subnet*

	Type	Protocol	Source	Destination
1	Stateless	TCP	All ports	192.168.1.0/24 Port 5000

Figure 2-48 shows the ingress rules.

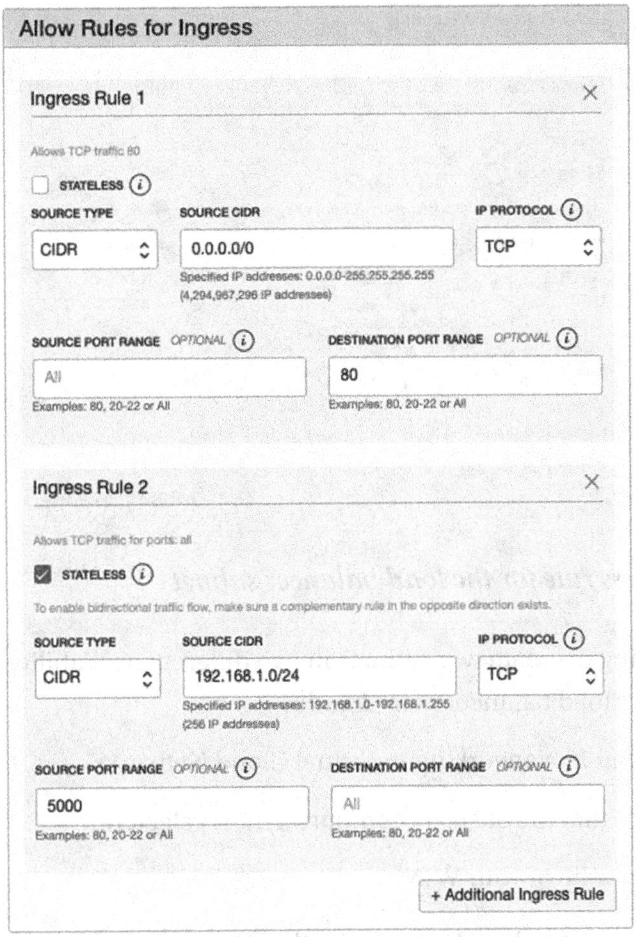

Figure 2-48. *Ingress rules for the load balancer subnets*

Figure 2-49 shows the expected egress rule.

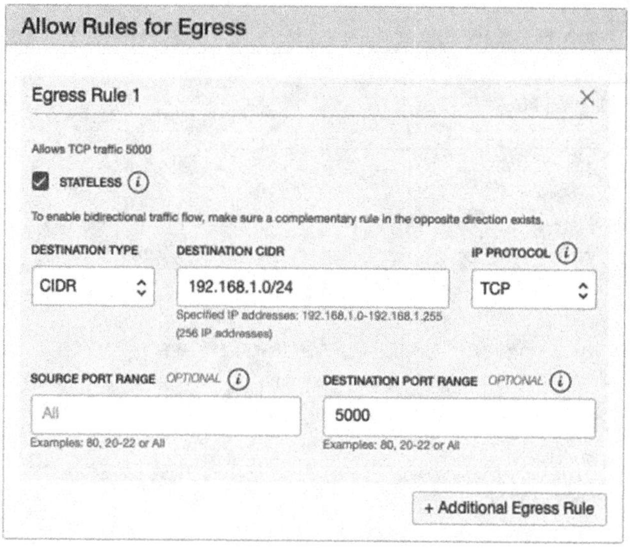

Figure 2-49. *Egress rule for the load balancer subnet*

We are now going to create two subnets in two different availability domains for a fault-tolerant public load balancer pair of nodes.

1. Go to Menu ➤ Networking ➤ Virtual Cloud Networks.

2. Make sure that the Sandbox compartment is selected.

3. Click the name of your VCN.

4. Click Subnets in the Resources menu.

5. Add two new public subnets, as defined in Table 2-3.

Table 2-3. *Load Balancer Subnets*

Name	AD	CIDR Block	DNS Label	Security List
c-net	1	192.168.1.32/29	c	lb-sl
d-net	2	192.168.1.40/29	d	lb-sl

We've just prepared the networking setup for our highly available public load balancer. Altogether with UUID API subnets, you should see four subnets in your VCN, as shown in Figure 2-50.

Name	▲	State	CIDR Block	Subnet Access	Created	
a-net		● Available	192.168.1.0/28	Public (feDV:EU-FRANKFURT-1-AD-1)	Mon, Jun 3, 2019, 4:03:09 PM UTC	⋮
b-net		● Available	192.168.1.16/28	Public (feDV:EU-FRANKFURT-1-AD-2)	Tue, Jun 4, 2019, 12:47:26 PM UTC	⋮
c-net		● Available	192.168.1.32/29	Public (feDV:EU-FRANKFURT-1-AD-1)	Tue, Jun 4, 2019, 1:31:17 PM UTC	⋮
d-net		● Available	192.168.1.40/29	Public (feDV:EU-FRANKFURT-1-AD-2)	Tue, Jun 4, 2019, 1:31:48 PM UTC	⋮
					Showing 4 Items 〈 Page 1 〉	

Figure 2-50. *Subnets in VCN*

As a matter of fact, the load balancing capability is delivered by a set of cooperating OCI resources encapsulated by a *load balancer* resource. Compute nodes or private IP addresses to which the requests are forwarded by the load balancer are considered as *backends* and grouped together into a *backend set* resource. A backend set is more than just a simple grouping of backends because it also defines the health check policy. The health check policy decides how the backends are judge to be operational or failing. Finally, a *listener* is required to accept the ingress traffic; otherwise, requests wouldn't be able to flow into the public load balancer from the Internet. Figure 2-51 shows a conceptual composition of OCI resources for the load balancer.

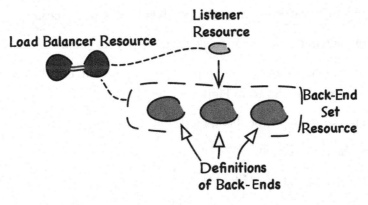

Figure 2-51. *Load balancer OCI resources*

Having outlined the resources that a load balancer is composed of, let's create them. When using the OCI Console, you can leverage a three-step all-in-one load balancer creation wizard. This is how you create a new load balancer resource:

1. Go to Menu ➤ Networking ➤ Load Balancers.

2. Make sure that the Sandbox compartment is selected.

3. Click Create Load Balancer.

4. In the Add Details step, provide the configuration, as shown in Figure 2-52:

    a. Name your load balancer **uuid-lb**.

    b. Set the visibility to Public.

    c. Select the Small shape: 100Mbps.

    d. Select Public Load Balancer.

    e. Set the VCN to the uuid-vcn VCN.

    f. Choose the load balancer subnets: c-net and d-net.

5. Click Next Step.

6. In the Choose Backends step, provide the configuration, as shown in Figure 2-53:

    a. Make sure Weighted Round Robin is selected.

    b. Click Add Backends and select both compute instances.

    c. For each backend instance, change the port to 5000.

7. Still in the Choose Backends step, provide the health check policy configuration, as shown in Figure 2-54:

    a. Make sure the protocol is set to HTTP.

    b. Set the port to 5000.

    c. Set the URL path to /identifiers.

    d. Make sure the status code is set to 200.

8. Click Next Step.

9. In the Configure Listener step, provide the configuration, as
    shown in Figure 2-55:

    a. Choose the HTTP protocol and set the port to 80.

    b. Name the listener **uuid-lb-listener**.

10. Click Create Load Balancer.

Figure 2-52 shows the expected load balancer configuration in the Load Balancer
Add Details step of the load balancer creation wizard in the OCI Console.

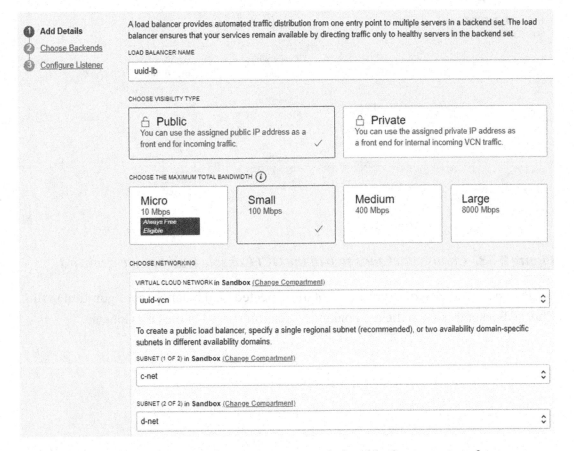

Figure 2-52. *Add Details step in the OCI console load balancer wizard*

Figure 2-53 shows the first part of the expected load balancer configuration in the
Choose Backends step of the load balancer creation wizard in the OCI Console.

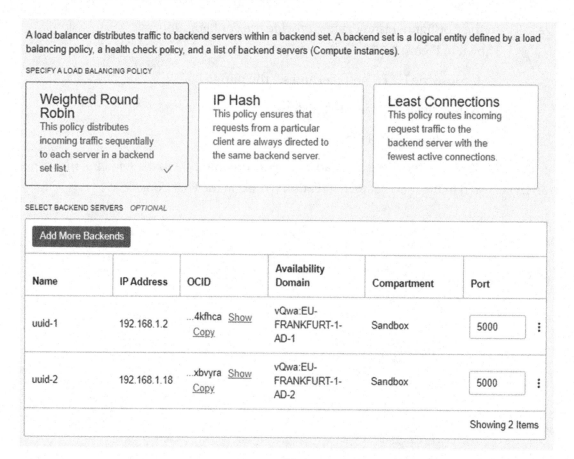

Figure 2-53. *Choose Backends step in the OCI Console load balancer wizard*

Figure 2-54 shows the second part of the expected load balancer configuration in the Choose Backends step of the load balancer creation wizard in the OCI Console.

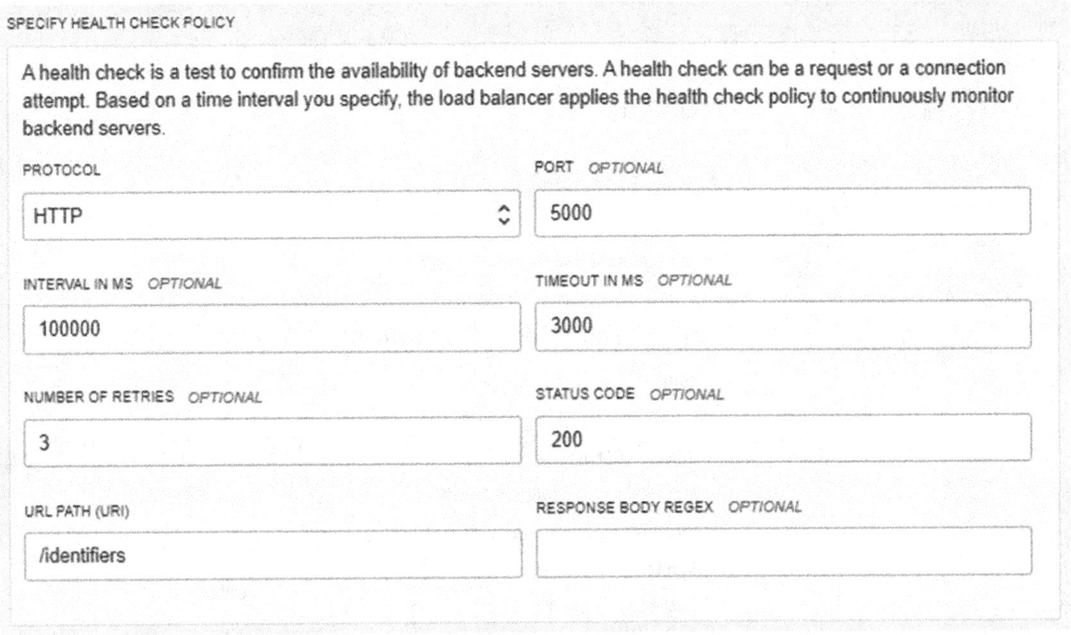

SPECIFY HEALTH CHECK POLICY

A health check is a test to confirm the availability of backend servers. A health check can be a request or a connection attempt. Based on a time interval you specify, the load balancer applies the health check policy to continuously monitor backend servers.

PROTOCOL

HTTP

PORT *OPTIONAL*

5000

INTERVAL IN MS *OPTIONAL*

100000

TIMEOUT IN MS *OPTIONAL*

3000

NUMBER OF RETRIES *OPTIONAL*

3

STATUS CODE *OPTIONAL*

200

URL PATH (URI)

/identifiers

RESPONSE BODY REGEX *OPTIONAL*

Figure 2-54. *Health check settings in the Choose Backends step*

Figure 2-55 shows the expected load balancer backend set configuration in the Configure Listener step of the load balancer creation wizard in the OCI Console.

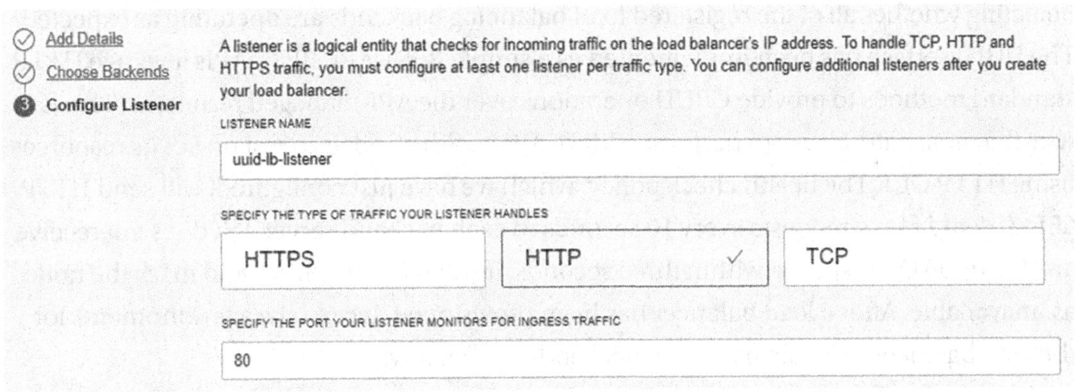

⊘ Add Details
⊘ Choose Backends
③ **Configure Listener**

A listener is a logical entity that checks for incoming traffic on the load balancer's IP address. To handle TCP, HTTP and HTTPS traffic, you must configure at least one listener per traffic type. You can configure additional listeners after you create your load balancer.

LISTENER NAME

uuid-lb-listener

SPECIFY THE TYPE OF TRAFFIC YOUR LISTENER HANDLES

| HTTPS | HTTP ✓ | TCP |

SPECIFY THE PORT YOUR LISTENER MONITORS FOR INGRESS TRAFFIC

80

Figure 2-55. *Configure Listener step in the OCI Console load balancer wizard*

Oracle Cloud Infrastructure will now provision a new public load balancer and attach a public IP address from a pool of Oracle Cloud addresses. We have to wait until the provisioning action has been completed to see something like in Figure 2-56.

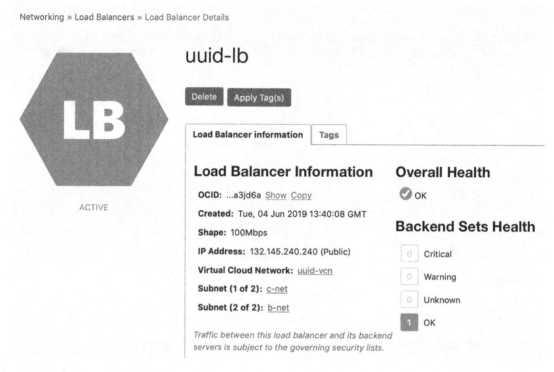

Figure 2-56. *Viewing load balancer information in the OCI Console*

The health check configuration we've defined is responsible for overseeing and detecting whether all of the registered load balancing backends are operating as expected. The UUID service has been implemented as a simple REST API. REST APIs leverage HTTP standard methods to provide CRUD operations over the API-managed resources. This is why the most natural way to perform a REST API health check is to test one of its resources using HTTP GET. The health check policy, which we have just configured, will send HTTP GET /identifiers requests every 10 seconds to each backend server. If it does not receive an HTTP 200 OK response within three seconds, it will retry two times and mark the node as unavailable. After a load balancer has been provisioned, it can take a few moments for the load balancer to confirm that the backends are healthy.

Tip   If you are observing the Unknown state for a prolonged period of time, do not worry, but move on to testing the load balancer. In some cases, after the load balancer launches, it can take minutes until the load balancer moves from the Unknown state to OK.

If needed, you can check the state of each individual backend, as shown in Figure 2-57. To do so, follow these steps:

1. Go to Menu ➤ Networking ➤ Load Balancers.

2. Click the name of your load balancer.

3. In the Resources section, click Backend Sets.

4. Click the name of the backend set.

5. In the Resources section, click Backends.

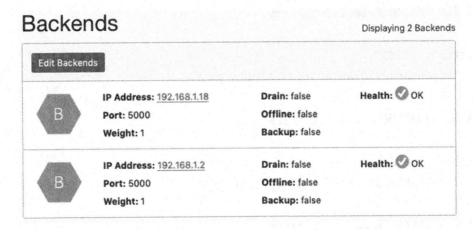

Figure 2-57. *Viewing backend health flags in the OCI Console*

If you should find one of the backends in a Critical state, follow this checklist to troubleshoot the issue:

- The target compute node is running.

- The UUID Service systemd service is started.

- The operating system firewall accepts connections on port 5000.

- There is an ingress stateful rule in the default security list that allows the incoming traffic to port 5000.

- The rules in the load balancer's subnet security list are correct.

- The load balancer set backends are properly defined.

- The load balancer backend set health check configuration is correct.

All in all, after a while, you will be able to perform the final test for this chapter. To do so, you need to identify the public IP address your load balancer has been given from the Oracle Cloud address pool. In my case, it is 132.145.240.240. When you send a few requests to the /identifiers resource on port 80 of your load balancer, they will be evenly routed in a round-robin manner to the first (uuid-1) and second (uuid-2) instances of the UUID service API. Every time you send a request to your load balancer, it is interchangeably served by one of the two UUID service instances, as proven by the generator JSON element in each response.

```
$ LB_INSTANCE=132.145.240.101
$ curl $LB_INSTANCE:80/identifiers
{
"generator":"uuid1",
"uuid":"709f6aac-0720-461a-9fd3-732748253bca"
}
$ curl $LB_INSTANCE:80/identifiers
{
"generator":"uuid2",
"uuid":"cfe329bd-cd2c-49a6-ae4f-29f23bf5d2fe"
}
$ curl $LB_INSTANCE:80/identifiers
{
"generator":"uuid1",
"uuid":"e22b5858-e70f-46ab-bd16-0da3d55aca73"
}
$ curl $LB_INSTANCE:80/identifiers
{
"generator":"uuid2",
"uuid":"1c9662d9-1426-4e2d-bae3-bd4207dbd73b"
}
```

We have completed the exercise. Before we move on, let's terminate the cloud resources. You can now terminate all resources you've created in this chapter, excluding the learning compartment that we are going to use in the next chapters.

Cleanup

To avoid unnecessary costs or trial credit consumption, no matter how low they are, let's terminate the resources we've created in this chapter. Some resources depend on other resources; therefore, it is important to stick to the required sequence when you delete them. This won't be a problem in future chapters because in many cases the automation will do it for us in one shot. In this chapter, however, we are doing everything manually in the OCI Console, so we have to follow these steps:

1. Go to Menu ➤ Networking ➤ Load Balancers.

2. Make sure that the Sandbox compartment is selected.

3. Click the three-dot menu, click Terminate, and wait until the resource is removed.

Figure 2-58 shows how to terminate a load balancer.

Figure 2-58. *Terminating a load balancer in the OCI Console*

Now, in a similar way, use the OCI Console to terminate (or delete) the remaining resources.

-   Both compute instances (Menu ➤ Compute ➤ Instances)

-   Custom image (Menu ➤ Compute ➤ Custom Images)

-   VCN with associated networking resources

Tip   When you terminate a compute instance, make sure you permanently delete the boot volume. If you forget to do so, you can always delete an abandoned boot volume later in Compute ➤ Boot Volumes.

This concludes the exercise in this chapter.

Summary

In this chapter, I drove you through the process of planning and running a simple cloud application on Oracle Cloud Infrastructure. First, we spent some time analyzing the application design and outlining the required cloud infrastructure resources. Subsequently, we used the OCI Console to provision each cloud resource step by step. The application itself was built and run on the instance by using cloud-init-powered automation. Next, we scaled the application out and added a public load balancer to evenly distribute the load to two compute nodes that host the application. At the end, I showed you how to perform a cleanup and remove the resources.

You may get the impression that the exercise in this chapter consisted of an enormous number of manual steps. Well, I warned you that I wanted to show you the manual way and teach you how to handle the OCI Console. The next chapter will introduce the OCI CLI and Terraform automation, and you will experience how to manage your cloud infrastructure as code faster. Read on.

## CHAPTER 3

Automating Cloud Infrastructure

Cloud computing cannot exist without *automation*. The entire concept of the rapid self-provisioning of pooled cloud resources (compute instances, storage, virtual networking, and many others) is built on an assumption that the whole provisioning process, from the beginning to the end, is fully automated. Simply because there are no manual steps involved, it is possible to represent the complete cloud infrastructure in the form of scripts and templates that are used to remotely manage cloud resources. Figure 3-1 shows a mind map of a few related operational characteristics that are enabled through the automation.

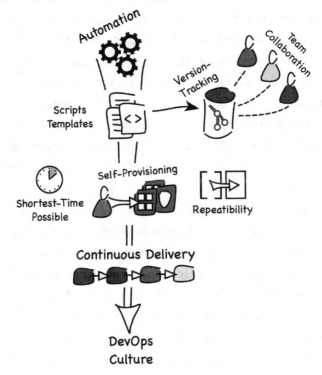

Figure 3-1. *Automation*

© Michał Tomasz Jakóbczyk 2020
M. T. Jakóbczyk, *Practical Oracle Cloud Infrastructure*, https://doi.org/10.1007/978-1-4842-5506-3_3

Scripts and templates can be treated as source code and stored in a version control system like Git. This boosts team collaboration as well as leads to faster delivery of enhancements and, as a consequence, problem resolution. New team members can furthermore understand the infrastructure just by reading the code that is always up-to-date, in contrast to the traditional documentation that can, as time goes by, easily skew from the real state. You prepare the scripts and templates, which, during execution, interact with the so-called cloud management plane through the interfaces covered in the next section. The cloud management plane provisioning engine is already automated by your cloud provider. It is responsible for creating, updating, and deleting the resources in the cloud. Again, there are absolutely no manual steps throughout the entire process. Everything considered together leads to the shortest provisioning time possible, repeatability, and self-service.

You can and actually should go beyond automating the cloud infrastructure management only. Cloud infrastructure is part of and, at the same time, a prerequisite for your cloud-based solutions. You indeed run business or platform software on cloud infrastructure. It makes therefore more sense to automate the entire solution delivery process. Imagine your developer checks in an application code change that effectively adds a new service. The service listens on a port that hasn't been used until now. The same commit can include an infrastructure script or template change that would add a new security list to allow the inbound traffic on that port. The new code revision is detected by the build server that creates the new security rule and reprovisions one or more virtual machines or containers that host the service in the test environment. Finally, the integration and regression tests are executed to assess the quality of the change. In this way, a simple code change can produce a tested deployment running in the cloud. This is called *continuous delivery*. The process does not need to end with the test environment. Some use cases would benefit from releasing a limited number of service instances in the newest version, known as a *canary release*, straight to the production environment to evaluate their behavior under real-world conditions.

Automation is the key enabler for continuous delivery that can become an important part of the *DevOps culture* in your organization. What does it mean, and what are its benefits? Looking only at the name, the Dev part comes from the word *development*, and the Ops part comes from the word *operations*. In the traditional model, developers handled deliverables to the operations team whose members prepared the configuration and deployed the artifacts to particular environments. This cascade often led to misunderstandings and errors, causing the delivery process to be longer than it should be.

DevOps breaks this approach and blends both roles. Processes related to the field of traditional operations are now fully automated and often triggered already by the actions done by application developers. In a popular understanding, a person who holds a DevOps role is responsible for building and maintaining the aforementioned automation. Repeatability, which is a result of thorough automation, decreases the risk of errors previously related to manual actions. Moreover, the time saved by automating the recurring manual tasks can be used to enhance the insights into running systems and provide better governance over the entire application landscape. The term *DevOps culture* is actually broader and goes far beyond the scope of this book.

Cloud Management Plane

To fulfill its duties, the cloud platform provides a set of secure interfaces you can interact with to control your cloud assets. These interfaces, referenced also as APIs, are your gateway to the *cloud management plane*, which is the engine that delivers cloud resources based on physical and virtual equipment in data centers. Clients send requests to API endpoints to remotely execute various operations in the cloud.

You need to remember that the cloud is by definition multitenant. Because manifold users interact with the same set of interface endpoints, the engine is not only responsible for managing and monitoring the cloud assets but also has to make sure that the resources used by different tenants (cloud accounts) are properly isolated. Moreover, the API is also responsible for protecting cloud assets from unauthorized access. This idea is conceptually presented in Figure 3-2.

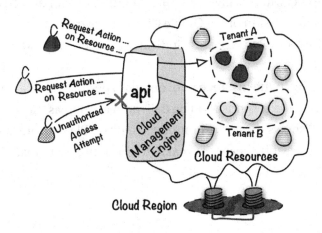

Figure 3-2. *Cloud management plane and multitenancy*

Oracle Cloud Infrastructure API

The most common way for cloud providers to offer their cloud interfaces is in the form of secure *REST APIs*. Cloud resources and their lifecycle events are represented as REST resources and corresponding HTTP methods (GET, PUT, POST, DELETE). A successfully authenticated and authorized client can order the cloud management plane to perform an operation on one or more cloud resources on his behalf. This is done by sending a properly formed request over HTTPS. The cloud management plane validates and translates the request to a set of operations performed on virtual and/or physical resources to accomplish the requested action.

How does it actually work in practice from a client's point of view? Let's take a quick look at Listing 3-1, which presents a simplified API request that would eventually list the details of a particular instance pool. To increase the clarity of this example, I've used parameter placeholders for the OCID of the instance pool cloud resource ({ic-id}) and the OCID of the compartment ({c-id}). In a real request, you would replace them with the correct Oracle Cloud identifiers.

Listing 3-1. Simplified API Request

```
GET /20160918/instancePools/{ic-id}?compartmentId={c-id} HTTP/1.1
Host: iaas.eu-frankfurt-1.oraclecloud.com
Accept: application/json
Authorization: ...
```

The request shown in Listing 3-1 asks for the instance pool details of a specified instance pool that exists within a given compartment. The first part of the REST resource, /20160918, denotes the version of the Oracle Cloud Infrastructure API, while the second segment, namely, instancePools, clearly indicates the type of cloud resource we are dealing with.

The operation to fetch the instance pool details is performed in a synchronous way, which means that the response will be delivered as soon as the results have been collected. Listing 3-2 shows the corresponding response. Please note that I've shortened the OCIDs and the request ID header to make the structure more readable.

Listing 3-2. Simplified API Response

```
HTTP/1.1 200 OK
Content-Type: application/json
Content-Length: 931
opc-request-id: /D8613...

{
  "id" : "ocid1.instancepool....",
  "compartmentId" : "ocid1.compartment....",
  "definedTags" : { },
  "displayName" : "instance-pool",
  "freeformTags" : { },
  "instanceConfigurationId" : "ocid1.instanceconfiguration....",
  "lifecycleState" : "RUNNING",
  "placementConfigurations" : [ {
    "availabilityDomain" : "feDV:EU-FRANKFURT-1-AD-1",
    "primarySubnetId" : "ocid1.subnet...."
  }, {
    "availabilityDomain" : "feDV:EU-FRANKFURT-1-AD-2",
    "primarySubnetId" : "ocid1.subnet...."
  } ],
  "size" : 4,
  "timeCreated" : "2018-12-21T18:47:29.767Z"
}
```

Depending on the type of the requested action, the cloud management plane engine may perform either a synchronous or an asynchronous operation. Synchronous operations result in blocking calls, which means that the client waits for the results that are returned in the corresponding response. In the case of an asynchronous operation, you would immediately receive a response that contains a work request ID you can use to track the state of the requested operation. At the time of writing, three capabilities support work requests and perform some operations in an asynchronous way.

- Container Engine for Kubernetes

- Object storage

- Load balancing

Using APIs for these three capabilities entails the need for careful design decisions an API client has to make when implementing the procedural provisioning scripts. This applies when using custom API calls, SDKs, and the CLI. Luckily, you do not need to worry about this design aspect if you manage your infrastructure as code using the declarative approach with Terraform.

The APIs are intended to deliver the richest set of operations that can be performed on the cloud resources. In other words, if you cannot find an API resource for a particular operation, the operation either is not supported at the moment or can be achieved through a sequence of multiple API calls that perform more granular actions on cloud assets.

Tip   You can find the comprehensive reference of the available Oracle Cloud Infrastructure REST APIs at `https://docs.cloud.oracle.com/iaas/api`.

Securing API Calls

You may wonder how secure the remote management of cloud resources is when using REST APIs. Well, if it wasn't secure, there would be no cloud computing I guess. There are three aspects of API calls security we have to briefly discuss.

- Transport layer security

- Authentication

- Authorization

First, the data packets that travel through the public Internet over HTTPS are encrypted. TLS 1.2 protocol mechanisms protect the communication from being eavesdropped on or altered while on the way. This industry-standard protocol provides *transport layer security* transparently, and no involvement from the cloud team is required.

The enforcement of *authentication*, which is a way to validate who the request sender really is, requires a different approach. Each request has to be signed using the sender's private key and the RSA-SHA256 algorithm. The signature is eventually included within the request's `authorization` header. Listing 3-3 shows the detailed structure of the header, including placeholders for user- and tenancy-specific data.

Listing 3-3. Authorization Header with Request Signature

```
Authorization: Signature version="1",keyId="{tenancy-ocid}/{user-ocid}/
{public-key-fingerprint}",algorithm="rsa-sha256",headers="(request-target)
date host",signature="{signature}"
```

To generate a signature, you first need to build a *signing string* that is composed of the parts of the request including, but not limited to, a resource target, such as /20160918/vcns, and a hash of a request payload, when present. The signing string is then encrypted using the private key and gets encoded to text using the Base64 algorithm. Yes, it does sound a bit complex, but do not worry. You do not need to perform these steps in your daily job on your own, unless you really want. You nearly always use software development kit (SDK) for a particular language or specialized provisioning tools (CLI, Terraform) that prepare the authorization header and invoke the OCI API for you.

Not every successfully authenticated user should be allowed to perform a particular operation. For example, if there are multiple projects maintained under the same cloud account, you will probably prefer to keep the resources that belong to project A isolated from project B users. Even for a single project, it may still make sense to limit some access rights to specific sets of resources for particular groups of users. This will be the task of the *authorization* function, which verifies what an authenticated user is really entitled to do. In the next chapter, you will learn about identity and access management users, groups, and policies that altogether let you configure the authorization mechanisms for your cloud account.

At this stage, it is crucial to highlight that every API call is always made on behalf of a named Oracle Cloud Infrastructure IAM user. For each request, in the authorization header, a client declares a tenancy OCID, a user OCID, and a fingerprint of a public key that has been uploaded to Oracle Cloud Infrastructure for this particular IAM user. Moreover, the signature, which is also part of the header, is encrypted with the corresponding private key. This all leads to the conclusion that you need to possess a keypair, called an *API signing keypair*, before you sign the API requests. The public key will have to be uploaded to Oracle Cloud Infrastructure and associated with a user of your choice. In this way, OCI will know how to decrypt your request.

API Signing Key

In this section, we are going to generate a new keypair that will serve as an API signing keypair and upload the public key to Oracle Cloud Infrastructure under a particular IAM user. In this way, we will empower anyone with the private key to leverage the OCI API and manage OCI resources remotely on behalf of this IAM user. The private key will be additionally secured with a password. Every time you try using the private key, you will be prompted for password, unless you persist it in your local configuration.

Note   The code snippets from this book have been tested on macOS and Windows Subsystem for Linux. Moreover, all commands should work on major Linux distributions. If you are using Windows and do not want to use Windows Subsystem for Linux, you can always run Linux on a VM. Furthermore, the majority of code snippets may also work in Git Bash on Windows.

Generate a Keypair

The API signing keypair must be an RSA keypair in PEM format. PEM format uses human-readable characters, which makes it slightly easier to work with (especially copying the public key) than when working with binary formats. We are going to use the openssl program to generate a new keypair that consists of two related 2,048-bit keys: one private to sign the request and one public to verify the genuineness of the request. This is how you generate a new keypair using openssl that should be available out of the box on your Linux, macOS, and Windows Subsystem for Linux:

```
$ mkdir ~/.apikeys
$ cd ~/.apikeys
$ openssl genrsa -out oci_api_pem -aes128 2048
Generating RSA private key, 2048 bit long modulus
.............+++
..+++
```

```
e is 65537 (0x10001)
Enter pass phrase for oci_api_pem:
Verifying - Enter pass phrase for oci_api_pem:
```

```
$ chmod go-rwx oci_api_pem
```

```
$ ls -l | grep pem | awk '{ print $1" "$9 }'
-rw------- oci_api_pem
```

```
$ openssl rsa -pubout -in oci_api_pem -out oci_api_pem.pub
Enter pass phrase for oci_api_pem:
writing RSA key
```

```
$ ls -l | grep pem | awk '{ print $1" "$9 }'
-rw------- oci_api_pem
-rw-r--r-- oci_api_pem.pub
```

It is recommended that you restrict the access permissions to your private key so that only the file owner is entitled to read or amend the file. You can perform this operation using the chmod command, as shown in the code snippet. At this stage, the keypair is ready. Listing 3-4 shows the public key we've just generated.

Listing 3-4. API Signing Keypair Public Key

```
$ cat oci_api_pem.pub
-----BEGIN PUBLIC KEY-----
MIIBIjANBgkqhkiG9w0BAQEFAAOCAQ8AMIIBCgKCAQEAy7QqyKkIM1UWOlBs3h04
OIxCNbAc1YpqLmd/ZQGwNFoC9L7kpkARjOTMQg/XY9VgFhTFwkhv/sP7aOwYZjVD
BMltp3e0Xzu1BGe4AQF3xL+euqZW9dBRlvZqb1ubEse4RnKDCWvYpqQS/vQU48TM
nRObefTsZH1xg2RfO2mFHuGEZhJKrVIjHTJvjisAIZgOdPaVD8Ee+julutCnDHcP
QWlfe2e4OtYvvki5Wwu5Uz4Zq6ZSf55oX25pDGyw/WB5oDFg4v6RsZ7kQZYTBsqA
gF7RnG+q5JnxFfuDvEZoUOsB5hRWujhhSZtE9FjU9UndMU5iaa8kNE6Ua3eOp4ZG
RwIDAQAB
-----END PUBLIC KEY-----
```

Uploading the Public Key

We've reached the point when we need to decide on whose behalf the API requests are sent. In other words, we have to select an existing IAM user and upload the public key that will get associated with this user. If you are working with a new trial or PAYG account, you are probably logged in as the default IAM user who represents the tenancy owner and belongs, out of the box, to the Administrators group. This group will let you perform all the exercises described in this chapter.

Tip   If you are using some other IAM user, given to you by your cloud team, who isn't a member of the Administrators group, please talk to your cloud team admin to verify what kind of actions you are entitled to perform or jump to Chapter 4 to understand what the IAM policies assigned to your IAM group mean.

This is how you upload a public key using the OCI Console:

1. Go to Menu ➤ Identity ➤ Users.

2. Click the name of your tenancy administrator user.

3. Click API Keys in the Resources menu.

4. Click Add Public Key.

5. Paste the public key.

6. Click Add.

Figure 3-3 presents the OCI Console window, which you use to add a new public key for an IAM user.

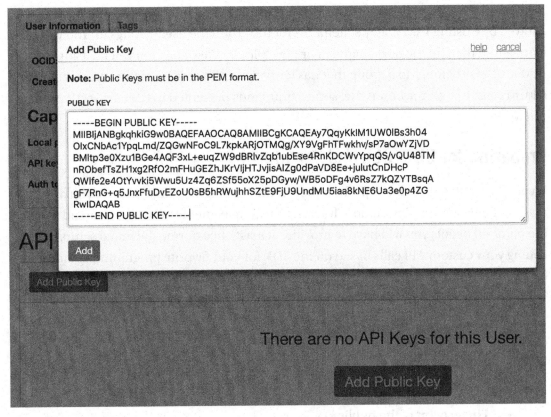

Figure 3-3. *Adding a public key in the OCI Console*

You can have up to three public API keys for each IAM user. The API will recognize which is the right one to use for each incoming request based on a *fingerprint* of the public key included in the `authorization` header of the request. The fingerprint is displayed in the OCI Console, as shown in Figure 3-4.

Figure 3-4. *Fingerprint of the public key*

The user is allowed to perform only the operations on cloud resources that are allowed by existing IAM policy statements for the group the user belongs to. You will learn about them in the next chapter. For now, please make sure you will be using an IAM user who belongs to a group that has tenancy administration rights, such as default Administrators group; otherwise, some commands presented in the next sections may not work.

Preparing for SDK, CLI, and Terraform

If you've completed all the steps described in the "API Signing Key" section, you are ready to begin automating cloud infrastructure management tasks. Let's wrap up and list the required details you will have to provide, at least once during the initial setup, when coding your custom API calls based on the SDK for your favorite programming language or, more often, running CLI scripts or provisioning infrastructure configuration with Terraform. These are the details you should prepare or know where to find them:

- **API Signing Keypair** in PEM format:

  - Public key

  - Private key

- **Fingerprint** of the public key

- **IAM User OCID**, available under Menu ➤ Identity ➤ Users

- **Tenancy OCID**, available under Menu ➤ Administration ➤ Tenancy Details

- **Region Identifier**, available under Menu ➤ Administration ➤ Region Management on the Infrastructure Regions tab

We are now ready to discuss and apply the three most popular automation techniques. We will talk about SDKs first.

SDK

The OCI SDK is a library for a particular programming language that lets your software interact with the Oracle Cloud Infrastructure cloud management plane. The SDK exposes the OCI API calls as functions or methods that are easier to use and faster to work with for a developer. In this way, custom logic that manages and monitors OCI resources can be embedded in your applications. Figure 3-5 illustrates this concept.

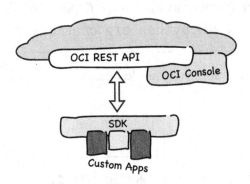

Figure 3-5. *SDK*

At the time of writing, Oracle Cloud Infrastructure delivers four SDKs implemented as open source projects.

- **Python**: https://github.com/oracle/oci-python-sdk

- **Go**: https://github.com/oracle/oci-go-sdk

- **Java**: https://github.com/oracle/oci-java-sdk

- **Ruby**: https://github.com/oracle/oci-ruby-sdk

If you needed an SDK for a different language, you could consider writing one on your own. You would first implement the API request signing logic and start wrapping into library functions or class methods these REST API calls that you need for your software. Later, you could incrementally add support for further API resources. In reality, especially in the age of microservices-oriented design and containers, there is little probability that you would need to build a new SDK because you could implement groups of cooperating microservices using different programming languages.

In this section, I am going to present the basics of the Python SDK for Oracle Cloud Infrastructure.

Installation

Because of historical reasons, Python is parallelly maintained in two major versions at the moment: 2 and 3. The SDK works with both, but I recommend using the newest major version as a best practice. I am going to use Python 3. Please check if Python 3 is already present on the machine that you are using to work on the exercises from this book. If it isn't, please install it and choose the newest Python 3.x available for your platform.

Note   The way you are going to install Python depends on the operating system you are using. Please visit `www.python.org` for more details.

After a successful installation, you should be able to see something like this:

```
$ python3 --version
Python 3.7.2
```

Note   The code snippets from this book were tested in the macOS Console and Windows Subsystem for Linux. All of the commands should easily work on all major Linux distributions. If you are using Windows, please run the exercises either on a guest VM with Linux or on Windows Subsystem for Linux.

Out of the box, Python 3 comes with the venv module, which lets developers create multiple virtual environments on a single machine. A virtual environment maintains self-contained Python binaries and a library of Python modules that serve as dependencies to your application. All modules installed using a dedicated, environment-specific instance of Package Installer for Python (pip) will be stored within the virtual environment's file hierarchy. This is especially useful if you are working on multiple projects and need to avoid module version conflicts. I am going to create a new virtual environment called ocidev and activate it by sourcing the bin/activate file.

Tip   I highly recommend you visit the Git repository for this book: `https://github.com/mtjakobczyk/oci-book`. Each chapter comes with a dedicated directory that holds the chapter's `README.md` file. The file contains all the code snippets in an easy-to-copy form.

This is how you do it on macOS or Linux:

```
$ python3 -m venv ocidev
$ ls -1 ocidev/bin/
activate
activate.csh
activate.fish
easy_install*
easy_install-3.7*
pip*
pip3*
pip3.7*
python@
python3@
$ source ocidev/bin/activate
(ocidev) $
```

You can see that the command prompt has changed to indicate the active virtual environment. Each time you open a new Terminal session, you need to activate the virtual environment so that variables are set to work with binaries and paths from the subdirectories of the chosen virtual environment.

Tip   The venv module is available only in Python 3. If you still want to use Python 2, there are analogous packages that support virtual environments, for example, `virtualenv`.

The Python SDK for Oracle Cloud Infrastructure is available as a module in the Python Package Index (PyPI) repository. You can download the oci module using the pip package management for Python, which is already included and can be found in your virtual environment's path. Let's upgrade the pip utility before we download and install the oci module.

```
(ocidev) $ python3 -m pip install --upgrade pip
Successfully installed pip-19.1.1
(ocidev) $ python3 -m pip --version
pip 19.1.1 from /Users/mjk/ocidev/lib/python3.7/site-packages/pip (python 3.7)
```

Now, I am going to use the `pip freeze` command to list the packages installed in this particular virtual environment.

```
(ocidev) $ python3 -m pip freeze
```

As you can see, there are no packages in our virtual environment. It is time to change this and install the Python SDK for Oracle Cloud Infrastructure.

```
(ocidev) $ python3 -m pip install oci
Successfully installed (...) oci-2.2.13 (...)
(ocidev) $ python3 -m pip freeze
asn1crypto==0.24.0
certifi==2019.3.9
cffi==1.12.3
configparser==3.7.4
cryptography==2.7
oci==2.2.13
pycparser==2.19
pyOpenSSL==19.0.0
python-dateutil==2.8.0
pytz==2019.1
six==1.12.0

(ocidev) $ deactivate
```

Together with the `oci` module, `pip` has installed its dependencies. Now, we need to discuss how to prepare the configuration that will store the details used by the SDK while signing the API requests.

Configuration

The Python SDK for Oracle Cloud Infrastructure is just a Python module that delivers a collection of several client classes with methods that invoke the OCI REST API to manage various types of OCI resources, for example:

- **oci.core.ComputeClient** class methods are used to manage compute instances.

- **oci.core.VirtualNetworkClient** class methods are used to manage VCN-related resources.

- **oci.load_balancer.LoadBalancerClient** class methods are used to manage load balancer resources.

As you create an instance object of a particular client class, you have to provide a dictionary (a set of key-value pairs) that stores the API signing details for the SDK. The following code snippet shows conceptually how it is done. Do not try executing these commands because one of them is still incomplete:

```
$ source ocidev/bin/activate
(ocidev) $ python3
>>> config = dict([('tenancy', '...'), ('region', '...'), ('user', '...'),
('fingerprint', '...'), ('key_file', '...'), ('pass_phrase', '...')])
>>> import oci
>>> compute = oci.core.ComputeClient(config)
```

It is also possible to load the configuration from a config file. A config file will include the details required for the SDK to be able to sign API requests it sends to the Oracle Cloud Infrastructure REST API on behalf of a named IAM user. The default name for the config file is config. The default location for the config file is the ~/.oci directory. The file must have the permissions set in such a way that it is only the file owner who is able to read the contents of the file. Listing 3-5 shows the structure of the config file.

Listing 3-5. Python SDK for OCI Config File

```
[DEFAULT]
tenancy=ocid1.tenancy.oc1..aa.........abcdef
region=eu-frankfurt-1
user=ocid1.user.oc1..aa.........ghijkl
fingerprint=12:78:5b:60:65:cf:dc:b1:04:fd:3d:31:2b:a7:88:12
key_file=/Users/mjk/.apikeys/oci_api_pem
pass_phrase=secret
```

A tenancy (tenancy) and an IAM user (user) have to be provided as valid OCIDs, while the region (region) must use a region identifier, for example, eu-frankfurt-1. The key file (key_file) should be the path to the private key in PEM format that belongs to the API signing keypair whose public key you've uploaded and associated with the IAM user. The private key password (pass_phrase) as well as the public key fingerprint (fingerprint) are also stored in the config file. This is why it is crucial to set the proper permissions on the config file to limit the visibility of its contents. You can store multiple named configuration profiles in one config file. In our example, there is only the DEFAULT profile present.

I have prepared a template of the config file for you. You will find the template file at this path: chapter03/1-sdk/config.template. Please copy and save it in the default location as the ~/.oci/config file.

```
$ mkdir ~/.oci
$ cp ~/git/oci-book/chapter03/1-sdk/config.template ~/.oci/config
$ chmod go-rwx ~/.oci/config
$ ls -l ~/.oci
-rw-------  1 mjk  staff   758B Jun 10 20:21 config
```

Now, adjust the properties and use the values that correspond to your environment. You can use vi or any other text editor.

```
$ vi ~/.oci/config
```

Let's activate the virtual environment and start the Python interpreter again. You can use the oci.config.from_file function in the configuration associated with a named profile. In our case, this will be the DEFAULT profile. Finally, you can test the creation of a compute client class instance.

```
$ source ocidev/bin/activate
(ocidev) $ python3
>>> import oci
>>> config = oci.config.from_file("~/.oci/config","DEFAULT")
>>> compute = oci.core.ComputeClient(config)
>>> quit()
(ocidev) $ deactivate
$
```

Using the SDK

As soon as you know how to prepare and load the configuration file, you are ready for the first simple test. Let's list the availability domains visible for your tenancy and the IAM user you've chosen.

```
$ source ocidev/bin/activate
(ocidev) $ python3
>>> import oci
>>> config = oci.config.from_file("~/.oci/config","DEFAULT")
```

```
>>> identity = oci.identity.IdentityClient(config)
>>> ads_list = identity.list_availability_domains(config['tenancy']).data
>>> for ad in ads_list:
...     print(ad.name)
...
feDV:EU-FRANKFURT-1-AD-1
feDV:EU-FRANKFURT-1-AD-2
feDV:EU-FRANKFURT-1-AD-3
```

Now, I will show you how to create a virtual cloud network in one of your non-root compartments. Before you proceed, please write down the OCID of a non-root compartment, such as Sandbox, in which you would like the VCN to be created. The OCID can be found in the OCI Console under Identity ➤ Compartments, as explained in the "Compartment" section in Chapter 2. To successfully test the script that follows, please replace the value of the cid variable with the OCID of the Sandbox compartment.

```
>>> cid = "ocid1.compartment.oc1..aa.........gzwhsa"
>>> kwargs = { "cidr_block": "10.5.0.0/16", "display_name": "sdk-vcn",
    "compartment_id": cid }
>>> create_vcn_details = oci.core.models.CreateVcnDetails(**kwargs)
>>> print(create_vcn_details)
{
  "cidr_block": "10.5.0.0/16",
  "compartment_id": "ocid1.compartment.oc1..aa.........gzwhsa",
  "defined_tags": null,
  "display_name": "sdk-vcn",
  "dns_label": null,
  "freeform_tags": null
}
>>> vcn = oci.core.VirtualNetworkClient(config)
>>> response = vcn.create_vcn(create_vcn_details)
>>> response.data
{
  "cidr_block": "10.5.0.0/16",
  "compartment_id": "ocid1.compartment.oc1..aa.........gzwhsa",
  "default_dhcp_options_id": "ocid1.dhcpoptions.oc1. ...",
  "default_route_table_id": "ocid1.routetable.oc1. ...",
```

```
    "default_security_list_id": "ocid1.securitylist.oc1. ...",
    "defined_tags": {},
    "display_name": "sdk-vcn",
    "dns_label": null,
    "freeform_tags": {},
    "id": "ocid1.vcn.oc1.eu-frankfurt-1.aa.........74vj5a",
    "lifecycle_state": "AVAILABLE",
    "time_created": "2019-06-13T20:56:53.200000+00:00",
    "vcn_domain_name": null
}
```

As a first step to creating a new VCN using the Python SDK for Oracle Cloud Infrastructure, we prepared an instance of a model class `CreateVcnDetails`. Model class objects are used to encapsulate the configuration parameters for the API calls done by the instances of client classes. In our case, we instantiated the model class with just three VCN resource parameters: the CIDR block, the display name, and an OCID of a target compartment. Subsequently, we passed the `CreateVcnDetails` object as an argument to the `create_vcn` method of the `VirtualNetworkClient` client class instance. The method sent a request to the OCI REST API to get the VCN created in a synchronous manner. You may have spotted that it took a moment to return a response. Finally, as we printed the `response.data` attribute, we were able to see the OCID (`id`) of the newly created VCN as well as all other VCN attributes. Figure 3-6 shows the new VCN in the OCI Console.

Name	State	CIDR Block	Default Route Table
sdk-vcn	● Available	10.5.0.0/16	Default Route Table for sdk-vcn

Figure 3-6. *VCN created using the SDK*

To delete the VCN, you can use the `delete_vcn` method like this:

```
>>> response.data.id
'ocid1.vcn.oc1.eu-frankfurt-1.aa.........74vj5a'
>>> vcn.delete_vcn(response.data.id)
```

To quit the Python interpreter and leave the virtual environment, you can issue the following commands:

```
>>> quit()
(ocidev) $ deactivate
$
```

In this section, we've briefly covered the introductory aspects of the Python SDK for Oracle Cloud Infrastructure. If you would like to learn more, please refer to the comprehensive documentation available at `https://oracle-cloud-infrastructure-python-sdk.readthedocs.io`.

CLI

The OCI *command-line interface* (CLI) is a command-line utility that lets you interact with Oracle Cloud Infrastructure REST APIs in a convenient, scripted way. The CLI is slightly more powerful than the OCI Console because you may find features available as CLI commands that are not implemented in the OCI Console. Furthermore, it is usually faster to execute a script instead of clicking your way through the graphical interface of the OCI Console. If you look closer at the CLI, you will discover that it is built on the Python SDK for Oracle Cloud Infrastructure. In other words, the OCI CLI is implemented in Python as the `oci-cli` module, which uses the classes from the `oci` module. Figure 3-7 illustrates this concept.

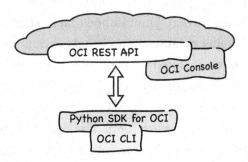

Figure 3-7. *OCI CLI*

The CLI is implemented as an open source project with code available on GitHub at `https://github.com/oracle/oci-cli`. It can be installed on the Linux, macOS, and Windows operating systems.

Installation

You install the CLI using a script dedicated to your operating system. The scripts can be downloaded from the GitHub account for the OCI CLI. As a matter of fact, there are two scripts available.

- A shell script for Linux/macOS/Windows Subsystem for Linux

- A PowerShell script for native CLI execution on Windows

If executed, each of the two scripts performs similar steps.

To install the CLI on Linux, macOS, or Windows Subsystem for Linux, open a Terminal window and execute this command:

```
$ bash -c "$(curl -L https://raw.githubusercontent.com/oracle/oci-cli/
master/scripts/install/install.sh)"
```

Note   The code snippets from this book were tested in the macOS Console and on Windows Subsystem for Linux. All of the commands should easily work in all major Linux distributions. If you are using Windows, please run the exercises either on a guest VM with Linux or on Windows Subsystem for Linux.

In the first place, the presence of Python binaries in the PATH variable is verified, and any missing native package dependencies are downloaded and put in place, if needed. The installer will prefer Python 3 to Python 2. Yet, the CLI works fine with any of the two. In the previous section, I mentioned that the CLI is basically a Python module. This is why the installer creates a new virtual environment dedicated to the CLI so that its dependencies are isolated from any other Python-based development you may be working on in the meantime. During the installation process, you will be asked to provide a directory path for the virtual environment and another path to store a lightweight oci utility. The utility can be thought of as the CLI executable, which exposes the oci-cli Python module classes in the form of a convenient command-line utility. You can leave the defaults if you do not have any specific directory in mind. At the end, the installer will update your PATH variable so that you can execute the oci utility in a straightforward manner. In some shells, the oci utility might not be visible right after installation. In such a case, you have to either restart the console or simply source the file in which the CLI added itself to the PATH variable. On Linux and Windows Subsystem for Linux, it is usually ~/.bashrc, while on Mac it is usually the ~/.bash_profile file.

```
$ oci --version
Command 'oci' not found.

$ source ~/.bashrc
```

As soon as the installation has been completed, you should be able to check the version of the CLI.

```
$ oci --version
2.6.6
```

The first line of the oci utility script will tell you the location of the virtual environment. This code snippet shows how to activate the virtual environment of your CLI and list the SDK version the CLI is using:

```
$ head -n 1 `which oci`
#!/Users/mjk/lib/oracle-cli/bin/python3
$ cd ~/lib/oracle-cli/
$ source bin/activate
(oracle-cli) $ python3 -m pip freeze | grep oci
oci==2.5.1
oci-cli==2.6.6

(oracle-cli) $ deactivate
$
```

We have done this to illustrate the CLI relationship to the Python SDK. In your daily work with the CLI, you won't explicitly activate the virtual environment but will use the oci utility instead.

Configuration

The CLI config file is a simple properties file that stores the details required for signing the API requests that are sent to the Oracle Cloud Infrastructure REST API on behalf of a named IAM user. If you expect that the CLI configuration is similar to the configuration file used in the context of the Python SDK for OCI, you are right. Listing 3-6 shows the structure of the CLI config file.

Listing 3-6. OCI CLI Config File

```
[DEFAULT]
tenancy=ocid1.tenancy.oc1..aa........
region=eu-frankfurt-1
user=ocid1.user.oc1..aa........
fingerprint=12:78:5b:60:65:cf:dc:b1:04:fd:3d:31:2b:a7:88:12
key_file=/Users/mjk/.apikeys/oci_api_pem
pass_phrase=secret
```

The structure is the same as the one used in the previous section about the SDK. Moreover, the CLI expects the configuration file at the same default ~/.oci/config path.

If you still have the ~/.oci/config file in place, the CLI is ready to be used.

Caution   If you have created the .oci/config file for use with the SDK, as described in the preceding section, *skip* the oci setup config step that is explained in the following text because the configuration is already present.

If you skipped the section about the SDK or have removed the configuration, do not worry. You can use a simple built-in CLI configuration wizard. You will need to provide the same information I've listed in the "Preparing for SDK, CLI, and Terraform" section. Additionally, you will be given an opportunity to create a new API signing keypair, in case you didn't prepare one earlier.

```
$ oci setup config
Enter a location for your config [/Users/mjk/.oci/config]:
Enter a user OCID: ocid1.user.oc1..aa........
Enter a tenancy OCID: ocid1.tenancy.oc1..aa........
Enter a region (e.g. ap-seoul-1, ap-tokyo-1, ca-toronto-1, eu-frankfurt-1,
uk-london-1, us-ashburn-1, us-gov-ashburn-1, us-gov-chicago-1, us-gov-
phoenix-1, us-langley-1, us-luke-1, us-phoenix-1): eu-frankfurt-1
Do you want to generate a new RSA key pair? (If you decline you will be
asked to supply the path to an existing key.) [Y/n]: n
Enter the location of your private key file: /Users/mjk/.apikeys/oci_api_pem
Enter the passphrase for your private key:
```

```
Fingerprint: e6:99:f5:82:db:a9:75:fb:cd:3c:30:74:00:b3:61:2b
Do you want to write your passphrase to the config file? (if not, you will
need to supply it as an argument to the CLI) [y/N]: y
Config written to /Users/mjk/.oci/config
```

If you have decided to generate a new API signing keypair using oci setup config, please remember to upload the public key to the cloud for your IAM user. If you do not remember how to do it, please go back to the "Uploading the Public Key" section earlier in this chapter.

Storing the password for your private key is optional. If you decide against doing it, you will be prompted for the password every time you issue a CLI command. If you decide in favor, please remember not to copy this file anywhere else also to keep its permissions restricted to the file owner.

```
$ ls -l .oci
-rw------- 1 mjk  staff   322B Jun 13 21:26 config
```

Now, you should be ready to test the CLI. We are going to list the available versions of Ubuntu-based images. Such a query is run in the context of the root compartment whose OCID is the same as the OCID of the tenancy. Luckily, we already stored the root compartment OCID in the CLI configuration file and can use a combination of grep and sed tools to extract this value. This is how you run your first OCI command that sends a request to the OCI REST API:

```
$ TENANCY_OCID=`cat ~/.oci/config | grep tenancy | sed 's/tenancy=//'`

$ oci compute image list --compartment-id $TENANCY_OCID --operating-system
"Canonical Ubuntu" --output table --query "data [*].{Image:\"display-name\"}"
+---------------------------------------------+
| Image                                       |
+---------------------------------------------+
| Canonical-Ubuntu-18.04-Minimal-2019.05.15-0 |
| Canonical-Ubuntu-18.04-Minimal-2019.04.15-0 |
| Canonical-Ubuntu-18.04-Minimal-2019.03.11-0 |
| Canonical-Ubuntu-18.04-2019.05.15-0         |
| Canonical-Ubuntu-18.04-2019.04.15-0         |
| Canonical-Ubuntu-18.04-2018.12.10-0         |
```

```
| Canonical-Ubuntu-16.04-Minimal-2019.05.15-0  |
| Canonical-Ubuntu-16.04-Minimal-2019.04.15-0  |
| Canonical-Ubuntu-16.04-Minimal-2019.03.11-0  |
| Canonical-Ubuntu-16.04-Gen2-GPU-2019.05.15-0 |
| Canonical-Ubuntu-16.04-Gen2-GPU-2019.04.15-0 |
| Canonical-Ubuntu-16.04-Gen2-GPU-2019.03.20-0 |
| Canonical-Ubuntu-16.04-2019.05.15-0          |
| Canonical-Ubuntu-16.04-2019.04.15-0          |
| Canonical-Ubuntu-16.04-2019.03.20-0          |
| Canonical-Ubuntu-14.04-2019.05.15-0          |
| Canonical-Ubuntu-14.04-2019.05.02-0          |
| Canonical-Ubuntu-14.04-2019.03.19-0          |
+----------------------------------------------+
```

The OCI REST API uses JSON for the payload. The CLI will also output JSON as its default format. You can change it and use a tabular output by applying the --output table option. If you want to limit what gets printed, you can use the --query option that consumes a valid *JMESPath*, which is a query language for JSON.

Tip   If you have ever worked with XML before, you can think of JMESPath as something like XPath but for JSON.

Nearly every CLI command requires a compartment OCID. If you know that you are going to work with one given compartment for the majority of time, you can define a default value for the --compartment-id option. Default values for CLI commands options can be defined in the ~/.oci/oci_cli_rc file. Listing 3-7 presents a minimalistic oci_cli_rc file with just one profile with a single default value.

Listing 3-7. OCI CLI RC File

```
[DEFAULT]
compartment-id = ocid1.compartment.oc1..aa.........
```

The [DEFAULT] part is the name of the profile. This also applies to the configuration file shown in Listing 3-6. You can store multiple profiles in one configuration file (or in the file with default values) and dynamically select the profile with the --profile option when you issue a CLI command. For example, you can have a separate profile for each compartment. This can be helpful when you work with just a few compartments and want to simplify the way you choose them as you execute CLI commands. Listing 3-8 presents this configuration.

Listing 3-8. OCI CLI RC File with Multiple Profiles

```
[DEFAULT]
compartment-id = ocid1.compartment.oc1..aa.........abc
[SANDBOX]
compartment-id = ocid1.compartment.oc1..aa........def
```

Actually, there is more than just the default values you can store in the oci_cli_rc file. For example, it is possible to create named JMESPath queries and reference them as you use CLI commands. We are going to test this now.

Please copy the template of the oci_cli_rc file to the ~/.oci/ directory and edit the file to replace the value of the compartment_id property with the OCID of your Sandbox compartment.

```
$ cp ~/git/oci-book/chapter03/2-cli/oci_cli_rc.template ~/.oci/oci_cli_rc
$ vi ~/.oci/oci_cli_rc
```

Listing 3-9 presents the oci_cli_rc file. The DEFAULT profile includes the compartment-id for your Sandbox compartment. The predefined section called OCI_CLI_CANNED_QUERIES is used to store common queries that can be reused in your CLI calls. A query called list_ubuntu_1804 can be used to filter the results based on the version of the operating system and display image names only.

Listing 3-9. OCI CLI RC File with Predefined Query

```
[DEFAULT]
compartment-id = ocid1.compartment.oc1..aa........gzwhsa
[OCI_CLI_CANNED_QUERIES]
list_ubuntu_1804 = data[?"operating-system-version"=='18.04'].
{Image:"display-name"}
```

Now, you can reuse this predefined query as you type the CLI command. Remember to prefix the value for the `--query` parameter with the `query://` string.

```
$ oci compute image list --operating-system "Canonical Ubuntu" --output
table --query query://list_ubuntu_1804
+------------------------------------+
| Image                              |
+------------------------------------+
| Canonical-Ubuntu-18.04-2019.05.15-0 |
| Canonical-Ubuntu-18.04-2019.04.15-0 |
| Canonical-Ubuntu-18.04-2018.12.10-0 |
+------------------------------------+
```

Tip   If you are using both the CLI and the SDK for other projects, you can either maintain multiple configuration files and explicitly pass their filesystem path or base on dedicated, named profiles in a single configuration file under the default path.

If you want to learn more about CLI configuration, you can refer to the official documentation at `https://docs.cloud.oracle.com/iaas/Content/API/SDKDocs/cliconfigure.htm`.

Using the CLI

I mentioned before that the CLI may offer features that are not available in the OCI Console, but if something is possible with the OCI Console, it is also possible when using the CLI. This is why if you see that there are some repeatable tasks you perform in the OCI Console and they cost you too much time, you may consider automating them using the CLI. In this section, you will see how to launch a compute instance using the OCI CLI.

I am assuming that you already created the `oci_cli_rc` file, as described in the previous section. Listing 3-10 shows the minimal content required from now on. The OCID value of the Sandbox compartment is present within the DEFAULT profile.

Listing 3-10. OCI CLI RC File with Compartment for the Infrastructure

```
[DEFAULT]
compartment-id = ocid1.compartment.oc1..aa.........gzwhsa
```

Let's start by making sure we are about to provision OCI resources in the correct compartment. You should see the name of the Sandbox compartment as a result of this command:

```
$ oci iam compartment get --output table --query "data.
{CompartmentName:\"name\"}"
+------------------+
| CompartmentName |
+------------------+
| Sandbox          |
+------------------+
```

If you read Chapter 2, you may remember that a compute instance must exist within a subnet that is part of a VCN. This is a CLI command that creates a new VCN, named cli-vcn, which uses the 192.168.3.0/24 address space:

```
$ vcn_ocid=`oci network vcn create --cidr-block 192.168.3.0/24 --display-
name cli-vcn --query "data.id" | tr -d '"'`
$ echo $vcn_ocid
ocid1.vcn.oc1.eu-frankfurt-1.aa.........lg4b7w
```

I've filtered the output using the --query parameter, removed the parentheses with the tr program, and saved the newly generated VCN OCID as a bash variable named vcn_ocid. Why? We will need the VCN OCID as an input parameter when we create an Internet gateway and a subnet. This is a CLI command that provisions a new Internet gateway within the VCN:

```
$ igw_ocid=`oci network internet-gateway create --vcn-id $vcn_ocid
--display-name cli-igw --is-enabled true --query "data.id" | tr -d '"'`
$ echo $igw_ocid
ocid1.internetgateway.oc1.eu-frankfurt-1.aa.........2ptvoa
```

To enable the connectivity with the Internet, we will add a routing rule that directs all outbound traffic from the VCN to the Internet gateway. This is the command that adds a new routing table with the relevant route rule:

```
$ route_rules="[{\"cidrBlock\":\"0.0.0.0/0\", \"networkEntityId\":\"$igw_ocid\"}]"
$ rt_ocid=`oci network route-table create --vcn-id $vcn_ocid --display-name
cli-rt --route-rules "$route_rules" --query "data.id" | tr -d '"'`
$ echo $rt_ocid
ocid1.routetable.oc1.eu-frankfurt-1.aa........ukqcjq
```

Before invoking the oci network route-table create command, a supplementary variable called route_rules with a single route rule referencing the Internet gateway has been created. Again, we are persisting the cloud identifier of the route table in a variable. We will need it while creating a subnet. This is how you create a subnet using the CLI:

```
$ ad1=`oci iam availability-domain list --query data[0].name | tr -d '"'`
$ echo $ad1
feDV:EU-FRANKFURT-1-AD-1
$ subnet_ocid=`oci network subnet create --vcn-id $vcn_ocid --display-name
cli-vcn --cidr-block "192.168.3.0/30" --prohibit-public-ip-on-vnic false
--availability-domain $ad1 --route-table-id $rt_ocid --query data.id | tr
-d '"'`
$ echo $subnet_ocid
ocid1.subnet.oc1.eu-frankfurt-1.aa........sqyz6a
```

This time, we made two calls to the OCI REST API using the CLI. Initially, we fetched the name of the first availability domain in our current region and saved it to a new variable. Second, we created a new AD-specific subnet with a narrow addressing space of 192.168.3.0/30, which gives us just a single usable IPv4 address: 192.168.3.2. Why just one? OCI reserves the first two addresses and the last address in each VCN subnet.

We are ready to provision a new compute instance. Please make sure there is an SSH public key present under ~/oci_id_rsa.pub. You created an SSH keypair in Chapter 2. The keypair will be required to enable remote access to the instance. This is how you launch a new compute instance using the CLI:

```
$ image_ocid=`oci compute image list --shape "VM.Standard2.1" --operating-
system "CentOS" --operating-system-version 7 --sort-by TIMECREATED --query
data[0].id | tr -d '"'`
```

```
$ echo $image_ocid
ocid1.image.oc1.eu-frankfurt-1.aa........hl2cma
$ vm_ocid=`oci compute instance launch --display-name cli-vm --availability-
domain "$ad1" --subnet-id "$subnet_ocid" --private-ip 192.168.3.2 --image-
id "$image_ocid" --shape VM.Standard2.1 --ssh-authorized-keys-file
~/oci_id_rsa.pub --wait-for-state
RUNNING --query data.id | tr -d '"'`
Action completed. Waiting until the resource has entered state: RUNNING
$ echo $vm_ocid
ocid1.instance.oc1.eu-frankfurt-1.ab........wsbmoq
```

Each compute instance must be based on an image that provides an operating system and, optionally, additional preinstalled software. The OCI CLI command that launches a compute instance requires an OCID of the image. This is why we query for the OCID of the newest shape-compatible CentOS 7 base operating system image in the first place. Subsequently, we issue the `oci compute instance launch` command providing a display name (`--display-name`) to be used, a preferred private IP address (`--private-id`), and a desired shape (`--shape`) that defines the profile of the allocated hardware resources and identifiers for the subnet (`--subnet-id`) and the image (`--image-id`). A target availability domain (`--availability-domain`) must be the same as the one used for the subnet. Finally, we tell OCI to wait until the instance enters the RUNNING state. If we had skipped that part, the CLI would have returned before the provisioning process had completed. Figure 3-8 presents the instance in the RUNNING state as shown in the OCI Console.

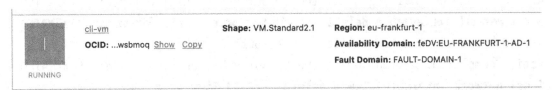

Figure 3-8. *Compute instance provisioned with the CLI*

Do you remember that we discussed the `oci_cli_rc` configuration file? Have you spotted any parameter that was always the same while we were executing the commands to launch a compute instance? Each command defined a `--query` parameter with the same `data.id` string as a value. In theory, looking at this usage pattern, you could consider adding it to the `oci_cli_rc` configuration file. In reality, this query is a bit too trivial to be stored in the `oci_cli_rc` file, but feel free to do so, if you want.

As a matter of fact, you will use the CLI more often to query for data. The compute instance we've just launched is running in a public subnet and has been assigned an ephemeral public IPv4 address. Let's find out the exact value of this public IP address. As we've saved the OCID of the compute instance as a variable (vm_ocid), we can reuse this value now. This is how you query for a public IP address of a compute instance running in a public subnet:

```
$ oci compute instance list-vnics --instance-id "$vm_ocid" --query
data[0].\"public-ip\" --raw-output
130.61.89.229
```

The CLI is based on a *procedural approach* when provisioning resources or querying for data. You specify the actions in a particular sequence that is taken by the CLI. These actions, issued as the CLI commands, are often mapped 1:1 into OCI REST API requests. Dependencies between resource types must be respected and taken into consideration in planning the action sequence. Similarly, if you delete the resources, the sequence must be usually inverted. This is how you terminate and delete previously created resources:

```
$ oci compute instance terminate --instance-id $vm_ocid --wait-for-state TERMINATED
Are you sure you want to delete this resource? [y/N]: y
Action completed. Waiting until the resource has entered state: TERMINATED
$ oci network subnet delete --subnet-id $subnet_ocid --wait-for-state TERMINATED
Are you sure you want to delete this resource? [y/N]: y
Action completed. Waiting until the resource has entered state: TERMINATED
$ oci network route-table delete --rt-id $rt_ocid --wait-for-state TERMINATED
Are you sure you want to delete this resource? [y/N]: y
Action completed. Waiting until the resource has entered state: TERMINATED
$ oci network internet-gateway delete --ig-id $igw_ocid --wait-for-state
TERMINATED
Are you sure you want to delete this resource? [y/N]: y
Action completed. Waiting until the resource has entered state: TERMINATED
$ oci network vcn delete --vcn-id $vcn_ocid
Are you sure you want to delete this resource? [y/N]: y
```

In the procedural approach, the responsibility to understand what actions have to be taken and in which sequence is delegated to the programmer. This can increase the complexity of the scripts, especially if you want to implement various types of changes to the state of an existing infrastructure. In such a case, you need to begin with finding out what the current state is, before you plan the actions that would bring the infrastructure to the expected state. It would have been much easier just to define the expected state and let a provisioning tool detect what kind of actions have to be taken depending on the current state of the infrastructure. This would be a declarative approach.

Terraform

Terraform is an infrastructure-as-code provisioning tool that tracks the state of the infrastructure it is managing to enable the *declarative approach*. Instead of defining and sequencing actions, as you are doing while working with the CLI, Terraform lets you define the expected state of your infrastructure. Next, it becomes the job of Terraform to detect what kind of actions, and in which sequence, have to be taken to bring the cloud resources to the expected state. You do not need to worry about any intermediary states. Only the result matters.

Terraform supports a diverse range of cloud providers through a set of plugins called *providers*. When you initiate a new project using the `terraform init` command, Terraform reads your configuration files in this directory, detects which provider to use, and downloads the newest version of a particular provider plugin. It is the provider plugin that is responsible for interacting with, in our case, Oracle Cloud Infrastructure REST APIs, as shown in Figure 3-9.

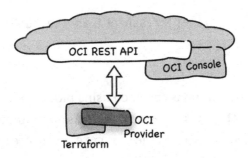

Figure 3-9. Terraform

Let's take a closer look at the concept of infrastructure as code.

Infrastructure as Code

The concept behind *infrastructure as code* is simple. You define your target cloud infrastructure, which consists of virtual cloud networks, compute instances, instance pools, custom images, various types of storage, managed database instances, managed Kubernetes clusters, and other cloud resources, in one or more configuration files. We often say that you write the *infrastructure code*. If you are using Terraform, the configuration files, or simply the infrastructure code, use JSON-like HashiCorp Language (HCL) syntax. Listing 3-11 presents a sample compute instance definition in HCL syntax.

Listing 3-11. Terraform HCL for a Compute Instance

```
resource "oci_core_instance" "bastion_vm" {
  compartment_id = var.compartment_ocid
  display_name = "bastion-vm"
  availability_domain = var.ads[0]
  source_details {
    source_id = "var.compute_image_ocid
    source_type = "image"
  }
  shape = "VM.Standard2.2"
  create_vnic_details {
    subnet_id = oci_core_subnet.bastion_ad1_net.id
    assign_public_ip = true
  }
  metadata = {
    ssh_authorized_keys = file("~/.ssh/oci_id_rsa.pub")
  }
}
```

Every cloud resource definition is specified using blocks of data. Resource block headers have a `resource <type> <name>` structure. As an example, Oracle Cloud Infrastructure compute instances are of the `oci_core_instance` type. If you look closer at Listing 3-11, you will spot that some attribute values use references to variables (`var.compartment_ocid`), attributes of other resources (`oci_core_subnet.bastion_ad1_net.id`), and even file paths in the local filesystem (`file(...)`). This leads to a conclusion that some resources depend on the others. It is pretty clear that a dependency chain is important for the sequence of various actions such as creation or destruction performed on groups of related resources. Terraform builds a graph that tracks all these dependencies and uses it to decide which actions can be done in parallel, shortening the overall provisioning time, and which actions have to be performed in a sequence.

The infrastructure code you write is understood as the *expected state*. You can change the code back and forth and apply these changes multiple times. Every time you do it, Terraform compares the expected state with the so-called *current state* that correspondes to the infrastructure deployed during the previous provisioning. The calculated difference is used to create an *execution plan* that consists of a series of steps that entail various OCI REST API calls that cause the real provisioning. Selected steps can run in parallel, as long as it does not impact the dependency chain. An execution plan can include actions that create new cloud resources, alter the existing ones, or terminate the resources that have to be removed. Sometimes, a small change in just one resource attribute will terminate the instance and launch a completely new one. For example, such a situation will take place when you change the compute instance shape of an existing instance. The shape specifies the hardware configuration for a compute instance. Other changes can cause nondestructive amendments such as adding a new security rule to an existing security list.

What we've just done in this section was a brief Terraform provider for Oracle Cloud Infrastructure crash course. If you feel that we've just scratched the surface of something complex, you are absolutely right, but don't worry. We will use Terraform in all the further chapters in this book so that you will have lots of opportunities to practice. Last but not least, I will explain Terraform features on the fly, as they appear in the course of the book.

Tip You can find the Terraform documentation at `www.terraform.io/docs/index.html`.

I bet you are now asking yourself how to put your hands on Terraform-driven automation for Oracle Cloud Infrastructure. What about installing the software first?

Installation

At the time of writing, you just download a single, executable binary file with the Terraform version that matches your operating system. To install Terraform, follow these steps:

1. Go to www.terraform.io/downloads.html.

2. Download the binary file for your operating system.

3. Move the downloaded terraform file to the directory where you are storing software binaries, and remember to add this directory to your PATH variable, unless you've already done it.

4. Test the installation by issuing a version check command.

All these steps can be automated. Just be careful to identify the correct path to the newest binary before you do them. At the time of writing, the newest binary is the 0.12.9 version.

```
$ wget https://releases.hashicorp.com/terraform/0.12.2/terraform_0.12.9_
linux_amd64.zip
$ sudo unzip terraform_0.12.9_linux_amd64.zip -d /usr/local/bin
$ terraform -v
Terraform v0.12.9
```

Tip   If you are using Windows Subsystem for Linux, you have to download the Terraform binary for Linux. Use the preceding code snippet, and execute it within the WSL Console.

As you probably expect, this simplicity comes at the cost of *manual upgrades*. You need to download a new binary and replace the file you've been using every time you see a message like this:

```
$ terraform -v
Terraform v0.12.8

Your version of Terraform is out of date! The latest version
is 0.12.9. You can update by downloading from www.terraform.io/downloads.html
```

This is pretty much everything you need to know about the installation. All further aspects have to be considered in the context of particular provider plugins you are going to work with. Let me explain what I mean in the next section.

Configuration

As a matter of fact, the expression *Terraform configuration* refers to the entire set of files with infrastructure code. Each project contains at least one provider block in one of the infrastructure code files. Based on this block, Terraform knows which provider plugin binary to use. If Terraform doesn't find the corresponding provider plugin binary in the cross-project default directory, it will download the binary and place it in the .terraform/plugins subdirectory of the project.

To explore the simplest Terraform-based infrastructure project, go to the chapter03/3-terraform/1-provider-only directory.

```
$ cd git/oci-book/chapter03/3-terraform/1-provider-only
```

This project directory contains two files, as shown in Listing 3-12.

Listing 3-12. Terraform Project Structure (1-provider-only)

```
1-provider-only/
├── provider.tf
└── vars.tf
```

The content of the provider.tf file is shown in Listing 3-13.

Listing 3-13. Terraform Provider Configuration Referencing Variables

```
# provider.tf
provider "oci" {
  tenancy_ocid = var.tenancy_ocid
  user_ocid = var.user_ocid
  region = var.region
  fingerprint = var.fingerprint
  private_key_path = var.private_key_path
  private_key_password = var.private_key_password
}
```

Because Terraform eventually sends API requests to the OCI REST API, it needs the same set of connection parameters required by the SDK and the CLI to sign the request. The "Preparing for SDK, CLI, and Terraform" section describes where you can find them. In theory, you could store the values relevant to your cloud environment directly in the

153

provider.tf file. This is discouraged, however, because these consist of, to some extent, sensitive data, and you do not want to store the data in a version-control system.

To avoid storing the values required by the provider block inside any of the infrastructure code files, we will inject them using variables. We still need to declare these variables. You could consider adding variable declarations to the same provider.tf file. It would be absolutely fine. Yet, to keep the project assets well structured, there exists another file for that purpose: the vars.tf file. It is shown in Listing 3-14.

Listing 3-14. Terraform Variables Configuration

```
# vars.tf
variable "tenancy_ocid" {}
variable "user_ocid" {}
variable "region" {}
variable "fingerprint" {}
variable "private_key_path" {}
variable "private_key_password" {}
```

There are four basic ways to supply the values for variables.

- Providing each variable with a value at the prompt when executing Terraform commands

- Providing each variable individually with the -var argument when executing a Terraform command

- Using a variable definition file .tfvars whose file path is passed as the -var-file argument when executing a Terraform command

- Using environment variables prefixed with TF_VAR_

You could supply the values for variables every time you issue the terraform command, but I am sure it would become annoying even to the most patient person in the planet. More often, you will end up defining them in a variable definition file or using environment variables.

Any environment variable prefixed with TF_VAR_ will be taken into account by Terraform. For example, the TF_VAR_region will be treated as the source for the variable region. This is why you will find it useful to keep your input variables in some sort of shell script. You would then execute this script and, as a result, set these variables every time you are about to work on a Terraform-based project. Let's prepare a file like that. First, copy the following template:

```
$ cp ~/git/oci-book/chapter03/3-terraform/tfvars.env.template.sh ~/tfvars.env.sh
```

Now, please edit the newly created `tfvars.env.sh` file and remember to properly replace all the values. For the `TF_VAR_compartment_ocid`, please use the OCID of the Sandbox compartment.

```
# Terraform
export TF_VAR_tenancy_ocid=ocid1.tenancy.oc1..aa.........abcdef
export TF_VAR_user_ocid=ocid1.user.oc1..aa.........ghijkl
export TF_VAR_fingerprint=12:78:5b:.........:a7:88:12
export TF_VAR_region=eu-frankfurt-1
export TF_VAR_private_key_path=/Users/mjk/.apikeys/oci_api_pem
export TF_VAR_private_key_password=secret
export TF_VAR_compartment_ocid=ocid1.compartment.oc1..aa.........
```

Again, you can use `vi` or some other text editor to edit the file.

```
$ vi ~/tfvars.env.sh
```

Tip   You can peek into the SDK/CLI config file available at the `~/.oci/config` path and copy the values for use, this time in the `tfvars.env.sh` file for Terraform. In addition, please remember to use the OCID of the Sandbox compartment.

If you've chosen not to store the password for the private API signing key as one of your environment variables, Terraform will prompt you for this missing variable like this:

```
var.private_key_password
  Enter a value:
```

It can be pretty annoying to be honest. If you feel comfortable storing your private API signing key password in a file you will later `source`, feel free to do it. In such a case, please remember to set the correct filesystem permissions to limit the read rights to the file owner only.

```
$ chmod go-rwx ~/tfvars.env.sh
```

If you want, you can source the file for each session. To do so, append the appropriate command to the end of the ~/.bashrc (Linux or Windows Subsystem for Linux) or ~/.bash_profile (macOS) file.

```
$ echo "source ${HOME}/tfvars.env.sh" | tee -a ${HOME}/.bash_profile
```

We are ready to initialize a new Terraform project. Issue the terraform init command. The tool will detect that you want to use the oci provider, download its binary in the newest version, and place the provider file in the .terraform/plugins subdirectory. Let's try it now.

```
$ source ~/tfvars.env.sh
$ cd ~/git/oci-book/chapter03/3-terraform/1-provider-only
$ terraform init

Initializing provider plugins...
- Checking for available provider plugins on https://releases.hashicorp.com...
- Downloading plugin for provider "oci" (3.45.0)...

* provider.oci: version = "~> 3.45"

Terraform has been successfully initialized!
```

Now, let's inspect the same project directory.

```
.
├── .terraform
│   └── plugins
│       └── darwin_amd64
│           ├── lock.json
│           └── terraform-provider-oci_v3.45.0_x4
├── provider.tf
└── vars.tf
```

As you can see, a new subdirectory has appeared. Are you curious how big the provider binary is that has just been downloaded by Terraform? Me too.

```
$ du -sh .terraform/
 41M  .terraform/
```

The size of the provider binary does differ a bit between platforms.

You are ready to create a simple, but this time additionally meaningful, Terraform-based project. It's a true infrastructure-as-code approach in action. Read on.

Using Terraform

In this section, we will create a small infrastructure-as-code project. The target setup will consist of a virtual cloud network with a single compute instance running in a public subnet. The virtual machine will be running an Apache HTTP Server instance. Security rules and operating system firewall rules will allow inbound traffic to the server's port 80. Figure 3-10 presents this architecture using Oracle Cloud Infrastructure notation.

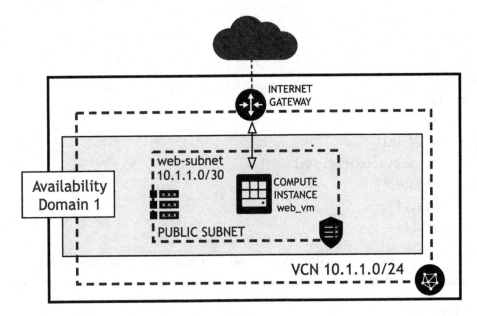

Figure 3-10. *Single server infrastructure*

Provisioning

Make sure you've installed Terraform. I will assume you have added the required connectivity-related variables to a file you've already sourced in your current Terminal session. You can check whether the variables are set correctly by issuing a command that lists all environment variables prefixed with TF_VAR_.

```
$ env | grep TF_VAR_
TF_VAR_tenancy_ocid={you-will-see-here-your-value}
TF_VAR_compartment_ocid={you-will-see-here-your-value}
```

```
TF_VAR_region={you-will-see-here-your-value}
TF_VAR_fingerprint={you-will-see-here-your-value}
TF_VAR_private_key_path={you-will-see-here-your-value}
TF_VAR_user_ocid={you-will-see-here-your-value}
TF_VAR_private_key_password={you-will-see-here-your-value}
```

Now, please enter this directory:

```
$ cd ~/git/oci-book/chapter03/3-terraform/2-simple-infrastructure
```

You should see the following files:

```
.
├── modules.tf
├── provider.tf
├── vars.tf
├── vcn.tf
└── web
    ├── cloud-init
    │   └── webvm.config.yaml
    ├── compute.tf
    ├── vars.tf
    └── vcn.tf
```

If you read the previous section, you already know what kind of content to expect in the provider.tf and vars.tf files. We will now initialize the infrastructure project.

```
$ terraform init
Initializing modules...
- module.web
  Getting source "web"

Initializing provider plugins...
- Checking for available provider plugins on https://releases.hashicorp.com...
- Downloading plugin for provider "oci" (3.45.0)...

* provider.oci: version = "~> 3.45"

Terraform has been successfully initialized!
```

Terraform downloads the newest plugin version for the oci provider.

Let's look at the directories again. Each directory that contains .tf files can be seen as an individual *module*. If you split your infrastructure configuration into groups of Terraform configuration files with dedicated folders and well-selected input parameters, you will be able to increase the code reusability across your projects. Our demonstrational project contains two modules.

- **root**: We define here the provider configuration, a VCN, an Internet gateway, and a module reference to the web module.

- **web**: We define here the route table, the security list, the subnet, and a compute instance that uses a cloud-init script to install and start the web server.

If you open the vars.tf file, you will see that it defines one more variable, namely, compartment_ocid, when compared to the file with the same name that we saw in the previous section.

```
## Provider-specific Variables
variable "tenancy_ocid" {}
variable "user_ocid" {}
variable "region" {}
variable "private_key_path" {}
variable "fingerprint" {}
variable "private_key_password" {}

## Project-specific input variables
variable "compartment_ocid" {}
```

Nearly every OCI resource lives inside a compartment. This means you will be expected to provide an OCID of a particular compartment you would like your resources to exist within. The corresponding environment variable is already present in the tfvars.env.sh file.

The compute instance resource definition inside the web/compute.tf configuration file assumes you have an existing SSH keypair with a public key available at ~/.ssh/oci_id_rsa.pub. Please generate a new keypair in the ~/.ssh/ or copy the existing keypair, which was created in Chapter 2, to that folder.

We will now provision the infrastructure. As soon as we see it up and running, I will explain the configuration files in detail. Please make sure you are in the 2-simple-infrastructure directory and issue the terraform apply command like this:

```
$ terraform apply
data.oci_core_images.centos_image: Refreshing state...
data.oci_identity_availability_domains.ads: Refreshing state...

An execution plan has been generated and is shown below.
Resource actions are indicated with the following symbols:
  + create
 <= read (data resources)

Terraform will perform the following actions:

+ oci_core_internet_gateway.web_igw
+ oci_core_virtual_network.web_vcn
<= module.web.data.oci_core_vnic.web_vnic
<= module.web.data.oci_core_vnic_attachments.web_vnic_attachment
  + module.web.oci_core_instance.web_vm
  + module.web.oci_core_route_table.web_rt
  + module.web.oci_core_security_list.web_sl
  + module.web.oci_core_subnet.web_subnet

Plan: 6 to add, 0 to change, 0 to destroy.

Do you want to perform these actions?
  Terraform will perform the actions described earlier.
  Only 'yes' will be accepted to approve.

  Enter a value:
```

Terraform will create a provisioning plan and ask you for permission to proceed. Provide yes as an input and confirm with Enter. The provisioning begins. Terraform uses the logic implemented in the plugin for the OCI provider and issues a series of OCI REST API calls. Whenever possible, the API requests will be sent in parallel.

```
Do you want to perform these actions?
  Terraform will perform the actions described earlier.
  Only 'yes' will be accepted to approve.
```

Enter a value: **yes**

```
oci_core_virtual_network.web_vcn: Creating...
oci_core_virtual_network.web_vcn: Creation complete after 0s
oci_core_internet_gateway.web_igw: Creating...
module.web.oci_core_security_list.web_sl: Creating...
oci_core_internet_gateway.web_igw: Creation complete after 1s
module.web.oci_core_route_table.web_rt: Creating...
module.web.oci_core_security_list.web_sl: Creation complete after 1s
module.web.oci_core_route_table.web_rt: Creation complete after 0s
module.web.oci_core_subnet.web_subnet: Creating...
module.web.oci_core_subnet.web_subnet: Creation complete after 0s
module.web.oci_core_instance.web_vm: Creating...
module.web.oci_core_instance.web_vm: Still creating... (10s elapsed)
module.web.oci_core_instance.web_vm: Still creating... (20s elapsed)
module.web.oci_core_instance.web_vm: Still creating... (30s elapsed)
module.web.oci_core_instance.web_vm: Still creating... (40s elapsed)
module.web.oci_core_instance.web_vm: Still creating... (50s elapsed)
module.web.oci_core_instance.web_vm: Creation complete after 56s
module.web.data.oci_core_vnic_attachments.web_vnic_attachment: Refreshing
state...
module.web.data.oci_core_vnic.web_vnic: Refreshing state...

Apply complete! Resources: 6 added, 0 changed, 0 destroyed.

Outputs:

web_instance_public_ip = 130.61.127.53
```

Let's take a closer look at the preceding code snippet. You can see that the virtual cloud network (web_vcn) was the first cloud resource created. Next, the creation process started in parallel for the Internet gateway (web_igw) and the security list (web_sl). This is pretty clear. Both exist within a VCN and have no dependencies between them. The route table (web_rt), however, had to wait until the Internet gateway has been successfully created. The reason behind this is that the route rule we included in the route table pointed to the Internet gateway as its target. In other words, the route table depended on the existence of the Internet gateway. The creation of the subnet (web_ subnet) began immediately after the route table and security list were created. Finally, the provisioning of a compute instance (web_vm) started and took nearly a minute to complete. Figure 3-11 presents the dependency tree.

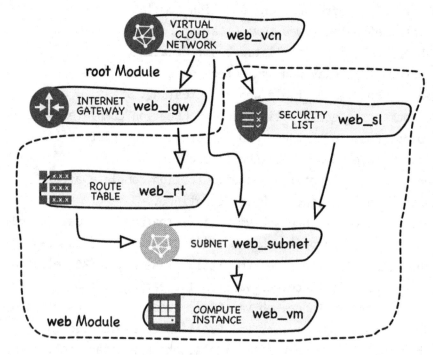

Figure 3-11. *Resource dependency tree*

The last two entries (web_vnic_attachment and web_vnic) annotated with the Refreshing state text mean that read-only requests were sent to the OCI REST API to fetch some information. In this case, Terraform queried OCI for the public IP address that had been assigned to the newly launched compute instance. Note this address (in my case, it is 130.61.127.53, but you will most probably see a different value, unless you are lucky to get the same address assigned from the pool). We will need it, in a moment, to test the deployment.

Congratulations! You've just provisioned your first Terraform-based cloud solution using the infrastructure-as-code approach. If you want, you can go to the OCI Console to see it, as shown in Figure 3-12.

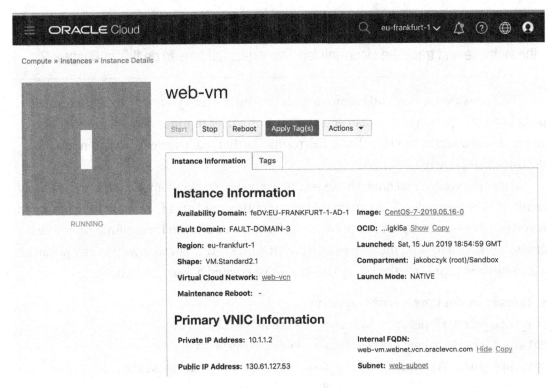

Figure 3-12. *web-vm compute instance in the OCI Console*

The fact that an instance is up and running does not mean that the booting process has completed. Cloud-init scripts, especially those that download and install new software, can take some time to complete. I explained this in Chapter 2. Try sending a standard GET request a few times using curl until you see this:

```
$ VM_PUBLIC_IP=`terraform output web_instance_public_ip`
$ echo $VM_PUBLIC_IP
130.61.127.54
$ curl $VM_PUBLIC_IP
Greetings from the Cloud
```

If you've read the greeting, it means you've successfully tested our simple cloud application. Hurrah!

> **Tip**   If you get bored by waiting for the cloud-init script to complete, you can log into the instance and trace the cloud-init log. I've explained how to do this in Chapter 2.

The infrastructure-as-code approach really shines when you need to update small pieces of a complex cloud infrastructure. Terraform tries to minimize the number of changes and alter (or re-create) only the resources that really have to be amended (or destroyed and newly launched).

Assuming you've had enough fun testing your simple cloud application, we will now terminate the resources. You can do this by executing the `terraform destroy` command. If you use the `--auto-approve` option, Terraform won't ask you for the final permission and will proceed to send the requests to the OCI REST API. This is how you can perform a cleanup and terminate the infrastructure we've created a moment ago:

```
$ terraform destroy --auto-approve
oci_core_virtual_network.web_vcn: Refreshing state...
data.oci_core_images.centos_image: Refreshing state...
data.oci_identity_availability_domains.ads: Refreshing state...
oci_core_security_list.web_sl: Refreshing state...
oci_core_internet_gateway.web_igw: Refreshing state...
oci_core_route_table.web_rt: Refreshing state...
oci_core_subnet.web_subnet: Refreshing state...
oci_core_instance.web_vm: Refreshing state...
data.oci_core_vnic_attachments.web_vnic_attachment: Refreshing state...
data.oci_core_vnic.web_vnic: Refreshing state...
module.web.oci_core_instance.web_vm: Destroying...
module.web.oci_core_instance.web_vm: Still destroying...10s elapsed
module.web.oci_core_instance.web_vm: Still destroying... 20s elapsed
module.web.oci_core_instance.web_vm: Still destroying... 30s elapsed
module.web.oci_core_instance.web_vm: Still destroying... 40s elapsed
module.web.oci_core_instance.web_vm: Still destroying... 50s elapsed
module.web.oci_core_instance.web_vm: Still destroying... 1m0s elapsed
module.web.oci_core_instance.web_vm: Still destroying... 1m10s elapsed
module.web.oci_core_instance.web_vm: Still destroying... 1m20s elapsed
module.web.oci_core_instance.web_vm: Destruction complete after 1m25s
module.web.oci_core_subnet.web_subnet: Destroying...
```

```
module.web.oci_core_subnet.web_subnet: Destruction complete after 1s
module.web.oci_core_route_table.web_rt: Destroying...
module.web.oci_core_security_list.web_sl: Destroying...
module.web.oci_core_security_list.web_sl: Destruction complete after 0s
module.web.oci_core_route_table.web_rt: Destruction complete after 0s
oci_core_internet_gateway.web_igw: Destroying...
oci_core_internet_gateway.web_igw: Destruction complete after 1s
oci_core_virtual_network.web_vcn: Destroying...
oci_core_virtual_network.web_vcn: Destruction complete after 0s

Destroy complete! Resources: 6 destroyed.
```

The resources are destroyed in the reversed sequence to how the resources were created. You can verify that the compute instance really has been terminated. In the OCI Console, you should see something like what is shown in Figure 3-13.

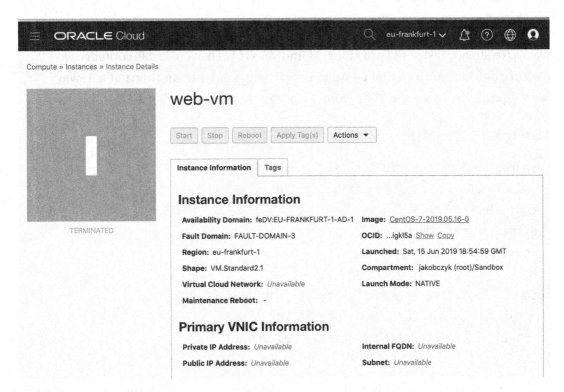

Figure 3-13. *Terminated instance*

Infrastructure Code

In this section, we will discuss the resources we've defined in the Terraform configuration files (suffixed with .tf). Let's take another look at the files our project consists of:

```
.
├── modules.tf
├── provider.tf
├── vars.tf
├── vcn.tf
└── web
    ├── cloud-init
    │   └── webvm.config.yaml
    ├── compute.tf
    ├── vars.tf
    └── vcn.tf
```

We've already discussed provider.tf and vars.tf. The vcn.tf file contains two resource definitions: a virtual cloud network (web_vcn) and an Internet gateway (web_igw). You can see the definitions for both resources in Listing 3-15.

Listing 3-15. vcn.tf (Root Module)

```
resource "oci_core_virtual_network" "web_vcn" {
  compartment_id = var.compartment_ocid
  cidr_block = "10.1.1.0/24"
  display_name = "web-vcn"
  dns_label = "vcn"
}
resource "oci_core_internet_gateway" "web_igw" {
  compartment_id = var.compartment_ocid
  vcn_id = oci_core_virtual_network.web_vcn.id
}
```

The Internet gateway (web_igw) references the OCID of the VCN (vcn_id) it exists within. It does that with the help of Terraform syntax that empowers you to reference the attributes of resources, variables, data sources, local values, and other types of Terraform configurations as well as use functions and mathematical calculations. If you want to reference a resource, you will use an expression that follows this structure: `type.name.attribute`, for example, `oci_core_virtual_network.web_vcn.id`. If you want to reference a variable, you will use this structure: **var**`.variable_name`, for example, `var.compartment_ocid`.

The root module does not define any other resources. On the other hand, it does include a module definition. You can find it in the `modules.tf` Terraform configuration file. Its contents are shown in Listing 3-16.

Listing 3-16. modules.tf (Root Module)

```
data "oci_identity_availability_domains" "ads" {
  compartment_id = var.tenancy_ocid
}

data "oci_core_images" "centos_image" {
  compartment_id = var.tenancy_ocid
  operating_system = "CentOS"
  operating_system_version = 7
  shape = "VM.Standard2.1"
}

module "web" {
  source = "./web"
  compartment_ocid = var.compartment_ocid
  vcn_ocid = oci_core_virtual_network.web_vcn.id
  vcn_igw_ocid = oci_core_internet_gateway.web_igw.id
  vcn_subnet_cidr = "10.1.1.0/30"
  ads = data.oci_identity_availability_domains.ads.availability_domains[*].name
  compute_image_ocid = data.oci_core_images.centos_image.images[0].id
}

output "web_instance_public_ip" { value = module.web.web_public_ip }
```

This file has about three times more lines than the previous one we've discussed. Terraform uses *data sources* to deliver a read-only view to the resources that already exist in the cloud or are computed on the fly during provisioning. The first configuration block defines a data source called ads that is used to query OCI to get the list of availability domains. The second configuration block defines another data source called centos_image

that is responsible for fetching the list of available CentOS 7 base images. New versions
of operating system base images are released monthly, so this will always get you a
reference to a currently existing version. In production, you can hard-code OCIDs of
particular images to avoid unexpected changes in infrastructure when newer images are
released. In our case, we are fine with fetching the OCID of the newest image on each
Terraform execution.

Terraform uses *modules* to gather multiple Terraform configuration files and serve
them as reusable and customizable pieces for use across various projects. Each directory
that contains .tf files can be seen as a module. If you look at the root directory of our
project, you can see two directories that can serve as modules. The modules.tf file,
which we are discussing right now, exists within the directory we called the root module.
The third configuration block in this file defines a module (web) and tells Terraform to
instantiate the resources within the directory provided as the source attribute, which
in our case refers to the web subdirectory. To customize a module instance, we can use
attributes of our choice as long as they are defined as variables within the referenced
module directory. It may sound a bit confusing at the beginning. Let me explain with
an example. If you look at the modules.tf configuration file again, you will see that I am
passing the OCID of a VCN as a custom, arbitrarily named vcn_ocid module attribute.
The source module attribute points to the web subdirectory as the module directory. If
you open the web/vars.tf configuration file, you will see that the variable definitions
have exactly the same names as module attributes in modules.tf. For your convenience,
I've decided to show this relation in Figure 3-14.

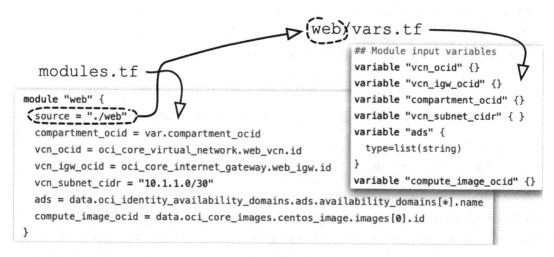

Figure 3-14. *Input variables and module attributes*

Both the VCN and the Internet gateway are referenced by the resources defined within the web module; therefore, we have to provide their OCIDs as attribute values to the module. This is done through the vcn_ocid and vcn_igw_ocid module attributes that are seen as variables by the resources inside the module. Furthermore, we provide an address range block for the subnet through the vcn_subnet_cidr attribute/variable as well as the OCID of the compartment through the compartment_ocid attribute/variable.

We use interpolation on data sources that are defined at the beginning of the modules.tf file to pass the fetched values into the module. The compute_image_ocid module attribute is used to convey the OCID of an operating system base image to be used by the compute instance defined inside the web module. Please hold on a minute to understand what this interpolation expression does. Our goal is to pass a single OCID into the module, while the data source is defined to read all the available CentOS 7 images, showing the base operating system images first. To achieve our goal, we have to select the OCID of the first element in the list of CentOS 7 base images fetched by the data source. Figure 3-15 explains in detail what each part of the expression is responsible for.

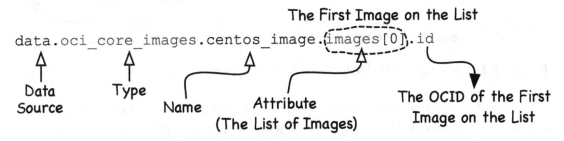

Figure 3-15. *Terraform data source interpolation example*

To be more precise, technically, the elements on the list returned by data sources in the OCI provider are currently implemented as maps because they associate keys that happen to be the list element attribute names with values that are the corresponding list element attribute values. This allows us to use another lookup-based syntax in our interpolation expression. I am going to present this alternative right now with an example based on the second data source.

Note   The Terraform provider for Oracle Cloud Infrastructure is implemented as an open source project in the Go language. You can find the source code on Github at https://github.com/terraform-providers/terraform-provider-oci.

The `ads` module attribute provides the input to a variable with the same name inside the `web` module. This time, the variable is of a `list` type. In this way, we can store multiple values that can be accessed based on the list index in this variable. The `ads` data source of the `oci_identity_availability_domains` type returns a list of availability domains. Although we launch only one compute instance in our simple project and could have lived with passing just a single name of a particular availability domain, I've decided to provide the module with a list that contains the names of all availability domains returned by the API. In this way, the choice of a particular availability domain for the compute instance is delegated to the internals of the module. To construct a list storing the values that belong to one attribute of all elements in another list, we are using the *splat expression*, explained in Figure 3-16.

Creating a New List of Availability Domain Names

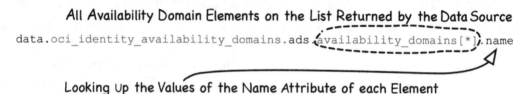

Figure 3-16. *Terraform lookup interpolation example*

Listing 3-17 presents the contents of the `vcn.tf` file that exists inside the `web` module directory. It contains the configuration for the route table (`web_rt`), the security list (`web_sl`), and a subnet (`web_subnet`).

Listing 3-17. web/vcn.tf (Web Module)

```
resource "oci_core_route_table" "web_rt" {
  compartment_id = var.compartment_ocid
  vcn_id = var.vcn_ocid
  route_rules {
    destination_type = "CIDR_BLOCK"
    destination = "0.0.0.0/0"
    network_entity_id = var.vcn_igw_ocid
  }
  display_name = "web-rt"
}
```

```
resource "oci_core_security_list" "web_sl" {
  compartment_id = var.compartment_ocid
  vcn_id = var.vcn_ocid
  egress_security_rules {
    stateless="false"
    destination="0.0.0.0/0"
    protocol="all"
  }
  ingress_security_rules {
    stateless="false"
    source="0.0.0.0/0"
    protocol="6"
    tcp_options {
      min=22
      max=22
    }
  }
  ingress_security_rules {
    stateless="false"
    source="0.0.0.0/0"
    protocol="6"
    tcp_options {
      min=80
      max=80
    }
  }
  display_name = "web-sl"
}

resource "oci_core_subnet" "web_subnet" {
  compartment_id = var.compartment_ocid
  vcn_id = var.vcn_ocid
  display_name = "web-subnet"
  availability_domain = var.ads[0]
  cidr_block = var.vcn_subnet_cidr
  route_table_id = oci_core_route_table.web_rt.id
```

```
  security_list_ids = [ oci_core_security_list.web_sl.id ]
  prohibit_public_ip_on_vnic = "false"
  dns_label = "webnet"
}
```

The route table (`web_rt`) defines a single route rule that directs the entire outbound traffic (`0.0.0.0/0`) that is destined to travel outside the VCN to the Internet gateway that has been defined in the `root` module and whose OCID has been passed as a module attribute.

The security list (`web_sl`) defines one stateful egress rule that allows the entire outbound traffic and two stateful ingress rules that allow the inbound traffic on ports 22 (SSH) and 80 (HTTP). As a reminder, if a stateful security rule permits the traffic in the direction it oversees, the corresponding packets that return as part of the same TCP session will also be allowed.

The subnet (`web_subnet`) resource exists within the VCN that has been defined in the `root` module and whose OCID has been passed as a module attribute. It references the route table and the security list created in the `web` module and briefly described in two previous paragraphs. The value for the `availability_domain` attribute shows how to access a list variable using an index: `var.ads[0]`. The `prohibit_public_ip_on_vnic` attribute set to `false` makes this subnet public. It is worth noting that even though we use just one security list for this subnet, we still have to pass its OCID as a list element because the `security_list_ids` attribute expects a list. It comes from the fact that a subnet can reference more than one security list.

Listing 3-18 presents the contents of the `compute.tf` file that exists inside the `web` module directory. It contains the resource configuration for the compute instance (`web_vm`), which runs an Apache web server, as well as two data sources (`web_vnic_attachment` and `web_vnic`) used to fetch the public IP assigned to the instance during provisioning. At the bottom of the file, you will find an output configuration block (`web_public_ip`), which I will explain in a few moments.

Listing 3-18. web/compute.tf (Web Module)

```
resource "oci_core_instance" "web_vm" {
  compartment_id = var.compartment_ocid
  display_name = "web-vm"
  availability_domain = var.ads[0]
  source_details {
```

```
    source_id = var.compute_image_ocid
    source_type = "image"
  }
  shape = "VM.Standard2.1"
  create_vnic_details {
    subnet_id = oci_core_subnet.web_subnet.id
    assign_public_ip = true
  }
  metadata = {
    ssh_authorized_keys = file("~/.ssh/oci_id_rsa.pub")
    user_data = base64encode(file("web/cloud-init/webvm.config.yaml"))
  }
}

data "oci_core_vnic_attachments" "web_vnic_attachment" {
  compartment_id = var.compartment_ocid
  instance_id = oci_core_instance.web_vm.id
}

data "oci_core_vnic" "web_vnic" {
  vnic_id = data.oci_core_vnic_attachments.web_vnic_attachment.vnic_
  attachments[0].vnic_id
}

output "web_public_ip" {
  value = data.oci_core_vnic.web_vnic.public_ip_address
}
End
```

The compute instance (web_vm) is launched in the subnet that has been defined
in the same module. The resource definition references the image based on the OCID
that had been fetched in the root module and supplied as an input variable to the web
module. The create_vnic_details.assign_public_ip attribute set to true will cause
OCI to assign an ephemeral public IP address from the pool of the public addresses to
the primary vNIC of the instance. The authorized_keys file on an instance will include
a public key read as a string from the file provided as a path to the file function that is
used in the expression for the metadata.ssh_authorized_keys attribute.

The `metadata.user_data` attribute specifies a base64-encoded cloud-config configuration for the cloud-init tool that can be used to effectively customize the initialization of a compute instance. We use it to install the Apache HTTP Server, replace the default `index.html` file, open port 80 on the machine, and start the HTTP server. Listing 3-19 shows the contents of the cloud-config file used by the cloud-init tool on the instance's first startup.

Listing 3-19. web/cloud-init/webvm.config.yaml (Web Module)

```
#cloud-config
packages:
  - httpd
write_files:
  - content: |
      Greetings from the Cloud
    path: /var/www/html/index.html
runcmd:
  - [ "firewall-offline-cmd", "--add-port=80/tcp" ]
  - [ "systemctl", "restart", "firewalld" ]
  - [ "systemctl", "enable", "httpd" ]
  - [ "systemctl", "start", "httpd" ]
final_message: "$HOSTNAME initialization has been completed"
```

The public IP address is dynamically assigned to the compute instance from a pool of available public IP addresses. We learn the exact address as soon as the instance has been provisioned. A compute instance can have more than one vNIC. The first data source (`web_vnic_attachment`) fetches the list of vNICs. In our case, our compute instance has only a single vNIC. We use the OCID of this first vNIC found in the list returned by the first data source as an input to the second data source (`web_vnic`), which, eventually, returns a map with the public IP address defined as a value for the `public_ip_address` key. We use the output configuration (`web_public_ip`) to pass this value to the `root` module where another output configuration (`"web_instance_public_ip"`) defined at the bottom of the `modules.tf` file gets the value printed to the output of the Terraform build.

As we issued the `terraform apply` command, Terraform prepared an execution plan that consisted of actions to be taken to bring the *current state*, which was based on the information stored in the *state file*, to the *expected state* that was based on the contents of the configuration files (`.tf`) in the `root` module and in the `web` modules. It is time to briefly discuss the way Terraform manages state.

State

Terraform uses a *state file* to keep track of the real infrastructure it has provisioned, the intermediary values it has computed, and the dependency graph between resources. You can think of all these elements as the current state. State existence is the key enabler for Terraform to serve its purpose. Terraform compares the expected state as defined across the configuration files (.tf) that build up your infrastructure code with the current state stored in the state file to produce an execution plan that eventually leads to API calls. Figure 3-17 illustrates this concept.

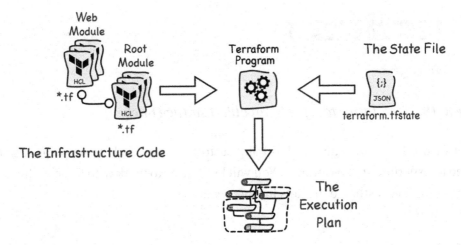

Figure 3-17. *Terraform state*

As you issued the terraform apply command for the first time, earlier in this chapter, Terraform created a terraform.tfstate file in the root module directory. This JSON file will get updated each time you run selected Terraform commands such as refresh, plan, apply, and others. Manual changes inside this file are discouraged unless you really know what to do. In such case, it is recommended that you back up the file and familiarize yourself with the capabilities of the terraform state command. By default, Terraform stores the state file locally in a form of a terraform.tfstate file, like in our case. This can lead to two problems: backup strategies and team collaboration.

First, it is not a good idea to back up the local state file in any kind of version control system because the file can contain some sensitive data. Second, working concurrently with multiple copies used by various team members will, sooner or later, lead to synchronization problems.

You can leverage Oracle Cloud Infrastructure object storage with the Terraform http backend type to take the *remote state* approach, instead of using a local state file, which is prone to the problems I mentioned before. If you do so, your state file will be stored as an object in an object storage bucket, encrypted at rest and protected from unauthorized access. Your team members will be able to collaborate, thanks to the locking mechanism provided by the http backend type. Figure 3-18 shows a Terraform state file in an object storage bucket.

Figure 3-18. *Terraform state file in an object storage bucket*

Storing the Terraform state in cloud object storage is beyond the scope of this book. Feel free to experiment on your own. You will learn how to work with Oracle Cloud Infrastructure object storage buckets in Chapter 5.

Best Practices

It is time to list a few recommendations I would like to share with you about automation. Figure 3-19 presents the automation options we've discussed in this chapter.

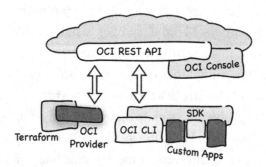

Figure 3-19. *Oracle Cloud Infrastructure automation landscape*

Use *Terraform* to manage the infrastructure as code and leverage a convenient and effective declarative approach to designing your cloud resources. This will let you version the infrastructure code and track changes so that you can always revert to a previous state.

Use *the CLI* to create read-only monitoring scripts and use them when you need to collect some information about the infrastructure on demand. Schedule these scripts, if needed, to collect the data at set intervals, and persist the results into a data store to allow future research and analysis. If you need to build a more sophisticated cloud monitoring utility, feel free to implement a custom tool using the SDK. Last but not least, you should first evaluate the built-in monitoring capabilities of OCI by using its dedicated cloud services. Then you can use the CLI to collect statistics straight from these services.

If you use Terraform, never perform any ad hoc changes on your cloud resources neither in the OCI Console nor using the CLI; otherwise, the Terraform *state file* that stores the current state may deviate from the real state or get changed with no warning. The latter can happen because prior to executing `terraform apply`, another command (`refresh`) that updates the state file based on the real state detected gets implicitly executed. In this way, you can unwillingly incorporate into your execution plan some destructive actions on the resources that had been created manually and wipe them out.

Do not store the Terraform state file (`terraform.tfstate`) in a version control system because the file may contain sensitive data. If you are using Git, make sure you've included the following lines in your `.gitignore`:

```
.terraform/
terraform.state*
```

Use *remote state* to avoid this problem and make smooth team collaboration possible, especially if the remote state backend supports a proper locking mechanism. If you cannot rely on remote state, consider running Terraform builds on dedicated build servers, as a part of the continuous delivery pipeline, so that the state file is stored on a single, remote machine with limited access. In this case, you will still need to address the issue of the state file backups. Alternatively, you can use the *Oracle Cloud Infrastructure Resource Manager*, which is one of the OCI services that is beyond the scope of this book.

Split the infrastructure code you write into *reusable modules*. Carefully consider what kind of module attributes will let you customize and reuse the module you are working on in various projects. Think about the output values that may be useful in the parent module as well as in the Terraform output.

Last but not least, make sure that your compute instances always *use the same image versions*, no matter if newer versions are introduced in the meantime, until you are ready to upgrade your running instances and know how to do it. You can do this by using variables with the hard-coded image OCIDs. In this chapter, we've used data sources to dynamically fetch the OCID of a CentOS 7 image. While this approach is absolutely fine for a short-living PoC or demo, you mustn't allow this to be the case for production systems. If you dynamically fetch the OCID and a newer image version is introduced in between your builds, your instances may be terminated and relaunched simply because Terraform changed its base image. A similar recommendation to provide the values as hard-coded variables has been issued for availability domains.

Summary

This chapter introduced the three ways to automate Oracle Cloud Infrastructure. At the beginning, I explained the role of the OCI REST API with a special focus on the security. You learned what information is required to sign a request and how to prepare the necessary API signing keys. Next, you read about the Python SDK for Oracle Cloud Infrastructure, starting from installation going through the configuration up to the point where you executed two simple actions on OCI from the interactive Python shell. Going further, you familiarized yourself with the CLI, discovering similarities with the Python SDK it is based on. The largest part of this chapter focused on applying the infrastructure-as-code principles using Terraform. You provisioned a simple, one-server infrastructure, performed a smoke test, and destroyed this sample setup. Afterward, I explained the infrastructure code in detail. Following that, you learned about the role of a Terraform state file. Finally, you read some recommendations related to automation. In the next chapter, we will look closer at identity and access management in the context of project environment management.

CHAPTER 4

Cloud Security and Project Environments

In this chapter, we will take a top-down approach and think about how to properly organize your cloud resources around projects, environments, and solutions you are about to design and run on Oracle Cloud Infrastructure.

Projects, Environments, and Systems

Throughout the years, we have gotten used to delivering information technology solutions in a collaborative effort that follows a particular organizational process. The process is usually built around more or less a formal plan and lasts until the moment when specific goals are achieved or conditions are met. To reference the entire endeavor, we typically call it a *project*. What is characteristic about nearly every project is its temporariness. The beginning, any optional intermediate goals (sometimes called *milestones*), and the expected ultimate end goal have well-defined expected completion dates. Contemporary cloud-oriented information technology projects generally aim either at transforming an existing on-premise solution and bringing its functionality to the cloud or at designing a completely new cloud-native solution.

The product of a cloud-oriented project is most commonly a set of applications running on a virtual cloud infrastructure. The software landscape of an organization can be indeed complex. The larger or more technology-oriented an organization is, the greater the number and types of applications are. To avoid ambiguity and be able to reference the applications or groups of tightly associated applications, we can use the term *system*. All in all, the application landscape consists of a number of systems that are eventually used to power a broad range of business processes. Usually, the majority of systems are interconnected with each other and require some degree of integration.

179

© Michał Tomasz Jakóbczyk 2020
M. T. Jakóbczyk, *Practical Oracle Cloud Infrastructure*, https://doi.org/10.1007/978-1-4842-5506-3_4

The software development lifecycle is nearly always iterative because complex problems can be truly solved only if they are split into manageable phases. Developers gradually build or migrate applications step by step in small chunks of features. In some cases, incremental changes can introduce some regression, understood as defects that make previously working functionality simply fail. To alleviate the risk of regression, it is crucial that the entire solution gets fully tested at least once on each milestone. This is done through the so-called regression tests. Furthermore, some major milestones and the final handover have to be approved by the customer. As a result, the software becomes the subject of the so-called acceptance tests. While developers change the software they are building frequently, the regression and acceptance tests do require some degree of stability. The traditional approach solves that through the use of different *environments* for different purposes. Developers work with one or more *development environments* where they deploy all intermediary versions of software. Even if you rely on good coverage of automated unit tests, these environments may still be rather unstable. This is why only selected versions are elevated to the so-called releases and deployed in a *test environment* where more sophisticated, either manual or automated, regression and acceptance tests take place.

Successfully tested and approved releases are usually elevated to an environment where all the production systems operate. We often reference this environment as the *production environment*. What is worth noting is the fact that production systems are the subject of routine operations, and, in the general run of things, we no longer talk about them in the context of individual projects. Furthermore, you can have multiple projects that contribute to a single production environment but impact only relatively loosely coupled production systems each. This is conceptually shown in Figure 4-1.

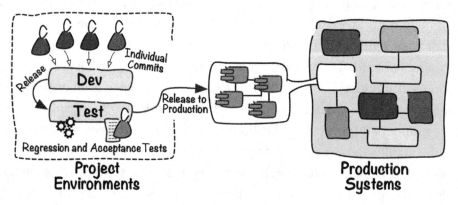

Figure 4-1. *Project environments and production systems*

The cloud resources, such as compute instances, object storage buckets, or virtual networks, used across different project environments and production systems require separate *management permissions*. While you can let a large group of developers manage the cloud resources used across various development and test environments, you would rather appoint a much smaller group of people to look after your production systems. Moreover, it is usually not necessary for developers working on one project to see the cloud resources used by other projects. To enforce the proper access levels, you have to be able to group selected cloud resources in some kind of logical groups to which you can attach dedicated permission polices that will decide who can take what kind of actions on the cloud resources a particular group contains. The metered usage of selected types of cloud resources such as compute instances or load balancers incur financial costs. From a financial point of view, nearly all organizations prefer to *measure the costs* incurred by individual projects and production systems. The more granular cost split, the better. In this way, the cloud charges can be properly assigned to their appropriate cost centers and eventually accounted in a correct way. Again, you need to be somehow able to group selected cloud resources to calculate the charges these groups cause.

Compartments

Oracle Cloud Infrastructure uses *compartments* to group related cloud resources. Nearly every cloud resource, such as compute instance, object storage bucket, or managed Kubernetes cluster, must belong to just one compartment. You decide in which compartment a newly created cloud resource will exist while creating that resource. If you find out you need to move a resource to a different compartment, you will have to terminate the old one and provision a new one with the same configuration in a target compartment, unless the particular cloud resource type supports moving between compartments. Compartments provide logical isolation, which makes it much easier to govern the management permission policies and track the costs incurred by the related groups of resources. The isolation is purely logical. This means that it is still technically possible to let the resources, for example, compute instances, in one compartment communicate with the resources, for example, other compute instances and object storage buckets, in another compartment. There are three reasons to use compartments.

- Easier resource management
- Granular access control
- Cost split

First, it is easier to understand what the assets in your cloud tenancy are and manage these resources if you logically group the related resources. In this way, you are able to apply more precise filters to your queries and receive shorter and more accurate lists of results. This becomes even more visible as the number and the variety of your cloud resources start to grow. Second, compartments normally become the primary scope of your access control policy statements. The statements are stored in documents called identity and access management *policies*. Each statement will allow some kind of access to a particular type of cloud resource that exists in a given compartment. At this stage, it is worth noting that child compartments inherit the access management policies from their parent compartments. Third, you can *filter costs* by compartment and know what cloud resource consumption costs are incurred by each project environment and production system as long as you choose to use different compartments for each of them.

Compartments are global, and every individual compartment spans all regions your cloud account is subscribed to. It is possible and in many cases advised to arrange your compartments in a hierarchical structure that can consist of up to six levels of child compartments. If you are working on a single proof-of-concept project or are just learning OCI, you will most probably store all your cloud resources in a single compartment. You could call it Sandbox or anything more meaningful to you. As soon as you consider working with multiple projects and running a set of production systems in your cloud tenancy, you ought to carefully plan the compartment hierarchy. How would you usually approach this task? Well, it is easy to spot that the most natural candidates to derive your compartment hierarchy from are project environments and production systems. Why? Simply because they are the ones that usually provide the typical context for resource management, access control, and cost tracking—the three main reasons to use compartments. This approach is illustrated in Figure 4-2.

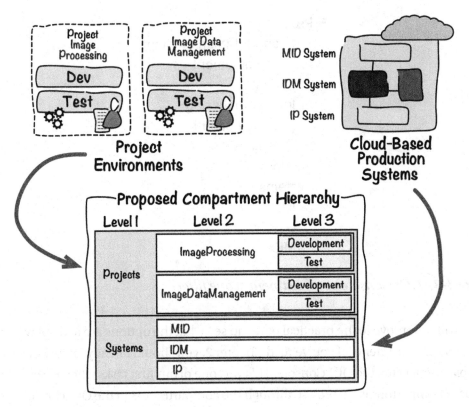

Figure 4-2. *Deriving compartment hierarchy*

There is always one root compartment in your cloud account. This is the root node in our compartment hierarchy as well. If we were to follow the example, we would create two separate compartments: one for projects (`Projects`) and one for production systems (`Systems`). Next, we would create three child compartments inside the `Systems` compartment: `MID`, `IDM`, and `IP`. In this way, the cloud resources that logically belong to the IDM production system would reside in the `Systems/IDM` compartment. Similarly, we would create two child compartments inside the `Projects` compartment: `ImageProcessing` and `ImageDataMangement`. Subsequently, we would finally create two further child compartments in each project-specific compartment for the development and test environments. Again, this would let you keep the assets specific to the Image Processing project and its development environment inside the `Projects/ImageProcessing/Development` compartment. It's as simple as that. Figure 4-3 presents the expected compartment structure as you would see it in the OCI Console compartment scope filter.

- Projects
    - ImageDataManagement
        - Development
        - Test
    - ImageProcessing
        - Development
        - Test
    - Sandbox
- Systems
    - IDM
    - IP
    - MID

Figure 4-3. *OCI Console compartment scope filter*

We will now move to the practical part and see what the options are to display, create, and delete compartments. If you've read Chapter 2, you should already know how to create a compartment using the OCI Console. This was one of our first tasks when we created a Sandbox compartment. To browse through the compartments in the OCI Console, you need to go to Menu ➤ Identity ➤ Compartments.

What you are going to see is a list of your level 1 compartments, as shown in Figure 4-4.

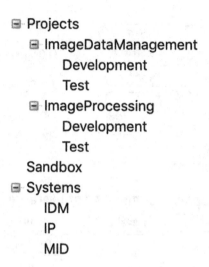

Figure 4-4. *Compartment list (level 1) in the OCI Console*

You need to click the name of a particular compartment to see its details as well as a detailed list of the child compartments it contains. Here, you can alter the name and description of a compartment, check its OCID, and manage its child compartments. Figure 4-5 presents the Compartment Details view for the Sandbox compartment.

Figure 4-5. *Compartment Details view in the OCI Console*

To add a new child compartment in the OCI Console, you just need to click the Create Compartment button and provide the required details.

Note   The code snippets from this book have been tested on macOS and Windows Subsystem for Linux. Moreover, all commands should work on the major Linux distributions. If you are using Windows and do not want to use Windows Subsystem for Linux, you can always run Linux on a VM. Furthermore, the majority of code snippets may also work in Git Bash on Windows.

As expected, you can use the OCI CLI to create a new compartment. If you've completed all the steps described in Chapter 3, your CLI should be already configured to work with the Sandbox compartment by default. Run this command to output the name of the compartment set in your CLI settings as the default:

```
$ oci iam compartment get --output table --query 'data.{Name:"name"}'
+---------+
| Name    |
+---------+
| Sandbox |
+---------+
```

If you see a different name and would still like to create a child compartment in the Sandbox compartment, you can either adapt the oci_cli_rc file or use the -c parameter that takes any valid compartment OCID. The second option is faster and gives you more flexibility. I have described both ways in the previous chapter. For example, to run the same command in the context of a different compartment, you can do the following:

```
$ oci iam compartment get -c "ocid1.compartment.oc1..aa.........bpfl6q"
--output table --query 'data.{Name:"name"}'
+---------+
| Name    |
+---------+
| Systems |
+---------+
```

Tip   You can use the -c parameter with every CLI command to set the context of that individual command to any compartment of your choice.

As soon as we make sure that our CLI commands are executed in the context of the expected compartment, we are ready to create a new child compartment. To do so, just run this command and do not forget to use the -c parameter if needed:

```
$ EXP_COMPARTMENT_OCID=`oci iam compartment create --name Experiments
--description "Sandbox area for experiments" --query "data.id" | tr -d '"'`
```

The preceding command has created a new compartment called Experiments as a child compartment to the Sandbox compartment. At this stage, you should be able to see the newly created compartment in the list of child compartments for the Sandbox compartment, as shown in Figure 4-6.

Name	Status	OCID	Authorized	Created
Experiments	● Active	...qhslia	Yes	Thu, 21 Feb 2019 18:23:26 GMT

Figure 4-6. *Child compartment in the OCI Console*

From now on, it is possible to create various cloud resources inside this compartment in any region and any availability domain of your choice. The only thing to remember is to choose this compartment for the context of your actions. In the case of the OCI Console, you do it by selecting the compartment name in the List Scope combo box shown in Figure 4-7.

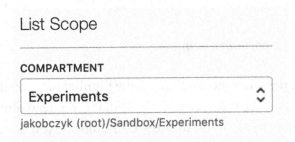

Figure 4-7. *Selecting the compartment in the OCI Console*

Like every other Oracle Cloud Infrastructure resource, compartments are uniquely identified through OCIDs. You can read more about them in Chapter 2. At any time, you can easily change a compartment's name and description, but its OCID remains immutable.

Tip   If you've made a typo in the compartment's name, do not delete it, but just rename it.

It is possible to delete unneeded compartments. You can perform this operation both in the Console or using the CLI. The action is asynchronous and usually takes some time. Prior to that, you still have to terminate and delete all resources and subcompartments inside the compartment you are about to delete; otherwise, you won't be allowed to do so. This is a command that initiates compartment deletion:

```
$ oci iam compartment delete -c "$EXP_COMPARTMENT_OCID"
Are you sure you want to delete this resource? [y/N]: y
{
  "opc-work-request-id": "ocid1.identityworkrequest.oc1..aa.........rejw7a"
}
```

The output indicates the asynchronous nature of this action. Furthermore, if you look at the list of child compartments to the Sandbox compartment, you will probably see that the Experiments subcompartment is still being deleted, as shown in Figure 4-8.

Name	Status	OCID	Authorized	Created
Experiments	● Deleting	...qhslia	Yes	Thu, 21 Feb 2019 18:23:26 GMT

Figure 4-8. *Deleting a compartment*

Last but not least, there is a service limit on the number of compartments. At the time of writing, it is set to 50 per tenancy. If you find out you need more, you can always request a service limit increase. To do so in the OCI Console, you need to follow these steps:

1. Go to Menu ➤ Governance ➤ Limits, Quotas and Usage.

2. Click "Request a service limit increase".

3. Fill in the form and click Submit Request.

Earlier in this section, I mentioned that one of the main motivations to use compartments is to be able to analyze the costs of individual production systems, projects, or even environments. In the OCI Console, you can do the following:

1. Go to Menu ➤ Account Management ➤ Cost Analysis.

2. Select a compartment in the filter.

3. Choose the desired period of time.

4. Click Apply Filters.

Figure 4-9 presents the costs incurred by the Sandbox compartment since the beginning of the calendar year in Polish Zloty (PLN), which is the local currency in my home country.

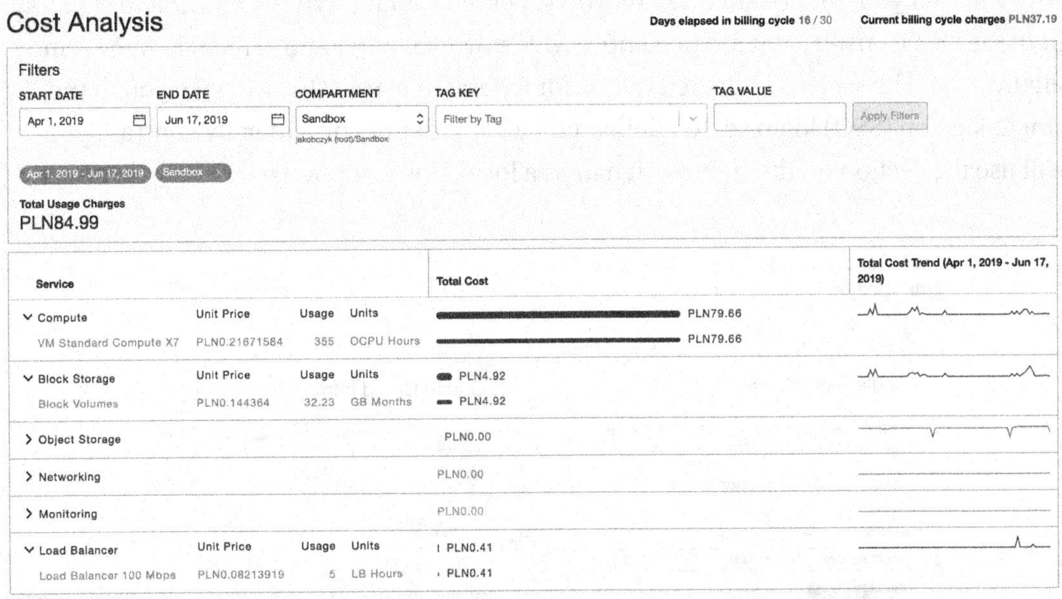

Figure 4-9. *Viewing costs per compartment in the OCI Console*

We are now ready to move to another important topic, which is the user management.

Users

Each action performed on Oracle Cloud Infrastructure resources is always done on behalf of a named user. As you read Chapter 3, you learned that every API call requires the OCID of a user simply to be able to sign a request. No matter if you are using the Console, API, SDK, CLI, or Terraform, you will always need a user account. Oracle Cloud Infrastructure supports two types of user accounts.

- Local users

- Federated users

When you subscribe to a new cloud account, there is a *default administrator user for the cloud account* created in the Oracle Identity Cloud Service (IDCS). The e-mail address that is used during registration becomes the username of this global administrator user. This is a federated user account. As a matter of fact, all tenancies are by default federated with IDCS, but you are free to switch to any other SAML-compliant identity provider or create nonfederated users that are local to OCI. If you are not sure whether you understand, do not worry. Let me explain. When you want to sign in to the OCI Console, you are presented with a two-section login screen, as shown in Figure 4-10. The section in the left part is for federated users. This will take you to the single-sign on (SSO) login screen delivered by your identity provider. By contrast, you will use the section on the right to sign in as a local, nonfederated user.

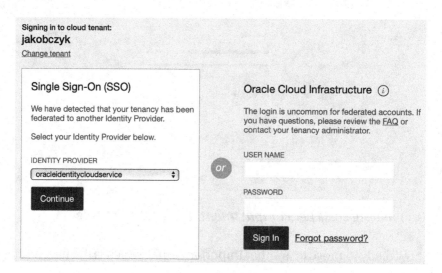

Figure 4-10. *Sign-in screen in the OCI Console*

Throughout this book, until this point, I've assumed you were using the default administrator user. This is going to change now because we are about to create and switch to a less-privileged, compartment administrator user. To demonstrate access policies in action, we are going to create a second local user with nearly no access rights. In the course of the book, we will be granting more and more access rights to this second local user depending on the resources used in various exercises.

Caution   If you are not the tenancy owner, you were probably given a user by your administrator. Yet, it is still possible that your user has been added to the tenancy's Administrators group in IDCS. If this is not the case and you want to complete the exercises in this book, you need to ask your tenancy administrator to put your user into an OCI group that has full control over a chosen compartment. In this case, you will need to work with this particular compartment.

First, we are going to create a new, local, nonfederated user who will become the Sandbox administrator. This operation is typically performed in the OCI Console or using the CLI. This is how you apply the first method:

1. Go to Menu ➤ Identity ➤ Users.

2. Click Create Users.

3. Provide **sandbox-admin** as the name, add some description, and click Create.

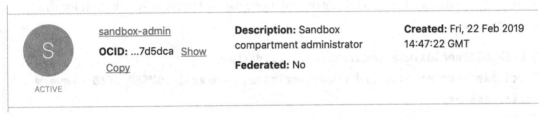

Figure 4-11. *Nonfederated user in the OCI Console*

A new user will be shown, as in Figure 4-11, in the OCI Console. This will be the local administrator for the Sandbox compartment. Now, we are going to create another local user, sandbox-user, this time using the CLI. The command we are about to use requires the tenancy OCID to be used as one of the parameters. You should be able to find this value in your CLI configuration file, most probably available at the path ~/.oci/config unless you've used a custom path for the CLI configuration file. Alternatively, you can also find this in the OCI Console under Menu ➤ Administration ➤ Tenancy Details. We are now ready to execute the following CLI command:

```
$ TENANCY_OCID=`cat ~/.oci/config | grep tenancy | sed 's/tenancy=//'`
$ oci iam user create --name sandbox-user --description "Sandbox user"
--query "data.id" -c $TENANCY_OCID
"ocid1.user.oc1..aa...........dzqpxa
```

First, we assigned the tenancy OCID to a bash variable to simplify the syntax of the CLI command that follows. Finally, we used an iam user create command that leverages a JMESPath query to output the newly assigned user OCID.

Let me use this opportunity to show you how to build some more advanced JMESPath queries. We are going to list the names of all OCI users whose names start with the sandbox word. We expect to see a list of two names of the users we've just created. Again, we have to pass the tenancy OCID as a parameter.

```
$ oci iam user list -c $TENANCY_OCID --query "data [?starts_
with(name,'sandbox')].name" --all
[
  "sandbox-admin",
  "sandbox-user"
]
```

At this point of the time, there are two new nonfederated local users ready. We still have to generate a one-time password for them; otherwise, neither of them would be able to sign in to the OCI Console as one of these users. This is how you do it for the sandbox-user user:

```
$ USER_OCID=ocid1.user.oc1..aa.........dzqpxa
$ oci iam user ui-password create-or-reset --user-id $USER_OCID --query
"data.password"
"&gDX9F)iAP_[2E16XD)r"
```

Now, you are ready to open another browser and try to sign in, this time as a nonfederated user, as presented in Figure 4-12. Because this is the first login attempt after the password has been reset, you will be prompted to provide a new password.

Figure 4-12. *Signing in as a nonfederated user*

At first glance, the OCI Console looks the same. To make sure you've accessed it as one of the new users, please click the circular silhouette icon in the top-right corner to expand the active user menu, as shown in Figure 4-13. You should see there the user name, in our case sandbox-user. Click the name or User Settings to open the user profile.

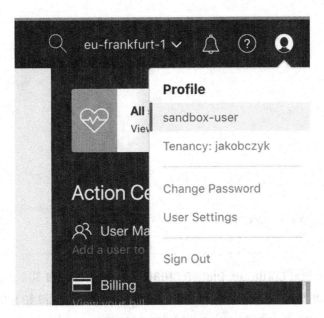

Figure 4-13. *Active user menu in the OCI Console*

Oracle Cloud Infrastructure IAM prohibits the newly created users from having any access to cloud resources by default. The only things you are able to do, as a newly created user who is not assigned to any group, are just the basic changes in the user settings such as a password change or an API key upload. If you try to list any kind of cloud resources in various compartments or list the existing users, you will see nothing, as shown in Figure 4-14.

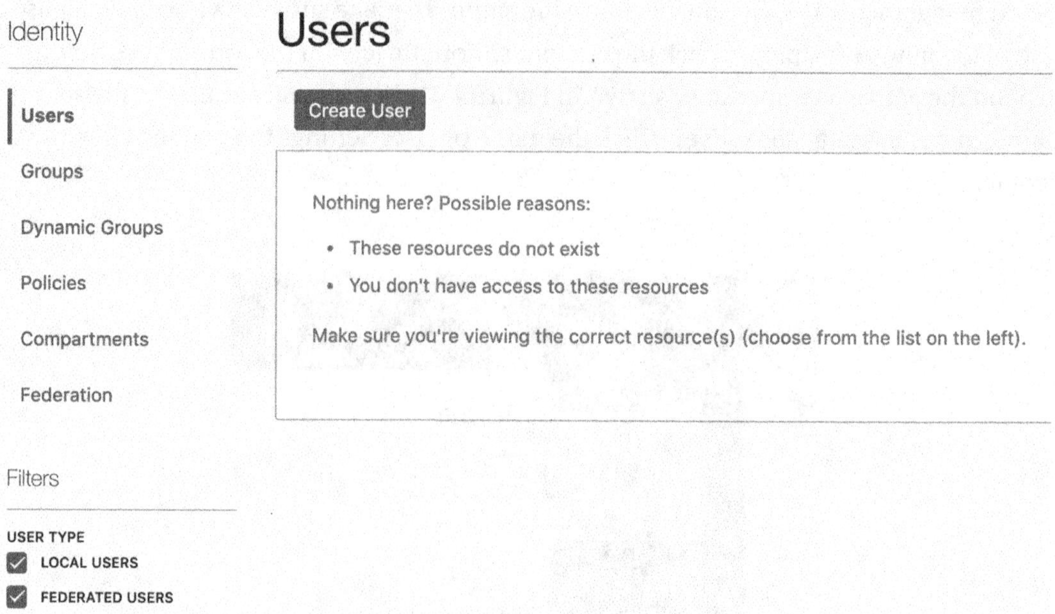

Identity

Users

| Users |
| Groups |
| Dynamic Groups |
| Policies |
| Compartments |
| Federation |

Create User

Nothing here? Possible reasons:

- These resources do not exist
- You don't have access to these resources

Make sure you're viewing the correct resource(s) (choose from the list on the left).

Filters

USER TYPE
- ☑ LOCAL USERS
- ☑ FEDERATED USERS

Figure 4-14. *Insufficient access in the OCI Console*

Caution   Before you continue, please create a password for the `sandbox-admin` user and log in for the first time to reset it so that you are able to sign in to the OCI Console. This is exactly what you've just done for the `sandbox-user` user. You do not need to use the CLI again. It is also possible to reset the user password in the OCI Console in the user details view for a given user.

We are going to let the two new users make remote API calls. You will need to generate two API signing keypairs, one for each of the two new local users, and upload their public keys under their accounts. You can find more information about the API signing keys in Chapter 3. This is the fast track:

```
$ cd ~/.apikeys
$ openssl genrsa -out api.sandbox-user.pem -aes128 2048
Generating RSA private key, 2048 bit long modulus
.........+++
..+++
```

```
e is 65537 (0x10001)
Enter pass phrase for api.sandbox-user.pem:
Verifying - Enter pass phrase for api.sandbox-user.pem:
$ chmod go-r api.sandbox-user.pem
$ openssl rsa -pubout -in api.sandbox-user.pem -out api.sandbox-user.pem.
pub
Enter pass phrase for api.sandbox-user.pem:
writing RSA key

$ openssl genrsa -out api.sandbox-admin.pem -aes128 2048
Generating RSA private key, 2048 bit long modulus
.................................+++
.........................................+++
e is 65537 (0x10001)
Enter pass phrase for api.sandbox-admin.pem:
Verifying - Enter pass phrase for api.sandbox-admin.pem:
$ chmod go-r api.sandbox-admin.pem
$ openssl rsa -pubout -in api.sandbox-admin.pem -out api.sandbox-admin.pem.
pub
Enter pass phrase for api.sandbox-admin.pem:
writing RSA key
$ ls -l | awk '{print $1, $9}'
total
-rw------- api.sandbox-admin.pem
-rw-r--r-- api.sandbox-admin.pem.pub
-rw------- api.sandbox-user.pem
-rw-r--r-- api.sandbox-user.pem.pub
```

Now, you can upload the public keys (.pub suffix) to the corresponding user accounts. We are going to use the CLI, but, if you want, you can do it in the OCI Console as well. First, make sure the TENANCY_OCID bash variable is still set to the tenancy OCID.

```
$ echo $TENANCY_OCID
ocid1.tenancy.oc1..aa........
```

To upload a public key, you need to know the OCID of the user. You can either read it in the OCI Console or use the CLI to make a query, just like this:

```
$ SANDBOX_ADMIN_OCID=`oci iam user list -c $TENANCY_OCID --query
"data[?name=='sandbox-admin'] | [0].id" --all --raw-output`
ocid1.user.oc1..aa.........7d5dca
```

Now, let's upload the public key for the sandbox-admin user.

```
$ oci iam user api-key upload --user-id $SANDBOX_ADMIN_OCID --key-file
~/.apikeys/api.sandbox-admin.pem.pub --query "data.fingerprint"
"91:64:1b:4e:4e:35:4a:06:b2:8f:6f:53:ae:7d:0d:ee"
```

Typically, you configure the CLI on your machine to send API requests on behalf of just a single user. As a result, you are using only the default profile in your ~/.oci/config file. Listing 4-1 displays how the structure of this file looks at the moment, after having completed the exercises from Chapter 3.

Listing 4-1. OCI CLI Configuration File

```
[DEFAULT]
tenancy=...
region=...
user=...
fingerprint=...
key_file=...
pass_phrase=...
```

There is only one profile, which is the default profile. Every OCI CLI command uses the details from the default profile to sign requests and make API calls. If you've followed the exercises from Chapter 3, the default configuration profile corresponds to the tenancy administrator superuser.

Luckily for us, it is possible to create more profiles. In this way, you will be able to execute different CLI commands on behalf of different OCI users on a single machine. Open the config file in a chosen text editor.

```
$ vi ~/.oci/config
```

Under the default profile, please add a new profile called SANDBOX-ADMIN and provide the user details for the sandbox-admin user, which you can find in this section. The new part is shown in bold in Listing 4-2.

Listing 4-2. OCI CLI Configuration File with Multiple Profiles

```
[DEFAULT]
tenancy=...
region=...
user=...
fingerprint=...
key_file=...
pass_phrase=...
[SANDBOX-ADMIN]
user=ocid1.user.oc1..aaaaaaaa3n5.........7d5dca
fingerprint=91:64:1b:4e:4e:35:4a:06:b2:8f:6f:53:ae:7d:0d:ee
key_file=~/apikeys/api.sandbox-admin.pem
pass_phrase=put-here-sandbox-admin-private-key-password
```

From now on, every time you add `--profile SANDBOX-ADMIN` to your CLI command, the CLI will use the four parameters (`user`, `fingerprint`, `key_file`, and `pass_phrase`) from the SANDBOX-ADMIN profile and the remaining two (`tenancy` and `region`) from the DEFAULT profile.

If you try executing one of the commands, but this time as the `sandbox-admin` user through the use of the SANDBOX-ADMIN profile, you will encounter an error.

```
$ oci iam user list -c $TENANCY_OCID --query "data [?starts_
with(name,'sandbox')].name" --all --profile SANDBOX-ADMIN
ServiceError:
{
    "code": "NotAuthorizedOrNotFound",
    "message": "Authorization failed or requested resource not found",
    "opc-request-id": "DE........./411.........E1F/B6A.........A8B",
    "status": 404
}
```

The reason is obvious. Oracle Cloud Infrastructure denies any kind of access to cloud resources by default. The `sandbox-admin` user does not belong to any group; therefore, there are no access policies that would grant some access rights to this user. It is time to discuss how the policies work.

Note   If you are still logged into the OCI Console as either the `sandbox-user` or the `sandbox-admin` user, please log out and log in again as the tenancy superuser. Alternatively, you can use a different browser.

One more important remark: before you read on, please upload the public key as a new API key for the `sandbox-user` user. You have already learned how. Please do it straightaway. We will need it in the future chapters.

Groups and Policies

The access to various types of cloud resources is given to the *groups*, not the individual users. We will focus on local groups only, but you may benefit from knowing that it is also possible to map your identity provider groups to the local groups. Policy statements define what kind of access is allowed to whom and in which scope. We will take a closer look at policy statements in a second. First, let's discuss groups.

Groups

A group is basically a collection of users. A user can belong to more than one group. It is possible to dynamically add and remove users from groups. You create groups in a similar manner as you've created users usually using the Console or the CLI. It is time to create a new group for the `sandbox-admin` user.

1. Go to Menu ➤ Identity ➤ Groups.

2. Click Create Group.

3. Provide `sandbox-admins` as the group name, description, and click Create.

Figure 4-15 presents the groups in your cloud tenancy. The `Administrators` group is the default group present in every cloud account. At any given time, Oracle Cloud Infrastructure enforces that there must be at least one user in this group; otherwise, you could easily get unintentionally locked out from your account.

Figure 4-15. *User groups in the OCI Console*

You may remember as I mentioned that cloud resources in Oracle Cloud Infrastructure are uniquely identified not by their names but by the OCIDs. This is true for the groups as well, with one small exception. While it is usually technically possible to provision multiple cloud resources of the same type with the same name, you cannot do it either with the groups or with the users. There is an additional constraint that does not allow any name duplicates among groups or users.

We are going to create another group, this time for the regular users for the Sandbox compartment such as the sandbox-user. This time, for the sake of variety, we will use the CLI. Please remember to make sure the TENANCY_OCID bash variable value is still set to the OCID of your tenancy before running this command:

```
$ oci iam group create --name sandbox-users --description "Group for the regular
users of the Sandbox compartment" --query "data.id" -c $TENANCY_OCID
"ocid1.group.oc1..aa.........rj2sba"
```

Run this CLI command to list the groups whose names start with sandbox. We are going to format the output as a table.

```
$ oci iam group list -c $TENANCY_OCID --all --query "data[?starts_
with(name,'sandbox')].{Name:name,OCID:id}" --output table
+----------------+------------------------------------+
| Name           | OCID                               |
+----------------+------------------------------------+
| sandbox-admins | ocid1.group.oc1..aa.........hlotwa |
| sandbox-users  | ocid1.group.oc1..aa.........rj2sba |
+----------------+------------------------------------+
```

The two new groups are still empty. In the OCI Console, adding or removing users from a group can be done in two ways. The first option is to use the group details view, just like this:

1. Go to Menu ➤ Identity ➤ Groups.

2. Click the name of the group to which you want to add a user.

3. On the Group Members tab, click Add User to Group.

4. Select the user you want to add to the group.

Alternatively, you can perform the same operation from the user details screen.

1. Go to Menu ➤ Identity ➤ Users.

2. Click the name of the user you want to add to a group.

3. On the Groups tab, click Add User to Group.

4. Select the group to which you want to add to the user.

Finally, you are more than welcome to do this task using the CLI. The `iam group add-user` command requires the user OCID and the group OCID, so either find them in the OCI Console or run these two queries:

```
$ USER_OCID=`oci iam user list -c $TENANCY_OCID --query
"data[?name=='sandbox-admin'] | [0].id" --all --raw-output`

$ GROUP_OCID=`oci iam group list -c $TENANCY_OCID --query
"data[?name=='sandbox-admins'] | [0].id" --all --raw-output`
```

To add a user to a group, use the `oci iam group add-user` CLI command.

```
$ oci iam group add-user --user-id $USER_OCID --group-id $GROUP_OCID
```

The `sandbox-admin` user gets immediately added to the `sandbox-admins` group. You can verify it in the OCI Console in the group details view, as shown in Figure 4-16.

Group Members

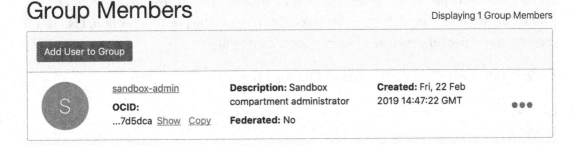

Displaying 1 Group Members

Figure 4-16. Group members in the OCI Console

Furthermore, it is feasible to employ the CLI command `iam group list-users` to fetch the list of group members of a particular group. To do so, please use the following command:

```
$ oci iam group list-users --group-id $GROUP_OCID --query "data[*].name" -c
$TENANCY_OCID --all
[
  "sandbox-admin"
]
```

Now, before you read on, please add the `sandbox-user` user to the `sandbox-users` group. We will need it in the future chapters. At this stage, you should have the two users added to their corresponding groups. Each user should have its unique keypair already in place and the public key uploaded. The expected setup is conceptually shown in Figure 4-17.

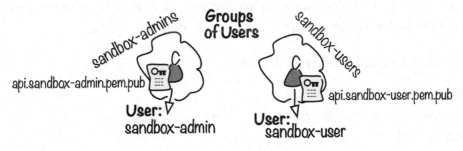

Figure 4-17. Users and groups for Chapter 4

As a next step, please add a new profile for the sandbox-user user to the ~/.oci/ config file like you've done for the sandbox-admin user in the previous section. Listing 4-3 presents the expected structure of your ~/.oci/config file.

Listing 4-3. OCI CLI Configuration File for Chapter 4

```
[DEFAULT]
tenancy=...
region=...
user=...
fingerprint=...
key_file=...
pass_phrase=...
[SANDBOX-ADMIN]
user=ocid1.user.oc1..aaaaaaaa3n5.........7d5dca
fingerprint=91:64:1b:4e:4e:35:4a:06:b2:8f:6f:53:ae:7d:0d:ee
key_file=~/apikeys/api.sandbox-admin.pem
pass_phrase=put-here-sandbox-admin-private-key-password
[SANDBOX-USER]
user=ocid1.user.oc1..aaaaaaaatimmpj37ao............cdzqpxa
fingerprint= 61:68:a5:1c:40:ef:51:fd:1a:74:6b:d9:9f:1c:b2:b8
key_file=~/apikeys/api.sandbox-user.pem
pass_phrase=put-here-sandbox-user-private-key-password
```

Last but not least, we are going to create two profiles in the ~/.oci/oci_cli_rc file to set the default compartment for each CLI query. Please replace the OCIDs in Listing 4-4 with the OCID of your Sandbox compartment. If you do not remember what kind of file that is, you will find more information in Chapter 3.

Listing 4-4. OCI CLI RC File for Chapter 4

```
[DEFAULT]
compartment-id = ocid1.compartment.oc1..aa.........gzwhsa
[SANDBOX-ADMIN]
compartment-id = ocid1.compartment.oc1..aa.........gzwhsa
[SANDBOX-USER]
compartment-id = ocid1.compartment.oc1..aa.........gzwhsa
```

All set? Let's explore how the access control to cloud resources is organized.

Policy Statements

How does privilege management work? You define which group is entitled to perform particular actions on specific cloud resource types using *policy statements*. Each policy statement refers either to one particular compartment or to the entire tenancy. Figure 4-18 illustrates a simple policy statement that grants read-only access (read policy verb) over selected cloud resource types that belong to the instance-family aggregate resource type to the members of the groupABC. The aggregate resource type is a logical grouping of real cloud resource types such as compute instances or instance images. The sample policy statement refers only to the cloud resources that exist inside the projectABC compartment.

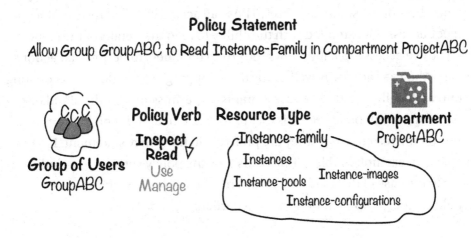

Figure 4-18. *IAM policy statement*

While it should be pretty clear to understand what roles are played by a group of users and a compartment in a policy statement, you may still need some additional explanation of the policy verb and the resource type.

There are various types of cloud infrastructure resources you can provision in your cloud account. A compute instance and an object storage bucket are examples of cloud resources. Some cloud *resource types* are more related to each other than the others. An instance image is used to provision compute instances. The instances can be managed in pools. To launch an instance pool, an instance configuration is required. As you can see, there is some degree of interdependency between all four resource types I've given as an example. From the access control point of view, you will usually grant the same access permissions to all resource types that belong to one family of related resource types. For this reason, Oracle Cloud Infrastructure defines the so-called aggregate cloud resources, such as `instance-family` or `virtual-network-family`, that are logical groupings of the existing cloud resource types.

Tip   It makes little sense to include the list of all available resource types that can be used in your policy statements because the list is steadily growing. Please refer to the policy reference in the official documentation.

A *policy verb* defines the access level to a cloud resource. There are four levels available: inspect, read, use, and manage. The `inspect` access is basic and usually lets the group members only list the resources. The `read` access includes the same scope as the `inspect` access but extended with the ability to read the details of the cloud resources. The `use` access typically allows the group members to perform all actions in the scope of the `read` access as well as starting, stopping, and updating the existing cloud resources. Finally, the `manage` access grants all permissions for the cloud resource type. The key thing about policy verbs is that their exact meaning is highly contextual and depends on the resource type they are prefixing in the policy statement. Let me explain it using an example. Table 4-1 presents how the policy verbs map to individual permissions in the case of the `load-balancers` resource type. Each permission effectively allows the group members to call a particular set of APIs.

Table 4-1. *Policy Verbs for the load-balancers Resource Type*

Verb	Permissions	Covered APIs
inspect	LOAD_BALANCER_INSPECT	ListLoadBalancers ListShapes ListPolices ListProtocols
read	inspect permissions + LOAD_BALANCER_READ	inspect APIs + GetLoadBalancer and others
use	read permissions + LOAD_BALANCER_UPDATE	read APIs + UpdateLoadBalancer CreateBackendSet DeleteBackendSet UpdateBackendSet and others
manage	use permissions + LOAD_BALANCER_CREATE LOAD_BALANCER_DELETE	use APIs + CreateLoadBalancer DeleteLoadBalancer

As you can see in Table 4-1, in the case of the load-balancers resource type, the inspect policy verb maps to just one LOAD_BALANCER_INSPECT permission, which essentially gives access to four APIs: ListLoadBalancers, ListShapes, ListPolicies, and ListProtocols. These four APIs give some basic insights into the available load balancer policies, shapes, protocols, and load balancers present in the scope of the given compartment. Usually, the API names are self-explanatory, but if you want to be sure what kind of operation on cloud resources the APIs really let you perform, you can always read the API reference.

If you look at the table again, you will spot that a load balancer can be created or deleted only by the group members whose group was granted the manage policy verb over the load-balancers resource type. This is not a big surprise. What is more interesting is the fact that a backend set can be created or deleted already when there is a policy statement with the use policy verb. How should we understand it? Well, a backend set can exist only in the context of a load balancer as its child resource. In this way, you could delegate the creation of backend sets to the users of the load balancer just as you let them update an existing load balancer. However, the creation or termination of the parent resource, namely, the load balancer, is limited to the managers.

Tip Policy verbs are highly contextual, and their exact meaning depends on the resource type they are prefixing in the policy statement. You need to refer to the documentation to find out more: `https://docs.cloud.oracle.com/iaas/Content/Identity/Reference/policyreference.htm`.

Let's discuss a couple of examples for IAM policy statements. I would like you to get some general view before we move into creating the statements for our new IAM groups. If your intention is to grant all kinds of permissions over a particular compartment to the group of admins for that compartment, you can do it with just one *IAM policy statement*.

```
allow group sandbox-admins to manage all-resources in compartment Sandbox
```

Let's look at another example. To allow the members of the `sandbox-users` group to perform all load-balancer-specific operations in the Sandbox compartment, you would simply create this policy:

```
allow group sandbox-users to manage load-balancers in compartment Sandbox
```

What if you would like to explicitly deny some selected permissions that belong to the policy verb you are using? For example, the manage policy verb in the context of the load-balancers resource type will let you perform all actions, including load balancer creation and deletion. If you would like to exclude the LOAD_BALANCER_DELETE permission, you can use *policy statement condition*.

```
allow group sandbox-users to manage load-balancers in compartment Sandbox
where request.permission != 'LOAD_BALANCER_DELETE'
```

Policy statement conditions can be defined for permissions (e.g., `request.permission != 'LOAD_BALANCER_DELETE'`) as well as individual API operations (e.g., `request.operation != 'DeleteLoadBalancer'`). In this way, it is possible to tune the policy statements and make them as granular as needed. Sometimes, you may even build more complex conditions that reference more than one permission or operation. I will give now further examples. This policy statement permits the group members to list the load balancers (`ListLoadBalancers` operation), even though the policy verb inspect would normally allow more operations, such as listing the available shapes (ListShapes operation) or protocols (ListProtocols operation).

```
allow group sandbox-admins to inspect load-balancers in compartment Sandbox
where all { request.operation != 'ListShapes', request.operation !=
'ListProtocols', request.operation != 'ListProtocols' }
```

The where all clause is used to make sure that all conditions are met. This approach is taken if you want to explicitly deny multiple permissions or operations. If you would prefer to explicitly allow multiple permissions or operations, you can use the where any clause. In the next example, the policy statement permits the group members to perform only three operations (ListShapes, ListPolicies, and ListProtocols), although the policy verb inspect would normally allow one operation more.

```
allow group sandbox-admins to inspect load-balancers in compartment
Sandbox where any { request.operation = 'ListShapes', request.operation =
'ListPolicies', request.operation = 'ListProtocols' }
```

As a result, the fourth remaining operation (ListLoadBalancers) that falls into the inspect policy verb for the load-balancers resource type will be denied.

In this section, we've been discussing individual policy statements. I have not mentioned, however, how they are actually created in Oracle Cloud Infrastructure. We are going to do this now.

Policies

Individual policy statements cannot exist on their own but have to be contained in the so-called policies. A *policy* is a cloud resource that consists of one or more statements that determine the access a group of users has over a particular class of cloud resources in a particular compartment or the entire tenancy. Individual policy statements cannot exist outside of a policy; therefore, you will always work with policy statements contained in policies. At this stage, we need to highlight one important notion. The users and groups do exist in the scope of the entire tenancy. We can say they are global. Policies, on the other hand, are created in compartments, just like the majority of regular cloud resources such as compute instances or virtual networks. At the time of writing, a new cloud account arrives with two policies by default. To see them using the OCI Console, take these steps:

1. Go to Menu ➤ Identity ➤ Policies.

2. Make sure that the root compartment is selected.

Figure 4-19 shows the two default policies. Looking at the creation time of the two policies, you can even guess around what time my cloud tenancy was actually brought into existence.

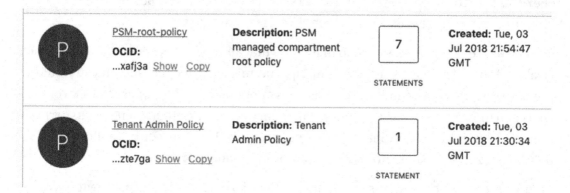

Figure 4-19. *Default policies in the OCI Console*

If you prefer to use the CLI, this is the query to list the policies that are present in the root compartment:

```
$ oci iam policy list -c $TENANCY_OCID --all --query 'data[*].{Name:name,St
atements:length(statements)}' --output table
+----------------------+------------+
| Name                 | Statements |
+----------------------+------------+
| PSM-root-policy      | 7          |
| Tenant Admin Policy  | 1          |
+----------------------+------------+
```

As you can see, I am using the tenancy OCID to point to the root compartment in the CLI command (-c $TENANCY_OCID). The OCID of the root compartment of your tenancy is the same as the OCID of your tenancy.

The Tenant Admin Policy contains only one, but important, statement.

```
$ oci iam policy list -c $TENANCY_OCID --all --query "data[?name=='Tenant
Admin Policy'].statements[0]"
[
  "ALLOW GROUP Administrators to manage all-resources IN TENANCY"
]
```

The role of this policy is to let the members of the default group `Administrators` manage all cloud resources in your tenancy. This policy is protected; you neither can delete it nor can add any other statements.

The second default policy visible in your root compartment, namely, the `PSM-root-policy` policy, allows various Oracle Cloud Platform services to be provisioned on Oracle Cloud Infrastructure. I am not going to discuss them in this work.

Earlier in this chapter, we created a new user called `sandbox-admin` and added him to the newly created `sandbox-admins` group. We also added a dedicated profile in the `~/.oci/config` file for this user. If we tried to execute any CLI command on behalf of this user, the command would fail with the `NotAuthorizedOrNotFound` service error because there are no policy statements that would allow the members of the `sandbox-admins` group to interact with the API. We are ready to change it by adding a new policy to the root compartment. The policy is going to ship with just a single statement that allows the members of the `sandbox-admins` group to perform all kinds of operations on all resources in the Sandbox compartment. This is how you do it using the CLI:

```
$ oci iam policy create -c $TENANCY_OCID --name sandbox-admins-
policy --description "Policy for the Sandbox compartment admins
group"  --statements '["allow group sandbox-admins to manage all-resources
in compartment Sandbox"]'
```

The command has created a new policy cloud resource called `sandbox-admins-policy`. Even though the policy was created in the root compartment, the scope of the statement refers to the Sandbox compartment. The IAM policy contains one statement.

```
allow group sandbox-admins to manage all-resources in compartment Sandbox
```

This statement is pretty powerful because it allows the members of the `sandbox-admins` group to perform all kinds of operations on the cloud resources in the Sandbox compartment, including the creation of policies with statements that grant other groups to take actions in the Sandbox compartment or its subcompartments.

Caution   Before continuing, please make sure you've added two profiles (SANDBOX-ADMIN and SANDBOX-USER) to the `~/.oci/config` and `~/.oci/oci_cli_rc` files, as described at the end of the "Groups" section in this chapter!

Let's try if the sandbox-admin user is able to access some APIs. Do not forget to apply the correct --profile switch so that the request is signed as the sandbox-admin user.

```
$ oci lb shape list --profile SANDBOX-ADMIN --query 'data[*].name'
[
  "100Mbps",
  "400Mbps",
  "8000Mbps"
]
```

Everything looks fine. We were able to list the available load balancer shapes. If you repeat the same command, but this time using the SANDBOX-USER profile, you will see an error because the other group, sandbox-users, is not mentioned in any policy for the Sandbox compartment.

```
$ oci lb shape list --profile SANDBOX-USER --query 'data[*].name'
ServiceError:
{
    "code": "NotAuthorizedOrNotFound",
    "message": "Authorization failed or requested resource not found.",
    "opc-request-id": "CF6..............7DC",
    "status": 404
}
```

To let the sandbox-user see the load balancer shapes, protocols, and load balancers in the Sandbox compartment, we need to grant the inspect policy verb over the load-balancers resource type to the proper group. As the sandbox-admin user, you will create a new policy, this time in the Sandbox compartment. I will additionally show you how to import the policy statements from a JSON file. This would let you manage the policy statements in version-controlled files if you want. First, we need a file with the IAM policy statement. You will find it at the chapter04/2-policies/sandbox-user-policy.json path. Listing 4-5 shows the contents of this policy file.

Listing 4-5. Policy Statements in JSON File

```
[
"allow group sandbox-users to inspect load-balancers in compartment Sandbox"
]
```

We will reference the `sandbox-user-policy.json` file, as we execute the `oci iam policy create` CLI command that adds a new policy in the Sandbox compartment with the statements read from the JSON file. Do not forget to use the SANDBOX-ADMIN profile when you execute the command.

```
$ cd ~/git/oci-book/chapter04/2-policies/
$ oci iam policy create --profile SANDBOX-ADMIN --name sandbox-users-policy
--description "Policy for regular Sandbox compartment users"  --statements
"file://~/sandbox-user-policy.json"
```

To verify whether the new `sandbox-users-policy` policy has been successfully created in the Sandbox compartment, you can run this command:

```
$ oci iam policy list --profile SANDBOX-ADMIN --all --query "data[*].{Name:
name,Statements:statements}"
[
  {
    "Name": "sandbox-users-policy",
    "Statements": [
      "allow group sandbox-users to inspect load-balancers in compartment
      Sandbox"
    ]
  }
]
```

For the final test, please try repeating the previously unsuccessful API call, again as the `sandbox-user` user, by applying the SANDBOX-USER profile in the CLI command.

```
$ oci lb shape list --profile SANDBOX-USER --query 'data[*].name'
[
  "100Mbps",
  "400Mbps",
  "8000Mbps"
]
```

If something went wrong, please make sure you've added the `sandbox-user` to the sandbox-users group. As you can see, as soon as the relevant policy statement has been added, the user is able to successfully reach the API.

In this section, we created two policies, as shown in Figure 4-20. The first one, called `sandbox-admins-policy`, was added to the root compartment and granted unlimited management-level access over all kinds of cloud resources in the scope of the Sandbox compartment to the `sandbox-admins` group members. The second policy, named `sandbox-users-policy`, was set up inside the Sandbox compartment and given limited inspect-level access just over load-balancer-specific resource types that exist in the scope of the Sandbox compartment to the `sandbox-users` group members.

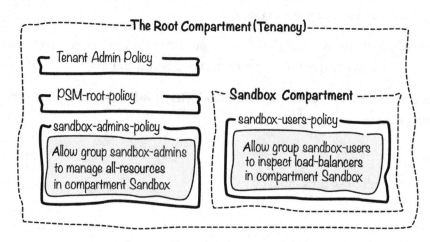

Figure 4-20. *Policies in different compartments*

The more users and compartments your tenancy contains, the more you may end up with the need for a pretty complex set of policies. This is why you should have in mind a well-organized pattern for the placement of policies and their statements structure from the beginning. Because of the implicit deny-all rule, I encourage you to gradually increase the access level to various cloud resources, as soon as you spot that users really need access to them. Throughout this book, we are going to follow this best practice in the case of the `sandbox-user` user. In each later chapter, I am going to add the required policy statements so that this user is able to perform the tasks included in a particular chapter.

We've covered the compartments, users, groups, and policies management by using the OCI Console and the CLI. You may wonder, especially after having read Chapter 3, whether it is possible to include these cloud resources in your Terraform infrastructure code. Well, technically, yes. Absolutely. For example, you would use the `oci_identity_policy` resource to define an access policy. However, I personally prefer to manage IAM cloud resources outside of my Terraform infrastructure code.

Audit and Search

As a cloud tenancy owner or a person responsible for the cloud account you manage, you need to keep an eye on all these different cloud resources that exist across different compartments at any given moment. In addition, you should be aware of the actions taken by the users. When I talk about an action over one particular or sometimes many cloud resources at once, I basically think about an interaction with the API. I mentioned this in the previous chapter, as I discussed the automation options. Any kind of activity, no matter if it is done in the OCI Console, with the use of API, SDK, CLI, or Terraform, results in an API call under the hood. In this section, I will introduce you briefly to the searching and auditing capabilities in Oracle Cloud Infrastructure, which are truly indispensable when you want to control things properly.

Searching

Imagine you want to find all users and groups whose display name contains the term *sandbox*. In the previous sections of the current chapter, I fetched the lists of all users and groups with two separate CLI commands: `iam user list` and `iam group list`. The JMESPath-powered filter I applied with the `--query` parameter parsed the data received in the response and displayed the matching elements locally on my client machine. What if my cloud tenancy had dozens of users? We would unnecessarily receive a really large response with all the users and only then apply a local JMESPath-powered filter. This does not seem like an effective solution. Furthermore, what if we wanted to *search* for cloud resources of various types that match a given name just using a single API call?

Oracle Cloud Infrastructure offers a dedicated Search API to perform cross-resource-type and cross-compartment full-text search or structured queries to simplify and enhance the way you collect information about cloud resources. This is especially useful when you need to find a broad range of resources that are scattered across different compartments. This is conceptually illustrated in Figure 4-21.

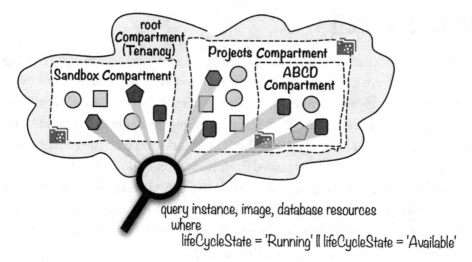

Figure 4-21. *Oracle Cloud Infrastructure Search API*

As long as there are policy statements that give access to these compartments and resource types to the group your user belongs to, you can easily search for the resources using the Search API. There are two types of searches supported.

- Free-text queries

- Structured queries

You will usually employ the free-text queries to get a brief overview of resources based on their metadata text-pattern match. The structured queries will be handier if you have already certain resource types or conditions in mind.

Free-Text Search

Free-text queries are nothing more than full-text searches performed over all cloud resource metadata indexed by Oracle Cloud Infrastructure. If a given search term is found in any of the indexed metadata fields, the cloud resource is included in the results, as long as this type of resource and its compartment scope are visible for the user who runs a free-text search. To run a free-text query in the OCI Console, place the searched term, for example, *sandbox*, in the search box present in the top bar, as shown in Figure 4-22. The results will be grouped into types and displayed altogether with the searched term highlighted, as presented in Figure 4-23.

Figure 4-22. *Free-text search in the OCI Console*

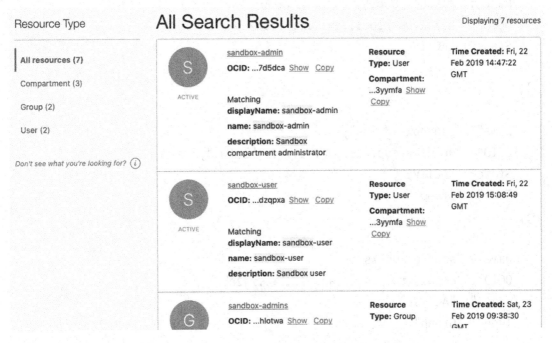

Figure 4-23. *Free-text search results in the OCI Console*

The same query can be run with the use of the CLI. To do so, we are going to leverage the `search resource free-text-search` command and specify the term that we are interested in finding using the `--text` parameter. Please note that we still can use JMESPath (the `--query` parameter) to locally filter and display only the fields we are really interested in.

```
$ oci search resource free-text-search --text sandbox --query 'data.
items[*].{Type:"resource-type",Name:"display-name",OCID:"identifier",State:
"lifecycle-state"}'
[
  {
    "Name": "sandbox-admin",
    "OCID": "ocid1.user.oc1..aa.........7d5dca",
```

```
    "State": "ACTIVE",
    "Type": "User"
  },
  {
    "Name": "sandbox-user",
    "OCID": "ocid1.user.oc1..aa.........dzqpxa",
    "State": "ACTIVE",
    "Type": "User"
  },
  {
    "Name": "sandbox-admins",
    "OCID": "ocid1.group.oc1..aa.........hlotwa",
    "State": "ACTIVE",
    "Type": "Group"
  },
  {
    "Name": "sandbox-users",
    "OCID": "ocid1.group.oc1..aa.........rj2sba",
    "State": "ACTIVE",
    "Type": "Group"
  },
  {
    "Name": "Sandbox",
    "OCID": "ocid1.compartment.oc1..aa.........gzwhsa",
    "State": "ACTIVE",
    "Type": "Compartment"
  }
}
```

As I said earlier, you will usually employ this type of search just to get some initial, high-level overview of these resources whose metadata match a particular text pattern. Depending on the term you are searching for, the result set can be really large. All in all, this is a full-text search over all kinds of cloud resources in your tenancy or the compartments your user has access to. This is why you should not forget about pagination, which you can control, in the case of CLI commands, with the --limit and --page parameters. You can read more about that in a dedicated section, later in this chapter.

Structured Queries

Structured queries, on the other hand, use a special query language that gives you more power and control over the types of resources and the compartment scope you would like to include in your search. For example, this is a query that will list all "running" or "terminating" compute instances in the Sandbox compartment:

```
query
  instance resources
    where ( lifeCycleState = 'RUNNING' || lifeCycleState = 'TERMINATING' ) &&
    compartmentId = 'ocid1.compartment.oc1..aa.........gzwhsa'
```

To run it in the OCI Console, open a free-text search page and click the Advanced Search button, or you can append `/search` to your URL to access this page directly. For example, if you are using the Frankfurt region, go to this URL: `https://console.eu-frankfurt-1.oraclecloud.com/search`. You will see the text box where you can put your query, as shown in Figure 4-24.

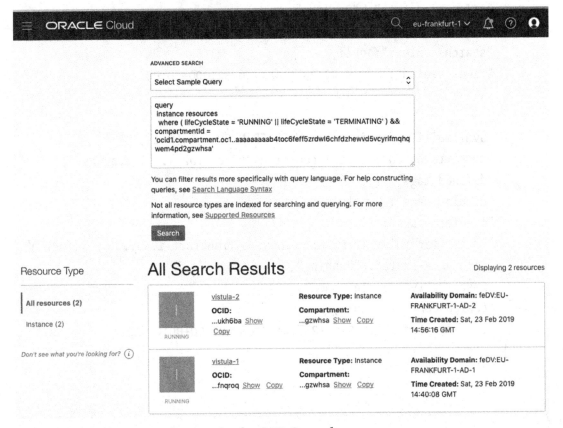

Figure 4-24. *Structured query in the OCI Console*

The same query can be run with the CLI using the search resource structured-search command. The query will then be passed as the --query-text parameter.

```
$ oci search resource structured-search --query-text "query instance resources
where ( lifeCycleState = 'RUNNING' || lifeCycleState = 'TERMINATING' )
&& compartmentId = 'ocid1.compartment.oc1..aa........gzwhsa'"
{
  "data": {
    "items": [
      {
        "availability-domain": "feDV:EU-FRANKFURT-1-AD-2",
        "compartment-id": "ocid1.compartment.oc1..aa........gzwhsa",
        "defined-tags": {},
        "display-name": "vistula-2",
        "freeform-tags": {},
        "identifier": "ocid1.instance.oc1.eu-frankfurt-1.ab........ukh6ba",
        "lifecycle-state": "Running",
        "resource-type": "Instance",
        "search-context": null,
        "time-created": "2019-02-23T14:56:16.521000+00:00"
      },
      {
        "availability-domain": "feDV:EU-FRANKFURT-1-AD-1",
        "compartment-id": "ocid1.compartment.oc1..aa........gzwhsa",
        "defined-tags": {},
        "display-name": "vistula-1",
        "freeform-tags": {},
        "identifier": "ocid1.instance.oc1.eu-frankfurt-1.ab........fnqroq",
        "lifecycle-state": "Running",
        "resource-type": "Instance",
        "search-context": null,
        "time-created": "2019-02-23T14:40:08.609000+00:00"
      }
    ]
  }
}
```

Note   Do not worry that there are no results in your case. This is because there are no running instances in the Sandbox compartment at the moment. Feel free to test this feature while working with various cloud resources in the exercises from the upcoming chapters.

Coming back to the initial task, namely, listing users and groups whose metadata such as display name or description contain the term *sandbox*, the following is the proper query:

```
query user, group resources matching 'sandbox-'
```

As you can see, instead of applying the where clause, we are incorporating the matching clause. This is an example of how you achieve a free-text query over a selected subset of resource types. If you've used the free-text search, you would see other types of resources as well.

Similarly to the free-text search, you can apply an additional JMESPath-powered filter to the result set also in case of the structured queries. Just do not confuse the --query-text parameter and the --query parameter. The first uses the Search API to find and return in a response only matching resources. The latter, namely, the --query parameter, applies the JMESPath formula to filter the results locally on your client machine.

```
$ oci search resource structured-search --query-text "query user, group
resources matching 'sandbox-'" --query 'data.items[*].{Type:"resource-
type",Name:"display-name",OCID:"identifier"}'
[
  {
    "Name": "sandbox-admin",
    "OCID": "ocid1.user.oc1..aa.........7d5dca",
    "Type": "User"
  },
  {
    "Name": "sandbox-user",
    "OCID": "ocid1.user.oc1..aa.........dzqpxa",
    "Type": "User"
  },
```

```
{
  "Name": "sandbox-admins",
  "OCID": "ocid1.group.oc1..aa.........hlotwa",
  "Type": "Group"
},
{
  "Name": "sandbox-users",
  "OCID": "ocid1.group.oc1..aa.........rj2sba",
  "Type": "Group"
}
]
```

To read more about the syntax of the query language for structured searches, please consult the official documentation. You will find it at `https://docs.cloud.oracle.com/iaas/Content/Search/Concepts/queryoverview.htm`.

Targeted searches done with the use of structured queries usually bring smaller result sets when compared to the free-text search. However, you may still benefit from employing proper pagination. Let's see how to do it.

Pagination

Result sets can be really large nowadays. You can find dozens, hundreds, thousands, or even more items that match your query. Sometimes, it makes sense to verify just a few initial results; in other cases, you need to carefully analyze the entire result set item by item. For example, to calculate the total number of CPUs of your running compute instances at a given time, you would need to process the entire result set of your query. Fetching all the results at once may seem costly and, in some cases, can crash the application because of memory reasons. This is why you should always think about *pagination*. Pagination assumes you fetch the result set in pages by making a sequence of related search calls. The items are sorted; therefore, if you continue collecting results page by page, you will eventually reach the end of the result set. In this way, you will know you've managed to process the entire result set. The OCI Console provides pagination out of the box. When using the CLI, you will need to define the `--limit` and `--page` parameters and base the contents of the `opc-next-` header field on each consequent request. It does not matter if you are using the search resource `structured-search` command or the search resource `free-text-search` command. In both cases, the mechanism works in the same way.

Let's see how it works with an example. We are going to run the same free-text query for the *sandbox* term. This time, we will apply pagination and list up to three items at once. Hence, as you can guess, the `--limit` parameter in the CLI command will take 3 as the value. If you look closer at the JMESPath filter, you will see I am additionally displaying the `opc-next-page` element under the `nextpage` name.

```
$ oci search resource free-text-search --text sandbox --query "{results:
data.items[*].{type: \"resource-type\", name: \"display-name\"}, nextpage:
\"opc-next-page\"}" --limit 3
{
  "nextpage": "eyJ.........cOY",
  "results": [
    {
      "name": "sandbox-admin",
      "type": "User"
    },
    {
      "name": "sandbox-user",
      "type": "User"
    },
    {
      "name": "sandbox-admins",
      "type": "Group"
    }
  ]
}
$ NEXTPAGE=eyJ.........cOY
```

Perfect. We've received the first three items from the result set. Now, in the next query, you will add the `--page` parameter to the CLI command and use the value received in the `nextpage` field of the previous query result.

```
$ oci search resource free-text-search --text sandbox --query "{results:
data.items[*].{type: \"resource-type\", name: \"display-name\"}, nextpage:
\"opc-next-page\"}" --limit 3 --page "$NEXTPAGE"
```

```
{
  "nextpage": null,
  "results": [
    {
      "name": "sandbox-users",
      "type": "Group"
    },
    {
      "name": "Sandbox",
      "type": "Compartment"
    }
  ]
}
```

Excellent. The next three items from the result set are delivered. This time, the nextpage field is set to null, which indicates that we've reached the end of the result set.

Auditing

Oracle Cloud Infrastructure collects information about every call to the API. As a result, any kind of interaction with the API, regardless of its origin, whether the OCI Console, SDK, CLI, or Terraform, is a subject of auditing. The audit logs are stored for 90 days, unless you change this value. You can retain the audit log entries for as long as 365 days. To search for the occurrence of a particular event that took place in a chosen timeframe in the OCI Console, take these steps:

1. Go to Menu ➤ Governance ➤ Audit.

2. Choose the compartment to which you would like to narrow the results.

3. Choose the start date and the end date for your timeframe.

4. Provide a search keyword such as LaunchInstance.

5. Click Search.

6. Click the Keep Searching label to make sure all audit log entries are processed.

Figure 4-25 shows the results of an audit event search.

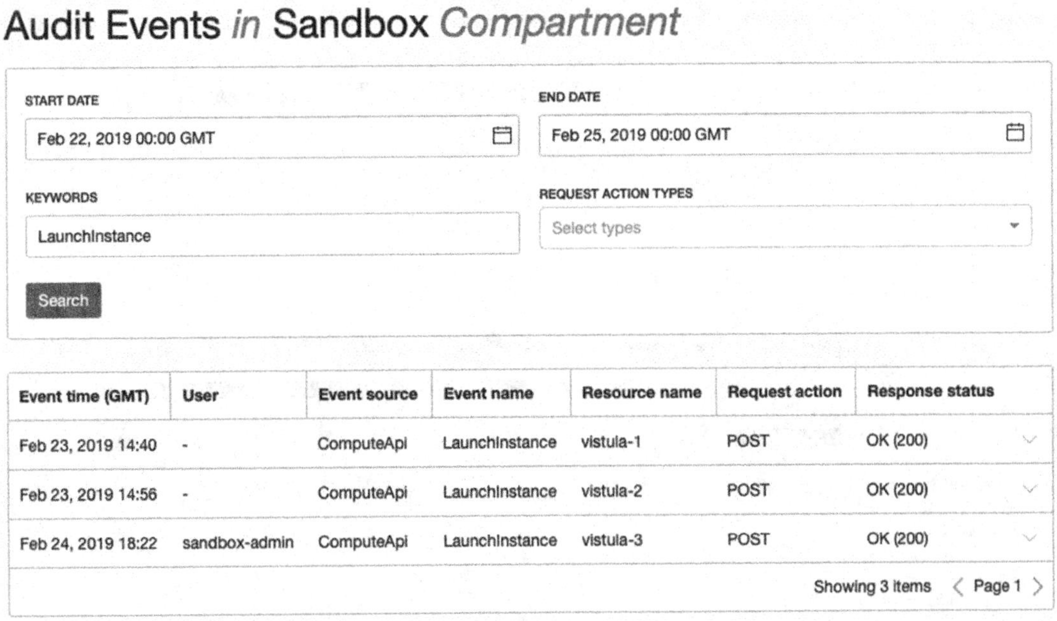

Audit Events *in* Sandbox *Compartment*

START DATE		END DATE	
Feb 22, 2019 00:00 GMT	📅	Feb 25, 2019 00:00 GMT	📅

KEYWORDS	REQUEST ACTION TYPES	
LaunchInstance	Select types	▾

Search

Event time (GMT)	User	Event source	Event name	Resource name	Request action	Response status	
Feb 23, 2019 14:40	-	ComputeApi	LaunchInstance	vistula-1	POST	OK (200)	⌄
Feb 23, 2019 14:56	-	ComputeApi	LaunchInstance	vistula-2	POST	OK (200)	⌄
Feb 24, 2019 18:22	sandbox-admin	ComputeApi	LaunchInstance	vistula-3	POST	OK (200)	⌄

Showing 3 items   ＜ Page 1 ＞

Figure 4-25. *Audit Events search in the OCI Console*

The first two entries show the events captured during the vistula-1 and vistula-2 compute instance provisioning. These two instances have been provisioned by the tenancy owner admin user, who happens to be a federated user. In the case of federated users, to find out who took the action, you would need to expand the event details and look at the principalId field. The third compute instance called vistula-3 was launched by the sandbox-admin user, which is a local, nonfederated user; therefore, you can see its name in the User column.

Note   Launching the vistula-* instances has not been described in this chapter, but feel free to search for the uuid-* instances you provisioned as part of the exercises from the chapter to experiment with the Audit Event search feature.

There are more details recorded for each audit log event than what you can see in the table shown in Figure 4-25. If you expand one of these entries, say the third one, you would see more information, as shown in Figure 4-26, including the OCID of the compute instance that was the subject of the LaunchInstance event.

```
Feb 24, 2019 18:22    sandbox-admin    ComputeApi    LaunchInstance    vistula-3           POST              OK (200)

⊖ "event" : {
    "tenantId" : "ocid1.tenancy.oc1..aaaaaaaaq2▬▬▬▬▬▬▬▬▬▬▬▬▬▬▬▬▬▬▬▬a"
    "compartmentId" : "ocid1.compartment.oc1..aaaaaaaaab4toc6feff5zrdwl6chfdzhewvd5vcyrifmqhqwem4pd2gzwhsa"
    "compartmentName" : "Sandbox"
    "eventId" : "88d968cc-5db1-4ba9-b1d7-2a76dfc0e6c8"
    "eventName" : "LaunchInstance"
    "eventSource" : "ComputeApi"
    "eventType" : "ServiceApi"
    "eventTime" : "2019-02-24T18:22:47.024Z"
    "principalId" : "ocid1.user.oc1..aaaaaaaa3n5yzrt7t7ezehmsderad2chkclrmuizmzfen5zxudptw57d5dca"
    "credentialId" : ""
    "requestAction" : "POST"
    "requestId" : "/02DD82E1B71A90D8198C85AD2F743137/DA6381E2655623A42CE2CE80849CEB96"
    "requestAgent" :
    "Mozilla/5.0 (Macintosh; Intel Mac OS X ▬▬▬▬▬▬▬▬▬▬▬▬▬▬▬▬▬▬▬▬▬▬▬▬▬▬... "
  ⊕ "requestHeaders" : {...}
    "requestOrigin" : "▬▬▬▬▬▬▬"
  ⊕ "requestParameters" : {}
    "requestResource" : "/20160918/instances/"
  ⊕ "responseHeaders" : {...}
    "responseStatus" : "200"
    "responseTime" : "2019-02-24T18:22:47.607Z"
  ⊖ "responsePayload" : {
        "resourceName" : "vistula-3"
        "id" : "ocid1.instance.oc1.eu-frankfurt-1.abtheljr5p2mqu7wvr3glp3ivvjyuglg5c5zjxi5lkcmz5vfh3nbep5rlspq"
    }
    "userName" : "sandbox-admin"
}
```

Figure 4-26. *Audit event details in the OCI Console*

As always, the same operation is also available in the form of a CLI command, this time called audit event list.

Summary

After having read this chapter, you should have a pretty clear understanding of how to prepare the logical containers called compartments for the cloud resources that belong to different projects environments and production systems. You know how to manage users and groups both in the Console and with the use of the CLI. You are aware of the importance of the policy statements and have knowledge of how to create and manage them using IAM policies. You are able to perform free-text searches and find resources using structured queries. Finally, you understand the concept of auditing and its importance in cloud tenancy custodianship.

CHAPTER 5

Data Storage in the Oracle Cloud

There are many ways to store data in Oracle Cloud. A lot will depend on the type of data, application context, and data usage patterns that apply to a particular use case or user story. This chapter will focus solely on one of the most popular approaches to store data in the cloud, namely, object storage.

Buckets and Objects

Imagine you are working for a real estate developer. You are dealing with various types of data items such as real estate marketing materials, apartment blueprints, parking lot plans, construction schedules, and so on. Even though each of these items is typically a file, you may generalize a bit and consider them *objects*. In other words, you can see these items as the content that your cloud-based application would process and serve. To ease the data asset management, it would be helpful to be able to group these objects. In this example, the grouping could be based on different real-estate projects, which own particular objects. Now, what if you were able to safely forget about nonbusiness tasks such as making sure the data is always available and securely replicated to survive any unexpected events? This would simply let you focus solely on the business nature of the individual data items as required by your business processes. This is where *object storage* comes into play. It takes the burden of various, purely technical activities that occur in the data lifecycle. The data items are automatically replicated. Furthermore, you do not need to worry about whether there is still enough space on a disk volume because you never consider individual disk volumes in this case. By contrast, from a user perspective, you work with a flat, nearly endless storage space. Last but not least, data is by default encrypted at rest using the 256-bit Advanced Encryption Standard (AES-256).

© Michał Tomasz Jakóbczyk 2020
M. T. Jakóbczyk, *Practical Oracle Cloud Infrastructure*, https://doi.org/10.1007/978-1-4842-5506-3_5

I've mentioned that you can group related objects such as, in the case of the earlier example, apartment blueprints and parking lot plans that belong to the same real estate project. To do so, you need some kind of logical container. Object storage lets you store the associated objects in logical containers called *buckets*. In the previous chapter, we talked about compartments and their role in isolating cloud resources based on the projects and systems maintained under your cloud account. The same rule applies here as well. Each bucket has to exist in exactly one compartment. This forces you to place the new bucket in the context of some particular project environment, production system, or general-purpose compartment such as Sandbox. Compartments and buckets may still be insufficient in more sophisticated ways to organize the objects as you would want. Often, we would prefer to deal with a hierarchical structure with a number of hierarchy levels to express a more detailed grouping. This can be achieved by prefixing object names in a proper way to simulate a folder-like multilevel hierarchy inside a bucket. You can prefix object names with /-separated "paths" and end up with complete object names such as /waw/bemowo/125.pdf or /waw/bemowo/245.pdf. This naming convention allows you to list the objects based on a particular prefix and perform various bulk operations on prefix-based subsets of objects in a bucket when using the CLI. Figure 5-1 illustrates the core components of object storage and their relation to compartments.

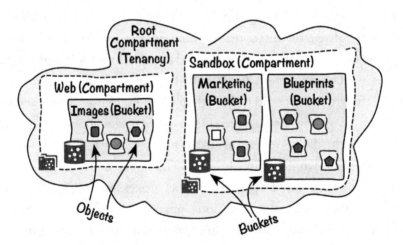

Figure 5-1. *Buckets and object hierarchies*

Each cloud tenancy comes with an own *namespace* in which the buckets exist. The namespace name is generated only once, at the very beginning, and cannot be changed. Object storage requires bucket names to be unique only within a single cloud account. There are no conflicts possible with the existing bucket names taken by other tenants. As a result, it becomes obvious that all direct and indirect (CLI, SDK, Terraform) API calls to the object storage endpoint have to be aware of the namespace.

Note   The code snippets from this book have been tested on macOS and Windows Subsystem for Linux. Moreover, all commands should work on the major Linux distributions. If you are using Windows and do not want to use Windows Subsystem for Linux, you can always run Linux on a VM. Furthermore, the majority of code snippets may also work in Git Bash on Windows. Remember to set up the CLI and Terraform exactly as described in Chapters 3 and 4.

You can find the name of the object storage namespace associated with your cloud tenancy in the Console like this:

1. Go to Menu ➤ Administration ➤ Tenancy Details.

2. Find the Object Storage Namespace label.

Alternatively, you can use the CLI to get the name of the object storage (os) namespace (ns) like this:

```
$ oci os ns get
{
  "data": "jakobczyk"
}
```

The object storage namespace name is immutable and does not change. The name of the object storage namespace is a random and unique string. Older tenancies, such as mine, may have their namespace name the same as tenancy name. You may recall that, in Chapter 2, I wrote that every Oracle Cloud Infrastructure cloud resource is uniquely identified with a structured identifier called an OCID. Well, there are exceptions to that rule: buckets and objects are uniquely identified by names. They are always named in the context of the namespace dedicated to your cloud tenancy, as shown in Figure 5-2.

/n/<namespace>/b/<bucket>/o/<object>

/n/weq324dfwef/b/blueprints/o/waw/bemowo/l25.pdf

Figure 5-2. *Namespace, bucket, and object*

At this stage, I need to note that object storage in Oracle Cloud Infrastructure is regional in scope. This basically means that a particular bucket, together with the objects it stores, resides in the region in which the bucket was initially created. If you find yourself needing to perform cross-regional object transfers to another bucket located in a different region, there is an API that supports this kind of operation.

Working with Objects

Buckets in which objects reside are either public or private. To protect the data most of the time, you will be using private buckets, but you are free to create public buckets whenever you want. There are two types of authenticated groups that can access objects in private buckets.

- IAM users

- Instance principals

I will explain each of these two types of access in the upcoming sections. In addition, you are able to let unauthenticated clients access particular objects in private buckets by issuing pre-authenticated requests that are valid for a given period of time. Anyone who knows the link is able to access the particular object. Pre-authenticated requests will be covered at the end of this chapter.

To prepare for the exercises, we need a quick recap. In the previous chapter, I asked you to create two users, `sandbox-admin` and `sandbox-user`, and two corresponding groups, `sandbox-admins` and `sandbox-users`. Then, in the root compartment, we created a new IAM policy (`sandbox-admins-policy`) with a single *IAM policy statement* that granted the full administration access over the Sandbox compartment to the members of `sandbox-admins` group.

```
allow group sandbox-admins to manage all-resources in compartment Sandbox
```

Please make sure this setup is still in place before proceeding. You will need it in order to complete the walk-throughs in this chapter. To demonstrate some basic features of object storage, you are going to create a bucket and upload a set of files using CLI as the sandbox-user user. Next, we will use other commands for bulk operations, prefix-based lists with paging, and custom metadata. You will also learn how to handle concurrent updates. All CLI commands use Oracle Cloud Infrastructure REST APIs that are conceptually illustrated in Figure 5-3.

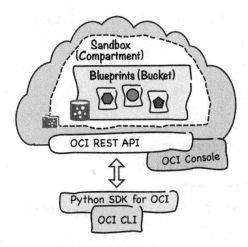

Figure 5-3. *Interacting with the object storage API*

Let's look at the basic interactions with object storage. We will perform them using the CLI. Again, the CLI commands you are about to issue will simply result in API requests, as described in Chapter 3.

Basics

Objects can be thought of as data entities. This implies that there is a standard set of operations that can be performed on them such as create, read, update, and delete, commonly known as CRUD. No surprise here. Similar operations can be performed on buckets. We are now going to use the oci os bucket create CLI command to create a new bucket called blueprints in the Sandbox compartment. To stick to the best practices, we will perform this and a few consecutive operations as the sandbox-admin user. To do so, remember to apply the proper CLI profile.

```
$ oci os bucket create --name blueprints --profile SANDBOX-ADMIN
{
  "data": {
    "approximate-count": null,
    "approximate-size": null,
    "compartment-id": "ocid1.compartment.oc1..aa.........gzwhsa",
    "created-by": "ocid1.user.oc1..aa.........7d5dca",
    "defined-tags": {},
    "etag": "7115bc55-b18c-4232-80f7-363643c327b9",
    "freeform-tags": {},
    "kms-key-id": null,
    "metadata": {},
    "name": "blueprints",
    "namespace": "jakobczyk",
    "object-lifecycle-policy-etag": null,
    "public-access-type": "NoPublicAccess",
    "storage-tier": "Standard",
    "time-created": "2019-03-07T15:25:52.065000+00:00"
  },
  "etag": "7115bc55-b18c-4232-80f7-363643c327b9"
}
```

There are a couple of interesting elements in the response that are worth explaining. The only parameter we provided the CLI command with was the bucket name. This is why the bucket took the default configuration values whenever needed. As a result, the newly created bucket has been provisioned as a standard storage tier bucket with no public access allowed.

There are two *storage tiers*: standard and archive. They do not differ much. The *archive storage tier* is basically cheaper at the cost of no immediate access to the objects that have to be restored first. This is an operation that can take a few hours. What would you use the archive storage for? Think about rarely accessed data that has to be stored for a given period of time because of some regulatory or compliance reasons. Another example could be old logs or measurements you do not necessarily need at the moment but would prefer to keep somewhere just in case. In this chapter, we are going to deal with standard storage tier buckets.

No public access allowed means the bucket is private and the objects can be accessed only by authenticated IAM users, by instance principals, or through pre-authenticated requests. If we had been dealing with a public bucket, the objects would have been visible and downloadable for everyone. Figure 5-4 shows the bucket details in the OCI Console.

Figure 5-4. Viewing bucket details in the OCI Console

This is the CLI command that lists the buckets present in an active compartment and displays them in a form of a table:

```
$ oci os bucket list --query 'data[*].{Bucket:name}' --output table
--profile SANDBOX-ADMIN
+------------+
| Bucket     |
+------------+
| blueprints |
+------------+
```

Moving to the next step, we want to create permissions that allow the members of the sandbox-users group to list the objects that exist in this bucket as well as be able to add new and delete existing objects. To do so, prepare a file with the relevant policy statements first, as shown in Listing 5-1. I've called this file sandbox-users.policies.storage.json, but the name doesn't matter as long as you reference it properly in the next command. Alternatively, you can find this file in the Git repository at the following path: chapter05/1-policies/sandbox-users.policies.storage.json.

Listing 5-1. sandbox-users.policies.storage.json

```
[
"allow group sandbox-users to read buckets in compartment Sandbox where
target.bucket.name='blueprints'",
"allow group sandbox-users to manage objects in compartment Sandbox where
target.bucket.name='blueprints'"
]
```

The read policy verb for buckets allows the users to list the buckets and get the detailed configuration of each bucket. Yet, we are using a condition with the target.bucket.name variable that basically limits the permission and allows the users to work only with the bucket named blueprints. Similarly, we are using the manage policy verb for objects to grant all kinds of operations in the scope of objects, but only those that are present in the blueprints bucket.

As soon as the file is ready, we can create a new policy in the Sandbox compartment using the oci iam policy create CLI command in the same way we added new policies in the previous chapter. Working as the sandbox-admin, you are only able to create policies in the Sandbox compartment. In Chapter 4, we set the Sandbox compartment as the default compartment for the SANDBOX-ADMIN profile in the ~/.oci/ oci_cli_rc file. In this way, you can skip the required --compartment-id (or its -c alias) parameter because the CLI will be able to read and apply the default value. The following CLI command will create a new IAM policy based on the file supplied. I am assuming you have cloned the code related to the book; therefore, you can enter the directory that contains the policy file and execute the CLI command like this:

```
$ cd ~/git/oci-book/chapter05/1-policies
$ oci iam policy create --name sandbox-users-storage-policy --statements
file://sandbox-users.policies.storage.json --description "Storage-related
policy for regular Sandbox users" --profile SANDBOX-ADMIN
```

At this stage, you should see the new policy with two statements in the OCI Console, as shown in Figure 5-5.

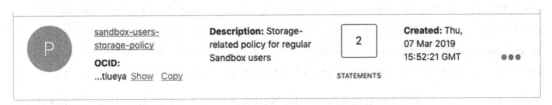

Figure 5-5. *New policy for sandbox-users related to object storage*

What about executing one of the most basic commands to put a file into the bucket? In the first place, we need a sample file. Real data is precious and should be protected nowadays, so let's generate a random, meaningless file that we will pretend is a real estate apartment blueprint PDF. This is how you generate a random binary file using Bash:

```
$ mkdir ~/data
$ cd ~/data
$ SIZE=$((4096+(10+RANDOM % 20)*1024))
$ head -c $SIZE /dev/urandom > 101.pdf
$ ls -lh 101.pdf | awk '{ print $9 " (" $5 ")" }'
101.pdf (21K)
```

Perfect. Now, be careful. From now on, the consecutive CLI commands will be invoked using another profile, the SANDBOX-USER profile. This is how you can use the CLI to put this file into the blueprints bucket:

```
$ oci os object put -bn blueprints --file 101.pdf --profile SANDBOX-USER
Uploading object  [####################################]  100%
{
  "etag": "06b2293c-72d9-4668-b236-bdb881472bd6",
  "last-modified": "Thu, 07 Mar 2019 18:42:25 GMT",
  "opc-content-md5": "urJobycygNAm2Z3fEf3tkw=="
}
```

It was pretty easy, wasn't it? We have used the oci os object put command to upload the 101.pdf file to the blueprints bucket. The CLI profile SANDBOX-USER authenticates as the sandbox-user user. This user belongs to the sandbox-users group. A few moments ago, we granted this group of users the manage-level access over objects in the blueprints bucket in the Sandbox compartment. As a careful reader, you may wonder how the CLI knows the name of the target object storage namespace. The name is stored neither in the CLI config file nor in the oci_cli_rc file. The answer is it does not. As a result, the CLI must query the API for the default object storage namespace associated with the tenancy, in the background, using the same API as the one we queried with the oci os ns get command. If you want to avoid this additional internal call to the API, you can pass the namespace name to object storage CLI commands using the -ns option like this:

```
$ oci os object put -ns jakobczyk -bn blueprints --file 101.pdf --profile
SANDBOX-USER
```

To download the object to your local drive and save it under a different name, for example, 101-copy.pdf, execute this CLI command:

```
$ oci os object get -bn blueprints --name 101.pdf --file 101-copy.pdf
--profile SANDBOX-USER
Downloading object  [###################################]   100%
```

Finally, to delete the file from the bucket, use this CLI command:

```
$ oci os object delete -bn blueprints --name 101.pdf --profile SANDBOX-USER
Are you sure you want to delete this resource? [y/N]: y
```

What about updating an object? You have to be aware that the objects are immutable. To update an object, you basically need to overwrite it, effectively replacing the old version with the new one.

Alright. These were the basics.

Object Name Prefixes

What if we are going to store the blueprints from different real estate projects in one bucket? A property in the Bemowo district in Warsaw can have an apartment on sale with the same number as another apartment in a different property in the Wola district. We could use name prefixes to avoid mixing up these two apartments. This time, we are going to generate an entire set of files that we will pretend are apartment blueprints. We are going to use three groups of files. The first group will consist of blueprints of apartments in a property in the Bemowo district in Warsaw.

```
$ mkdir -p warsaw/bemowo
$ for i in 101 102 105 107 115; do SIZE=$((4096+(10+RANDOM % 20)*1024));
head -c $SIZE /dev/urandom > warsaw/bemowo/$i.pdf; done
```

The second group will imitate the blueprint files of apartments in building A that belong to a property in the Wola district in Warsaw.

```
$ mkdir -p warsaw/wola/a
$ for i in 115 120 124 130; do SIZE=$((4096+(10+RANDOM % 20)*1024)); head
-c $SIZE /dev/urandom > warsaw/wola/a/$i.pdf; done
```

The third group will pretend to be the blueprint files of flats in building B in the same property in the Wola district in Warsaw.

```
$ mkdir -p warsaw/wola/b
$ for i in 119 120 121; do SIZE=$((4096+(10+RANDOM % 20)*1024)); head -c
$SIZE /dev/urandom > warsaw/wola/b/$i.pdf; done
```

Good. You should end up with something like this:

```
$ find warsaw -type f -exec ls -lh {} + | awk '{ print $9 " (" $5 ")"}'
warsaw/bemowo/101.pdf (29K)
warsaw/bemowo/102.pdf (30K)
warsaw/bemowo/105.pdf (18K)
warsaw/bemowo/107.pdf (23K)
warsaw/bemowo/115.pdf (33K)
warsaw/wola/a/115.pdf (32K)
warsaw/wola/a/120.pdf (21K)
warsaw/wola/a/124.pdf (15K)
warsaw/wola/a/130.pdf (31K)
warsaw/wola/b/119.pdf (21K)
warsaw/wola/b/120.pdf (29K)
warsaw/wola/b/121.pdf (18K)
```

The CLI comes with a convenient trio of *bulk commands* that let you upload, download, and delete objects in groups. We are now going to upload the blueprints from the warsaw/bemowo local directory to the blueprints bucket as new objects prefixed with the waw/bemowo/ string like this:

```
$ oci os object bulk-upload -bn blueprints --src-dir warsaw/bemowo/
--object-prefix "waw/bemowo/" --include "*.pdf" --profile SANDBOX-USER
{
  "skipped-objects": [],
```

```
    "upload-failures": {},
    "uploaded-objects": {
      "waw/bemowo/101.pdf": {...}
      "waw/bemowo/102.pdf": {...},
      "waw/bemowo/105.pdf": {...},
      "waw/bemowo/107.pdf": {...},
      "waw/bemowo/115.pdf": {...}
  }
}
```

If you want, you can use the --include option to limit the uploaded files from the
source directory to the ones that match a given pattern.

In a similar way, we will upload the files from the warsaw/wola directory, this time
prefixing the objects with the waw/wola/a and waw/wola/b strings depending on the local
subdirectory in which each file was originally located.

```
$ oci os object bulk-upload -bn blueprints --src-dir warsaw/wola/a
--object-prefix "waw/wola/a/" --profile SANDBOX-USER
{
    "skipped-objects": [],
    "upload-failures": {},
    "uploaded-objects": {
      "waw/wola/a/115.pdf": {...},
      "waw/wola/a/120.pdf": {...},
      "waw/wola/a/124.pdf": {...},
      "waw/wola/a/130.pdf": {...}
  }
}
$ oci os object bulk-upload -bn blueprints --src-dir warsaw/wola/b
--object-prefix "waw/wola/b/" --profile SANDBOX-USER
{
    "skipped-objects": [],
    "upload-failures": {},
    "uploaded-objects": {
      "waw/wola/b/119.pdf": {...},
```

```
    "waw/wola/b/120.pdf": {...},
    "waw/wola/b/121.pdf": {...}
  }
}
```

Figure 5-6 illustrates the operations we've just performed. Prefixes are indeed helpful because they let you re-create a folder-like hierarchy in a particular bucket. The ListObject Object Storage Service API offers a convenient query parameter called prefix that lets you specify a subset of objects to be listed based on the object name prefix. You can access this API using the oci os object list CLI command like this:

```
$ oci os object list -bn blueprints --prefix "waw/wo" --query 'data[*].
name' --profile SANDBOX-USER
[
   "waw/wola/a/115.pdf",
   "waw/wola/a/120.pdf",
   "waw/wola/a/124.pdf",
   "waw/wola/a/130.pdf",
   "waw/wola/b/119.pdf",
   "waw/wola/b/120.pdf",
   "waw/wola/b/121.pdf"
]
$ oci os object list -bn blueprints --prefix "waw/wola/b" --query 'data[*].
name' --profile SANDBOX-USER
[
   "waw/wola/b/119.pdf",
   "waw/wola/b/120.pdf",
   "waw/wola/b/121.pdf"
]
$ oci os object list -bn blueprints --prefix "waw/wola/b/12" --query
'data[*].name' --profile SANDBOX-USER
[
   "waw/wola/b/120.pdf",
   "waw/wola/b/121.pdf"
]
```

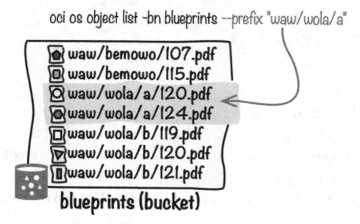

Figure 5-6. *Prefix-based filtering*

Listing Objects in Pages

In your daily work, you may easily encounter buckets that contain hundreds or thousands of objects. Listing all of them at once is impossible. You need to revert to the *paging mechanism*. You may remember the Search API and its paging mechanism that I described in the previous chapter. The bad news is that, at the time of writing, the Search API does not support object storage objects. The good news is that the Object Storage ListObjects API features its own paging mechanism, which is actually slightly simpler than the one used in the Search API. If you decide to use the `limit` parameter, in the response besides the list of objects you will receive the `next-start-with` element that is nothing more than the name of the next object. In every subsequent query, you can take the value of the previous `next-start-with` element and use the `start` parameter to instruct the API where to start listing the elements, as shown in this code snippet:

```
$ oci os object list -bn blueprints  --limit 5 --query '{names:data[*].
name, next:"next-start-with"}' --profile SANDBOX-USER
{
  "names": [
    "waw/bemowo/101.pdf",
    "waw/bemowo/102.pdf",
    "waw/bemowo/105.pdf",
    "waw/bemowo/107.pdf",
    "waw/bemowo/115.pdf"
  ],
```

```
  "next": "waw/wola/a/115.pdf"
}
$ oci os object list -bn blueprints  --limit 5 --start "waw/wola/a/115.pdf"
--query '{names:data[*].name, next:"next-start-with"}' --profile SANDBOX-USER
{
  "names": [
    "waw/wola/a/115.pdf",
    "waw/wola/a/120.pdf",
    "waw/wola/a/124.pdf",
    "waw/wola/a/130.pdf",
    "waw/wola/b/119.pdf"
  ],
  "next": "waw/wola/b/120.pdf"
}
$ oci os object list -bn blueprints  --limit 5 --start "waw/wola/b/120.pdf"
--query '{names:data[*].name, next:"next-start-with"}' --profile SANDBOX-USER
{
  "names": [
    "waw/wola/b/120.pdf",
    "waw/wola/b/121.pdf"
  ],
  "next": null
}
```

Object Metadata

Another useful aspect related to storing files of different kinds and business purposes
in object storage buckets is the possibility to attach *custom metadata*. In this way, you
can provide additional contextual information by annotating selected objects without
changing their content. Back to our example scenario with the real estate projects, we
could decide to annotate the blueprints that refer to two-level apartments. Because
we do not want to change the object content, we can leverage custom metadata that
basically consists of key-value pairs that you associate with an existing object. This is how
you put a new object with some custom metadata (apartment-levels key) into a bucket:

```
$ head -c 4096 /dev/urandom > warsaw/wola/a/122.pdf
$ METADATA='{ "apartment-levels": "2" }'
$ oci os object put -bn blueprints --name "waw/wola/a/122.pdf" --file
warsaw/wola/a/122.pdf --metadata "$METADATA" --profile SANDBOX-USER
Uploading object  [####################################]  100%
{
  "etag": "b899ed57-baca-4aff-85ba-5e1fe925c437",
  "last-modified": "Sat, 09 Mar 2019 10:46:34 GMT",
  "opc-content-md5": "kZ6fEuo46zGMm+Tymcumaw=="
}
```

At first glance, nothing particular seems to have happened. Yet, if you view object details in the OCI Console, you will see a new custom key-value pair, as shown in Figure 5-7.

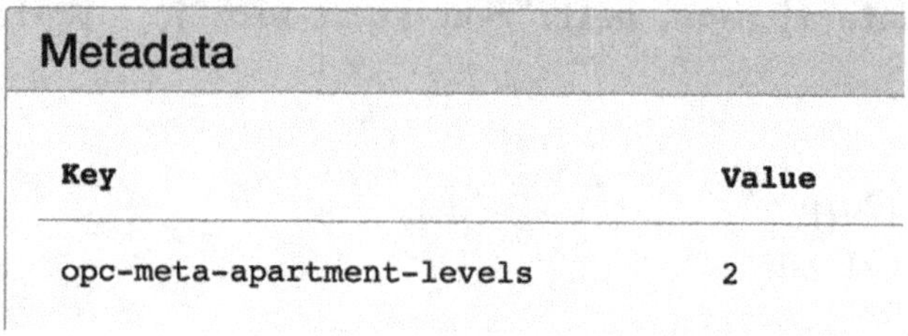

Metadata	
Key	**Value**
opc-meta-apartment-levels	2

Figure 5-7. *Custom metadata of an object*

If you consider programmable interactions with the API, there is no need to download a particular file to inspect its custom metadata. The HeadObject API lets you read only the object's metadata and the entity tag. We will talk about the importance of entity tags in the next section. This is how you access this API using the oci os object head CLI command:

```
$ oci os object head -bn blueprints --name "waw/wola/a/122.pdf" --profile
SANDBOX-USER
{
  ......
  "content-length": "4096",
  "content-md5": "kZ6fEuo46zGMm+Tymcumaw==",
  "content-type": "application/octet-stream",
  "date": "Sat, 09 Mar 2019 11:40:41 GMT",
  "etag": "b899ed57-baca-4aff-85ba-5e1fe925c437",
  "last-modified": "Sat, 09 Mar 2019 10:46:34 GMT",
  ......
  "opc-meta-apartment-levels": "2",
  ......
}
```

In both cases, you can see that any custom key will be prefixed with the opc-meta-prefix to avoid conflicts with any standard metadata such as content-length or content-type. You need to be aware that the objects are immutable; therefore, to attach new metadata to an object already present in a bucket, we have to replace the object. It does not matter if the new version contains the same content.

Concurrent Updates

Let's discuss something called *race conditions*. Suppose there are two applications that want to update the same object, at the same time, incrementally adding their partial changes. If they fetch the object straight one after another, they will be processing the same base version, each unaware of the fact that there is another application working on the same object in parallel. Everything seems fine until the moment in which both applications decide to upload a new version of the object, effectively replacing the base version. The result is easy to predict. The application that performs an update second will wipe out the changes done by the application that saved the object first. This situation can be called a *lost update* and is conceptually presented in Figure 5-8.

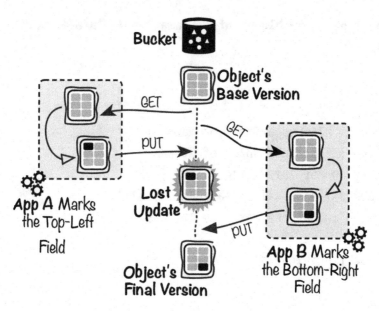

Figure 5-8. *Lost update problem*

The impact of a lost update depends on the business scenario. Think of application logic that changes underground parking lot maps by coloring the parking spaces that have been sold. In this case, a lost update would result in showing some parking spaces as available even though they have been sold. Usually, we would prefer to completely eliminate that kind of issue. The object storage API addresses this problem with *entity tags* (ETags) that can be used to implement optimistic concurrency control. An ETag is an identifier generated for each version of the object, no matter whether the content has changed or remained the same. If you put the same object twice, effectively overwriting it with the same content during the second upload, you will still end up having two different ETags generated, as shown in this code snippet:

```
$ head -c 8096 /dev/urandom > warsaw/bemowo/parking.pdf
$ oci os object put -bn blueprints --name waw/bemowo/parking.pdf --file
warsaw/bemowo/parking.pdf --profile SANDBOX-USER
Uploading object  [###################################]  100%
{
  "etag": "d5ded03a-64ca-4af2-8185-563f658f4021",
  "last-modified": "Sat, 09 Mar 2019 16:43:31 GMT",
  "opc-content-md5": "upvy5Ns5flwg053S8WJG1w=="
}
```

```
$ oci os object put -bn blueprints --name waw/bemowo/parking.pdf --file
warsaw/bemowo/parking.pdf --profile SANDBOX-USER
WARNING: This object already exists. Are you sure you want to overwrite it?
[y/N]: y
Uploading object  [###################################]  100%
{
  "etag": "4f893925-455a-4ea5-8890-2b39f8523d82",
  "last-modified": "Sat, 09 Mar 2019 16:43:41 GMT",
  "opc-content-md5": "upvy5Ns5flwgO53S8WJG1w=="
}
```

How would you include the *optimistic concurrency control* in your application logic to avoid race conditions? An update operation on an object can be performed in steps. First, the current object's ETag is read, and the object content gets downloaded. Next, the application changes the object locally. Finally, the API is told to put a new version of the object into the bucket, effectively overwriting the old version, but only if the ETag hasn't changed in the meantime. Such a conditional PUT can be achieved using the If-Match HTTP header, as shown in Figure 5-9.

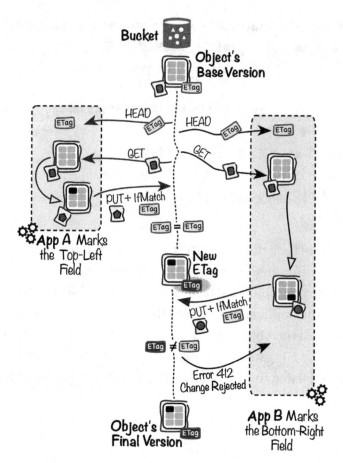

Figure 5-9. *Implementing optimistic concurrency*

Let me demonstrate this scenario using the CLI:

```
$ ETAG=`oci os object head -bn blueprints --name waw/bemowo/parking.pdf
--query 'etag' --profile SANDBOX-USER --raw-output`

$ echo $ETAG
6836145f-2b37-4538-885d-bd7f242d5a34

$ oci os object get -bn blueprints --name waw/bemowo/parking.pdf --file
local.parking.pdf --profile SANDBOX-USER
Downloading object  [####################################]  100%
$ ls -lh local.parking.pdf | awk '{ print $9 " (" $5 ")" }'
local.parking.pdf (7.9K)

$ head -c 2048 /dev/urandom >> local.parking.pdf
```

```
$ ls -lh local.parking.pdf | awk '{ print $9 " (" $5 ")" }'
local.parking.pdf (9.9K)

$ oci os object put -bn blueprints --name waw/bemowo/parking.pdf --file
local.parking.pdf --if-match "$ETAG" --profile SANDBOX-USER
WARNING: This object already exists. Are you sure you want to overwrite it? [y/N]: y
Uploading object  [####################################]  100%
{
  "etag": "0698bdb4-ddd0-4d12-a030-cd7e55dc25af",
  "last-modified": "Sat, 09 Mar 2019 17:56:35 GMT",
  "opc-content-md5": "z2gpBufEwHkU2SsbutTQsA=="
}
```

We began with reading the ETag of a particular object. The `oci os object head` CLI command uses a lightweight `HeadObject` API, which fetches only the metadata associated with an object including the ETag. In our case, we found out that the current ETag has the value ending with `bd7f242d5a34`. In the second step, we downloaded the object's content using the `oci os object get` CLI command and appended 2KB of random data to the local copy to simulate a local change. In the last part, we used the `oci os object put` CLI command with the `--if-match` option to make sure that the object gets overwritten only if it hasn't been altered since we fetched the ETag at the beginning. In the response to the conditional PUT operation, we can see that the new object version has been assigned a completely new ETag that ends with `cd7e55dc25af`. If another application tried to issue the conditional PUT command using an ETag that is no longer in sync, it would receive an error with status HTTP 412 (Precondition Failed).

```
$ head -c 1024 /dev/urandom >> local.parking.pdf
$ ls -lh local.parking.pdf | awk '{ print $9 " (" $5 ")" }'
local.parking.pdf (11K)
$ oci os object put -bn blueprints --name waw/bemowo/parking.pdf --file
local.parking.pdf --if-match "$ETAG" --profile SANDBOX-USER
ServiceError:
{
    "code": null,
    "message": "The service returned error code 412",
    "opc-request-id": "f3fee86d-8e97-93b4-1c5e-da3ed572ed35",
    "status": 412
}
```

Programming Object Storage

To interact with the object storage API, we have been using CLI commands in the examples presented in this chapter until that point. In the real world, however, the great majority of all API calls to the object storage comes from applications. In this section, I will show you how to use one of the SDKs, namely, the OCI SDK for Python, to let your applications use Oracle Cloud Infrastructure object storage. I will also take this opportunity and explain how to deal with large files by employing a multipart file upload method.

In Chapter 3, I guided you through a simple process of SDK installation and configuration. In Chapter 4, we created new groups and users as well as added two new profiles to the SDK/CLI configuration file: SANDBOX-ADMIN and SANDBOX-USER. Finally, in the first part of this chapter, we created the required policies in this way to allow the group members of the sandbox-users group to manage objects in the blueprints bucket. I am assuming all of this is still in place.

All operations performed on object storage cloud resources with the use of the OCI SDK for Python are done through the methods of the ObjectStorageClient class. You can find a comprehensive documentation of this class at https://oracle-cloud-infrastructure-python-sdk.readthedocs.io/en/latest/api/object_storage/client/oci.object_storage.ObjectStorageClient.html.

Multipart Uploads

When dealing with very large files such as those bigger than 100MB, it is recommended that you split the original file into smaller parts and leverage the *multipart upload* API to divide the file into manageable chunks to the cloud. This approach makes the upload process less prone to the negative impact of any network issues because you would just need to reupload the single part that failed to be delivered to the cloud. Furthermore, the multipart upload mechanism makes it possible to parallelize the upload of individual parts, which results in a faster completion of the upload operation. At the time of writing, the maximum size for an uploaded object is 10TB. Additionally, each individual part must be smaller than 50GB. You can create up to 10,000 parts.

A multipart upload operation consists of four phases, which are conceptually illustrated in Figure 5-10. First, you have to split a large file into smaller parts (1). The way you do this is up to you and the tools of your choice. Next, you make your first API call by sending a `CreateMultipartUpload` request to start a new multipart upload (2). In the request, you specify the storage namespace, bucket name, and target object name. In the response, you will be provided with an upload ID of the newly activated multipart upload. At this stage, you can begin uploading the parts (3). For each part, you are sending an `UploadPart` request to the object storage API. The sequence does not matter. As I mentioned, you can even upload multiple parts in parallel. In addition to the storage namespace, the bucket name, the target object name, and the upload ID, the `UploadPart` operation expects you to provide an upload part number, different for each part. In other words, you are responsible for numbering the parts. The part numbers do not need to be contiguous. The parts will be eventually combined to form a target object based on the ascending sequence of part numbers. The `UploadPart` operation returns a unique entity tag (ETag) for each part you upload. Make sure you collect the entity tags because you will need them as soon as you are ready to commit the multipart upload. To have the target object built by object storage from the uploaded parts, you need to commit the multipart upload (4). You do this by sending a `CommitMultipartUpload` request to the API. In the request, you specify a list of pairs where each pair contains an assigned part number and the corresponding ETag. Only the parts included in the list will be used to build the target object, no matter how many parts you've uploaded in total.

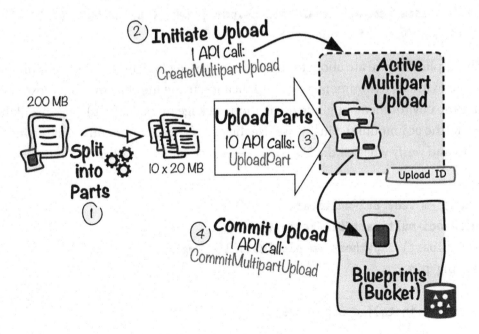

Figure 5-10. *Multipart upload*

If your application cancels an ongoing multipart upload, it sends an AbortMultipartUpload request to the API. In this way, object storage would close the multipart upload, effectively removing the parts that have already been uploaded. What would have happened if you just closed the application without aborting the upload in a correct manner? Well, the multipart upload would technically remain active and ready to accept further parts. In such a case, you would be constantly charged for the uploaded parts until the moment you aborted the upload. Do not worry about keeping track of your multipart uploads. It is possible to list active uploads by sending ListMultipartUploads requests to the API. If you expect to have many application instances that perform multipart updates, it may be smart to implement a recurring job that uses this method to keep an eye on ongoing and abandoned uploads.

Let's prepare a test file. This time, we are going to generate a larger file (25M), call it visualizations.pdf, and place it in the warsaw/bemowo local directory. You can easily imagine this to be a sales catalog with colorful pictures and visualizations of a particular property that belongs to a real estate project. Such files are typically considerably large in size. This is how you generate the file:

```
$ cd ~/data
$ SIZE=$((25*1024*1024))
$ head -c $SIZE /dev/urandom > warsaw/bemowo/visualizations.pdf
$ ls -lh warsaw/bemowo/visualizations.pdf | awk '{ print $9 " (" $5 ")" }'
warsaw/bemowo/visualizations.pdf (25M)
```

The application we are about to run will use the OCI SDK for Python. Let's prepare an isolated virtual environment for this application using the venv module. Next, we activate the environment, upgrade the Python package manager (pip), and install the OCI SDK (the oci module). Finally, we use the pip freeze command to list the installed modules and verify whether the SDK has been successfully installed.

```
$ cd
$ python3 -m venv oci-multipart
$ source oci-multipart/bin/activate
(oci-multipart) $ python3 -m pip install --upgrade pip
Collecting pip
.........
Successfully installed pip-19.2.3
```

```
(oci-multipart) $ python3 -m pip install oci
Collecting oci
.........
Successfully installed asn1crypto-0.24.0 certifi-2019.9.11 cffi-1.12.3
configparser-4.0.2 cryptography-2.7 oci-2.5.1 pyOpenSSL-19.0.0
pycparser-2.19 python-dateutil-2.8.0 pytz-2019.2 six-1.12.0
(oci-multipart) $ python3 -m pip freeze | grep oci
oci==2.5.1
```

Assuming the blueprints bucket still exists and all credentials are in place, we are
ready to execute the application. Access the application code fetched earlier from my
GitHub account, adapt the paths to the visualizations.pdf and config files, and run
the program.

```
(oci-multipart) $ cd ~/git/oci-book/chapter05/2-multipart-upload
(oci-multipart) $ chmod u+x multipart.py
(oci-multipart) $ FILE="$HOME/data/warsaw/bemowo/visualizations.pdf"
(oci-multipart) $ CONFIG="$HOME/.oci/config"
(oci-multipart) $ ./multipart.py "$FILE" 10 "waw/bemowo/visualizations.pdf"
                  "blueprints" "$CONFIG" SANDBOX-USER
Upload ID: 7de81d8f-44ba-4178-4269-5c25f7d03a86
Part File: /Users/mjk/warsaw/bemowo/visualizations.pdf.part0
Part ETag: 8489D285131C4A32E053C21DC20AAE16
Part File: /Users/mjk/warsaw/bemowo/visualizations.pdf.part1
Part ETag: 84897E38465648C8E053C21DC20AB5FF
Part File: /Users/mjk/warsaw/bemowo/visualizations.pdf.part2
Part ETag: 84897DC3EF364AEEE053C21DC20AF0F0
(oci-multipart) $ deactivate
$
```

The application split the original file into three parts, as shown in the output of the
following command:

```
$ ls -lh ~/data/warsaw/bemowo/visual* | awk '{ print $9 " (" $5 ")" }'
data/warsaw/bemowo/visualizations.pdf (25M)
data/warsaw/bemowo/visualizations.pdf.part0 (10M)
data/warsaw/bemowo/visualizations.pdf.part1 (10M)
data/warsaw/bemowo/visualizations.pdf.part2 (5.0M)
```

The newly created object has been built from these parts by committing the multipart upload. To verify whether it is really the same, download the object and use the `diff` tool.

```
$ cd ~/data
$ oci os object get -bn blueprints --name "waw/bemowo/visualizations.pdf"
--file visualizations.downloaded.pdf --profile SANDBOX-USER
Downloading object  [################################]  100%
$ ls -lh visualizations.downloaded.pdf | awk '{ print $9 " (" $5 ")" }'
visualizations.downloaded.pdf (25M)
$ diff visualizations.downloaded.pdf warsaw/bemowo/visualizations.pdf
$
```

No output from the `diff` command means the files have identical content.

It is time to look at the code you've just executed. As shown in Listing 5-2, we have encapsulated the main program logic within a traditional if __name__ == '__main__' Python block. In this way, the code is executed only if we run this file directly. Python lets you treat `.py` files as importable modules and, in this way, reuse already implemented logic. In such case, you typically want to be able to call the imported functions, ignoring the main program logic. When a file is imported as a module by another module, the __name__ variable no longer has the __main__ value but holds the name of the module (file), effectively leaving out the main program logic. We've run the program directly; therefore, the main program logic is executed and calls two functions. First, we use the `split_large_file` function to split the file into smaller parts. Then, we use the `upload_to_oci` function to perform the multipart upload.

Listing 5-2. multipart.py: The Main Function

```python
if __name__ == '__main__':
    filepath = str(sys.argv[1])
    part_size_mb = int(sys.argv[2])
    object_name = str(sys.argv[3])
    bucket_name = str(sys.argv[4])
    config_path = str(sys.argv[5])
    config_profile = str(sys.argv[6])
    part_list = split_large_file(filepath, part_size_mb*1024*1024)
    upload_to_oci(part_list, object_name , bucket_name, config_path,
        config_profile)
```

Listing 5-3 presents the split_large_file function. It is worth noting the returned object. In our case, we not only split the content of the original file into smaller chunks but collect the filenames of newly created files that store the chunks. This lets us return the list of the paths to the files that store the parts.

Listing 5-3. multipart.py: split_large_file Function

```python
def split_large_file(file_path, part_size):
    """Splits a file into parts"""
    part_list = []
    part_number = 0
    with open(file_path, 'rb') as file_stream:
        part = file_stream.read(part_size)
        while part != b"":
            part_file_path = file_path+'.part'+str(part_number)
            with open(part_file_path, 'wb') as part_stream:
                part_stream.write(part)
            part_list.append(part_file_path)
            part_number += 1
            part = file_stream.read(part_size)
    return part_list
```

Listing 5-4 presents the upload_to_oci function. The first input argument is the list of parts, returned from the split_large_file function. We do this to instruct the function where the part files can be found. At the beginning, the oci.config.from_file method reads the connection details from the configuration file (the config_path input argument) using the profile selected (the config_profile input argument). Immediately afterward, an instance of the oci.object_storage.ObjectStorageClient class is created and called client. All interactions with the OCI object storage API are done using the methods of this class. Before we begin the multipart upload, we still have to obtain the object storage namespace assigned to the cloud account. We perform this task using the client.get_namespace method. Next, we call our local create_multipart_upload function that starts the new multipart upload and returns the generated upload ID. Subsequently, we iterate over the list of parts and call the upload_part function for each part. This is not a very effective way, though, because we are doing it in a blocking, sequential manner. However, for the purpose of this example, it is easier to understand

if I had used a parallel function execution. During each iteration, we collect the object
returned by the upload_part function and aggregate all objects in a list called part_
details_list. Finally, we pass this list together with other input arguments such as the
upload ID and the object storage client class instance to the commit_multipart_upload
local function, which commits the multipart upload.

Listing 5-4. multipart.py: upload_to_oci Function

```
def upload_to_oci(part_list, object_name, bucket_name, config_path, config_
profile):
    """Performs a multi-part upload to OCI object storage"""
    config = oci.config.from_file(config_path, config_profile)
    client = oci.object_storage.ObjectStorageClient(config)
    storage_namespace = client.get_namespace().data

    upload_id = create_multipart_upload(storage_namespace, bucket_name,
    object_name, client)

    part_number = 1
    part_details_list = []
    for part in part_list:
        part_details = upload_part(storage_namespace, bucket_name, object_
        name, upload_id, part_number, part, client)
        part_details_list.append(part_details)
        part_number += 1

    commit_multipart_upload(storage_namespace, bucket_name, object_name,
    upload_id, part_details_list, client)
```

Listing 5-5 presents the create_multipart_upload function that uses the
client.create_multipart_upload method to begin the upload. As you can see,
the CreateMultipartUpload API request takes the object storage namespace, the
target bucket, and the target object name as input arguments. The object name,
though, has to be passed encapsulated in an instance of a model class called
CreateMultipartUploadDetails using a keyword argument dictionary conventionally
named kwargs. Last but not least, the function returns the upload ID that has been
generated for this multipart upload.

Listing 5-5. multipart.py: create_multipart_upload Function

```
def create_multipart_upload(storage_namespace, bucket_name, object_name, client):
    kwargs = { "object": object_name }
    details = oci.object_storage.models.CreateMultipartUploadDetails(**kwargs)
    upload_id = client.create_multipart_upload(storage_namespace, bucket_
    name, details).data.upload_id
    print('Upload ID: '+upload_id)
    return upload_id
```

Listing 5-6 presents the upload_part function, which is the primary workhorse of the entire multipart upload process. It takes the path to a part file (the part input argument) and an assigned part number (the part_number input argument) as input arguments along with the upload ID, object storage namespace, bucket, object name, and client class instance. The file is opened as a read-only, binary stream and passed to the client.upload_part method, which under the hood sends the UploadPart API request. I mentioned earlier that at the end we need to specify the list of parts to be included in the multipart upload commit. The list will contain CommitMultipartUploadPartDetails objects that effectively store the part number and corresponding entity tag each. To populate the list back in the upload_to_oci function, we create the details object for each part in the upload_part function based on the known part number and the returned ETag header that stores the entity tag for the uploaded part.

Listing 5-6. multipart.py: upload_part Function

```
def upload_part(storage_namespace, bucket_name, object_name, upload_id,
part_number, part, client):
    print('Part File: '+part)
    kwargs = {}
    with open(part, 'rb') as part_stream:
        rsp = client.upload_part(storage_namespace, bucket_name, object_
        name, upload_id, part_number, part_stream)
        kwargs = { "part_num": part_number, "etag": rsp.headers['ETag'] }
        print('Part ETag: '+rsp.headers['ETag'])
    return
    oci.object_storage.models.CommitMultipartUploadPartDetails(**kwargs)
```

Listing 5-7 presents the `commit_multipart_upload` function that takes
the list of `CommitMultipartUploadPartDetails` objects, wraps it into a
`CommitMultipartUploadDetails` object, and uses the `client.commit_multipart_`
`upload` method to send a `CommitMultipartUpload` request to the API.

Listing 5-7. multipart.py: commit_multipart_upload Function

```
def commit_multipart_upload(storage_namespace, bucket_name, object_name,
upload_id, part_details_list, client):
    kwargs = { "parts_to_commit": part_details_list }
    details = oci.object_storage.models.CommitMultipartUploadDetails(**kwargs)
    client.commit_multipart_upload(storage_namespace, bucket_name, object_
    name, upload_id, details)
```

I've built this sample application to illustrate both the way to use the OCI SDK and
a program multipart upload. To release such an application into production, you would
need to add error handling logic that aborts an ongoing multipart upload in the case
of severe failure. You could also consider adding a retry mechanism for the upload of
individual parts. Finally, the upload of individual parts can be done in parallel to speed
up the entire process.

As a matter of fact, if you are happy to rely on the OCI CLI embedded in your scripts,
you can use the convenient `oci os put` CLI command. This is the same you've already
used earlier in this chapter. Any file larger than what you define with the `--part-size`
argument is effectively uploaded using the multipart upload API, unless you explicitly
use the `--no-multipart` option. Moreover, you can define the number of parallel part
uploads with the `--parallel-upload-count` argument, which defaults to 3.

In this section, you've worked with an application that uses the SDK/CLI config file
to let the SDK sign the API calls as an IAM user. This can be annoying because you need
to distribute in some way things like the API signing key and the OCID of a user to the
hosts where your application is supposed to run. Luckily, you do not need to do it for the
applications that are hosted on compute nodes running in the Oracle Cloud. In this case,
you do not even need any dedicated IAM user. Instead, you can leverage the so-called
dynamic groups whose members are compute instances that match certain conditions.
You will learn about them in the next section.

Instance Principals

In the context of IAM, each compute instance in Oracle Cloud has its own identity based on the certificates that are automatically generated for, added to, and rotated on the instance. In other words, a compute instance is seen as an *instance principal*, an independent actor, and is allowed to call OCI APIs with its own name. Instance principals can be members of *dynamic groups* only. You have already learned that we use policies to specify the allowed access over cloud resources for a particular group of users. Similarly, we can define policies that specify the permitted access for a particular dynamic group that consists of instance principals. Why do we call dynamic groups "dynamic"? Simply because they use matching rules to dynamically add or remove their members, as shown in Figure 5-11.

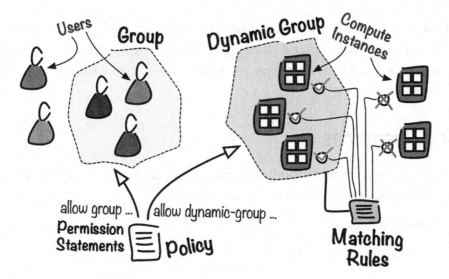

Figure 5-11. *Instance principals and dynamic groups*

You formulate matching rules using easy syntax to define the conditions an instance must meet to be treated as a member of a given dynamic group. Let me give you an example. This is the *matching rule* condition that would include all compute instances that exist in a particular compartment:

```
instance.compartment.id = 'ocid1.compartment.oc1..aaaaa.........gzwhsa'
```

You can also point to the instances based on their precise OCIDs.

```
instance.id = 'ocid1.instance.oc1.........kurtua'
```

The most convenient and truly dynamic way, though, is to rely on defined tags that are attached to compute instances. This is a condition that includes all compute instances that have the `project.realestate` custom tag attached.

```
tag.project.realestate.value
```

You can create complex conditions as well. The `all` word will make sure that all individual conditions have to be met, while the word `any` will treat the rule as fulfilled as long as at least one condition is met. This is a condition that includes all compute instances that exist in a particular compartment and have the `project.name` custom tag attached. In this case, the tag value must be set to `realestate`.

```
all { instance.compartment.id = 'ocid1.compartment.oc1..aaaaa........
gzwhsa', tag.projects.name.value = 'realestate' }
```

Wait a minute? A "custom tag"? Yes. Correct. I haven't mentioned this before. In Oracle Cloud, you can attach *user-defined tags* to compute instances and many other types of cloud resources. This is a simple yet powerful feature that lets you organize and track your cloud resources.

Tagging Resources

Many types of cloud resources including compute instances and object storage buckets can have custom tags attached. There are two types of tags.

- Free-form tags
- Defined tags

We are going to focus on defined tags because they offer more functionality including dynamic group matching rules support. Defined tags must be grouped within *tag namespaces*. To be precise, a tag namespace contains *tag keys*. You then attach tags from a given namespace with a given key to cloud resources such as compute instances, object storage buckets, or load balancers. While doing this, you can optionally assign a custom *tag value* to a particular tag key, but this is not mandatory. Although you create tag namespaces in compartments, tag namespace names must be unique within the entire tenancy. Furthermore, the names are case insensitive; therefore, it is a good practice to keep them either all in lowercase or all in uppercase for consistency. In contrast to many other types of cloud resources, you are allowed to move tag namespaces from one compartment to another.

Note   You can assign tags to object storage buckets, but not to the individual objects. In their case, use the custom metadata feature that was presented earlier in this chapter.

A tag key that is no longer needed can be made either retired or completely deleted. A retired tag key is marked as inactive and can no longer be attached to cloud resources. The existing attachments remain unaffected, however. Tag-specific operations will still take into account the retired tag keys attached to resources. Retiring a tag namespace effectively retires all tag keys that belong to the namespace.

Let's create a new tag namespace called test-projects in the Sandbox compartment. We are going to use the oci iam tag-namespace create CLI command. If you have configured the SANDBOX-ADMIN profile in the oci_cli_rc configuration file as instructed in Chapter 4, you can omit the --compartment-id option like I did in the following code snippet:

```
$ oci iam tag-namespace create --name "test-projects" --description "Test
tag namespace: projects" --profile SANDBOX-ADMIN
{
  "data": {
    "compartment-id": "ocid1.compartment.oc1..aa.........gzwhsa",
    "defined-tags": {},
    "description": "Test tag namespace: projects",
    "freeform-tags": {},
    "id": "ocid1.tagnamespace.oc1..aa.........6qu2eq",
    "is-retired": false,
    "name": "test-projects",
    "time-created": "2019-03-09T20:23:33.458000+00:00"
  },
  "etag": "4c49c30092918551319c46469d6051f47309f001"
}
```

The response body is self-descriptive. We can clearly see that tag namespace creation was successful. We can always verify whether everything went fine using the OCI Console, as shown in Figure 5-12. To do so follow these steps:

1.   Go to Menu ➤ Governance ➤ Tag Namespaces.

Tag Namespaces *in* Sandbox *Compartment*

Create Namespace Definition					
Name	**Status**	**OCID**	**Cost-tracking Tags**	**Created**	
test-projects	● Active	...6qu2eq	0	Sat, 09 Mar 2019 20:23:33 GMT	⋮
				Showing 1 Item(s) ‹ Page 1 ›	

Figure 5-12. *Viewing tag namespaces in the OCI Console*

Tip   If you've accidentally created the `tag-namespace` in the root compartment, do not retire it; just move it to the `Sandbox` compartment.

If you are asking yourself what the "cost-tracking tags" column means in the view presented in Figure 5-12, I will help you. You can designate up to 10 tag keys in total to be cost tracking enabled in a single moment. These tag keys will be available for selection in the billings cost analysis view in the OCI Console as an additional filter you apply to trace the costs in a more granular way. Based on that tags can be attached and detached from resources in a dynamic way, the cost tracking tags give you more flexibility in tracing the costs incurred by groups of related cloud resources across their compartments.

We are now going to create a new tag key. The key will be used in a matching rule to include a compute instance we are about to provision in a dynamic group. This will let us test instance principals in action. To create a new tag key within a given namespace, please execute the following CLI command, remembering to replace the tag namespace OCID:

```
$ TAG_NAMESPACE_OCID=`oci iam tag-namespace list --query
"data[?name=='test-projects'] | [0].id" --raw-output`

$ oci iam tag create --tag-namespace-id $TAG_NAMESPACE_OCID --name
realestate --description "Real-estate project" --profile SANDBOX-ADMIN
{
  "data": {
    "compartment-id": "ocid1.compartment.oc1..aa.........gzwhsa",
    "defined-tags": {},
    "description": "Real-estate project",
```

```
    "freeform-tags": {},
    "id": "ocid1.tagdefinition.oc1..aa.........mnlowa",
    "is-cost-tracking": false,
    "is-retired": false,
    "name": "realestate",
    "tag-namespace-id": "ocid1.tagnamespace.oc1..aa.........6qu2eq",
    "tag-namespace-name": "test-projects",
    "time-created": "2019-03-09T20:57:41.094000+00:00"
  },
  "etag": "83cfd4a247632b699c548886ac4c628891b4eecc"
}
```

Again, you can use the OCI Console to see your new tag by following these steps:

1. Go to Menu ➤ Governance ➤ Tag Namespaces.

2. Click the "test-projects" namespace name.

If you find the CLI more convenient, you can use the oci iam tag list CLI command to list all the keys within a given namespaces.

```
$ oci iam tag list --tag-namespace-id $TAG_NAMESPACE_OCID
qsmxlurkwx7pu6qu2eq --all --profile SANDBOX-ADMIN
{
  "data": [
    {
      "compartment-id": "ocid1.compartment.oc1..aa.........gzwhsa",
      "defined-tags": {},
      "description": "Real-estate project",
      "freeform-tags": {},
      "id": "ocid1.tagdefinition.oc1..aa.........mnlowa",
      "is-cost-tracking": false,
      "is-retired": false,
      "name": "realestate",
      "time-created": "2019-03-09T20:57:41.094000+00:00"
    }
  ]
}
```

Perfect. Now, we are ready to define a new dynamic group and its matching rule.

Dynamic Groups

The members of a *dynamic group* can be only the compute instances running in Oracle
Cloud Infrastructure that fulfill the conditions defined in the matching rule associated
with the dynamic group. The matching rule will be provided when a dynamic group is
created. We are going to accept, as the dynamic group members, all compute instances
that carry the `realestate` tag key defined in the `test-projects` namespace. This is a
matching rule we need to use:

```
tag.test-projects.realestate.value
```

Dynamic groups just like standard groups exist in the scope of the entire tenancy. As
a result, the `sandbox-admin` user won't be able to create a new dynamic group because
it can manage only the resources within the Sandbox compartment. This is why we are
going to use the default CLI profile that represents the tenancy administrator and create
a new dynamic group on behalf of the tenancy admin.

Tip   If you do not have access to the tenancy admin account, please ask your
cloud account admin to create this dynamic group for you.

To create a new dynamic group and explicitly indicate the tenancy-level scope, use
the `oci iam dynamic-group create` command like this:

```
$ TENANCY_OCID=`cat ~/.oci/config | grep tenancy | sed 's/tenancy=//'`

$ MATCHING_RULE="tag.test-projects.realestate.value"

$ oci iam dynamic-group create --name realestate-instances --description
"Instances related to the real-estate project" --matching-rule $MATCHING_
RULE -c $TENANCY_OCID
{
  "data": {
    "compartment-id": "ocid1.tenancy.oc1..aa.........3yymfa",
    "description": "Instances related to the real-estate project",
    "id": "ocid1.dynamicgroup.oc1..aa.........hkt7dq",
    "inactive-status": null,
    "lifecycle-state": "ACTIVE",
    "matching-rule": "tag.test-projects.realestate.value",
```

```
    "name": "realestate-instances",
    "time-created": "2019-03-20T20:59:36.353000+00:00"
  },
  "etag": "4c007061997871d3f5ac4a98a225f71be509ac25"
}
```

We have defined the matching rule as the MATCHING_RULE variable and passed it to the --matching-rule argument of the oci iam dynamic-group create CLI command. The command was issued with no explicit --profile; therefore, the CLI used the default profile that we configured, back in Chapter 3, to use the tenancy admin credentials. The new dynamic group was called realestate-instances.

With the new dynamic group in place, we are ready to add a new permission statement to an existing policy. The policy syntax for standard groups and dynamic groups is virtually the same, with the exception of using the dynamic-group term instead of the group term. This statement allows the instance principals of the newly created dynamic group to manage objects in the Sandbox compartment.

allow **dynamic-group realestate-instances** to manage objects in compartment Sandbox where target.bucket.name='blueprints'

We are going to reuse the same policy that was created earlier in this chapter. To perform an update, we need a file with all statements that are to be present within the policy. Listing 5-8 presents the two existing and the third, new statement.

Listing 5-8. sandbox-users.policies.storage.2.json

```
[
"allow group sandbox-users to read buckets in compartment Sandbox where
target.bucket.name='blueprints'",
"allow group sandbox-users to manage objects in compartment Sandbox where
target.bucket.name='blueprints'",
"allow dynamic-group realestate-instances to manage objects in compartment
Sandbox where target.bucket.name='blueprints'"
]
```

The file is available in the Git repository at oci-book/chapter05/1-policies/.

The policy we are about to update was originally created in the Sandbox compartment. To find this policy by name, we can use the `oci iam policy list` CLI command to additionally apply a local JMESPath filter to display only the policy OCID.

Let's execute the `oci iam policy update` CLI command from the directory that stores the `sandbox-users.policies.storage.2.json` file. We will reference the relative path to the file using the `--statements` argument. These are the commands:

```
$ cd ~/git/oci-book/chapter05/1-policies

$ POLICY_ID=`oci iam policy list --all --query "data[?name=='sandbox-users-
storage-policy'] | [0].id" --raw-output --profile SANDBOX-ADMIN`

$ oci iam policy update --policy-id $POLICY_ID --statements file://sandbox-
users.policies.storage.2.json --version-date "" --profile SANDBOX-ADMIN
WARNING: The value passed to statements will overwrite all existing
statements for this policy. The existing statements are as follows:
[
  "allow group sandbox-users to read buckets in compartment Sandbox where
  target.bucket.name='blueprints'",
  "allow group sandbox-users to manage objects in compartment Sandbox where
  target.bucket.name='blueprints'"
]
Are you sure you want to continue? [y/N]: y
{
  "data": {
    "compartment-id": "ocid1.compartment.oc1..aa.........gzwhsa",
    "defined-tags": {},
    "description": "Storage-related policy for regular Sandbox users",
    "freeform-tags": {},
    "id": "ocid1.policy.oc1..aa.........tiueya",
    "inactive-status": null,
    "lifecycle-state": "ACTIVE",
    "name": "sandbox-users-storage-policy",
    "statements": [
      "allow group sandbox-users to read buckets in compartment Sandbox
      where target.bucket.name='blueprints'",
```

```
        "allow group sandbox-users to manage objects in compartment Sandbox
        where target.bucket.name='blueprints'",
        "allow dynamic-group realestate-instances to manage objects in
        compartment Sandbox where target.bucket.name='blueprints'"
      ],
      "time-created": "2019-03-07T15:52:21.583000+00:00",
      "version-date": null
    },
    "etag": "79b1393841a75cb5cf8b22586d731e52b9617cda"
}
```

Additionally, at the time of writing, we have to pass the --version-date argument to the CLI command; otherwise, the validation fails. This parameter defines the effective policy verb and resource type scope. Using an empty value for the --version-date argument will include all future resource types added to the resource type family as well as changes in policy verb definitions. For the purpose of this exercise, it actually does not matter, but the parameter has to be set.

Until this point, we created a new tag namespace and a defined tag key. Next, we specified a new dynamic group with a matching rule that accepts a compute instance as a member of the dynamic group, provided that the instance carries the newly defined tag. Finally, we added to the existing policy a new statement to let the dynamic group members manage objects in the Sandbox compartment. We are ready to provision the infrastructure shipped with a custom application that will allow us to see an instance principal in action.

Accessing Storage from Instances

In this section, you are going to apply Terraform infrastructure code that provisions a simple set of cloud resources including a single CentOS-based virtual machine. On the machine, we will run a simple Python-based application wrapped into a systemd-based Linux operating system service. The application will list a set of objects in a particular bucket at regular intervals and create a summary text file in the same bucket. We are going to use the OCI SDK for Python to implement the logic. The application, or, to be more precise, the compute instance on which the application is running, will authenticate as the so-called instance principal. In this way, you will avoid storing passwords or keys on that compute instance. The application logic is conceptually shown in Figure 5-13.

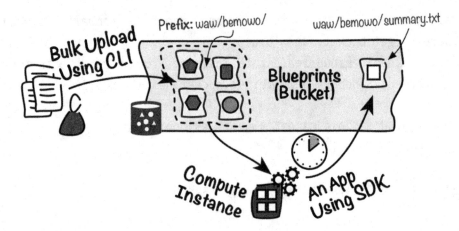

Figure 5-13. *Accessing object storage from the OCI instance*

Earlier in this chapter, you already experimented a bit with the OCI SDK for Python in the context of object storage APIs. The code you ran before was using your local OCI CLI/SDK configuration file and authenticated as the sandbox-user user. The application had to be able to access the private API signing key and know a couple of other details, such as the user OCID and region, to successfully sign each request. This is not a very portable setup, is it? This time we are going to let the application authenticate as an instance principal. In this way, we do not need to ship or define any keys or user details on the compute instance where our application is running. Instead, the application will make API calls on behalf of the compute instance. This increases security and makes the entire management simpler and the application more scalable.

The entire solution will be built in a fully automated way using the scripts I prepared. You just need to "press the button" and watch. The infrastructure is nearly the same as the one deployed in Chapter 3. Just a couple of names have changed. The cloud-init configuration file is completely new, though. I will explain everything later. First, let's see it in action.

I am assuming the environment variables used by Terraform are still in place. You can verify this using the env | grep TF_VAR Bash commands. If they are gone, you should be able to load them using the tfvars.env.sh script, which you created as part of the Chapter 3 exercise.

```
$ source ~/tfvars.env.sh
```

The Terraform code assumes the oci_id_rsa.pub public SSH key is present in the ~/.ssh directory and references the key from the compute.tf infrastructure code file. Having fulfilled the aforementioned prerequisites, run the terraform init command to download the newest OCI plugin and execute the terraform apply command to provision the infrastructure.

```
$ cd ~/git/oci-book
$ cd chapter05/3-instance-principals/infrastructure
$ find . \( -name "*.tf" -o -name "*.yaml" \)
./app/compute.tf
./app/vcn.tf
./app/cloud-init/appvm.config.yaml
./app/vars.tf
./modules.tf
./vcn.tf
./provider.tf
./vars.tf

$ terraform init
Initializing modules...
- module.app
  Getting source "app"

Initializing provider plugins...
- Checking for available provider plugins on https://releases.hashicorp.
  com...
- Downloading plugin for provider "oci" (3.45.0)...

* provider.oci: version = "~> 3.45"

Terraform has been successfully initialized!

$ terraform apply -auto-approve
data.oci_identity_availability_domains.ads: Refreshing state...
data.oci_core_images.centos_image: Refreshing state...
oci_core_virtual_network.app_vcn: Creating...
oci_core_virtual_network.app_vcn: Creation complete after 1s
oci_core_internet_gateway.app_igw: Creating...
module.app.oci_core_security_list.app_sl: Creating...
module.app.oci_core_security_list.app_sl: Creation complete after 0s
oci_core_internet_gateway.app_igw: Creation complete after 1s
module.app.oci_core_route_table.app_rt: Creating...
module.app.oci_core_route_table.app_rt: Creation complete after 0s
module.app.oci_core_subnet.app_subnet: Creating...
```

```
module.app.oci_core_subnet.app_subnet: Creation complete after 0s
module.app.oci_core_instance.app_vm: Creating...
module.app.oci_core_instance.app_vm: Still creating... (10s elapsed)
module.app.oci_core_instance.app_vm: Still creating... (20s elapsed)
module.app.oci_core_instance.app_vm: Still creating... (30s elapsed)
module.app.oci_core_instance.app_vm: Still creating... (40s elapsed)
module.app.oci_core_instance.app_vm: Still creating... (50s elapsed)
module.app.oci_core_instance.app_vm: Creation complete after 55s
module.app.data.oci_core_vnic_attachments.app_vnic_attachment: Refreshing
state...
module.app.data.oci_core_vnic.app_vnic: Refreshing state...

Apply complete! Resources: 6 added, 0 changed, 0 destroyed.

Outputs:

app_instance_public_ip = 130.61.18.158
```

Wait until you see the public IP assigned to your newly provisioned virtual machine. This time, in my case, it is 130.61.18.158. Even though the instance has been announced as created and ready, we have to remember that the boot process is, probably, still running. You may need to wait a couple of seconds until the ssh daemon starts accepting connections. Let's connect to the instance.

```
$ APP_VM_PUBLIC_IP=`terraform output app_instance_public_ip`
$ ssh -i ~/.ssh/oci_id_rsa opc@$APP_VM_PUBLIC_IP
The authenticity of host '130.61.18.158' can't be established.
ECDSA key fingerprint is SHA256:YJE8Q........./.........LSQxtM.
Are you sure you want to continue connecting (yes/no)? yes
Warning: Permanently added '130.61.18.158' (ECDSA) to the list of known hosts
```

The completion of tasks we've set for cloud-init can take up to a minute. You can always use the sudo tail -f /var/log/cloud-init.log command on the compute instance to trace the progress of cloud-init execution and debug any unexpected problems. You can periodically execute the systemctl status command, passing reportissuer as the service name. At some point of the time, you should be able to see a custom reportissuer service loaded and active. This is our Python application wrapped into a systemd unit. If you look at the service logs, you will see that every 30 seconds there is a report said to be generated.

```
[opc@app-vm]$ sudo systemctl status reportissuer
● reportissuer.service - Issue Report Job
  Loaded: loaded (/etc/systemd/system/reportissuer.service; enabled;
  vendor preset: disabled)
  Active: active (running) since Thu 2019-03-21 16:14:09 GMT; 5min ago
  Main PID: 13978 (python3.6)
  CGroup: /system.slice/reportissuer.service
          └─13978 python3.6 /home/opc/reportissuer.py

Mar 21 16:17:45 app-vm reportissuer.py[13978]: Creating a report
Mar 21 16:17:45 app-vm reportissuer.py[13978]: ### Report generated
2019-03-21 16:17:45.634197
Mar 21 16:18:15 app-vm reportissuer.py[13978]: Creating a report
Mar 21 16:18:16 app-vm reportissuer.py[13978]: ### Report generated
2019-03-21 16:18:16.170609
Mar 21 16:18:46 app-vm reportissuer.py[13978]: Creating a report
Mar 21 16:18:47 app-vm reportissuer.py[13978]: ### Report generated
2019-03-21 16:18:47.605280
Mar 21 16:19:17 app-vm reportissuer.py[13978]: Creating a report

[opc@app-vm]$ exit
```

If you look in the bucket, you should be able to see a new object called waw/
bemowo/summary.txt. This object gets generated and uploaded every 30 seconds by
the reportissuer service running on the compute instance you've just provisioned.
Figure 5-14 presents the new object in the OCI Console.

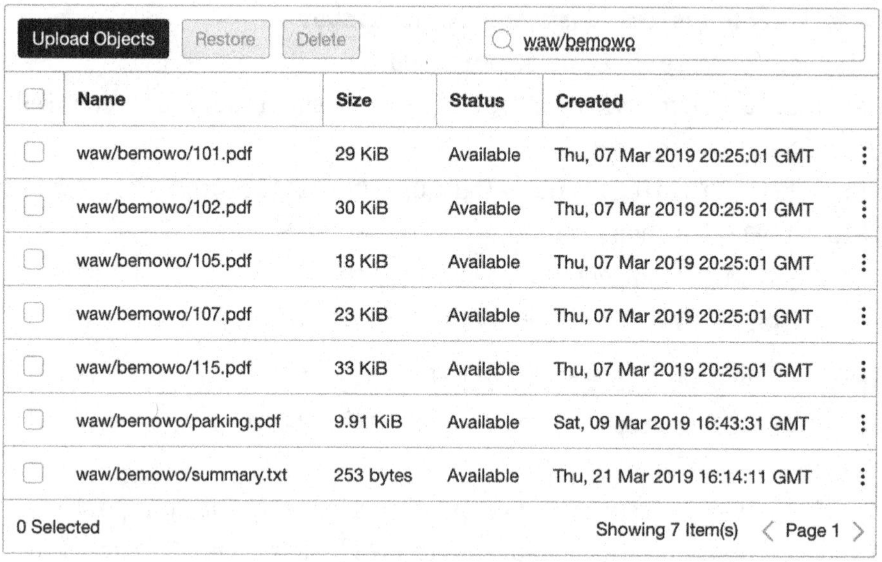

Figure 5-14. *Summary object uploaded by an instance principal*

Are you curious about the content of the report? Sure, you are. Return to your local command line closing the SSH connection to the compute instance. Use the `oci os object get` CLI command using the `--file -` option to dump the content of the `waw/bemowo/summary.txt` object to the standard output.

```
$ oci os object get -bn blueprints --name "waw/bemowo/summary.txt" --file -
--profile SANDBOX-USER
waw/bemowo/101.pdf (29.0K)
waw/bemowo/102.pdf (30.0K)
waw/bemowo/105.pdf (18.0K)
waw/bemowo/107.pdf (23.0K)
waw/bemowo/115.pdf (33.0K)
waw/bemowo/parking.pdf (9.90625K)
waw/bemowo/summary.txt (0.2470703125K)
### Report generated 2019-03-21 16:34:33.971448
```

As you can see, the report contains the names and sizes of all objects prefixed with the `waw/bemowo` string. The last line shows the report creation timestamp, the same as last logged by the `reportissuer` service that is running on the compute instance.

Listing 5-9 presents the cloud-config file that gets uploaded to the compute instance and processed by the cloud-init module. As a result, a series of steps takes place. First, there is a new unit file added to the compute instance filesystem at the following path: /etc/systemd/system/reportissuer.service. This unit file is a base for the new systemd service that encapsulates our application. It specifies a few variables that provide runtime configuration for the reportissuer.py script, which is the main service executable here. The runcmd section of the cloud config file defines further actions performed on the instance such as the installation of Python 3 and the OCI SDK, downloading the reportissuer.py script from the GitHub repository, and a few commands that altogether effectively add a new systemd service based on the unit file we've supplied.

Listing 5-9. appvm.config.yaml

```
#cloud-config
write_files:
-   content: |
      [Unit]
      Description = Issue Report Job
      After = network.target
      [Service]
      Environment=APP_BUCKET_NAME=blueprints
      Environment=APP_OBJECT_NAME=waw/bemowo/summary.txt
      Environment=APP_OBJECT_PREFIX=waw/bemowo
      Environment=APP_POLLING_INTERVAL_SECONDS=30
      Environment=PYTHONUNBUFFERED=1
      ExecStart = /home/opc/reportissuer.py
      User = opc
      [Install]
      WantedBy = multi-user.target
    path: /etc/systemd/system/reportissuer.service
runcmd:
  - [ yum, -y, install, "https://centos7.iuscommunity.org/ius-release.rpm" ]
  - [ yum, -y, install, python3 ]
  - [ yum, -y, install, python3-pip ]
  - [ python3, -m, pip, install, --upgrade, pip ]
  - [ python3, -m, pip, install, oci ]
```

- [wget, "https://raw.githubusercontent.com/mtjakobczyk/oci-book/master/chapter05/3-instance-principals/applications/reportissuer.py"]
- [mv, reportissuer.py, "/home/opc/"]
- [chown, "opc:opc", "/home/opc/reportissuer.py"]
- [chmod, "u+x", "/home/opc/reportissuer.py"]
- [ln, -s, "/etc/systemd/system/reportissuer.service", "/etc/systemd/system/multi-user.target.wants/reportissuer.service"]
- [systemctl, enable, reportissuer.service]
- [systemctl, start, reportissuer.service]

If you are interested in the implementation of the reportissuer service, especially in the way it authenticates as an instance principal, read on. Listing 5-10 shows the main function of the program.

Listing 5-10. reportissuer.py: The Main Function

```
if __name__ == '__main__':
    bucket_name = os.environ['APP_BUCKET_NAME']
    summary_object_name = os.environ['APP_OBJECT_NAME']
    object_prefix = os.environ['APP_OBJECT_PREFIX']
    polling_interval_seconds = int(os.environ['APP_POLLING_INTERVAL_SECONDS'])
    tmp_directory = os.environ['HOME']
    while True:
        print('Creating a report')
        signer = oci.auth.signers.InstancePrincipalsSecurityTokenSigner()
        client = oci.object_storage.ObjectStorageClient(config={},
        signer=signer)
        storage_namespace = client.get_namespace().data
        report_entry_list = prepare_report_entries(storage_namespace,
        bucket_name, object_prefix, client)
        upload_report(report_entry_list, tmp_directory, storage_namespace,
        bucket_name, summary_object_name, client)
        time.sleep(polling_interval_seconds)
```

The first few lines read the environment variables into the corresponding local program variables. The values have been defined in the Service section of the uploaded systemd unit file (`reportissuer.service`). The recurring nature of the process is implemented through an infinite `while` loop. At the end of each iteration, the process thread sleeps for the interval defined through the `APP_POLLING_INTERVAL_SECONDS` environment variable. The `prepare_report_entries` function is responsible for listing the objects and preparing a list for the `upload_report` function, which uploads a newly created summary file to the bucket. For each iteration, there is an instance of object storage client class created and set to use the instance principal security token signer. These two simple lines result in the use of instance-principal-based request signing:

```
signer = oci.auth.signers.InstancePrincipalsSecurityTokenSigner()
client = oci.object_storage.ObjectStorageClient(config={}, signer=signer)
```

All other SDK client classes can be used in the same way to leverage instance principals and dynamic groups. This can greatly simplify the authentication patterns for applications running on Oracle Cloud Infrastructure compute instances because you no longer need to supply keys and user details to every compute instance.

Let's take a brief look at the two functions that are called in the main function. Listing 5-11 presents the `prepare_report_entries` function. The `client.list_objects` method calls the object storage API to fetch the list of objects whose names start with a particular prefix. The keyworded argument `fields="name,size"` informs the API what fields we are interested in. If we've left it out, the API would not return the size field values in the response. We iterate over the returned objects and use concatenation to prepare a report entry. At the end, we return a list with the report entries we've created.

Listing 5-11. reportissuer.py: prepare_report_entries Function

```
def prepare_report_entries(storage_namespace, bucket_name, object_prefix, client):
    report_entries = []
    objects = client.list_objects(storage_namespace, bucket_name,
    fields="name,size", prefix=object_prefix).data.objects
    for obj in objects:
        entry = str(obj.name)+' ('+str(obj.size/1024)+'K)'
        report_entries.append(entry)
    return report_entries
```

Listing 5-12 covers the `upload_report` function, which takes the list of report entries and writes them to a new temporary file. To avoid name collisions, we include a newly generated UUID in the name of the file. The last line in the file contains the report creation timestamp. The same string is written to the standard output you saw in the systemd service status log a moment ago. The `client.put_object` method uploads the file contents as a new object. At the end, the temporary file is removed from the local filesystem.

Listing 5-12. reportissuer.py: upload_report Function

```python
def upload_report(report_entry_list, tmp_directory, storage_namespace,
bucket_name, object_name, client):
    tmp_report_filename = tmp_directory+'/bucket_report.'+str(uuid.
    uuid4())+'.txt'
    with open(tmp_report_filename, 'w') as stream:
        for entry in report_entry_list:
            stream.write(entry+'\n')
        report_timestamp_str = '### Report generated '+str(datetime.
        datetime.now())+'\n'
        stream.write(report_timestamp_str)
        print(report_timestamp_str)
    with open(tmp_report_filename, 'r') as stream:
        client.put_object(storage_namespace, bucket_name, object_name,
        stream)
    os.remove(tmp_report_filename)
```

This concludes the instance principal demonstration. You can now use the well-known `terraform destroy` command to terminate all cloud resources like this:

```
$ terraform destroy --auto-approve
oci_core_virtual_network.app_vcn: Refreshing state...
data.oci_identity_availability_domains.ads: Refreshing state...
data.oci_core_images.centos_image: Refreshing state...
oci_core_internet_gateway.app_igw: Refreshing state...
oci_core_security_list.app_sl: Refreshing state...
oci_core_route_table.app_rt: Refreshing state...
oci_core_subnet.app_subnet: Refreshing state...
```

```
oci_core_instance.app_vm: Refreshing state...
data.oci_core_vnic_attachments.app_vnic_attachment: Refreshing state...
data.oci_core_vnic.app_vnic: Refreshing state...
module.app.oci_core_instance.app_vm: Destroying...
module.app.oci_core_instance.app_vm: Destruction complete after 2m15s
module.app.oci_core_subnet.app_subnet: Destroying...
module.app.oci_core_subnet.app_subnet: Destruction complete after 0s
module.app.oci_core_route_table.app_rt: Destroying...
module.app.oci_core_security_list.app_sl: Destroying...
module.app.oci_core_security_list.app_sl: Destruction complete after 1s
module.app.oci_core_route_table.app_rt: Destruction complete after 1s
oci_core_internet_gateway.app_igw: Destroying...
oci_core_internet_gateway.app_igw: Destruction complete after 0s
oci_core_virtual_network.app_vcn: Destroying...
oci_core_virtual_network.app_vcn: Destruction complete after 0s

Destroy complete! Resources: 6 destroyed.
```

Oracle Cloud Infrastructure comes with rich monitoring capabilities with a broad variety of service-specific metrics. In the case of object storage, there are two metrics available for buckets: the number of objects and the aggregated size of a bucket. To view the monitoring data in the OCI Console, follow these steps:

1. Go to Menu ➤ Object Storage ➤ Object Storage.

2. Click the bucket name.

3. On the Resource tab, select Metrics.

If you click one of the charts, you will be presented with a detailed view, as shown in Figure 5-15.

273

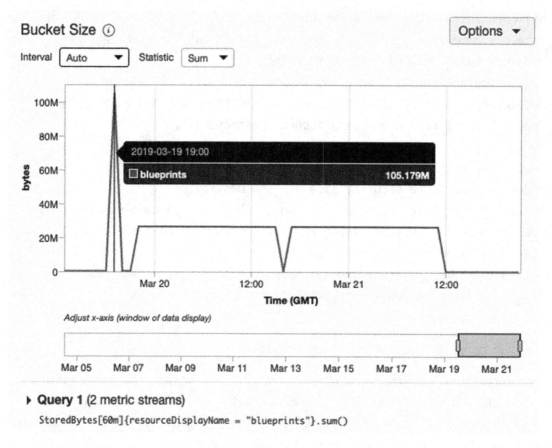

Figure 5-15. *Viewing object storage metrics*

Note   At the bottom of the detailed chart, you will see a query that was used to produce the displayed results. Oracle Cloud Infrastructure uses the Monitoring Query Language (MQL), which can be used to create custom charts.

Public Access

Sometimes, you may decide to designate selected buckets to allow anonymous read-only access to serve the content to the general public. This approach may be useful when building edge solutions such as mobile apps that rely on public content. For example, you could store selected images, videos, and articles in a bucket that allows everyone to download these objects. In such a case, you can simply use *public buckets*. When using the CLI, you employ the `--public-access-type` option to define whether a bucket is private or public. The default value, `NoPublicAccess`, results in creating a private bucket. There are two access modes a public bucket can have.

- `ObjectRead`

- `ObjectReadWithoutList`

Both will allow the unauthenticated, read-only access to the objects. The only difference is that `ObjectReadWithoutList` will disable object listings for unauthenticated users. This may be helpful to serve the objects only to the holders of exact links and avoid having your content scrapped, especially if you are using object names that are hard or impossible to guess. It is technically possible to change the public access type back and forth from public to private and vice versa, but it is not considered a best practice.

What if you have a bucket with a large number of objects and you find yourself in a situation where you would benefit from temporarily allowing unauthenticated read-write access to just one of these objects? In this and other scenarios, you may find *pre-authenticated requests* useful. A pre-authenticated request comes with a dynamically generated unique URL that remains active for a defined period of time. Anyone holding the URL can use the object storage in the scope allowed by the pre-authenticated request. If you create a pre-authenticated request for a particular object, you can choose from three access types.

- `ObjectRead`

- `ObjectWrite`

- `ObjectReadWrite`

The URLs are nearly impossible to guess. As long as your distribution channel is secure and you trust the applications at the edge, you could consider building a solution that relies on pre-authenticated requests to access the objects by applications that

275

neither use instance principals nor use authenticated users. This is how you create a pre-authenticated request for one of the PDF files in the blueprints bucket using the CLI:

```
$ date +"%Y-%m-%d"
2019-09-29
$ ONE_WEEK_LATER="2019-10-06"
$ MIDNIGHT="T00:00:00.000Z"
$ oci os preauth-request create -bn blueprints --name waw-bemowo-105-par
--access-type ObjectRead --time-expires "$ONE_WEEK_LATER$MIDNIGHT" -on waw/
bemowo/105.pdf --profile SANDBOX-ADMIN
{
  "data": {
    "access-type": "ObjectRead",
    "access-uri": "/p/nO218vRTg4FW5d1t1nV-uMPp471HFIxNccISzFiU2Qg/n/
    jakobczyk/b/blueprints/o/waw/bemowo/105.pdf",
    "id": "tk/aQTCjIGsF1EJ1SsMAMVOwPNW4RErVneNfLjR5LN8=:waw/bemowo/105.pdf",
    "name": "waw-bemowo-105-par",
    "object-name": "waw/bemowo/105.pdf",
    "time-created": "2019-09-29T23:16:20.599000+00:00",
    "time-expires": "2019-10-06T00:00:00+00:00"
  }
}
```

No matter if a pre-authenticated request is created through the OCI Console or with the use of CLI, you will see the generated access URI only once, so make sure that either you or your application code does read it. If you miss doing it, the pre-authenticated request will be useless. The --time-expires option indirectly defines the time window in which the access URI remains active. It is not possible to extend or shorten this period, but you are free to delete the existing request and create a new pre-authenticated request for the same object to alter the expiration time. Because of these reasons, before you build a solution that heavily relies on pre-authenticated requests, make sure you are able to implement a reliable distribution and notification channel to provide the applications with up-to-date pre-authenticated requests.

To use the access URI, you need to enrich the value returned in the `data.access-uri` field by prepending the region-specific base URL like in this code snippet:

```
https://objectstorage.eu-frankfurt-1.oraclecloud.com/p/n0218vRTg4FW5d1t1nV-
uMPp471HFIxNccISzFiU2Qg/n/jakobczyk/b/blueprints/o/waw/bemowo/105.pdf
```

You can try opening the link in a web browser. Do not forget to use your link instead of the one shown. The PDF file, or more precisely a random binary file that imitated a PDF file in this chapter, will get downloaded to your local machine, even though you have not authenticated yourself in any way.

You can use the OCI Console, as shown in Figure 5-16, or the CLI to list the existing pre-authenticated requests or delete some of them before the expiry time is reached, if needed.

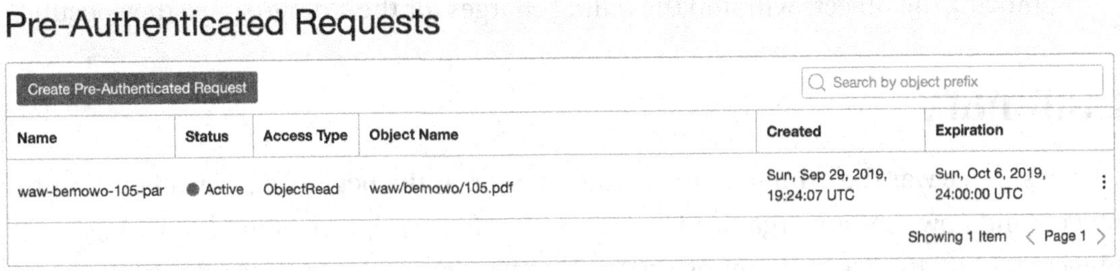

Pre-Authenticated Requests

Create Pre-Authenticated Request				Search by object prefix	
Name	**Status**	**Access Type**	**Object Name**	**Created**	**Expiration**
waw-bemowo-105-par	● Active	ObjectRead	waw/bemowo/105.pdf	Sun, Sep 29, 2019, 19:24:07 UTC	Sun, Oct 6, 2019, 24:00:00 UTC
				Showing 1 Item 〈 Page 1 〉	

Figure 5-16. *Viewing active pre-authenticated request in the OCI Console*

A pre-authenticated request can be created for a bucket as well. In this case, the only access type allowed is `AnyObjectWrite` the which effectively lets the URL holders manage all objects inside that bucket.

Cleanup

We will no longer need the object storage resources created during the exercises in this chapter. You can remove them. There is one exception to that. Do not remove the IAM policies. We will need them later.

This is how you can use the OCI CLI to remove the pre-authenticated request, the objects, and the blueprints bucket:

```
$ OS_PARID=`oci os preauth-request list -bn blueprints --query
"data[?name=='waw-bemowo-105-par'] | [0].id" --raw-output`
$ oci os preauth-request delete -bn blueprints --par-id $OS_PARID
Are you sure you want to delete this resource? [y/N]: y
$ oci os object bulk-delete -bn blueprints
WARNING: This command will delete 16 objects. Are you sure you want to
continue? [y/N]: y
$ oci os bucket delete -bn blueprints
Are you sure you want to delete this resource? [y/N]: y
```

Removing the objects will stop the billing charges for the storage space they occupy.

Summary

Object storage was the primary topic of this chapter. At the beginning, we talked about objects and how they are organized into buckets. Afterward, you learned some basic object manipulation techniques using the CLI. What came then was the discussion about the importance of object name prefixes and CLI-based examples on how to use them properly. Additionally, I described the bulk commands that come with the CLI and presented how to use the object storage API to list objects in pages and thus handle large sets of objects in a safe way. We also covered the aspect of concurrent updates and the role of ETags in this context. A large part of this chapter was devoted to programming object storage. You learned how to use the OCI SDK for Python to handle multipart uploads and let applications authenticate as instance principals. You were also able to familiarize yourself with the concept of defined tags and use them in a matching rule of a dynamic group. Finally, I briefly presented the ways to let anonymous users access the objects either thanks to public buckets or through pre-authenticated requests. In the next chapter, we will explore some fundamental patterns that you are going to apply to your compute and networking cloud resources in Oracle Cloud Infrastructure.

CHAPTER 6

Patterns for Compute and Networking

The practice of information technology attaches great importance to the notion of *reusability*, which does not limit itself to software libraries, modules, or services, but is often expressed in a form of *architectural patterns*. In this chapter, I am going to guide you through some basic cloud infrastructure patterns that are meant to help to solve the standard problems you often encounter while designing cloud solutions. This chapter is meant to be a loose discussion built around hands-on exercises. It is not supposed to be a comprehensive catalog with architectural patterns.

If you recall Chapter 2 and what you read there about planning cloud infrastructure in Oracle Cloud, it becomes clear that you start designing cloud infrastructure by preparing the appropriate compartment hierarchy and outlining virtual networking. In Chapter 4, I described aspects related to the use of compartments. Now, we are going to look at virtual cloud networks.

Virtual Networking

A *virtual cloud network* is a software-defined network used to organize and provide connectivity between compute instances. It has regional scope, which means that you create each VCN in one particular Oracle Cloud region. A VCN alone is useless unless you split it into *subnets*. Both VCNs and their subnets are conceptually close to traditional networks that employ IP addressing and address range division. If you've followed the previous chapters, you've already gained some hands-on experiences with VCN-related resources. Furthermore, you probably remember well that every compute instance must exist in the context of a particular virtual cloud network. To be more precise, every compute instance must be attached to at least one subnet through one

279

© Michał Tomasz Jakóbczyk 2020
M. T. Jakóbczyk, *Practical Oracle Cloud Infrastructure*, https://doi.org/10.1007/978-1-4842-5506-3_6

or more virtual network interface cards (VNICs). A subnet can be bound to a specific availability domain or span all availability domains within the entire region. The first type is known as an *AD-specifc subnet*, while the latter is known as a *regional subnet*. Both subnet types are shown in Figure 6-1.

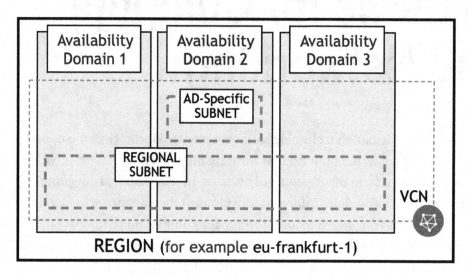

Figure 6-1. *Regional and AD-specific subnets*

The regional scope of a particular subnet is usually seen as more flexible because it makes it possible to create compute instances in different availability domains, simultaneously keeping them attached to the very same subnet. Why would we ever need to use an AD-specific subnet instead of a regional subnet? Initially, a subnet always had to be created within a particular availability domain. In other words, in the beginning, only AD-specific subnets were possible, which imposed the necessity to use multiple subnets when designing highly available solutions that rely on multiple ADs. With the arrival of regional subnets, you may stick to using them in the majority of cases. Moreover, Oracle recommends using regional subnets if possible. It does make sense to employ AD-specific subnets in a situation in which you want to add a layer of control that all instances attached to that subnet are always created in a particular AD.

Private IPs

As soon as a new compute instance has been launched, its VNIC receives a private IPv4 address from the IP address range of the subnet to which the VNIC is attached. This is the *primary private IP* address. The address itself can be chosen by you or automatically selected by the Oracle Cloud control plane. It is not possible to remove or change the primary private IP on an existing instance. Its lifecycle is strictly associated with the lifetime of the compute instance, which means that the primary private IP gets terminated on the instance's destruction. The private IP address lets your instance communicate with other instances, as presented in Figure 6-2, in the same or, what you will learn soon, other interconnected VCNs. Optionally, it is used in the data exchange with the machines in an on-premise network if FastConnect or VPN is in place.

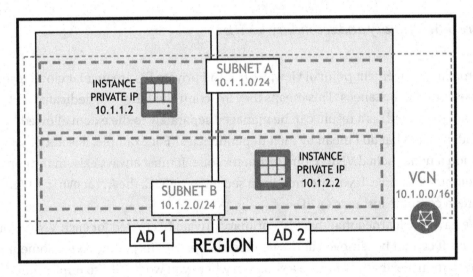

Figure 6-2. *Private IPs*

If there is a "primary" VNIC, there must be a notion of "secondary" VNIC; otherwise, the name wouldn't make a lot of sense, would it? Indeed, it is possible to create *secondary VNICs* on a single instance. This is actually the way to go if your intention is to attach an instance to more than one subnet. Figure 6-3 shows a list of VNICs of a single compute instance. Each VNIC is in this case attached to a different subnet. Adding a secondary VNIC is just a first step in providing multisubnet connectivity. Depending on instance shape and image, you will still have to configure a new network interface within the operating system.

Attached VNICs

Create VNIC

VNIC ATTACHED	**multisubnet-instance** *(Primary VNIC)* OCID: ...4pcqoa Show Copy **Attached:** Sun, 21 Apr 2019 22:04:32 GMT **Compartment:** Sandbox	**Private IP Address:** 10.1.1.4 **Fully Qualified Domain Name:** *Unavailable* **Public IP Address:** 130.61.89.6	**Subnet:** sub1 **Skip Source/Destination Check:** No **MAC Address:** 02:00:17:02:E9:A8 **VLAN Tag:** 1049	•••
VNIC ATTACHED	**sub2-vnic-multisubnet-instance** OCID: ...u4f35q Show Copy **Attached:** Sun, 21 Apr 2019 22:09:32 GMT **Compartment:** Sandbox	**Private IP Address:** 10.1.2.3 **Fully Qualified Domain Name:** *Unavailable* **Public IP Address:**	**Subnet:** sub2 **Skip Source/Destination Check:** No **MAC Address:** 02:00:17:02:AA:AF **VLAN Tag:** 1051	•••

Figure 6-3. *Primary and secondary VNICs*

From a management point of view, VNICs and private IPs are regular cloud resources just like compute instances. This means they are controlled through dedicated API endpoint paths and, as a result, can be managed separately to the extent allowed by their dependencies. What do I mean by their dependencies? For example, it is not possible to provision a nonattached VNIC cloud resource alone. It must always exist in the context of a compute instance. If you are creating a secondary VNIC, the `AttachVnic` API indeed requires a compute instance OCID.

We have just learned that there is a primary private IP created for each VNIC cloud resource. It cannot be removed and is deleted always with its parent VNIC. Sometimes, you need more flexibility. Imagine a situation where you would like to implement a floating IP architecture for the purpose of high availability. A floating IP is an IP address that can be moved from one compute instance to another, in this way enabling active-passive high availability. Should the current private IP holder abruptly fail, the passive instance, also known as the *standby*, would take over the floating IP, in this way securing service continuity. To implement such a scenario, you need to rely on a *secondary private IP* cloud resource in conjunction with cluster engine software such as Heartbeat or Corosync as well as a cluster resource manager such as Pacemaker. A secondary private IP can be added to any kind of VNIC (both primary and secondary). Another use case for attaching more than one private IP to an existing VNIC is having multiple services running on a single compute instance. Sometimes, you may find it useful to bind each of these services to a separate private IP. Figure 6-4 shows two private IP resources attached to a single VNIC.

Figure 6-4. *Primary and secondary private IP addresses*

Note   In most cases, you will be using compute instances with just a single VNIC and a single private IP each.

Public IPs

A compute instance may, but not need to, hold a public IP address. If you are using Oracle Cloud as a computing power extension or a managed database provider, it can be securely connected to your on-premise network using either FastConnect or VPN. In such a case, usually no direct connection to the Internet for your cloud instances is even desired. In such a situation, you access these compute instances from within your private on-premise network and the instances download updates and new software from some kind of a private artifact repository that stores various types of software such as RPM packages, npm and Maven libraries, Docker images, or even Helm charts. Nowadays, however, more and more especially newly established businesses are purely running in the cloud. In their case, access to the Internet is indispensable for at least a subset of compute instances.

Let's consider the simplest scenario for a solitary compute instance. The scenario that assumes a given instance has its own Internet identity, understood as a public IP address. There are usually three main reasons why an instance needs a public IP address.

- It hosts an application that exposes a public web service.

- Its operating system has to download updates or additional software.

- You want to establish an SSH connection to access terminal.

Public IP addresses can be assigned only to these compute instances that are attached to *public subnets*. You choose whether a subnet is public or private during subnet creation. In the OCI Console, this choice is pretty straightforward. You just have to tick the correct checkbox. You already trained it in the course of Chapter 2. When using an API, SDK, or CLI, on the other hand, you set the public or private nature of a particular subnet indirectly through a value of the `prohibitPublicIpOnVnic` element (API), the `prohibit_public_ip_on_vnic` key (Terraform), or the `--prohibit-public-ip-on-vnic` option (CLI). You already used it once if you followed Chapter 3. All in all, private subnets always prohibit attached instances from having a public IP on the VNIC attached to the private subnet.

In a simple scenario, to access the Internet, apart from a public IP attached to an instance, three further conditions must be met.

- A VCN contains an active Internet gateway (IGW).

- A route rule directs outbound traffic to the IGW.

- Security rules allow a particular type of inbound and outbound traffic.

In the course of the previous chapters, you had multiple opportunities to work with these resources in the Console as well as using the CLI and Terraform.

How is a public IP address actually attached to an instance? From a management point of view, a public IP cloud resource is always associated with a private IP cloud resource. For the majority of use cases, this happens in the background, and you do not even need to do anything special about that. Because there is a finite number of public IPv4 addresses, Oracle Cloud uses public IP address pools. By default, a newly created instance gets an available public IPv4 address from the Oracle Cloud address pool, as shown in Figure 6-5. After an instance has been terminated, the address goes back to the pool and may be reused in the future, also by other customers. This is called an *ephemeral public IP*. Its lifecycle is strictly tied to a particular compute instance.

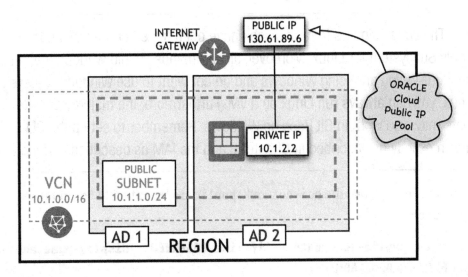

Figure 6-5. *Internet-facing compute instance*

For development purposes, it seems fine to rely on dynamically assigned and, to some extent, random public IPv4 addresses. If you consider production systems, however, you would truly benefit from gaining some more control over the public IP addresses. To do so, you can use *reserved public IPs*. Their lifecycle is completely independent from any other cloud resources. Furthermore, it is possible to attach them to and detach them from running compute instances. In contrary to an ephemeral public IP, a reserved public IP can remain unassigned, if you do not need it at a given point of time. This is how you reserve a new reserved public IP using the OCI Console:

1. Go to Menu ➤ Networking ➤ Public IPs.

2. Make sure that the Sandbox compartment is selected.

3. Click Create Reserved Public IP.

4. Provide a new display name, for example, **my-ip**.

5. Click Create.

From now on, a newly reserved public IP will be ready to be assigned to a compute instance of your choice.

> **Note**   The code snippets from this book have been tested on macOS and
> Windows Subsystem for Linux. Moreover, all commands should work on major Linux
> distributions. If you are using Windows and do not want to use Windows Subsystem
> for Linux, you can always run Linux on a VM. Furthermore, the majority of code
> snippets may also work in Git Bash on Windows. Remember to set up the CLI and
> Terraform exactly as described in Chapter 3 and the IAM as described in Chapter 4.

As always, you can use the `oci network public-ip create` CLI command to
perform the same action.

```
$ oci network public-ip create --lifetime RESERVED --display-name another-
ip --profile SANDBOX-ADMIN
{
  "data": {
    "assigned-entity-id": null,
    "assigned-entity-type": null,
    "availability-domain": null,
    "compartment-id": "ocid1.compartment.oc1..aa.........gzwhsa",
    "defined-tags": {},
    "display-name": "another-ip",
    "freeform-tags": {},
    "id": "ocid1.publicip.oc1.eu-frankfurt-1.aa.........mkawlq",
    "ip-address": "130.61.68.218",
    "lifecycle-state": "AVAILABLE",
    "lifetime": "RESERVED",
    "private-ip-id": null,
    "scope": "REGION",
    "time-created": "2019-04-22T16:50:41.982000+00:00"
  },
  "etag": "34e061ab"
}
```

If you read the previous chapter, you know that we have prepared and are using the SANDBOX-ADMIN profile to execute the CLI commands as the sandbox-admin user. The --lifetime RESERVED parameter is used to tell the API that we would like to create a new reserved public IP. Figure 6-6 presents the two new reserved public IP addresses in the OCI Console.

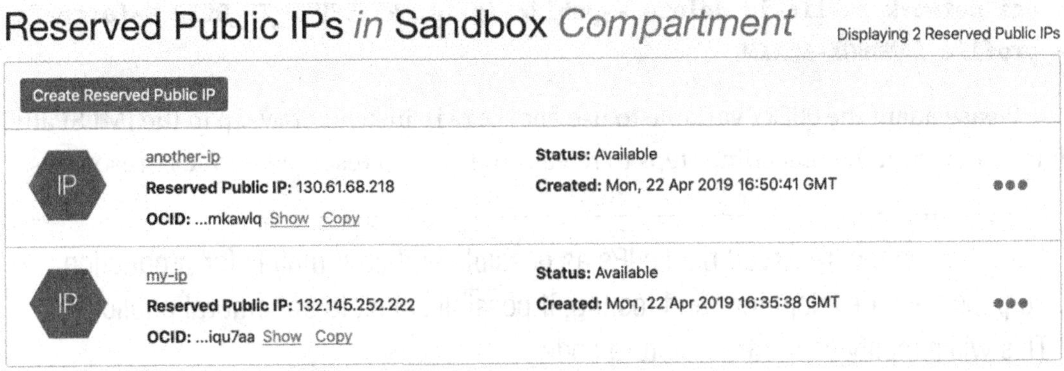

Reserved Public IPs *in* Sandbox *Compartment*   Displaying 2 Reserved Public IPs

Create Reserved Public IP

IP	another-ip	Status: Available	
	Reserved Public IP: 130.61.68.218	Created: Mon, 22 Apr 2019 16:50:41 GMT	•••
	OCID: ...mkawlq Show Copy		
IP	my-ip	Status: Available	
	Reserved Public IP: 132.145.252.222	Created: Mon, 22 Apr 2019 16:35:38 GMT	•••
	OCID: ...iqu7aa Show Copy		

Figure 6-6. Viewing reserved public IPs in the OCI Console

To list reserved public IPs using the CLI, you have to use the oci network public-ip list command like this:

```
$ oci network public-ip list --lifetime RESERVED --scope REGION --query
'data[*].{IP:"ip-address",Name:"display-name",State:"lifecycle-state"}'
--output table --all --profile SANDBOX-ADMIN
+-----------------+------------+-----------+
| IP              | Name       | State     |
+-----------------+------------+-----------+
| 130.61.68.218   | another-ip | AVAILABLE |
| 132.145.252.222 | my-ip      | AVAILABLE |
+-----------------+------------+-----------+
```

In the preceding example, I have employed the JMESPath filter and tabular output to increase the clarity of the response. To read more about it, please refer to the previous chapters.

We are now going to use the CLI to free up the two reserved public IPs because, in our exercises, we are going to use ephemeral public IPs. You can use the following CLI commands to terminate each reserved public IP cloud resource:

```
$ RESERVED_IP_NAME="my-ip"
$ QUERY="data[?\"display-name\" == '$RESERVED_IP_NAME'].id | [0]"
$ RESERVED_IP_OCID=`oci network public-ip list --scope REGION --lifetime
RESERVED --query "$QUERY" --all --profile SANDBOX-ADMIN | tr -d '"'`
$ echo $RESERVED_IP_OCID
ocid1.publicip.oc1.eu-frankfurt-1.aa.........6glghq
$ oci network public-ip delete --public-ip-id $RESERVED_IP_OCID --force
--profile SANDBOX-ADMIN
```

Please adapt the QUERY variable to use another-ip instead of my-ip in the JMESPath filter and repeat the preceding steps to release the second reserved public IP resources.

Tip   Use as few reserved public IPs as possible and do it mainly for production purposes. For development and testing, if possible, stick to ephemeral public IPs. This will simplify your infrastructure code.

In addition to compute instances, there are other cloud resource types that can use public IP addresses including public load balancers and NAT gateways. When you provision a public load balancer, a new reserved public IP address is automatically added to your account. You can see it in the OCI Console, in the same way as described in the previous paragraph. You cannot detach it from the load balancer, however. The lifecycle is tied to the load balancer, which means that the reserved public IP address that came together with a newly provisioned public load balancer will be deleted as soon as the load balancer has been terminated. NAT gateways use ephemeral public IP addresses. We are going to discuss that type of gateway in the next section.

We've mentioned that public subnets allow you to assign public IPs to the compute instances, while private subnets don't. This simple rule helps a lot when designing and governing your cloud infrastructure because you can be sure that all compute instances attached to private subnets never use public IPs. In this way, one possible breach path is closed.

Private Subnets, Bastion, and NAT

Private subnets isolate compute instances from the public Internet by design. The fact that an instance cannot use a public IP makes it, in a certain degree, invisible from the outside world. Earlier, I mentioned the three basic reasons for an instance to have a public IP.

- It hosts an application that exposes a public web service.

- Its operating system has to download updates or additional software.

- You want to establish an SSH connection to access the Terminal.

As a matter of fact, it is possible to address all three, even if a particular instance is running without a public IP in an isolated, private subnet. To do so, we are going to apply the cloud infrastructure pattern that employs a *bastion host* and a *NAT gateway*. Let's consider two goals for applications hosted on compute instances.

- Running isolated workloads

- Exposing web services

Applications that execute *isolated workloads* may run periodic batch jobs over data in object storage or a managed database. Other more exciting examples are high-performance computing (HCP) tasks such as 3D rendering, fluid dynamics, or biological simulations. Hosts to which these applications are deployed rarely expose public web services. Instead, they can be treated as isolated backend systems. Yet, sometimes, you still want to access this instance over SSH in order to perform some housekeeping tasks. This becomes a task for a *bastion host*, a dedicated instance provisioned in a public subnet that holds a public IP. To access instances in private subnets, you simply tunnel your SSH connection over the bastion host. The next aspects are outbound connections from isolated instances. Operating systems and applications must at least be able to download updates. If no private artifact registry with proper mirrors is available within your private network, you may need to let these hosts access public repositories on the Internet. In your VCN, you deploy and redirect the outbound traffic to a *NAT gateway*. The gateway's public IP becomes the source IP address seen in the Internet for the isolated instances running in private subnets that send their outbound traffic to the gateway. In addition to the responses associated with the outbound traffic, a NAT gateway does not let any other inbound traffic enter your VCN. Simple and secure. Figure 6-7 presents a simplified infrastructure for an isolated workload use case, as described earlier.

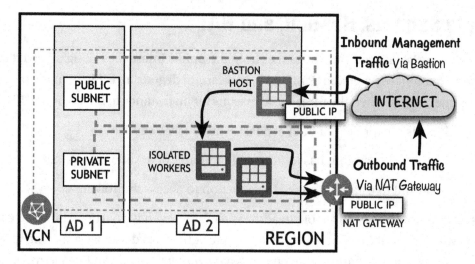

Figure 6-7. *Isolated workload infrastructure*

It is clear that applications that expose public web services must be reachable from the public Internet. In their case, you usually deploy a highly available load balancer to front the Internet and evenly distribute traffic to the application hosts grouped together in one or more backend sets. In this way, it is possible to place the backend set hosts in private subnets, reducing unnecessary exposure and public IP address consumption. To support remote management and access to updates, we rely on the bastion host and NAT gateway. Figure 6-8 presents this use case, as described earlier.

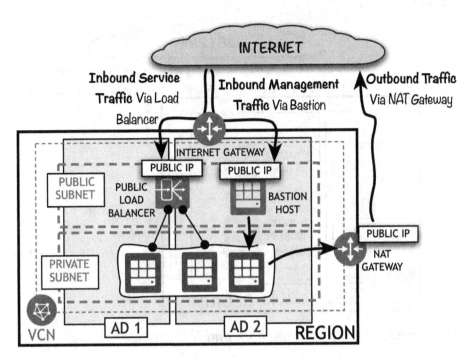

Figure 6-8. *Public web services infrastructure*

We are now going to provision a simplified infrastructure that supports the isolated workload use case. In a private subnet, we are going to launch a CentOS-based instance equipped with two OCPUs. This will be our worker node with no Internet identity and therefore no public IP address. To access the worker node over SSH, we are going to launch another, less powerful instance in a public subnet. This instance, called a *bastion host*, will hold a public IP address that will let us reach it from the Internet. In this way, we'll be able to tunnel SSH connections and access the worker node terminal. Finally, a NAT gateway will allow the worker node to access the Internet. The target infrastructure is presented in Figure 6-9.

Warning   Before doing the hands-on exercises covered in this chapter, you have to make sure your service limits allow you to launch at least one instance of the VM.Standard2.2 shape in each AD of the region you are working in. In the OCI Console, go to Menu ➤ Governance ➤ Limits, Quotas and Usage and search for *VM.Standard2.2*. If the limit is set to 0, please click Request a Service Limit Increase, fill in the form accordingly, and submit the form.

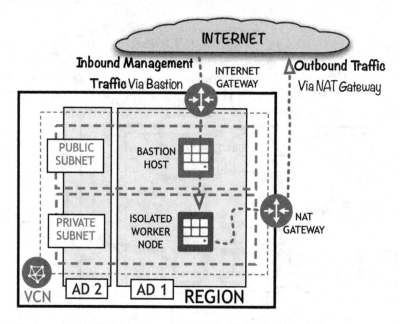

Figure 6-9. *Isolated worker, bastion host, and NAT gateway*

The infrastructure code is in a huge part identical to what we have already deployed a couple of times. You should be familiar with many elements. There are some new things, though. Go to the chapter06/1-bastion-nat directory. The infrastructure code assumes the SSH public key is located at the ~/.ssh/oci_id_rsa.pub path. You will also need the corresponding private key to access the provisioned compute instance remotely. In the infrastructure subfolder, run the terraform init command to download the newest OCI plugin and execute the terraform apply command to provision the infrastructure.

```
$ source ~/tfvars.env.sh
$ cd ~/git
$ cd oci-book/chapter06/1-bastion-nat/infrastructure/
$ find . -name "*.tf"
./modules.tf
./bastion/compute.tf
./bastion/vcn.tf
./bastion/vars.tf
./vcn.tf
./workers/compute.tf
./workers/vcn.tf
```

```
./workers/vars.tf
./provider.tf
./vars.tf
```

$ terraform init
```
Initializing modules...
- module.bastion
  Getting source "bastion"
- module.workers
  Getting source "workers"

Initializing provider plugins...
- Checking for available provider plugins on https://releases.hashicorp.com...
- Downloading plugin for provider "oci" (3.45.0)...

* provider.oci: version = "~> 3.45"

Terraform has been successfully initialized!
```

$ terraform apply -auto-approve
```
Apply complete! Resources: 11 added, 0 changed, 0 destroyed.

Outputs:

bastion_public_ip = 130.61.53.185
worker_public_ip = 10.0.1.130
image_name = CentOS-7-2019.04.15-0
```
$ BASTION_PUBLIC_IP=`terraform output bastion_public_ip`

Wait until you see the public IP assigned to your newly provisioned bastion host
that has been deployed in a public subnet. This time, in my case, it is 130.61.53.185. You
should now see the two new instances in the OCI Console, as shown in Figure 6-10: one
bastion host instance in a public subnet and one worker node in a private subnet.

Figure 6-10. *Viewing bastion and worker instances in the OCI Console*

You may need to wait a couple of seconds until the ssh daemon starts accepting connections. Let's connect to the worker node, jumping over the bastion host.

If you are working on Windows either using Windows Subsystem for Linux or using GitBash, you may need to start the ssh-agent first.

```
$ eval `ssh-agent -s`
Agent pid 290
```

Now, you should be ready to establish a connection to the worker node in the private subnet over the bastion host in a public subnet.

```
$ ssh-add ~/.ssh/oci_id_rsa
Identity added: /Users/mjk/.ssh/oci_id_rsa
```

```
$ ssh -J opc@$BASTION_PUBLIC_IP opc@10.0.1.130
[opc@worker-vm ~]$
```

To access the worker's terminal, we have added our private key to the authentication agent and executed ssh with the -J option to use the SSH ProxyJump technique. To verify whether the instance in a private subnet is indeed able to access the Internet, we will try to ping one of the Google's public DNS servers.

```
[opc@worker-vm ~]$ ping -c 3 8.8.8.8
PING 8.8.8.8 (8.8.8.8) 56(84) bytes of data.
64 bytes from 8.8.8.8: icmp_seq=1 ttl=123 time=24.0 ms
64 bytes from 8.8.8.8: icmp_seq=2 ttl=123 time=0.417 ms
64 bytes from 8.8.8.8: icmp_seq=3 ttl=123 time=0.377 ms
```

```
--- 8.8.8.8 ping statistics ---
3 packets transmitted, 3 received, 0% packet loss, time 2001ms
rtt min/avg/max/mdev = 0.377/8.294/24.088/11.168 ms
[opc@worker-vm ~]$ exit
$
```

As you can see, even though the worker instance doesn't have a public IP, it is both reachable over SSH via the bastion host and can access the Internet through the NAT gateway. It's time to take a brief look at the most interesting, from this section's point of view, resources in the infrastructure code. Listing 6-1 presents the vcn.tf file where we define the VCN, Internet gateway, and NAT gateway.

Listing 6-1. vcn.tf (Root Module)

```
resource "oci_core_virtual_network" "vcn" {
  compartment_id = var.compartment_ocid
  cidr_block = var.vcn_cidr
  display_name = "bastionnat-vcn"
  dns_label = "a"
}
resource "oci_core_internet_gateway" "igw" {
  compartment_id = var.compartment_ocid
  vcn_id = oci_core_virtual_network.vcn.id
  display_name = "internet-gateway"
}
resource "oci_core_nat_gateway" "natgw" {
  compartment_id = var.compartment_ocid
  vcn_id = oci_core_virtual_network.vcn.id
  display_name = "nat-gateway"
  block_traffic = false
}
```

Both types of gateways are created within the VCN. The Internet gateway (igw) effectively provides both inbound and outbound connectivity to these instances that are attached to public subnets whose route table contains a route rule that targets the Internet gateway for non-VCN traffic. The NAT gateway (natgw), in essence, is meant to serve only outbound traffic from instances in private subnets whose route table contains a route rule that targets the NAT gateway for non-VCN traffic. These roles are conceptually presented in Figure 6-11.

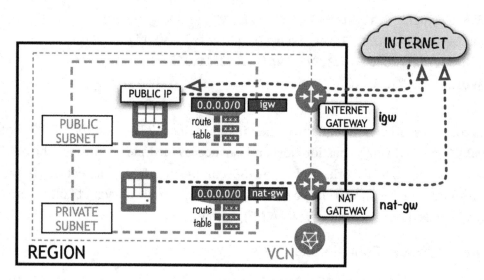

Figure 6-11. *Routing rules for Internet and NAT gateways*

To follow best practices, we have used modules in our infrastructure code. The bastion module is responsible for creating a public subnet with a dedicated route table and security list as well as launching the bastion instance attached to the public subnet. The workers module creates a private subnet, together with a dedicated route table and security list, and launches a worker instance that is attached to the private subnet. Because the routing rules are created within each module, we have to pass the OCID of both gateways as input variables. Listing 6-2 presents an excerpt from the modules.tf file that shows how it is done.

Listing 6-2. *modules.tf (Root Module)*

```
...
module "bastion" {
  source = "./bastion"
  compartment_ocid = var.compartment_ocid
  vcn_ocid = oci_core_virtual_network.vcn.id
  vcn_igw_ocid = oci_core_internet_gateway.igw.id
  vcn_cidr = oci_core_virtual_network.vcn.cidr_block
  vcn_subnet_cidr = "10.0.1.0/27"
  ads = data.oci_identity_availability_domains.ads.availability_domains[*].name
  image_ocid = data.oci_core_images.centos_image.images[0].id
}
```

```
module "workers" {
  source = "./workers"
  compartment_ocid = var.compartment_ocid
  vcn_ocid = oci_core_virtual_network.vcn.id
  vcn_nat_ocid = oci_core_nat_gateway.natgw.id
  vcn_cidr = oci_core_virtual_network.vcn.cidr_block
  vcn_subnet_cidr = "10.0.1.128/27"
  ads = data.oci_identity_availability_domains.ads.availability_domains[*].name
  image_ocid = data.oci_core_images.centos_image.images[0].id
}
...
```

The variable that carries the OCID of the Internet gateway into the bastion module is, in my case, called vcn_igw_ocid. You learned in Chapter 3 that the module input variable names are arbitrary. You just need to make sure you are referencing them properly within the module. If you look at the bastion/vcn.tf file, you will see that the OCID of the Internet gateway becomes a target for all non-VCN traffic. Listing 6-3 presents the relevant part of the bastion/vcn.tf file.

Listing 6-3. vcn.tf (Bastion Module)

```
resource "oci_core_route_table" "bastion_rt" {
  compartment_id = var.compartment_ocid
  vcn_id = var.vcn_ocid
  route_rules {
    network_entity_id = var.vcn_igw_ocid
    destination_type = "CIDR_BLOCK"
    destination = "0.0.0.0/0"
  }
  display_name = "bastion-rt"
}
```

Similarly, we are using the vcn_nat_ocid variable to pass the OCID of the NAT gateway, this time into the workers module. Listing 6-4 shows the definition of the route table used by the private subnet to which the worker node is attached.

Listing 6-4. vcn.tf (Workers Module)

```
resource "oci_core_route_table" "workers_rt" {
  compartment_id = var.compartment_ocid
  vcn_id = var.vcn_ocid
  route_rules {
    network_entity_id = var.vcn_nat_ocid
    destination_type = "CIDR_BLOCK"
    destination = "0.0.0.0/0"
  }
  display_name = "workers-rt"
}
```

If you ever need to temporarily block the outbound traffic from your private instances to the public Internet, you can do this using just one simple switch. NAT gateways can be set to block traffic. To test this feature, go to the vcn.tf file in the root module and set the block_traffic attribute to true, as shown in Listing 6-5.

Listing 6-5. vcn.tf (Root Module)

```
...
resource "oci_core_nat_gateway" "natgw" {
  compartment_id = var.compartment_ocid
  vcn_id = oci_core_virtual_network.vcn.id
  display_name = "nat-gateway"
  block_traffic = true
}
```

As soon as you apply changes, Terraform will detect that the expected state represented by your .tf files is different from what it finds in the refreshed state file. The calculated plan will perform the relevant API call(s) to set the NAT gateway to block the traffic.

```
$ terraform apply -auto-approve
...
oci_core_nat_gateway.natgw: Modifying... (ID: ocid1.natgateway.oc1.eu-
frankfurt-1.........6n76gq)
  block_traffic: "false" => "true"
oci_core_nat_gateway.natgw: Modifications complete after 0s
```

Apply complete! Resources: 0 added, 1 changed, 0 destroyed.

Outputs:

```
bastion_public_ip = 130.61.53.185
worker_public_ip = 10.0.1.130
image_name  = CentOS-7-2019.04.15-0
```

You can now verify in the OCI Console that the NAT gateway has been effectively disabled. To do so, follow these steps:

1. Go to Menu ➤ Networking ➤ Virtual Cloud Networks.

2. Make sure that the Sandbox compartment is selected.

3. Click the VCN name (bastionnat-vcn).

4. In the Resources section, click NAT Gateways.

You should see the NAT gateway grayed out with its status set to blocking traffic, as shown in Figure 6-12. The public IP you see for the NAT gateway is an ephemeral public IP.

Figure 6-12. *Viewing how to disable NAT gateway in the OCI Console*

This time, you should not be able to ping the Google public DNS server. Let's test it. Connect to the worker instance using SSH over the bastion host and issue the ping command.

```
$ ssh -J opc@$BASTION_PUBLIC_IP opc@10.0.1.130
...
[opc@worker-vm ~]$ ping -c 5 8.8.8.8
PING 8.8.8.8 (8.8.8.8) 56(84) bytes of data.

--- 8.8.8.8 ping statistics ---
5 packets transmitted, 0 received, 100% packet loss, time 3999ms
[opc@worker-vm ~]$ exit
$
```

This concludes the hands-on exercise with a bastion host and NAT gateway. You can now terminate the infrastructure.

```
$ terraform destroy -auto-approve
...
Destroy complete! Resources: 11 destroyed.
```

In addition to the two route rules we have created for each subnet, there are also dedicated security lists. This will be the last element we are going to discuss based on the infrastructure code you've just terminated.

Security Rules

Security rules provide an additional layer of a virtual firewall that protects compute instances by explicitly allowing the traffic they describe. Virtual cloud networks follow the deny-all principle by default; therefore, to let different kinds of specialized traffic pass through, proper security rules must be put in place. Security lists and rules were already briefly introduced at the beginning, back in Chapter 2. In the course of this book, you used them every time you deployed and tested the cloud infrastructure with compute instances. You already know that every subnet must have at least one associated *security list*, which is a collection of security rules. *Security rules* always define what is allowed, so to deny a particular type of traffic, you just need to make sure there are no rules that allow it. The rules are enforced before packets reach the compute instance. Security rules are categorized based on their direction as *ingress* (inbound) and *egress* (outbound). Security rule statelessness impacts how response traffic is handled. For a *stateful* rule, if outbound traffic is allowed based on an egress rule, the corresponding response packets are automatically allowed. In the case of a *stateless* rule, we still need an explicit stateless rule in the opposite direction, as conceptually illustrated in Figure 6-13.

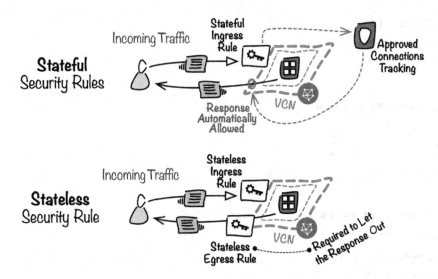

Figure 6-13. *Stateless and stateful security rules*

It is no surprise that Oracle Cloud has to track the connections allowed by stateful rules to be able to automatically permit the corresponding responses. This comes at a cost of a slight increase in latency. Furthermore, every type of instance shape has a limit for the allowed number of tracked connections.

Tip   Use stateless rules whenever possible to avoid the connection tracking performance penalty that occurs for the stateful rules and avoid hitting. In this way, you will avoid hitting the limit on the number of tracked connections.

If there are two security rules, one stateless and one stateful, that overlap for some particular traffic, the stateless rule takes priority, and you must make sure that there is a corresponding stateless rule that will allow related response traffic.

Listing 6-6 presents the definition of a security list element from the bastion/vcn.tf file.

Listing 6-6. vcn.tf (Bastion Module)

```
...
resource "oci_core_security_list" "bastion_sl" {
  compartment_id = var.compartment_ocid
  vcn_id = var.vcn_ocid
  egress_security_rules {
```

```
        stateless=true
        destination=var.vcn_cidr
        protocol="all"
    }
    egress_security_rules {
        stateless=false
        destination="0.0.0.0/0"
        protocol="all"
    }
    ingress_security_rules {
        stateless=true
        source=var.vcn_cidr
        protocol="all"
    }
    ingress_security_rules {
        stateless=false
        source="0.0.0.0/0"
        protocol="6"
        tcp_options {
            min=22
            max=22
        }
    }
    display_name = "bastion-sl"
}
...
```

The bastion_sl security list contains one *stateless* (stateless=true) *ingress rule*
that allows the entire (protocol = "all") incoming traffic from instances in the same
VCN (source=var.vcn_cidr) to which the subnet belongs and one *stateless egress rule*
that, similarly, accepts the entire outgoing traffic to the instances attached to any subnet
in the same VCN (destination=var.vcn_cidr) to which the bastion public subnet
belongs. The resulting rules are shown in Figure 6-14.

Stateless Security Rules for the Intra-VCN (10.0.1.0/24)Traffic

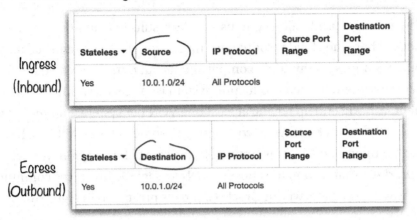

Figure 6-14. *Intra-VCN traffic stateless rules for the bastion subnet*

To allow two-way communication initiated by the incoming SSH connections (protocol="6" tcp_options { min=22 max=22 }) from any host (source="0.0.0.0/0"), the security list contains one *stateful* (stateless=false) *ingress rule*. Finally, the bastion host alone benefits from a *stateful egress rule* that allows any kind (protocol = "all") of two-way packet exchange initiated by the outbound traffic sent to any host (destination="0.0.0.0/0") and coming from the public subnet the instance is attached to. The resulting rules are shown in Figure 6-15.

Stateful Security Rules for All Remaining Traffic

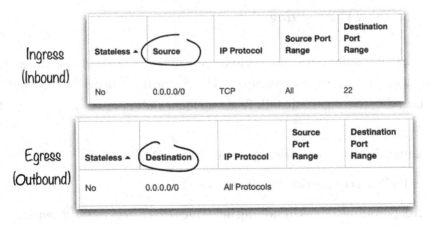

Figure 6-15. *Stateful rules for the bastion subnet*

VCN Peering

Working with multiple production systems usually results in a number of separate compartments where the cloud resources for these production systems reside. The VCN cloud resource cannot span multiple compartments but must be created inside one particular compartment. If each production system is managed within its own dedicated compartment, you will end up having at least one VCN per system. Sooner or later, you are going to face the challenge of connecting to some of these systems, based on business requirements. For systems running in the same cloud region, you will use the *local VCN peering* to connect to the chosen VCNs and let the instances communicate using their private addresses within Oracle Cloud, as presented in Figure 6-16.

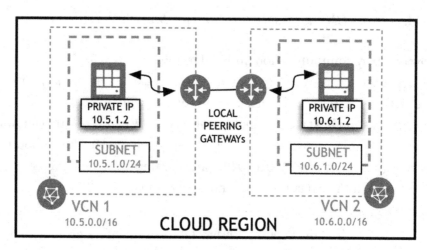

Figure 6-16. *Local VCN peering*

An important requirement that has to be considered already during the early planning stage is the fact that two connected VCNs must not use overlapping IP address ranges. If they did, routing would fail. To set up local VCN peering, you need to do the following:

- Create *local peering gateways* (LPG) in both VCNs.

- Establish a connection between LPGs.

- Adapt routing tables by adding new rules that direct traffic intended for the other VCN to LPGs.

- Make sure the security rules allow traffic to and from the other VCN.

A local peering gateway is just an ordinary cloud resource that is created within the VCN just like the Internet gateway or NAT gateway you've already worked with. If your user is entitled to manage both VCNs, creating a connection is pretty straightforward. You just need to point to the other LPG and the peering status should indicate a successful connection, as shown in Figure 6-17.

Name	State	Peering Status	Route Table ⓘ	Peer Advertised CIDR
idm-lpg	● Available	Peered - Connected to a peer.		10.5.0.0/16

Figure 6-17. *Connected local peering gateway*

When dealing with production systems, however, there is some chance that the other VCN is managed by someone else. In such a case, you need to agree on who is going to initiate the connection. If the admin users do not have full management access to their own compartments, you have to make sure that the requestor belongs to a group that holds the manage local-peering-from rights. The acceptor belongs to a group that holds the managed local-peering-to rights. Both IAM policy resource types (local-peering-from and local-peering-to) belong to the virtual-network-family. To learn more about IAM policies, please refer to Chapter 4.

As soon as the LPGs have been successfully connected, the VCN peering is in place. Now, you have to adapt the routing tables in both VCNs. Basically, new route rules that direct the traffic intended for the other VCN must be added on both sides. The target network entity is the LPG, as shown in Figure 6-18, where the other VCN uses the 10.6.0.0/16 address range.

Destination	▲	Target Type	Target
0.0.0.0/0		Internet Gateway	idm-igw
10.5.0.0/16		Local Peering Gateway	idm-lpg

Showing 2 Item(s)

Figure 6-18. *Route rules for local VCN peering*

The last elements to add are the security rules. There is no exception here. Just like you would add new security rules for different subnets in the same VCN, you have to do the same for the subnets from the peered VCN. Please consider using stateless rules to avoid unnecessary connection tracking related to stateful rules.

VCN peering is a point-to-point connection. Any given VCN can be locally peered with up to ten other VCNs. In other words, you can have up to ten LPGs per VCN where each LPG represents one peered VCN, as shown in Figure 6-19. It does not sound very scalable, does it? Another important characteristic of peering to remember is the fact that instances in one VCN cannot use the Internet gateway in the peered VCN to access the Internet.

Name	State	Peering Status	Route Table (i)	Peer Advertised CIDR
ip-lpg-to-idm	● Available	Peered - Connected to a peer.		10.6.0.0/16
ip-lpg-to-mid	● Available	Peered - Connected to a peer.		10.7.0.0/16

Figure 6-19. *One LPG per one peered VCN*

In the case of a complex application landscape, you may either end up with a hard-to-manage local peering VCN spaghetti or hit the maximum limit of local peering connections. To alleviate these problems, there are two alternative architectures to consider.

- Using a dedicated compartment just for cloud networking

- Using a messaging platform as a service

Figure 6-20 presents a high-level sketch of an architecture in which there is a *dedicated networking compartment* with one large VCN that contains multiple subnets. Each subnet is dedicated to one production system. Production system instances are launched in their own compartments but, at the same time, are attached to subnets from the VCN in the networking compartment. This setup completely eliminates the need for local VCN peering, but this benefit may come at a cost of more complex IAM policies, especially if there are different compartment admin groups in place.

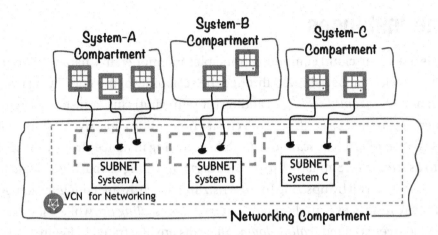

Figure 6-20. *Architecture based on a dedicated network compartment*

Another recommended way to go in the case of complex application landscapes that involve multiple production systems is to use a messaging platform as a service. Production systems send their messages to a messaging cluster that under the hood consists of multiple message brokers. If you choose a managed service, you won't need to worry about cluster management. To find out more, explore Oracle Cloud Infrastructure Streaming to see if it fits your purpose.

Until now, we discussed local VCN peering that assumed all connected VCNs are located in the same cloud region. To connect VCNs that reside in two different Oracle Cloud regions, you will employ *remote VCN peering*. This technique is to some extent similar but involves another type of cloud resource called a *dynamic routing gateway* (DRG). In rare cases, you might even want to connect to a VCN that resides in a different tenancy. *Cross-tenancy VCN peering* is also possible and requires granting additional IAM policies in both tenancies. You can find more information in the official documentation.

Up to that point, we focused on networking. We discussed cloud resources related to IP addresses, applied bastion host and NAT gateway patterns to allow private workers to securely communicate with the Internet, explained the types of security rules, and explored selected interconnectivity matters. Now, we will look closer at the aspects related to compute instances.

Scaling Instances

Elasticity is one of the cloud computing principles mentioned in Chapter 1. We said there that elasticity can be achieved through the scalability of the underlying resources. We also defined *horizontal scaling* as adding (or removing) cluster instances of the same kind to increase (or decrease) the overall cluster processing capacity. Adding more instances is often referred as *scaling out*, while removing instances from a cluster is referred to as *scaling in*. Similarly, we defined *vertical scaling* as making a single instance more (or less) powerful by upsizing (or downsizing) its hardware configuration. Adding more hardware resources is traditionally referred to as *scaling up*, while using less powerful resources is called *scaling down*. All terms are illustrated in Figure 6-21.

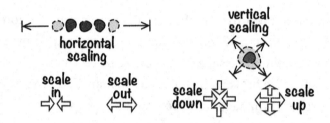

Figure 6-21. *Horizontal and vertical scaling*

In this section, we are going to discuss both types of scaling, first horizontal and then vertical.

Instance Pools and Autoscale

Horizontal scaling is typically performed against groups of homogeneous instances. Each of these instances uses the same hardware profile and base software stack. Furthermore, in the case of clustered applications whose members cooperate, the instance initialization logic should tell each member how to find others and establish the correct connections. To be able to rapidly scale out by launching new instances, we need some kind of instance template, something more than just a custom image you worked with in Chapter 2. This kind of instance template understood as a combination of hardware profile (shape), base software stack (image), and initialization logic (cloud-config for cloud-init) accompanied with some basic networking details is called an *instance configuration*. The instances provisioned based on an instance configuration are grouped into an *instance pool*. You can then set the expected number of instances for a particular pool and observe how the pool is scaled out (or in) by launching new (or terminating existing) instances. As time goes by, you can dynamically adjust the instance count so that the expected cluster processing capability is delivered. A single instance configuration can be used to provision multiple instance pools. You create instance configurations based on existing compute instances or, totally from scratch, using the API, usually through Terraform or the CLI. The relationship between an instance configuration and an instance pool is illustrated in Figure 6-22.

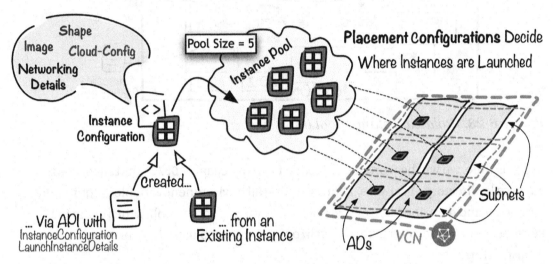

Figure 6-22. *Instance pool and instance configuration*

We are going to look closer at the way an instance pool works by provisioning a complete set of cloud resources. The pool will consist of instances launched in a private subnet and based on a custom instance configuration. To provide the isolated instances with proper connectivity to the Internet, we are going to employ the familiar pattern that relies on a bastion host and NAT gateway. The instance configuration will use the newest CentOS image, a simple cloud-init configuration that installs and executes a stress testing utility called `stress-ng`, the SSH public key, as well as some basic hardware profile info such as shape and VNIC details. Figure 6-23 presents the expected infrastructure for our exercise.

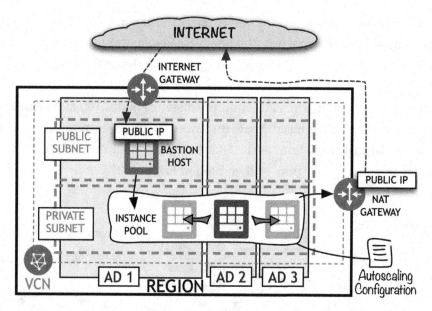

Figure 6-23. *Isolated instance pool infrastructure*

This time, we will be working with code from the chapter06/2-instance-pool-autoscale directory. As always, I am assuming all environment variables required by Terraform and described in Chapter 3 are present. The same applies the public SSH key that should be located at the ~/.ssh/oci_id_rsa.pub path. Let's provision the infrastructure.

```
$ cd ~/git
$ cd oci-book/chapter06/2-instance-pool-autoscale/infrastructure
$ find . \( -name "*.tf" -o -name "*.yaml" \)
./modules.tf
./bastion/compute.tf
./bastion/vcn.tf
./bastion/vars.tf
./vcn.tf
./workers/compute.tf
./workers/vcn.tf
./workers/cloud-init/worker.config.yaml
./workers/vars.tf
./provider.tf
./vars.tf
```

```
$ terraform init
Initializing modules...
- module.bastion
  Getting source "bastion"
- module.workers
  Getting source "workers"

Initializing provider plugins...
- Checking for available provider plugins on https://releases.hashicorp.com...
- Downloading plugin for provider "oci" (3.30.0)...

* provider.oci: version = "~> 3.30"

Terraform has been successfully initialized!

$ terraform apply -auto-approve
Apply complete! Resources: 13 added, 0 changed, 0 destroyed.

Outputs:

bastion_public_ip = 130.61.122.251
image_name = CentOS-7-2019.04.15-0

$ BASTION_PUBLIC_IP=`terraform output bastion_public_ip`
```

Before we connect to the worker node over the bastion host, let's see some of the newly provisioned cloud resources in the OCI Console.

1. Go to Menu ➤ Compute ➤ Instance Pools.

2. Make sure that the Sandbox compartment is selected.

You should see a new instance pool called workers-pool, as shown in Figure 6-24. The pool's placement configuration includes all three availability domains (ADs) in my default region (eu-frankurt-1). Whenever a new instance is added to the pool, it will be created in one of these ADs. If you look at Target Instance Count, you will see that, in our case, we started small by having only one target instance.

Name	Status	Availability Domain	Target Instance Count	Instance Configuration
workers-pool	● Running	AD-1, AD-2, AD-3	1	instance-config

Figure 6-24. *Viewing an instance pool in the OCI Console*

To find out more about the instance that is a member of the pool, follow these steps:

1. Click the name of the instance pool.

2. In the Resources section, make sure Created Instance is selected.

You should now see something similar to what is shown in Figure 6-25. This time, the worker instance landed in AD-1.

Name	Status	Availability Domain	Fault Domain	Instance Configuration
inst-pu327-workers-pool	● Running	AD-1	FD-3	instance-config

Figure 6-25. *Viewing the instance pool member in the OCI Console*

Let's inspect the instance in more detail. We are now going to find out the private IP assigned to the instance as well as monitor its current load. To do so, follow these steps:

1. Click the name of the instance.

2. Read the Private IP Address setting from the Primary VNIC Information section on the Instance Information tab of the Instance Details view. In my case, it is 10.1.2.2.

3. In the Resources section, make sure Metrics is selected.

4. Click the plot area of the CPU Utilization widget.

A new embedded window should appear in which you adjust the x-axis at the bottom to increase the readability of the plot even further. This is presented in Figure 6-26.

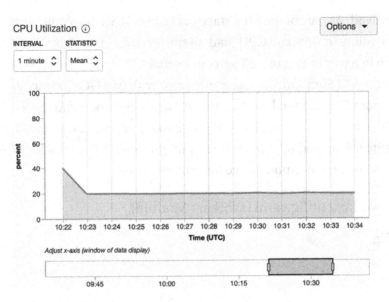

Figure 6-26. *Viewing instance CPU utilization in the OCI Console*

As you can see, the CPU consumption decreases from around 40 percent to 20 percent after the processes related to the initial boot have been completed. Why is an idle machine consuming 20 percent of the CPU? Is it actually idle? To see the reason, let's connect to the worker node. Of course, we have to rely on the bastion host because the worker node doesn't even have a public IP address.

```
$ ssh -J opc@$BASTION_PUBLIC_IP opc@10.1.2.2
[opc@inst-pu327-workers-pool ~]$ ps -axf -o %cpu,pid,command
%CPU    PID COMMAND
...
0.0 13531 /usr/bin/python /usr/bin/cloud-init modules -mode=final
 0.0 13776  \_ /bin/sh /var/lib/cloud/instance/scripts/runcmd
 0.0 13780      \_ stress-ng -c 0 -l 20
19.9 13785          \_ stress-ng -c 0 -l 20
20.0 13786          \_ stress-ng -c 0 -l 20
19.9 13787          \_ stress-ng -c 0 -l 20
19.9 13788          \_ stress-ng -c 0 -l 20
```

Mystery solved. As part of the final stage of cloud-init, we have intentionally executed the `stress-ng` utility to simulate CPU load on the instance. The `stress-ng` utility has been executed in a way to create a 20 percent overall CPU load on each vCPU. Because we have used the VM.Standard2.2 shape that ships with two OCPUs, the operating systems sees four vCPUs in total. As a result, the stress-ng forked four processes, each consuming 20 percent of a particular vCPU processing capacity. Listing 6-7 presents the cloud-config file referenced by the instance configuration that served as the template for the instances in the instance pool we've just provisioned.

Listing 6-7. worker.config.yaml (Workers Module)

```
#cloud-config
packages:
 - stress-ng
runcmd:
 -  [ stress-ng, -c, 0, -l, 20 ]
```

Let's take a look at the infrastructure code and go through the new resources you haven't had an opportunity to see until now. Listing 6-8 shows the first part of the `workers/compute.tf` file and covers the instance configuration resource.

Listing 6-8. compute.tf (Workers Module): Instance Configuration

```
...
resource "oci_core_instance_configuration" "worker_config" {
  compartment_id = var.compartment_ocid
  instance_details {
    instance_type = "compute"
    launch_details {
      compartment_id = var.compartment_ocid
      create_vnic_details {
        assign_public_ip = false
      }
      metadata = {
        ssh_authorized_keys = file("~/.ssh/oci_id_rsa.pub")
        user_data = base64encode(file("workers/cloud-init/worker.config.yaml"))
      }
```

```
    shape = "VM.Standard2.2"
    source_details {
      source_type = "image"
      image_id = var.image_ocid
    }
  }
}
display_name = "instance-config"
}
...
```

The oci_core_instance_configuration resource defines an instance configuration that, as we mentioned earlier, is a template applied by an instance pool while launching new instances. The most important details are defined in the launch_details object. As a matter of fact, their definition is similar to the oci_core_instance resource, which is the standard compute instance Terraform resource. The resulting instance configuration can be seen in the OCI Console, as shown in Figure 6-27.

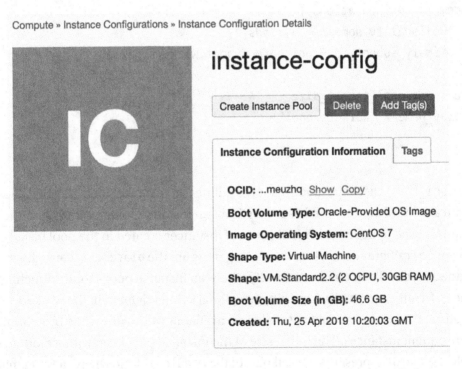

Compute » Instance Configurations » Instance Configuration Details

instance-config

Create Instance Pool   Delete   Add Tag(s)

Instance Configuration Information | Tags

OCID: ...meuzhq Show Copy

Boot Volume Type: Oracle-Provided OS Image

Image Operating System: CentOS 7

Shape Type: Virtual Machine

Shape: VM.Standard2.2 (2 OCPU, 30GB RAM)

Boot Volume Size (in GB): 46.6 GB

Created: Thu, 25 Apr 2019 10:20:03 GMT

Figure 6-27. *Viewing instance configuration details in the OCI Console*

Listing 6-9 shows the second part of the `workers/compute.tf` file and covers the instance pool resource.

Listing 6-9. compute.tf (Workers Module): Instance Pool

```
...
resource "oci_core_instance_pool" "worker_pool" {
  compartment_id = var.compartment_ocid
  instance_configuration_id = oci_core_instance_configuration.worker_
  config.id
  placement_configurations {
      availability_domain = var.ads[0]
      primary_subnet_id = oci_core_subnet.workers_net.id
  }
  placement_configurations {
      availability_domain = var.ads[1]
      primary_subnet_id = oci_core_subnet.workers_net.id
  }
  placement_configurations {
      availability_domain = var.ads[2]
      primary_subnet_id = oci_core_subnet.workers_net.id
  }
  size = var.pool_target_size
  display_name = "workers-pool"
}
...
```

The `oci_core_instance_pool` resource defines an instance pool. The `instance_configuration_id` argument takes the OCID of an instance configuration, and the `size` argument is used to define the initial count of instances created in the pool based on that instance configuration. Other interesting parts are the `placement_configurations` embedded blocks. Their elements specify where an instance pool should launch its instances. In our case, I am using a single regional subnet defined in the workers module and instruct the instance pool to use all three availability domains while provisioning any subsequent instances. The initial size of the instance pool is set with a module input variable. Listing 6-10 presents a small part of the `modules.tf` file where, among many different input parameters, you can see the value for the initial instance pool size.

Listing 6-10. modules.tf (Root Module)

```
...
module "workers" {
  source = "./workers"
  compartment_ocid = var.compartment_ocid
  vcn_ocid = oci_core_virtual_network.vcn.id
  vcn_nat_ocid = oci_core_nat_gateway.natgw.id
  vcn_cidr = oci_core_virtual_network.vcn.cidr_block
  vcn_subnet_cidr = "10.1.2.0/24"
  ads = data.oci_identity_availability_domains.ads.availability_domains[*].
  name
  image_ocid = data.oci_core_images.centos_image.images[0].id
  pool_target_size = 1
}
...
```

We are now going to explore the autoscaling capability of the instance pool we are working with. First, we are going to add much more CPU load on our worker node to simulate a heavy processing batch or a considerable peak of incoming requests. While still connected to the worker node, launch another stress-ng process.

```
[opc@inst-pu327-workers-pool ~]$ nohup stress-ng -c 0 -l 80 &
[1] 10834
[opc@inst-pu327-workers-pool ~]$ ps -axf -o %cpu,pid,command
%CPU   PID COMMAND
...
 0.0  5598 /usr/sbin/sshd -D
 0.1 10769  \_ sshd: opc [priv]
 0.0 10772      \_ sshd: opc@pts/1
 0.0 10773          \_ -bash
 0.0 10834              \_ stress-ng -c 0 -l 80
71.5 10835              |   \_ stress-ng -c 0 -l 80
71.0 10836              |   \_ stress-ng -c 0 -l 80
71.0 10837              |   \_ stress-ng -c 0 -l 80
71.1 10838              |   \_ stress-ng -c 0 -l 80
 0.0 10849                  \_ ps -axf -o %cpu,pid,command
```

```
0.0 13531 /usr/bin/python /usr/bin/cloud-init modules --mode=final
0.0 13776  \_ /bin/sh /var/lib/cloud/instance/scripts/runcmd
0.0 13780      \_ stress-ng -c 0 -l 20
19.9 13785         \_ stress-ng -c 0 -l 20
19.9 13786         \_ stress-ng -c 0 -l 20
19.9 13787         \_ stress-ng -c 0 -l 20
19.9 13788         \_ stress-ng -c 0 -l 20
...
[opc@inst-pu327-workers-pool ~]$ exit
```

To add some more CPU load, we launched a new stress-ng process instance. The preceding nohup command was used to let the stress-ng process continue even if we disconnect from the machine. After two or three minutes, the CPU utilization for the instance will report a large increase in load, as shown in Figure 6-28. Very good. Everything goes as expected.

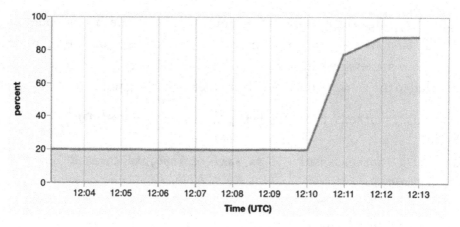

Figure 6-28. *Viewing increased CPU utilization in the instance's Metrics window*

In the meantime, we will look at the third part of the compute.tf file in the workers module, namely, the autoscaling configuration resource. The code is shown in Listing 6-11.

Listing 6-11. compute.tf (Workers Module): Autoscaling Configuration

```
...
resource "oci_autoscaling_auto_scaling_configuration" "workers_pool_
autoscale" {
```

```
compartment_id = var.compartment_ocid
auto_scaling_resources {
    id = oci_core_instance_pool.worker_pool.id
    type = "instancePool"
}
cool_down_in_seconds = 300
policies {
  capacity {
    initial = var.pool_target_size
    max = 3
    min = 1
  }
  policy_type = "threshold"
  rules {
    action {
      type = "CHANGE_COUNT_BY"
      value = 1
    }
    metric {
      metric_type = "CPU_UTILIZATION"
      threshold {
        operator = "GT"
        value = "70"
      }
    }
    display_name = "scale-out"
  }
  rules {
    action {
      type = "CHANGE_COUNT_BY"
      value = -1
    }
    metric {
      metric_type = "CPU_UTILIZATION"
      threshold {
        operator = "LT"
```

```
          value = "30"
        }
      }
      display_name = "scale-in"
    }
    display_name = "workers-pool-autoscale-policy"
  }
  display_name = "workers-pool-autoscale"
}
```

The oci_autoscaling_auto_scaling_configuration resource creates a new
autoscaling configuration and, at the same time, connects it to the instance pool.
Autoscaling adds some basic autonomous capabilities to an instance pool. You set the
criteria that define how an instance pool should react to changing conditions such as
increased (or decreased) processing load on instances that are instance pool members.
You could, for example, say that one new instance should be added to the pool whenever
the average instance pool CPU utilization performance metric exceeds 70 percent.
In an analogous way, one instance could be automatically taken down if the average
CPU utilization is lower than another threshold. The infrastructure code includes one
autoscaling policy with two rules. Both treat average instance pool CPU utilization as its
metric that drives autoscaling events. The first rule will cause the instance pool to scale
out by adding one instance if the average CPU utilization is greater than 70 percent. The
second rule will order the instance pool to scale in by terminating one instance if the
average CPU utilization falls below 30 percent. The policy is additionally responsible
for defining the minimum and maximum number of instances. In our case, they were
fixed to 1 and 3. The initial number of instances is set using the same module input
variable (pool_target_size) we used for the size of the instance pool. You can view the
autoscaling policy in the OCI Console. To do so, perform the following:

1. Go to Menu ➤ Compute ➤ Instance Pools.

2. Make sure that the Sandbox compartment is selected.

3. Click the name of the instance pool.

4. Click the link next to the Autoscaling Configuration label of the
   Instance Pool Information tab of the Instance Pool Details view.

5. Expand the policy.

Figure 6-29 presents the autoscaling policy in a more human-friendly format than the one used in the Terraform infrastructure code.

Policy Name	Policy Type	Performance Metric
workers-pool-autoscale-policy	Threshold	CPU Utilization

Scaling Limits	Scale-In Rule	Scale-Out Rule
Minimum Number of Instances: 1	Operator: Less than (<)	Operator: Greater than (>)
Maximum Number of Instances: 3	Threshold: 30%	Threshold: 70%
Initial Number of Instances: 1	Action: Remove 1 instance(s)	Action: Add 1 instance(s)

Figure 6-29. Viewing the autoscaling policy in the OCI Console

To avoid all too often and intermittent changes in the instance pool, the *cooldown period* was set to 300 seconds. You can find this value in infrastructure code as the `cool_down_in_seconds` parameter in Listing 6-11. The cooldown period begins when the instance pool enters a steady state. It happens for the first time during the initial provisioning of the pool. From that point of time, on regular intervals defined by the cooldown, the autoscaling engine checks the last three metric probes. By default, the metric probes are collected from the compute instances once a minute. Based on the probes, the instance pool calculates an average metric for a given timestamp. If another average value, this time for the last three consecutive instance pool averages, exceeds a particular autoscaling policy threshold, the autoscaling event is triggered, and the instance pool size is adjusted. At this stage, we can observe it for our pool as well.

Thanks to the `stress-ng` utility, we caused a 90 percent CPU load on the only instance pool member we had that time. Probably a few minutes have passed since that moment. Let's see if anything changed while you were reading. If you are lucky, you might still observe how the instance pool is being scaled out. The OCI Console views would show something like what was collected in Figure 6-30.

Name	Status	Availability Domain	Target Instance Count	Instance Configuration
workers-pool	● Scaling	AD-1, AD-2, AD-3	2	instance-config

PROVISIONING...	inst-3grzw-workers-pool OCID: ...xfb4yq Show Copy	Shape: VM.Standard2.2	Region: eu-frankfurt-1 **Availability Domain:** feDV:EU-FRANKFURT-1-AD-2 **Fault Domain:** FAULT-DOMAIN-1
RUNNING	inst-pu327-workers-pool OCID: ...sgqpaq Show Copy	Shape: VM.Standard2.2	Region: eu-frankfurt-1 **Availability Domain:** feDV:EU-FRANKFURT-1-AD-1 **Fault Domain:** FAULT-DOMAIN-3

Figure 6-30. *Viewing in the OCI Console how an instance pool is scaling out*

The second instance was created in a different availability domain than the first instance. This time, to see the monitoring metrics from multiple instances on one diagram, we are going to leverage the OCI Monitoring Service Metrics. To do so, perform the following in the OCI Console:

1. Go to Menu ➤ Monitoring ➤ Service Metrics.

2. Make sure that the Sandbox compartment is selected.

3. Click the plot area of the CPU Utilization widget.

4. Make sure the interval is set to 1 minute.

5. Adjust the x-axis, if needed.

At some point in time, displayed in your chart, you should observe a rapid increase in the CPU utilization of our compute instance. You saw this earlier in the "Metrics" section of the individual instance. As the cooldown period of five minutes has elapsed, the autoscaling engine evaluated the average of the last three CPU utilization metric probes aggregated from the entire instance pool, which that time contained only one instance. Because it was spotted that the 70 percent threshold was exceeded, a new compute instance was added to the pool. This is shown in Figure 6-31.

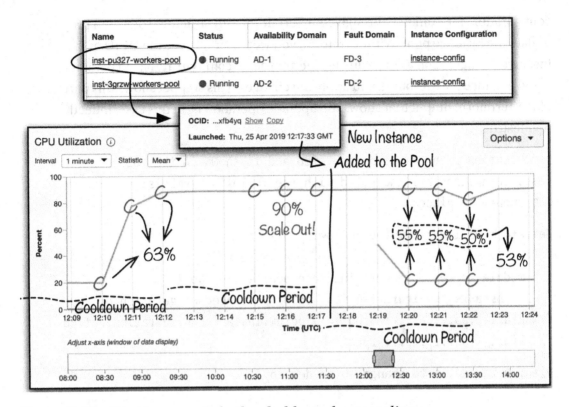

Figure 6-31. *Cooldown periods, thresholds, and autoscaling*

Because the new instance uses the same instance configuration as the first instance, both will be based on the same shape, base image, and cloud-config. Having the same cloud-config file, the cloud-init on the newly added instance will launch the `stress-ng` utility and causes 20 percent of the CPU load. From now on, the average instance pool CPU utilization will be calculated considering the probes from two instances.

At the time of writing, the autoscaling configuration policy rules in Oracle Cloud Infrastructure support only two types of metrics.

- CPU utilization

- Memory utilization

An interesting question refers to the lifecycle of an instance pool. Over time, especially for long-running instances, you may face the need to update the instance configuration that is used for a particular instance pool. The OCI Console seems not to support this operation at the moment, but the API does. To upgrade the instance configuration used by your instance pool, you just need to create the new instance configuration, for example, through your Terraform infrastructure code, and properly update the instance pool. With Terraform, you would simply use the OCID of the new instance configuration as the value for the `instance_configuration_id` parameter of the instance pool resource and apply the changes. This snippet shows this part of the Terraform output that shows the upgrade operation is, in this case, indeed nondestructive.

```
An execution plan has been generated and is shown in the following.
Resource actions are indicated with the following symbols:
  ~ update in-place

Terraform will perform the following actions:

  ~ module.workers.oci_core_instance_pool.worker_pool
      instance_configuration_id: "ocid1.instanceconfiguration.oc1.eu-
frankfurt-1.aa.........meuzhq" => "ocid1.instanceconfiguration.oc1.eu-
frankfurt-1.aa.........ijrpuq"

Plan: 0 to add, 1 to change, 0 to destroy.

Do you want to perform these actions?
  Terraform will perform the actions described earlier.
  Only "yes" will be accepted to approve.

  Enter a value: yes


Apply complete! Resources: 0 added, 1 changed, 0 destroyed.
```

After the successful update, new instances added to the pool will be created based on the new instance configuration, as shown in Figure 6-32. Already existing instances won't be impacted. You can always terminate them manually to let the instance pool engine provision their replacements, this time using the newest instance configuration.

Figure 6-32. *Viewing the instance pool with the updated instance configuration*

Another useful fact to mention about instance pools is their first-class capability to support *load balancers*. If there is a load balancer associated with a particular instance pool, an instance launched within the pool gets added to the backend set of the load balancer. You used a public load balancer with stand-alone instances in Chapter 2.

We are done with horizontal scaling. In the next section, we will discuss vertical scaling. Before moving on, do not forget to terminate the cloud infrastructure created in this section. To do so, make sure you are in the `chapter06/2-instance-pool-autoscale` directory and execute the following:

```
$ terraform destroy -auto-approve
```

Scaling Instance Vertically Up

In the previous section, we discussed and practically tested horizontal scaling on Oracle Cloud Infrastructure compute instances. To simplify the exercise, we focused on trivial tests with no real business software deployed on these instances. Things usually get more complicated as soon as you consider the application layer. Not every application, especially a legacy one, supports horizontal scaling pattern, though. To do so, systems will usually need to properly handle clustering, multinode distribution, replication, and synchronization, which is not as straightforward as you may think. In the past, a lot of systems were designed in a monolithic way. Some of them provided only active-passive high availability in which only one node could be active at a given moment, while the other waited as a standby. To increase the processing and storage capacity of that kind of systems, more hardware resources were added to existing servers, instead of adding new nodes. If you are adding more memory, storage, or CPU cores to an existing server, you are effectively *scaling* it (*vertically*) up. In this way, an application receives a more powerful host and, at least in theory, should be able to process more parallel threads even faster, as illustrated in Figure 6-33.

We are now going to launch a single compute instance with one OCPU, which actually provides the instance with two vCPUs. The cloud-config results in the creation of a new systemd service, which simulates two-core CPU utilization at 60 percent both. We will apply the same stress-ng utility we used for horizontal scaling tests. Finally, we are going to scale the machine up by upgrading its shape selection. As a result, the instance should see two OCPUs that effectively map to four vCPUs. Adding more CPU cores, for multithreaded applications running on the instance, would let them benefit from the increased processing capacity. In our case, after having doubled the number of cores, the overall average CPU utilization should fall from 60 percent to 30 percent, as illustrated in Figure 6-33.

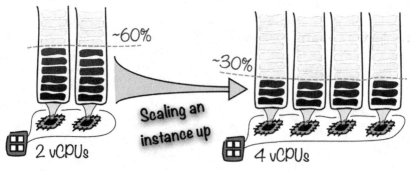

Figure 6-33. *Scaling an instance vertically*

The service that simulates a two-core CPU utilization at 60 percent is added by cloud-init based on the supplied cloud-config file, as shown in Listing 6-12.

Listing 6-12. vm.config.yaml (Root Module)

```
#cloud-config
packages:
 - stress-ng
write_files:
-   content: |
      [Unit]
      Description = Simulate CPU Utilization
      [Service]
      ExecStart = /usr/bin/stress-ng -c 2 -l 60
      User = opc
      [Install]
      WantedBy = multi-user.target
    path: /etc/systemd/system/stress.service
runcmd:
  - 'echo $(date) | tee /home/opc/datemarker'
  - [ "ln", "-s", "/etc/systemd/system/stress.service", "/etc/systemd/
    system/multi-user.target.wants/stress.service" ]
  - [ "systemctl", "enable", "stress.service" ]
  - [ "systemctl", "start", "stress.service" ]
```

The code available for this exercise is located in the chapter06/3-instance-scale-up directory. Again, before proceeding, make sure that all environment variables required by Terraform are set as needed. Furthermore, a public SSH key, as before, must be named oci_id_rsa.pub and located in the ~/.ssh directory. Let's begin and see the instance in action.

```
$ cd ~/git
$ cd oci-book/chapter06/3-instance-scale-up/infrastructure
$ find . \( -name "*.tf" -o -name "*.yaml" \)
./compute.tf
./vcn.tf
./data.tf
```

```
./provider.tf
./cloud-init/vm.config.yaml
./vars.tf
$ terraform init

Initializing provider plugins...
- Checking for available provider plugins on https://releases.hashicorp.
com...
- Downloading plugin for provider "oci" (3.30.0)...

* provider.oci: version = "~> 3.30"

Terraform has been successfully initialized!

$ terraform apply -auto-approve
Apply complete! Resources: 6 added, 0 changed, 0 destroyed.

Outputs:

image_name = CentOS-7-2019.04.15-0
vm_public_ip = 130.61.48.49

$ INSTANCE_PUBLIC_IP=`terraform output vm_public_ip`
```

At the time of writing, monitoring agents on compute instances send collected metric probes, including measured CPU utilization we are interested in, once per minute by default. To verify whether the average CPU utilization is really as expected, around 60 percent, we have to wait a couple of minutes. During that time, let's briefly discuss boot volumes. Go to the OCI Console and perform the following steps:

1. Go to Menu ➤ Compute ➤ Instances.

2. Make sure that the Sandbox compartment is selected.

   You should be able to see the newly provisioned instance, as shown in Figure 6-34. As promised, the current shape is VM.Standard2.1 and ships with one OCPU that effectively means two vCPUs visible for the operating system.

Figure 6-34. Viewing an instance before scaling up

3. Click the name of the newly provisioned instance to see the instance details.

4. In the Resources menu, select Boot Volume.

In front of your eyes appears the boot volume that is attached to the instance. What is a boot volume? Quite simple. A *boot volume* is a block volume where the operating system, the root file system, and sometimes additional software reside. It gets created based on the image you've chosen, whether it is just a base operating system image or a custom image with additional software. In other words, you could consider saying that a boot volume is a place where some part of the state of a particular instance is stored. Figure 6-35 shows the instance's boot volume.

Boot Volume

| | vm-1-OCPU (Boot Volume)
OCID:
...w37sra Show Copy
Image: CentOS-7-2019.04.15-0 | Size: 46.6 GB | Availability Domain:
feDV:EU-FRANKFURT-1-AD-1 | Attachment Type:
PARAVIRTUALIZED | In-transit Encryption:
Disabled |

Figure 6-35. Viewing the instance's boot volume

Boot volumes are created in the same availability domains as their initial parent instances. You can clearly see the image that served as a template for this boot volume. In my case, it was CentOS 7 (April 2019 build). Encryption at rest is enabled by default. For VM-based shapes, you may consider using the in-transit encryption. In many cases, it may not be required because the underlying iSCSI data exchange between the instance and block storage takes place on an internal network anyway. The size of a boot volume must be equal to or greater than the size of the image, but not smaller than 50GB, with some exceptions for selected base images. Last but not least, it is good to know that a volume can be resized, but this operation must be performed on a detached volume.

Even though boot volumes are created together with compute instances during instance launch, boot volumes are still regular cloud resources whose lifecycle can be separate from compute instances. This lets you *detach* a boot volume and *attach* it to a new compute instance, which may use a more powerful shape at the end of the day. In this way, you are doing nothing else but scaling an instance vertically up.

It is time to return to the instance metrics and confirm that the stress-ng-based service indeed generates around 60 percent of CPU utilization.

1. In the Resources menu, select Metrics.

2. Click the CPU Utilization widget, and adjust the x-axis.

If you wait a few minutes, you will be able to see, as shown in Figure 6-36, that the instance is busy to the degree we looked forward to, namely, 60 percent. As soon as we double the number of cores, the CPU utilization should fall to something around 30 percent.

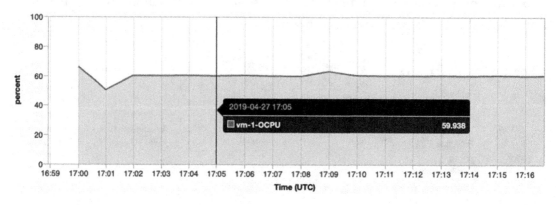

Figure 6-36. *Viewing an instance's (one OCPU) CPU utilization*

In January 2020 Oracle Cloud Infrastructure will introduce a convenient API-driven and fully-automated vertical scaling for compute instances. For majority of shapes, you will be able to use the *UpdateInstance* API to update any existing instance with a new, more or less powerful, shape. A running instance will be restarted but you should expect the instance's IP addresses, VNIC and volume attachments to remain unchanged. The CLI command to apply a new shape to a running instance will look something like this:

```
oci compute instance update --instance-id $INSTANCE_OCID --shape
VM.Standard2.2 --wait-for-state RUNNING
```

If you are reading this book late enough, this feature is already available. Yet, for the purpose of the incoming exercise, do not execute the *oci compute instance update* command at this stage. If you've already done it, please scale the instance back to the VM.Standard2.1 shape, before you continue.

Alternatively, there has always been another way to scale an instance vertically. This method involves detaching a boot volume, shutting down the old instance and launching a new instance reusing the boot volume. I am going to explain it using Terraform. Let's assume you have an idea to replace the shape name in the compute.tf infrastructure code file. Let me simulate such a change and explain the trap you can fall into. Shall we? You are just watching. I am commenting out the old line and adding a new one, this time with a more powerful shape (VM.Standard2.2) like this:

```
resource "oci_core_instance" "vm" {
...
#   shape = "VM.Standard2.1"
   shape = "VM.Standard2.2"
...
}
```

Running terraform plan provides the explanation of what would happen if I chose to apply this infrastructure code amendment:

```
$ terraform plan
...
Terraform will perform the following actions:

-/+ oci_core_instance.vm (new resource required)
...
boot_volume_id: "ocid1.bootvolume.oc1.........w37sra" => <computed>
...
image: "ocid1.image.oc1.........ai3kha" => <computed>
...
shape: "VM.Standard2.1" => "VM.Standard2.2" (forces new resource)
...
Plan: 1 to add, 0 to change, 1 to destroy.
```

Note   If you see *0 to add*, **1 to change**, *0 to destroy* it means that the convenient, fully-automated and API-driven vertical scaling feature has not only been enabled in the OCI API, but also in the Terraform Provider Plugin. In such a case, the problem described below does not apply anymore. Yet, you can still perform the semi-manual vertical scaling method as described below. As a matter of fact, it will still teach you how to detach and reattach boot volumes.

The output of the *terraform plan* command says **1 to add**, *0 to change*, **1 to destroy**. Well, at first glance, you may think we expected this compute instance to be terminated anyway and a new one, more powerful one launched. Correct. The problem here is that the new instance would also get a totally new boot volume built once again from the newest CentOS 7 base operating system image. This behavior is defined in the source_details object in this part of the infrastructure code:

```
# data.tf
...
data "oci_core_images" "centos_image" {
  compartment_id = var.tenancy_ocid
  operating_system = "CentOS"
  operating_system_version = 7
}
...
# compute.tf
resource "oci_core_instance" "vm" {
...
  source_details {
    source_id = data.oci_core_images.centos_image.images[0].id
    source_type = "image"
  }
...
}
```

Within the source_details object, the source_type still suggests that a new boot volume has to be created based on the image specified with the source_id attribute.

I hope you understand now why a simple shape replacement in the infrastructure code file won't work and may even be harmful because any application state persisted in the root file system would be lost. Talking about application state in the root file system, the cloud-config file has not only added a new stress-ng-based systemd service but also created a tiny text file containing the initial boot timestamp. We are going to use this timestamp to validate whether we are still using the same boot volume after having scaled the instance vertically up. First, connect to the instance and note the contents of this tiny file:

```
$ ssh -i ~/.ssh/oci_id_rsa opc@$INSTANCE_PUBLIC_IP
[opc@vm-1-ocpu ~]$ cat datemarker
Sat Apr 27 17:01:34 GMT 2019
[opc@vm-1-ocpu ~]$ exit
```

To scale an instance vertically, these are the steps you have to perform:

1. Stop the old instance while preserving the boot volume.

2. Detach the boot volume.

3. Create a new instance using the detached volume.

We are going to adapt the Terraform infrastructure code to transfer the instance into a stopped state. If you are on Linux or using Windows Subsystem for Linux, use the following sed command to uncomment currently commented blocks in the compute.tf file in the chapter06/3-instance-scale-up directory:

```
$ pwd
/Users/michal/git/oci-book/chapter06/3-instance-scale-up/infrastructure
$ sed -i 's/\/\*//; s/\*\///' compute.tf
```

If you are on macOS, use the following sed command:

```
$ sed -i '.bak' -e 's/\/\*//; s/\*\///' compute.tf
```

This will uncomment the code by removing all block comment marks (/* and */) in the compute.tf file, as shown in Listing 6-13.

Listing 6-13. compute.tf (Root Module) Part to Uncomment

```
resource "oci_core_instance" "vm" {
...
...
  # 1. Stop the instance
    state = "STOPPED"
    preserve_boot_volume = true
}
output "vm_bootvolume_ocid" {
  value = oci_core_instance.vm.boot_volume_id
}
```

Run terraform plan. You see something like this:

```
$ terraform plan
An execution plan has been generated and is shown in the following.
Resource actions are indicated with the following symbols:
  + create
  ~ update in-place

Terraform will perform the following actions:

~ oci_core_instance.vm
    preserve_boot_volume:            "" => "true"
     state:                          "RUNNING" => "STOPPED"
...
Plan: 0 to add, 1 to change, 0 to destroy.
```

Run terraform apply.

```
$ terraform apply -auto-approve
...
Apply complete! Resources: 0 added, 1 changed, 0 destroyed.

Outputs:

vm_public_ip = 130.61.48.49
image_name = CentOS-7-2019.04.15-0
vm_bootvolume_ocid = ocid1.bootvolume.oc1....w37sra
```

We have output the OCID of the boot volume. Now, we are moving to detach the volume from the instance. For this task, we are going to employ the OCI CLI.

Note   It is of course possible and really quick to use the OCI Console to detach a particular boot volume, but in the course of the book, we prefer automation over manual interactions with the user interface.

Why can we not stay consistent and continue using Terraform alone for this action as well? If you look into each infrastructure code file, you won't find any resource representing the boot volume that came with the instance. At the time of provisioning, the lifecycle of the instance and its boot volume were not separated. Therefore, we cannot use Terraform alone. This is one of the cases where a solid blend of a declarative infrastructure code (Terraform) approach and imperative programming techniques (CLI) are both required to accomplish the task. To detach the boot volume from an instance, follow these steps:

```
$ BOOTVOLUME_OCID=`terraform output "vm_bootvolume_ocid"`

$ echo $BOOTVOLUME_OCID
ocid1.bootvolume.oc1....w37sra

$ BOOTVOLUME_AD=`oci bv boot-volume get --boot-volume-id $BOOTVOLUME_OCID
--query 'data."availability-domain"' --profile SANDBOX-ADMIN | sed 's/["]//g'`

$ echo $BOOTVOLUME_AD
feDV:EU-FRANKFURT-1-AD-1

$ BOOTVOLUME_ATTACHMENT_OCID=`oci compute boot-volume-attachment list
--availability-domain $BOOTVOLUME_AD --boot-volume-id $BOOTVOLUME_OCID
--query 'data[0].id' --profile SANDBOX-ADMIN | sed 's/["]//g'`

$ echo $BOOTVOLUME_ATTACHMENT_OCID
ocid1.instance.oc1....gnzzyq

$ oci compute boot-volume-attachment detach --boot-volume-attachment-id
$BOOTVOLUME_ATTACHMENT_OCID --wait-for-state DETACHED --force --profile
SANDBOX-ADMIN
Action completed. Waiting until the resource has entered state: DETACHED
```

We began by using the `terraform output` command to persist one of the outputs that contains the OCID of the boot volume into a variable. In the next step, we used the `oci bv boot-volume get` CLI command to extract the name of the availability domain in which both the instance and the volume are located. Consequently, we used the `oci compute boot-volume-attachment list` CLI command to fetch the name of the boot volume attachment. At the time of writing, the OCID of the boot volume attachment is the same as the OCID of the instance, but to avoid problems in the case of any future changes, we followed the most reliable procedure to obtain the OCID of the attachment. Finally, we issued the `oci compute boot-volume-attachment detach` CLI command to trigger the asynchronous job that detaches the volume. We applied the `--wait-for-state DETACHED` option to keep the steps blocking and thus make it effectively synchronous. Additionally, we used the `--force` option to skip the confirmation prompt. You will find both options useful in case you decide to automate these steps as a single "scale-up" pipeline together with Terraform-based steps. All in all, the few commands will eventually cause the detachment operation of a boot volume, as shown in Figure 6-37.

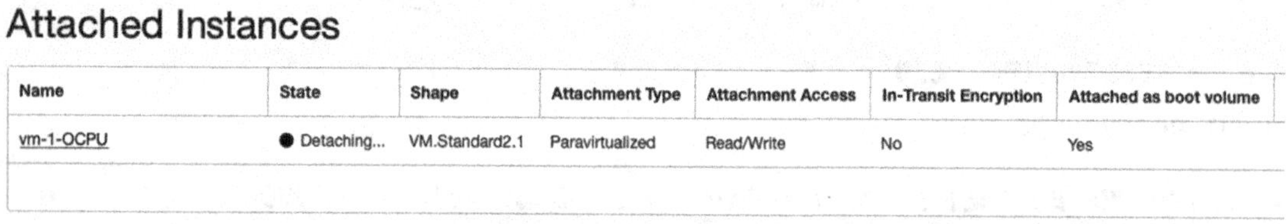

Attached Instances

Name	State	Shape	Attachment Type	Attachment Access	In-Transit Encryption	Attached as boot volume
vm-1-OCPU	● Detaching...	VM.Standard2.1	Paravirtualized	Read/Write	No	Yes

Figure 6-37. Observing a boot volume while detaching

To view the boot volume in OCI Console, you have to perform the following:

1. Go to Menu ➤ Compute ➤ Boot Volumes.

2. Make sure that the `Sandbox` compartment is selected.

Although the volume has been detached, it is still listed as present. It is shown in Figure 6-38. This was exactly our goal.

Boot Volumes *in* Sandbox *Compartment*

Name	State	Size	Availability Domain
vm-1-OCPU (Boot Volume)	● Available	47 GB	feDV:EU-FRANKFURT-1-AD-1

Figure 6-38. *Viewing a boot volume in the OCI Console*

If you open the boot volume details view and choose the Attached Instances in the Resources menu, you will see that there are no compute instances attached to that volume anymore. At the same time, the original instance we launched earlier, together with the boot volume, reports that the boot volume is effectively detached, as shown in Figure 6-39.

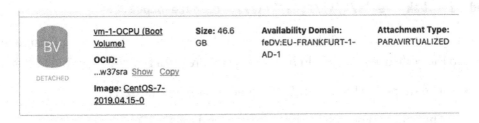

Figure 6-39. *Viewing a detached boot volume*

We are now ready to terminate the old and launch a new, more powerful compute instance using the boot volume we've just detached from the old instance. The new instance must be launched in the same availability domain.

Caution   You have to be careful not to re-initialize the new instance with cloud-init. Otherwise, you may corrupt the application state on this new instance, which is provisioned using an existing boot volume. In our case, the new, more powerful instance attached to an existing boot volume will use no cloud-config at all.

For provisioning, we will use declarative approach with Terraform. Before executing `terraform apply`, you have to do the following:

1. Comment the contents or simply remove the entire `compute.tf` file to terminate the older instance that was stopped a few moments ago.

2. Uncomment the contents of the `compute-ocpu2.tf` file (by removing the `/*` clause at the beginning of the file and the `*/` clause at the end of the file). This will provision the new instance.

These two tasks are easy to script. To perform them on Linux or Windows Subsystem for Linux, execute the following code:

```
$ rm compute.tf
$ sed -i 's/\/\*//; s/\*\///' compute-ocpu2.tf
```

If you are on macOS, you need to use the `sed` command in a slightly different way.

```
$ rm compute.tf
$ sed -i '.bak' -e 's/\/\*//; s/\*\///' compute-ocpu2.tf
```

Listing 6-14 presents the infrastructure code for the new, more powerful instance. It is similar to the code used for the old instance, yet there are a few considerable differences.

- The shape (VM.Standard2.2 instead of VM.Standard2.1).

- The source type is set to `bootVolume`, and the OCID of the existing boot volume is supplied through a Terraform variable.

- There is no user data, and therefore no additional initialization on first boot with cloud-init is done for the new instance, so as not to alter what is present in the boot volume.

- The display name (vm-2-OCPU instead of vm-1-OCPU).

Listing 6-14. compute-2-ocpu.tf (Root Module)

```
variable "vm_2_ocpu_bootvolume_ocid" { }

# 2. Add the new instance
resource "oci_core_instance" "vm_2_ocpu" {
  compartment_id = var.compartment_ocid
  display_name = "vm-2-OCPU"
  availability_domain = data.oci_identity_availability_domains.ads.
  availability_domains[0].name
```

```
  source_details {
    source_id = var.vm_2_ocpu_bootvolume_ocid
    source_type = "bootVolume"
  }
  shape = "VM.Standard2.2"
  create_vnic_details {
    subnet_id = oci_core_subnet.net.id
    assign_public_ip = true
  }
  metadata = {
    ssh_authorized_keys = file("~/.ssh/oci_id_rsa.pub")
  }
}

output "new_vm_public_ip" { value = oci_core_instance.vm_2_ocpu.public_ip }
```

Here are the steps to apply the new infrastructure code. Please note that we are using the previous Terraform output captured as the BOOTVOLUME_OCID variable and using it to set and export (!) a new environment variable (TF_VAR_vm_2_ocpu_bootvolume_ocid) and, in this way, pass the OCID of the existing boot volume to Terraform.

```
$ echo $BOOTVOLUME_OCID
ocid1.bootvolume.oc1....w37sra

$ export TF_VAR_vm_2_ocpu_bootvolume_ocid=$BOOTVOLUME_OCID

$ echo $TF_VAR_vm_2_ocpu_bootvolume_ocid
ocid1.bootvolume.oc1....w37sra

$ terraform plan
An execution plan has been generated and is shown in the following.
Resource actions are indicated with the following symbols:
  + create
  - destroy

Terraform will perform the following actions:

  - oci_core_instance.vm

  + oci_core_instance.vm_2_ocpu
```

```
...
   availability_domain:                "feDV:EU-FRANKFURT-1-AD-1"
...
   source_details.#:                   "1"
   source_details.0.source_id:         "ocid1.bootvolume.oc1....w37sra"
   source_details.0.source_type:       "bootVolume"
...

Plan: 1 to add, 0 to change, 1 to destroy.
```

As long as the plan reports that the old instance will be destroyed and the new one built using an existing boot volume, we are ready to go.

```
$ terraform apply -auto-approve
...
Apply complete! Resources: 1 added, 0 changed, 1 destroyed.

Outputs:

new_vm_public_ip = 130.61.90.54
image_name = CentOS-7-2019.04.15-0

$ NEW_INSTANCE_PUBLIC_IP=`terraform output new_vm_public_ip`
```

Tip   Do not worry, if the *terraform apply* command produces the *Service Error: Conflict*. In such a case, the old instance has not been deleted before the creation of the new instance. This leads to the situation in which the boot volume, even though detached, is still seen as assigned to the old instance. To continue, just run the *terraform apply -auto-approve* command again.

If you follow the intermediary Terraform output, you will actually spot that the creation of the newer instance will effectively begin after the destruction of the older instance, as shown in Figure 6-40. This is happening because the boot volume, even though detached, is still registered by the older instance. As long as the Terraform timeout for the create operation is set large enough, you should experience no problems.

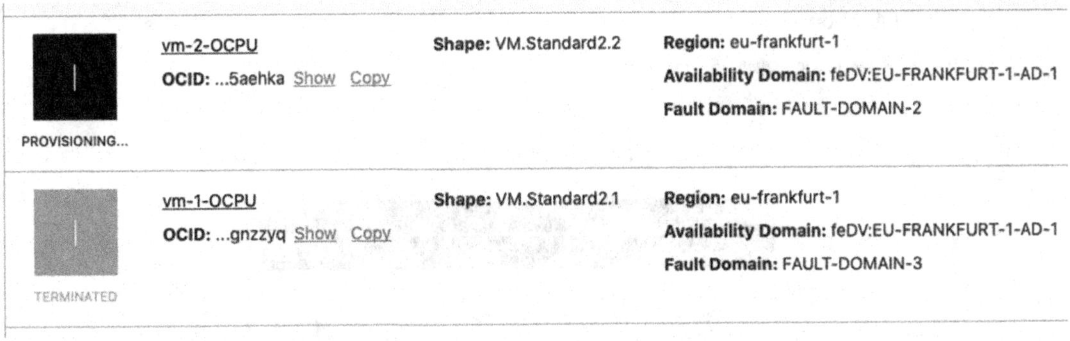

	vm-2-OCPU	Shape: VM.Standard2.2	Region: eu-frankfurt-1
	OCID: ...5aehka Show Copy		Availability Domain: feDV:EU-FRANKFURT-1-AD-1
PROVISIONING...			Fault Domain: FAULT-DOMAIN-2
	vm-1-OCPU	Shape: VM.Standard2.1	Region: eu-frankfurt-1
	OCID: ...gnzzyq Show Copy		Availability Domain: feDV:EU-FRANKFURT-1-AD-1
TERMINATED			Fault Domain: FAULT-DOMAIN-3

Figure 6-40. *Viewing the provisioning of a new scaled-up instance*

As soon as the new instance is ready and a few moments to start the ssh daemon have passed, feel free to connect to the instance and see whether the file written on the initial boot of the first instance survived the reattachment of the boot volume.

```
$ ssh -i .ssh/oci_id_rsa opc@$NEW_INSTANCE_PUBLIC_IP
[opc@vm-2-ocpu ~]$ cat datemarker
Sat Apr 27 17:01:34 GMT 2019
[opc@vm-2-ocpu ~]$ exit
```

Perfect. The fact that the file exists and the contents match what we checked earlier is proof that the boot volume has indeed survived the reattachment and effectively the scale-up operation.

The new instance comes with a doubled number of vCPUs, while our CPU utilization stress testing service parameters remain unchanged. As a result, we expect that this time instead of 60 percent of CPU utilization we see something around 30 percent of CPU utilization. Let's verify this. Go to the Metrics view of the new instance.

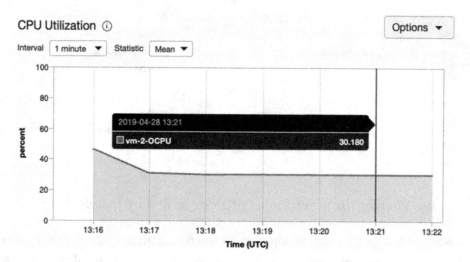

Figure 6-41. Viewing an instance's (two-OCPU) CPU utilization

After a couple of minutes, you should indeed see the CPU utilization stable around 30 percent. This proves that our scale-up operation has been successful. We have managed to reuse the same boot volume on a more powerful compute instance. If you automate the steps described in this section, you will see that the logic is rather simple here.

One more thing, if you look at the name of the boot volume, as shown in Figure 6-42, and compare it with the name of the new instance, you will see that the name of the boot volume is the same as the name of the older instance that has been terminated. Having the vm-1-OCPU boot volume attached to the vm-2-OCPU instance looks a bit odd, doesn't it?

Attached Instances

Name	State	Shape	Attachment Type	Attachment Access	In-Transit Encryption	Attached as boot volume
vm-2-OCPU	● Attached	VM.Standard2.2	Paravirtualized	Read/Write	No	Yes

Figure 6-42. Viewing the old name of the boot volume

Luckily, it is easy to rename the display name of a boot volume with no impact on data or instance downtime. All in all, the display name is just the metadata, isn't it? To rename a boot volume, you can use the `oci bv boot-volume update` CLI command with the `--display-name` option to set the new name like this:

```
$ oci bv boot-volume update --boot-volume-id $BOOTVOLUME_OCID --display-name vm-bv --profile SANDBOX-ADMIN
```

At this stage, this exercise is completed. Please use the `terraform destroy` command to free up the resources and stop the billing.

```
$ terraform destroy -auto-approve
```

The boot volume will be terminated with the new instance, as shown in Figure 6-43.

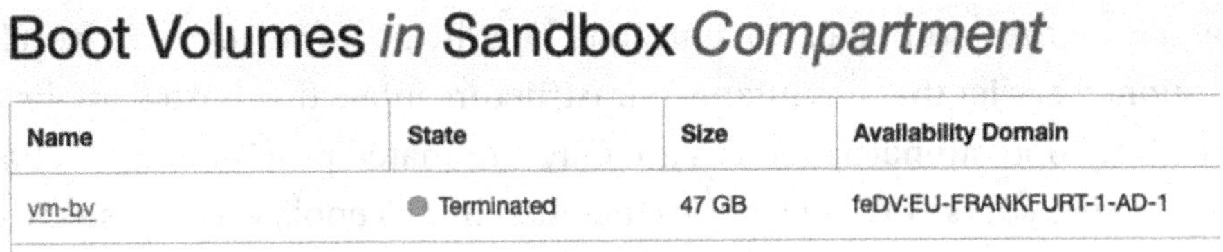

Boot Volumes *in* Sandbox *Compartment*

Name	State	Size	Availability Domain
vm-bv	● Terminated	47 GB	feDV:EU-FRANKFURT-1-AD-1

Figure 6-43. *Viewing the terminated boot volume*

Immutable Infrastructure

The high level of API-driven automation and the rapid self-provisioning of pooled infrastructure resources make cloud computing the key enabler for the *immutable infrastructure* pattern. The word *immutable* is synonymous to words such as *unchangeable, permanent,* or *fixed.* An infrastructure that does not change must be created in a relatively negligible time and ready to serve its business purpose straightaway. The latter implies that immutable infrastructure comes together with a preinstalled and already initialized application layer ready to deliver services and process data. Sooner or later, an upgrade of selected components will be required. This is where the word *immutable* comes into play. In contrast to the traditional server- and application lifecycle, the immutable infrastructure pattern assumes that a new set of cloud resources is provisioned based on the upgraded images and enhanced initialization code, and any incoming traffic is properly redirected and the old infrastructure simply terminated.

An immutable infrastructure can incorporate *autonomous intelligence* such as horizontal compute autoscale. The autoscale would then dynamically adapt the count of instances based on the metrics described earlier in this chapter. The key idea here is that no human intervention is needed, and because of that, the infrastructure can be considered immutable.

Because of the complexity of the application landscape, data flow dependencies, and various service continuity requirements, it would be rather utopic to think that the entire cloud infrastructure for all systems can be treated as a single set of immutable resources. In reality, you control multiple sets of cloud resources that are managed independently as immutable infrastructure. Furthermore, you usually decide that some cloud resources, especially managed platform services, won't be provisioned using this pattern. All in all, you should carefully pick a proper split of cloud resource groups having both of the ones that follow the immutable infrastructure pattern as well as the ones that rely on the traditional, dynamic, and long-living infrastructure lifecycle.

I mentioned earlier that immutable infrastructure infers that hosted applications and systems are operational as soon as the fully automated provisioning run has been completed. In the course of the exercises included in this book, we extensively used Terraform with cloud-config files processed and executed on instance boot by cloud-init. I am a great fan of cloud-init, but I admit that the more complex application initialization logic gets, the more inefficient it is to use cloud-init. The limitations of cloud-init become visible especially when you are initializing complex clustered systems where different nodes carry diverse roles, such as master or worker, and require a specific initialization sequence.

One option would be to use *Terraform provisioners* to execute scripts on remote cloud hosts in a particular sequence based on a predefined dependency tree. Some consider Terraform provisioners as if they were making Terraform infrastructure code no longer simple and readable. Well, Terraform infrastructure code is rather meant to be declarative. Using standard Terraform configurations such as resources, data sources, or modules is indeed purely declarative, which entails many benefits. First, you never worry about the execution steps needed to bring the actual state to the target state. This task is done by Terraform. If you are extending this clean declarative approach by using provisioners, you are adding the imperative nature and effectively mixing the two paradigms (declarative and imperative) in the same code base. In this way, the infrastructure code would become harder to understand and maintain.

Another option I would recommend for really complex architectures is to implement the immutable infrastructure by properly combining declarative

Terraform-based infrastructure code with imperative initialization logic orchestrated with Ansible. Ansible is an agent-less automation tool used to remotely manage compute instances. Its capabilities include not only system administration but also application deployment. Both Terraform and Ansible could be executed on the same build server and encapsulated as repeatable jobs within a complete CICD pipeline. The provisioning pipeline could consist of four stages, as illustrated in Figure 6-44 and understood as follows:

1. The cloud infrastructure is created based on the declared target infrastructure defined using Terraform configuration files.

2. Preinstalled applications and libraries can be shipped already included in the custom images used to launch instances.

3. Some initial operating system and application initialization logic is executed by cloud-init based on the supplied cloud-config user data.

4. More distributed and interdependent initialization tasks are finally performed through a set of Ansible-based playbooks.

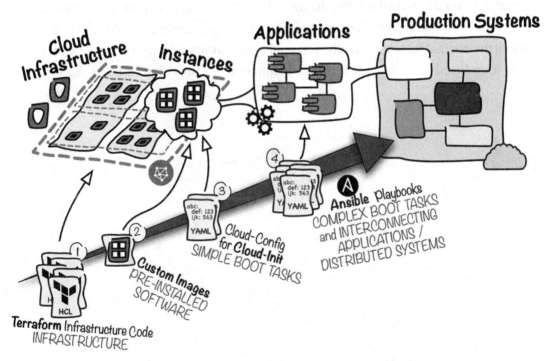

Figure 6-44. *Immutable architecture with Terraform and Ansible*

Summary

The main goal of this chapter was to familiarize you with some of the core cloud infrastructure patterns you will encounter while designing cloud-based solutions or migrating existing systems to the cloud. We began with discussing virtual networking by looking at VCNs, regional and AD-specific subnets, VNICs, and private IPs. Two types of public IPs, ephemeral and reserved, were subsequently covered in the context of Internet-facing instances. Next, we glanced over the bastion host and NAT gateway pattern applied to provide secure Internet connectivity to isolated instances attached to private subnets. You used Terraform to provision the corresponding infrastructure and see this pattern in action. We briefly looked at routing and spent some more time clarifying the differences between stateful and stateless security rules. You learned how to use local VCN peering to interconnect different VCNs in the same region. A dedicated network compartment pattern was given as an alternative to VCN peering, especially in the context of more complicated architectures. A large part of this chapter was devoted to elasticity delivered with horizontal and vertical instance scaling. You used instance pools, instance configurations, and autoscale configurations to experiment with horizontal scaling. You learned how to scale an instance vertically up by moving to a more powerful compute shape, while at the same time reusing the existing boot volume that had been created while booting the original instance. Finally, you read about immutable infrastructure and were briefly introduced to the tools you can use to implement a provisioning pipeline.

CHAPTER 7

Autonomous Database

Storing data can be challenging. There are many aspects to consider. In this chapter, we are going to explore one of the flagships of Oracle Cloud, a fully managed Oracle database available as a platform as a service in Oracle Cloud.

Relational Data Model

The way you structure and organize data is typically called a *data model*. A data model alone generally implies various relationships and integrity requirements between individual data entities. A data entity can represent an individual business object such as a product, a customer, or a sales item. Data entities are also used to embody technical data such as some kind of collected measurement probes. Each data entity must be eventually reflected in the form of physical data entry in a particular type of a database. The type of a database entails, to some extent, the primary physical data entry format. The following are a few popular database types:

- Relational model based on two-dimensional tables

- Document-oriented model based on JSON or XML documents

- Graphs

- Key-value stores

- Wide column stores

Two-dimensional tables are considered as the most popular and, historically, most prevalent way of organizing business-related data. Furthermore, business professionals are typically used to data representation in a tabular form because of their everyday work with spreadsheets. Looking at two-dimensional tables, *rows* correspond to individual data objects, and *columns* represent the attributes these objects have, as illustrated in Figure 7-1.

347

© Michał Tomasz Jakóbczyk 2020
M. T. Jakóbczyk, *Practical Oracle Cloud Infrastructure*, https://doi.org/10.1007/978-1-4842-5506-3_7

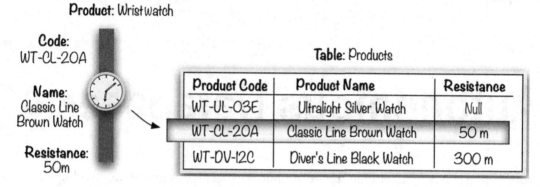

Figure 7-1. *Two-dimensional table*

Business data entities such as products, customers, or sales items rarely exist in isolation but nearly always happen to be somehow related to other entities. For example, sales items can refer to products they ship and customers who made the purchase. To express these relationships between two-dimensional tables, you leverage the relational data model that, by its design, truly helps database engines in

- Protecting data integrity

- Resolving and optimizing queries

What does it mean to protect data integrity? A particular sales item entity could be created, provided that the product entity it is referring to already exists. A relational database is able to enforce such a requirement and prohibit the creation of sales item table entries when the given product entries do not exist in the product table. This is called *referential integrity*. Relational databases really shine in this field. Even though relational databases technically can store duplicate rows, it is not desired in some workload types, especially operational ones. In their case, a single product usually should be represented by a single, easily identifiable data entry. To uniquely identify a selected product in a table, the data entry must have one or more columns whose values altogether uniquely identify the data entity. To prohibit the database from inserting duplicates, you create a *unique key* data integrity constraint over these columns. Any attempt to insert a new data row with an already existing set of values in unique-key columns will be rejected. Data integrity is protected based on the types of each individual column. Relational databases are traditionally based on tables with fixed-type columns. Each column is defined with a *column data type* that can be one of many supported character, numeric, date, and time datatypes. For example, the product name column could be of a Unicode-based variable-length character type with a maximum length expressed by the number of characters, while the sales item quantity column is defined using a nonnegative integer numeric type. Inserted values that do not comply with the column data type are rejected. Integrity checks can additionally enforce that a given column allows only the words that match a given regular expression or numeric values that belong to a particular range. This can be implemented using *check constraints*. In the real world, developers sometimes decide to build this kind of check for selected columns in the application layer instead. It all depends on the purpose and context a particular data model is created for. At this stage, it must be said that not every workload needs a data model with built-in integrity checks. As a matter of fact, there are use cases where data model flexibility is more valued than integrity enforcement. Yet, business-related data is typically in favor of having them.

Storing data is just one end of the stick. To use the persisted data, you have to be able to regularly and efficiently retrieve it from a database. To fetch the desired subset of data entries, you query the database engine. For a relational database, you usually precisely define what is to be returned using standardized *Structured Query Language* (SQL), sometimes extended with database-specific features. A SQL query is sent from a client to the database engine, which translates it into a query execution plan. Based on this plan, data is retrieved by the database engine and sent back to the client. Listing 7-1 presents a basic SQL query that selects product names and barcodes of all products whose barcode starts with 590 and category code is equal to REG.

Listing 7-1. SQL SELECT Statement

```
SELECT name,barcode
FROM products
WHERE barcode LIKE '590%' AND category_code = 'REG';
```

Queries may target single tables or span multiple tables, joining them as needed. Rows from different tables are joined based on the relationships defined in a particular data model. For example, if you want to collect all sales items that refer only to these products that are categorized as mathematical books, the database engine will have to join at least the sales items table with the products table and apply proper filters to sort out the other categories. How two tables are joined is derived from their logical design. The most popular type of relationship is when one table reflects entities that can be referenced by multiple entities from the second table. At the same time, each entity in the second table can reference only one entity from the first table. This is called a *one-to-many relationship*. This can be the relationship between the sales items table and the products table. Multiple sales items reference the same product, while only one product is referenced by a single sales item. This is implemented by storing the unique identifier of the referenced product in the sales items table for each entry, as shown in Figure 7-2. This key is typically called a *foreign key*.

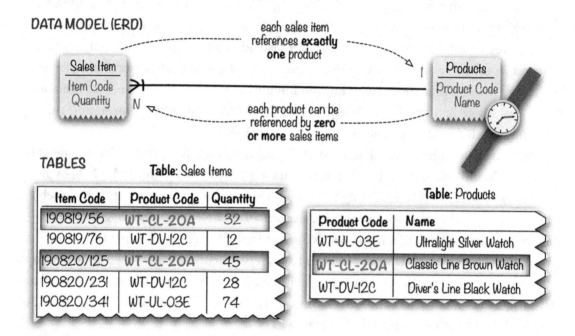

Figure 7-2. *Modeling one-to-many relationship*

To speed up queries that are expected to be frequently made, relational databases rely on additional data structures called *indexes*, which are used to bypass costly full-table searches and optimize table joins. A standard B-tree index is associated with a single table and created over one or more columns. The order of columns in an index matters. Queries that use these columns to filter the results as well as table joins that are based on these columns may benefit from a largely accelerated operation time. B-tree indexes point to a single row. Bitmap indexes are another type of index popular for implementing analytical data models. They are created over columns that store a small number of discrete values and enable complex searches that rely on set operations. Bitmap indexes point to multiple rows and in this way can be used to speed up aggregate queries. As soon as you create an index, its management is taken over by the database engine. Every time you issue an insert, update, or delete operation over a data row, the corresponding indexes will be brought up-to-date.

One of the key notions related to data-modifying operations against databases are *transactions*. A transaction makes sure that a set of data-modifying operations is either carried out as one or none of the transactions takes place. No intermediary states are allowed to impact the data set that is the subject of the data-modifying operations wrapped inside the transaction. When transaction is *committed*, all statements are applied in the database. If one of the statements fails or a transaction is intentionally *rolled back*, none of the statements will result in data set changes. This lets developers implement complex use cases and proper error handling in their applications that interact with databases. Transactions adhere to the so-called ACID properties, which means that transactions are

- Atomic

- Consistent

- Isolated

- Durable

Atomicity and consistency imply that either all or none of the operations are applied to the entire data set that is the subject of the transaction and no intermediary states of data entries are allowed in the database. Isolation means that it is possible to run multiple concurrent transactions, and the result of any given transaction is visible to other transactions only after it has been successfully committed. As a matter of fact, there are a few so-called isolation levels, and they decide how active concurrent transactions are handled. Last but not least, durability promises that any committed transaction is permanent and never lost, even in the case of database engine failure.

Oracle Database

Relational databases have been widely used as a data backbone across different industries for decades. Oracle Database was the first commercially available SQL-based relational database management system (RDBMS) introduced in 1979. A few years earlier, in 1970, the relational model of data was publicly introduced by Edgar F. Codd in his theoretical, mathematical-based paper "A Relational Model of Data for Large Shared Data Banks." This model eventually became the predominant database model for a few decades and made Oracle Corporation the dominant market leader in this field. Oracle Database has evolved for 40 years. During these years, Oracle ported the database code to the C language, hardened transaction support, enhanced transaction isolation consistency, moved to a client-server mode allowing network-based architectures, improved locking, introduced various backup strategies, added PL/SQL (which is a procedural extension to SQL), introduced triggers and stored procedures, offered high availability through clustering, leveraged compression to optimize the storage footprint, and included a countless number of other improvements such as XML and JSON support, in-memory and grid-computing support, Spatial and Graph, data masking for security and testing, advanced monitoring, REST data services, and many more. In 2013, multitenancy arrived with version 12c in the form of pluggable databases, and Oracle Database 12c was marketed as the world's first (relational) database designed for the cloud. Oracle Database can be used for both transactional (OLTP) and analytical (OLAP) workloads and meets a broad range of enterprise demands. Oracle Corporation is also the custodian of MySQL, one of the most popular open source relational databases that is often the first choice for small businesses and organizations with limited and rather nonenterprise requirements.

The abundance of features can result in rather challenging administration tasks especially in terms of initial setup, hardware selection, proper database tuning, and resource and performance monitoring. These activities are inevitable and must be carried out to deliver a production-ready database. The more demanding the expected workloads are, the more sophisticated setup that has to be put in place. All of these features depend on a skilled workforce and consume a lot of time. To alleviate this potential pain, more than a decade ago, Oracle introduced the *Exadata database machine* that combines database-optimized hardware, specialized system control software, and, of course, Oracle Database. The Exadata hardware leverages the InfiniBand networking fabric, NVMe SSD storage, and many more to provide extreme performance and support a gradual scale-up by enabling further CPU cores, installing more storage volumes, and even scaling out by placing additional racks. Customers can install the Exadata rack(s) in their data centers in order to still physically own data but leverage already-optimized hardware and software as well as delegate some lifecycle tasks to the built-in automation or Oracle advanced support experts who deploy and manage the infrastructure.

While operations team may be truly given some time to roll out the environment, developers usually don't want to wait. Years ago, Oracle enriched its portfolio with a free Oracle Database Express Edition (XE) that can be used to rapidly kick off Oracle-oriented application development and only later transition to working with the Enterprise Edition of Oracle Database. While Oracle Database Express Edition is fine to begin working with Oracle Database, it does not help in rapid database instance provisioning and management for production purposes.

Cloud computing brings to the market not only software-as-a-service or infrastructure-as-a-service options but also managed platform services. Managed platform services can be rapidly provisioned, decrease the overall administrational burden, and let teams focus on development and the use of a particular platform. Every Oracle Cloud region comes with a fully managed, highly automated, well-integrated, scalable Oracle database called *Autonomous Database* (ADB) available in two flavors: Autonomous Transaction Processing (ATP) and Autonomous Data Warehouse (ADW). ADB runs on Exadata hardware plugged into the Oracle Cloud Infrastructure backbone. ADB is marketed as self-driving, self-securing, and self-repairing, which basically indicates that it is a fully managed service with little if any administrational effort at all on the customer side. Responsibilities such as patching, upgrading, tuning, or backing up the database are automatically done in the background. This allows you to focus on data model design and development, leaving any database lifecycle tasks to Oracle-maintained automation, as illustrated in Figure 7-3.

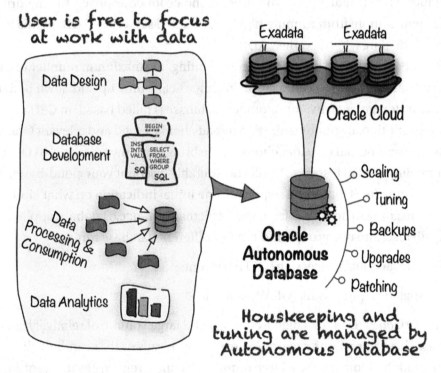

Figure 7-3. *Autonomous Database*

ADB is available in each Oracle public cloud region with two deployments choices.

- Serverless

- Dedicated

Serverless deployment is the simplest way to launch a managed Oracle Database. First you choose the target Oracle Cloud region, and then you just select the initial number of CPUs, storage capacity, admin credentials, and workload type (ATP or ADW). Later, you will still be able to scale up both the CPU and the storage. Furthermore, you can enable CPU autoscaling, if needed. Everything else, things such as patching, upgrades, auto-tuning, and backups, are fully automated in the background. All in all, the entire lifecycle is managed by Oracle-managed automation. The serverless deployment option follows the standard pattern widely used in the cloud, namely, multitenancy. What does this mean? There can be multiple ADB instances used by different cloud tenants, all running in the same Exadata machine. If higher isolation from other tenants is required, your enterprise will probably consider ADB in the *dedicated* deployment mode, which does require a bit more initial effort but lets your exclusive Exadata infrastructure run in completely isolated private virtual network in the Oracle public cloud. While a dedicated ADB is a good choice for enterprises, the majority of use cases will benefit more from running highly automated serverless ADB. In this book, we will be solely dealing with serverless ADB.

ADB can be really powerful. At the time of writing, the maximum number of CPU cores per instance is 128. You can scale an instance at any time up and down both for CPU count and for storage capacity. Autonomous Database is billed based on CPU and Exadata storage consumption. If your organization already holds a valid and relevant Oracle Database license, you can consider choosing the bring-your-own-license (BYOL) option when launching an ADB instance. It will considerably discount your cloud-based charges.

ADB can tune itself, but it still requires some initial indication on what kind of workloads are going to be served from the particular instance. Database applications are generally divided into two groups and require different database tuning.

- Transactional processing (OLTP) systems

- Analytical processing (OLAP) systems

OLTP workloads result in a high frequency and large volume of relatively small write operations. These operations can originate from hundreds or thousands of clients at the same time and therefore lead to a large number of concurrent writes that require proper transactional isolation. In some cases, data can be altered not only interactively but also based on batch data loads. Transaction processing has become even more significant for databases with the advent of e-commerce and is sometimes considered as the traditional domain for relational databases. Transactional databases usually employ highly normalized data models, which eliminate redundancy that could otherwise lead to significant data inconsistencies. You could say that one of the main goals for transaction processing workloads is to gather data and keep them up-to-date based on the incoming data modification operations. *Autonomous Transaction Processing* (ATP) is tuned to serve this type of workload.

OLAP workloads are characterized by the limited number of transactions in favor of planned and regular batch loading of large data volumes that often originate from multiple transactional databases. Data is transformed and consolidated from multiple normalized transactional databases to a highly denormalized, intentionally redundant, analytical data model. Analytical databases are tuned in such way to optimize the performance of both expected and completely ad hoc queries. Typical operations performed on analytical databases are pivoting, drilling down, rolling up, slicing and dicing, data selection, and sequencing. The main goal for OLAP systems is multidimensional aggregate data analysis performed to analyze trends based on historical data, discover various dependencies or correlations, and eventually provide fine-grained reporting. Autonomous Data Warehouse is tuned to serve this type of workload.

Workload types served by ATP and ADW are conceptually illustrated in Figure 7-4.

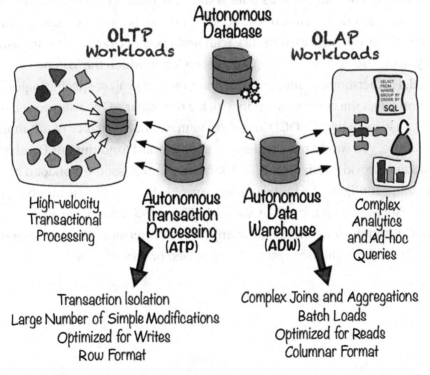

Figure 7-4. ATP and ADW

Autonomous Data Warehouse

Autonomous Data Warehouse is optimized to serve analytical processing in OLAP systems. It uses various Oracle tuning choices such as specific memory allocation, columnar data format, and parallelized queries to boost the performance of typical data warehousing tasks. In contrast to transactional systems, data is loaded into ADW nearly exclusively in batches at most once per day or even less frequently. We are going to simulate a simple data warehousing use case for the occurrence of various police-monitored road events across all major roads in Poland collected over a couple of years. As a matter of fact, the data you are going to use is completely artificial but may look somehow realistic and provide a good foundation for some data analytics. I have generated the data based on custom-choice parameters and the wide use of normal distribution randomness. To begin with, we have to provision a new ADW instance, set up a database schema, ingest data, and run our analytical queries to answer some of the business questions. Next, I will briefly explain what the options are to visualize these discoveries. In the course of this and consecutive sections, you will be introduced to some basic concepts of data warehousing and apply them in practice.

To provision a new Autonomous Data Warehouse instance, there are a few choices to be made and a few parameters to be set. ADW instances are region-specific and compartment-aware. In other words, like with nearly every Oracle Cloud Infrastructure resource, you have to choose the geographical region in which the instance will be provisioned. Furthermore, to support environment- and project-specific logical isolation, you select the compartment in which a particular ADW instance will be created. If you were to use the OCI Console to launch a new instance of Autonomous Data Warehouse, you would open a pretty straightforward Autonomous Database creation wizard, provide both display and database names, set the workload type to Data Warehouse, and configure the initial hardware profile by defining the number of CPUs and storage expressed in terabytes, as shown in Figure 7-5. You will be able to tune the number of CPUs and storage on the fly at any time. Furthermore, you could enable CPU autoscaling to let the database react to the increased processing needs.

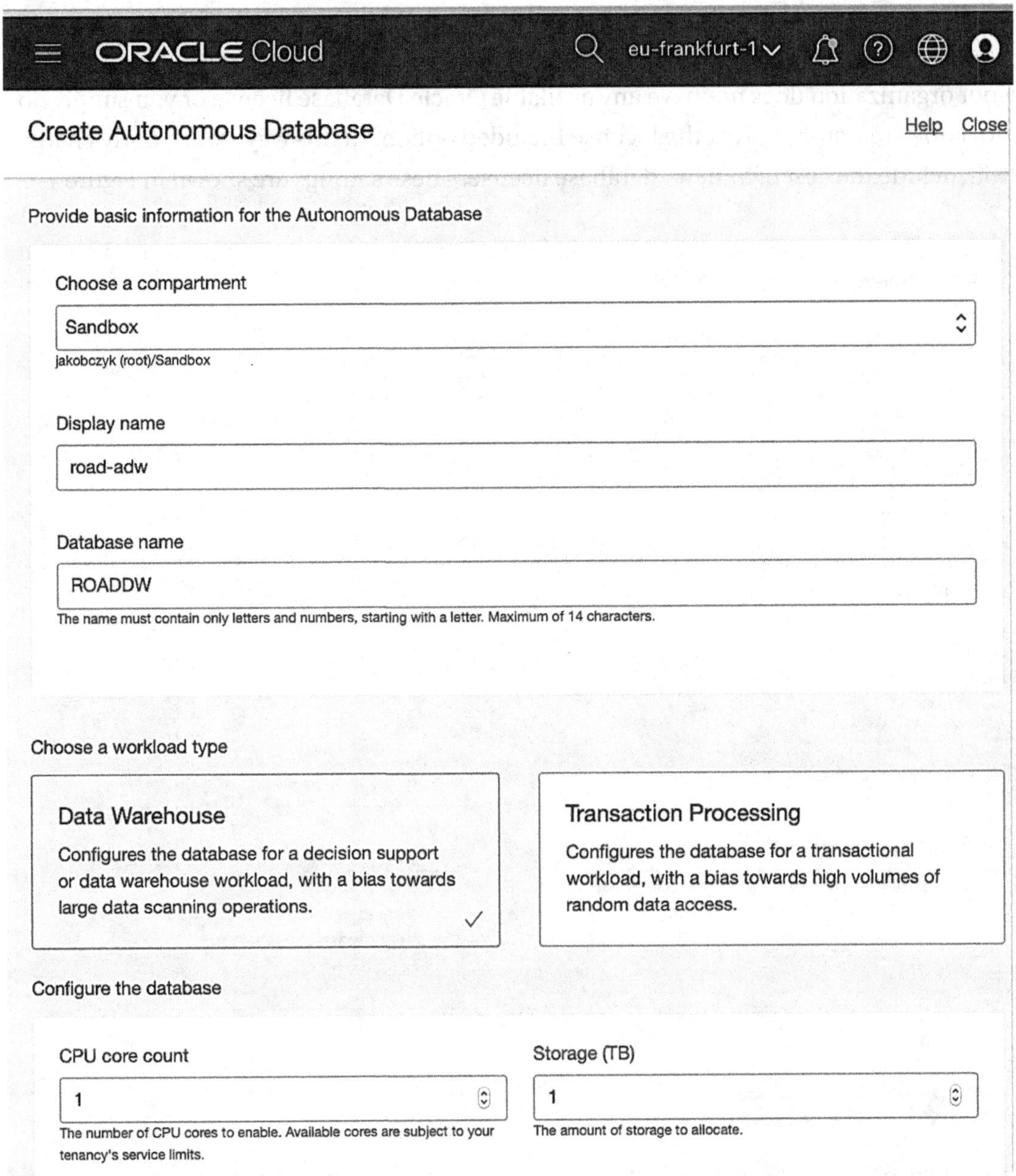

Figure 7-5. *Autonomous Database creation wizard in the OCI Console 1/2*

The database administrator user is called ADMIN. While working with the wizard, you have to set its password. Another important point is related to the licensing model. If your organization does not have any available Oracle Database license or you simply do not know, remember to set the License Included option. In this way, your hourly charge will include the cost of a "new" database license. These settings are shown in Figure 7-6.

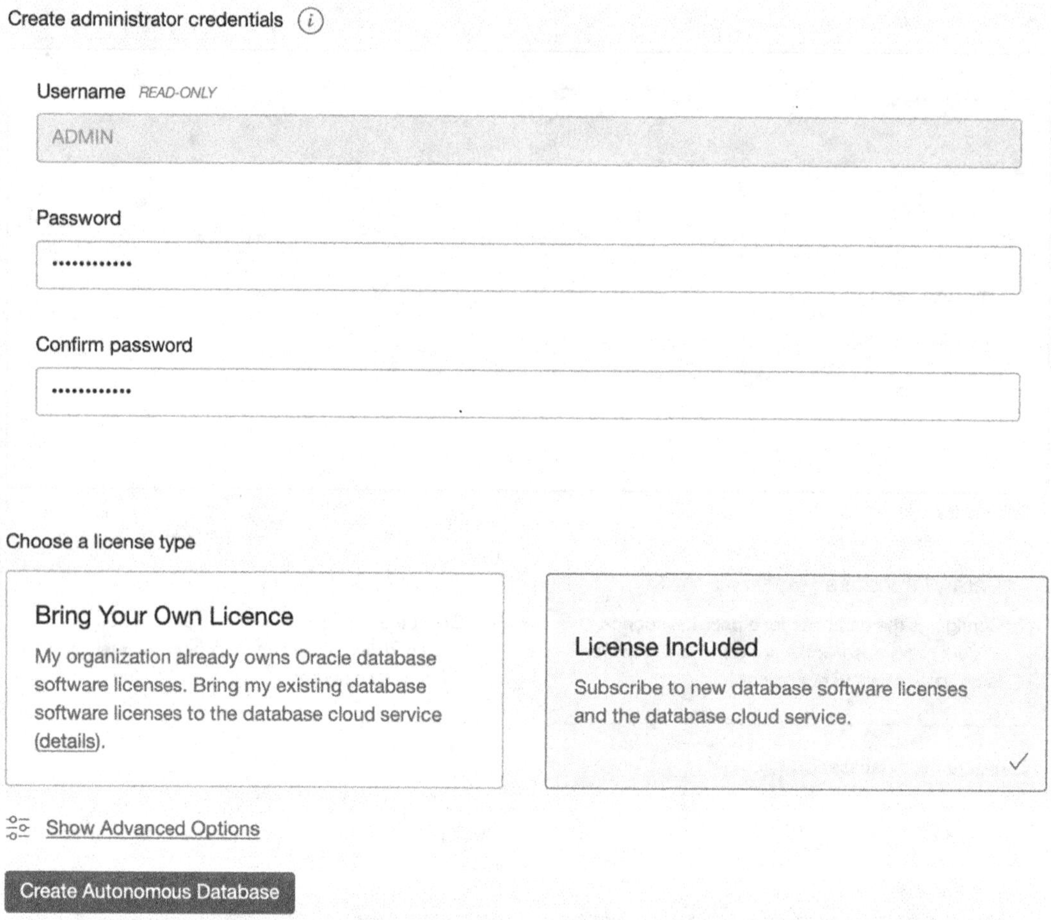

Create administrator credentials ⓘ

Username *READ-ONLY*

```
ADMIN
```

Password

```
••••••••••••
```

Confirm password

```
••••••••••••
```

Choose a license type

Bring Your Own Licence

My organization already owns Oracle database software licenses. Bring my existing database software licenses to the database cloud service (details).

License Included

Subscribe to new database software licenses and the database cloud service.

✓

⚙ Show Advanced Options

Create Autonomous Database

Figure 7-6. *Autonomous Database creation wizard in the OCI Console 2/2*

Like I mentioned, this book focuses on automation. We are therefore going to use the OCI CLI to launch a new instance of Autonomous Data Warehouse in the Sandbox compartment on behalf of the sandbox-admin user. I am assuming the SANDBOX-ADMIN CLI profile is set properly, as described in Chapter 4, with the corresponding section in the oci_cli_rc file that points to the Sandbox compartment as the default compartment for all CLI commands. Make sure you carefully choose the Admin password, which must adhere to the guidelines: be between 12 and 30 characters and contain at least one lowercase letter, one uppercase letter, and one number. To provision the ADW instance, remember to replace the password and use the db autonomous-database create CLI command like this:

```
$ ADW_ADMIN_PASS=evr43453fEWQ3@EF
$ oci db autonomous-database create \
    --db-name ROADDW \
    --display-name road-adw \
    --db-workload DW \
    --license-model LICENSE_INCLUDED \
    --cpu-core-count 1 \
    --data-storage-size-in-tbs 1 \
    --admin-password "$ADW_ADMIN_PASS" \
    --wait-for-state AVAILABLE \
    --profile SANDBOX-ADMIN
Action completed.
Waiting until the resource has entered state: AVAILABLE
```

Oracle has recently added a free tier marketed as Always Free. At the time of writing, you can provision up to two ADB instances limited to one OCPU and 20GB each. These instances won't incur any costs. To launch an Always Free ADB instance, use the --is-free-tier true option for the oci db autonomous-database create CLI command.

```
$ oci db autonomous-database create \
...
--is-free-tier true \
...
```

Tip   If you are working with a paid account, consider using the free tier to launch your ROADDW ADB instance for the purpose of running the exercises described in this chapter.

This will result in the creation of a new serverless Autonomous Database instance optimized for data warehousing and initially equipped with one CPU and 1TB of hardware capacity. The response shows a few interesting details including the Oracle Database version and the Service Console URL.

```
...
"cpu-core-count": 1,
"data-storage-size-in-tbs": 1,
"db-name": "ROADDW",
"db-version": "18c",
"db-workload": "DW",
"display-name": "road-adw",
"id": "ocid1.autonomousdatabase.oc1.eu-frankfurt-1.ab...hm23ea",
"is-auto-scaling-enabled": false,
"is-dedicated": false,
"license-model": "LICENSE_INCLUDED",
"lifecycle-state": "AVAILABLE",
"service-console-url": "https://adb.eu-frankfurt-1.oraclecloud.com/console/
index.html?tenant_name=OCID1.TENANCY.OC1..AA.........3YYMFA&database_
name=ROADDW&service_type=ADW",
...
```

ADW database can be used fully independently from the OCI Console; therefore, a separate dashboard is provided and called the ADB Service Console. You can bookmark and distribute the direct link as shown in the service-console-url element of the response to the db autonomous-database create CLI command. After accessing this link for the first time, you have to sign in as the ADB ADMIN user and provide the password you set for this user a few moments ago. The overview dashboard of the Service Console is shown in Figure 7-7.

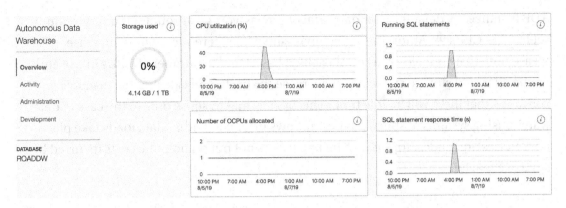

Figure 7-7. *Autonomous Database Service Console dashboard*

Let's take a step back and inspect the ADW instance details in the OCI Console. All instances that exist in a selected compartment are listed, as shown in Figure 7-8.

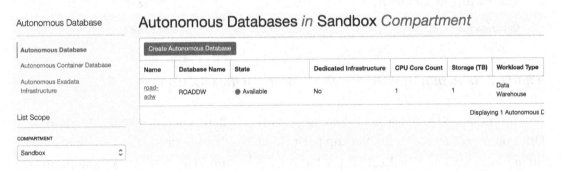

Figure 7-8. *Viewing ADB instances in the OCI Console*

To display the details of a particular ADB instance in OCI Console, do the following:

1. Go to Menu ➤ Database ➤ Autonomous Data Warehouse.

2. Make sure that the Sandbox compartment is selected.

3. Click the name (road-adw) of your ADW instance.

Apart from the instance information, you will spot a number of various buttons in the top part of the details view, as shown in Figure 7-9 and the backup area at the bottom. The Service Console, as the name suggests, will open the instance-specific console I've already introduced you to. The Scale Up/Down will let you tune the number of CPUs allocated to the instance and storage in 1TB increments. At the time of writing, you should be able to allocate up to 128 CPUs and up to 128TB of storage to a single

361

ADB instance. By default, a standard trial or pay-as-you-go account has a service limit set to eight CPUs for Autonomous Database, but you can request a limit increase. Please note that your cloud account is billed based on the number of CPUs in use and on the allocated storage capacity. To decrease the costs, you can stop the instance if you know that there will be idle time. This usually makes sense only in the case of data warehousing systems in specific time windows in which neither data loads take place nor queries are made. Stopping an instance does not put on hold the costs incurred by storage capacity.

Figure 7-9. *Available ADB instance actions in the OCI Console*

Autonomous Database is backed up every day with no user intervention required. Once per week, there is a full backup performed. On the remaining days, there are incremental backups made. All these backups are retained for 60 days. All automatic backups can be considered hot backups, which basically means that the database remains operative and available while a backup is being made. If something goes wrong such as there is a table accidentally truncated or an entire schema dropped, you can restore its state from a selected backup. The list of available backups is visible at the bottom of the ADB detail view in the OCI Console, as shown in Figure 7-10, and can be obtained with the OCI CLI as well.

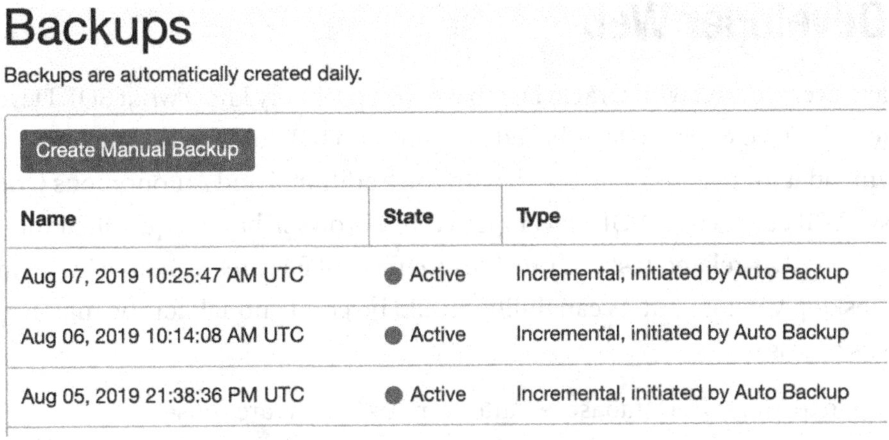

Backups

Backups are automatically created daily.

Create Manual Backup		
Name	**State**	**Type**
Aug 07, 2019 10:25:47 AM UTC	● Active	Incremental, initiated by Auto Backup
Aug 06, 2019 10:14:08 AM UTC	● Active	Incremental, initiated by Auto Backup
Aug 05, 2019 21:38:36 PM UTC	● Active	Incremental, initiated by Auto Backup

Figure 7-10. *ADB backups in the OCI Console*

Even though we could consider using the ADMIN user to make regular database queries, it would be against the approach generally recommended. Moreover, Oracle Database objects such as tables or views exist in the scope of schemas. A schema is associated with a database user. To create a few tables in the road schema, we need to create the road database user and grant all required privileges to that user. Autonomous Database is based on and compliant with the newest version of Oracle Database; therefore, we create database users just as we have done in the case of a traditional on-premise Oracle Database instance. We are now going to connect to the database as ADMIN, create a new user, and grant all the required privileges to that user.

SQL Developer Web

If you have ever worked with Oracle Database, you probably know what SQL Developer is. Oracle SQL Developer is a Java-based SQL desktop IDE for Oracle Database. You can download it for free and use it both with the traditional and Autonomous Oracle Database. ADB comes with SQL Developer Web, a browser-based equivalent that is optimized for ADB-related tasks. It provides a subset of features available in the more mature desktop version, but its capability should be good enough for the majority of SQL tasks. Let's access it.

1. Go to Menu ➤ Database ➤ Autonomous Data Warehouse.

2. Make sure that the Sandbox compartment is selected.

3. Click the name of your ADW instance.

4. Click the Service Console button.

Tip   If nothing happens after clicking the Service Console button, the new window might have been blocked by your browser. In your browser, you have to allow this page to open new windows.

---

5. Sign in as the ADMIN user.

6. Click Development.

7. Click SQL Developer Web.

If you are prompted to sign in again, use the same ADMIN credentials. You can paste the following query in the worksheet area and click the green Run Statement button to see something similar to what is shown in Figure 7-11:

```
SELECT CURRENT_TIMESTAMP FROM dual;
```

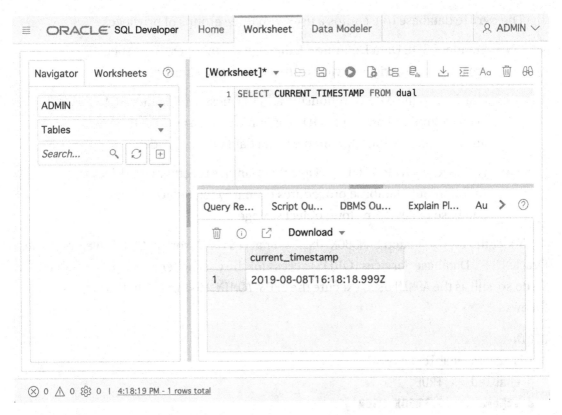

Figure 7-11. *SQL Developer Web*

Still in SQL Developer Web, paste the SQL statements shown in the following, adapt the password located after the `identified` clause, and run the queries:

```
CREATE USER SANDBOX_USER IDENTIFIED BY "y0uRp@55worD";
GRANT dwrole TO SANDBOX_USER;
ALTER USER SANDBOX_USER QUOTA 500M ON DATA;
```

A new database user called SANDBOX_USER will be created and given to the predefined ADW-specific database role called `dwrole`.

If you click the Script Output tab at the bottom, you should see two messages that announce the success of both operations.

```
User SANDBOX_USER created.
Grant succeeded.
```

The dwrole database role equips a user with three groups of privileges.

- Standard SQL Data Definition Language (DDL) operations such as creating tables, triggers, views, procedures, and similar

- Oracle-specific data warehousing and business intelligence SQL Data Definition Language (DDL) operations such as analytic views, attribute dimensions, hierarchies, and data mining models

- DBMS_CLOUD PL/SQL package that bundles together cloud-based Autonomous Database procedures primarily related to feeding database tables from cloud object storage

To let the newly created SANDBOX_USER user access and work in SQL Developer Web, Oracle REST Database Services (ORDS) access for the user schema has to be enabled. To do so, still as the ADMIN user, execute the ORDS_ADMIN.ENABLE_SCHEMA procedure as follows:

```
BEGIN
  ords_admin.enable_schema(
    p_enabled => TRUE,
    p_schema => 'SANDBOX_USER',
    p_url_mapping_type => 'BASE_PATH',
    p_url_mapping_pattern => 'sandbox',
    p_auto_rest_auth => TRUE
  );
  commit;
END;
```

There should be a message in the Script Output tab at the bottom saying the following:

```
PL/SQL procedure successfully completed.
```

The p_schema parameter references the newly created user, while the p_url_mapping_type parameter defines the user-specific part in the user-dedicated URL for SQL Developer Web. Figure 7-12 presents the typical structure of the SQL Developer Web URL.

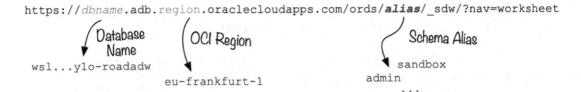

Figure 7-12. *SQL Developer Web URL structure*

Normally, you prepare the user-specific URL and deliver it to the user by replacing the schema-alias part with the URL mapping pattern value used earlier in the ORDS_ ADMIN.ENABLE_SCHEMA procedure. You can copy the base SQL Developer Web URL, while using this browser-based tool still as the ADMIN user. You have to replace the schema-alias part that, in this case, is originally set to the admin value and use the sandbox value instead.

Let's access the SQL Developer Web this time as the SANDBOX_USER. You can open the amended URL in a new browser tab.

Tip   As an alternative to switching tabs, you can use two different browsers for each SQL Developer Web session.

In this way, you will be able to continue working both as ADMIN in the first tab (or browser) and as SANDBOX_USER in the second tab (or browser), as shown in Figure 7-13.

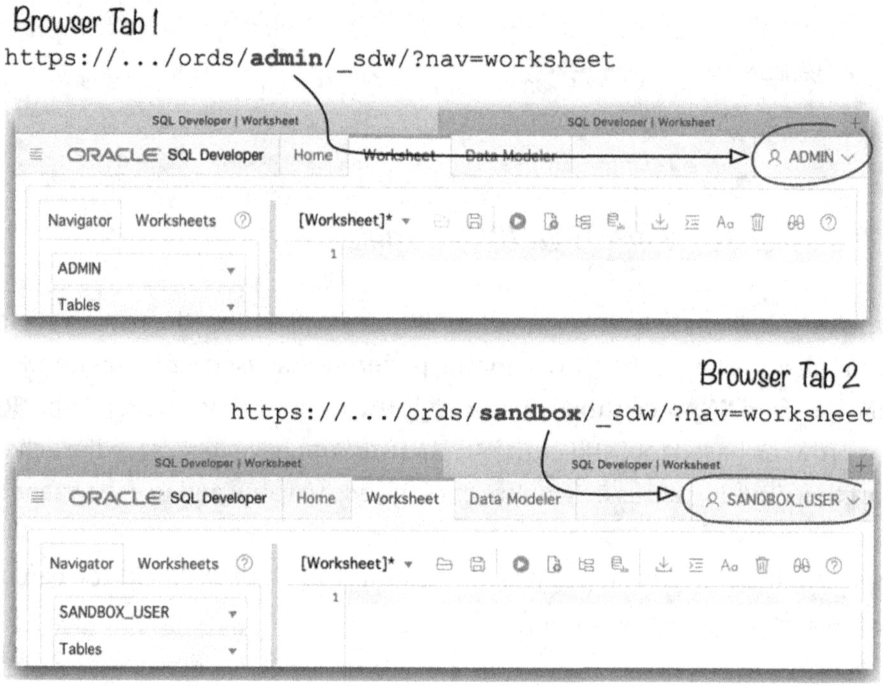
Browser Tab 1
https://.../ords/admin/_sdw/?nav=worksheet
SQL Developer | Worksheet
ORACLE SQL Developer
Home
Worksheet
Data Modeler
ADMIN
Navigator
Worksheets
[Worksheet]*
ADMIN
Tables
Browser Tab 2
https://.../ords/sandbox/_sdw/?nav=worksheet
SANDBOX_USER

Figure 7-13. *SQL Developer Web users*

Loading Data to ADW

Autonomous Database is a cloud-based managed database service. The recommended approach for loading data from files is to upload them to an object storage bucket and execute the DBMS_CLOUD.COPY_DATA procedure to parse these files and insert data into the database tables. This procedure is capable of loading data from the following:

- Oracle Cloud Infrastructure object storage
- Azure Blob Storage
- Amazon S3

The shortest data load time can be achieved from Oracle Cloud Infrastructure object storage buckets in the same region as the ADB instance, but other combinations are absolutely fine as well. The ADW instance accesses OCI object storage on behalf of a particular IAM user.

Database Credential

The DBMS_CLOUD.COPY_DATA procedure references a *Credential* database object that holds the authentication details required to access the cloud-based object storage. For OCI object storage, the IAM user must hold an active *Auth Token* that will be saved in this Credential object together with the username. A token is a relatively short Oracle-generated string. Any IAM user can have up to two Auth Tokens at a time. Tokens can be created by the users themselves or arbitrarily by administrators either using the OCI Console or leveraging API-based automation such as the OCI CLI.

This is how you generate an Auth Token as a sandbox-user in the OCI Console:

1. Log in to the OCI Console as the sandbox-user.

2. Go to the user profile by clicking the user name, as shown in Figure 7-14.

3. On the Resources tab, click Auth Tokens.

4. Click Generate Token.

5. Provide a description for your token, and click Generate Token.

6. Write down your token. You will see it only once.

Figure 7-14. *Accessing the user profile in the OCI Console*

It is crucial to remember that you see a newly generated Auth Token only once, as shown in Figure 7-15. If you lose it, you will have to delete the old token and generate a new one.

Figure 7-15. *Seeing a generated token*

To generate an Auth Token for a selected user programmatically, you can execute the following CLI commands on behalf of the tenancy admin by using the default profile (no `--profile` parameter). First you query for the OCID of a particular user, and then you are using the `iam auth-token create` CLI command for that user.

```
$ TENANCY_OCID=`cat ~/.oci/config | grep tenancy | sed 's/tenancy=//'`
$ IAM_USER_OCID=`oci iam user list -c $TENANCY_OCID --query
"data[?name=='sandbox-user'] | [0].id" --raw-output --all`
$ echo $IAM_USER_OCID
ocid1.user.oc1..aa........zqpxa
$ oci iam auth-token create --user-id $IAM_USER_OCID --description token-
adw --query 'data.token' --raw-output
B8.E_Ry7oOtN1KFOdo9x
```

No matter which way you choose, please make sure you have an Auth Token for the sandbox-user IAM user.

The new database user called SANDBOX_USER is completely independent from the sandbox-user IAM user we have been working with in the course of the previous chapters. We are now going to create a database Credential object to store the username and the Auth Token for the sandbox-user IAM user. These details will be stored in an encrypted format in the database. Every time you execute the DBMS_CLOUD.COPY_DATA procedure to load data from an object in object storage to a database table, you will provide the name of a Credential object to be used.

Tip   From now on, most of the SQL commands will have to be executed in SQL Developer Web on behalf of the SANDBOX_ADMIN. Make sure you open the correct SQL Developer Web instance, using a user-specific link as described a few paragraphs earlier.

Open SQL Developer Web as the SANDBOX_USER database user, place the SQL procedure in the worksheet, use your newly generated Auth Token as the value for the password parameter, and execute the following command:

```
BEGIN
  DBMS_CLOUD.CREATE_CREDENTIAL(
    credential_name => 'OCI_SANDBOX_USER',
    username => 'sandbox-user',
    password => 'B8.E_Ry7o0tN1KF0do9x'
  );
END;
```

The Credential objects exist in a particular user schema and can be accessed only by the users who have access to that schema. Each Oracle Database schema is by convention associated with a single database user of the same name. You can assume that, by default, only the Credential owner user is allowed to reference this Credential object. To delete an existing Credential object, you should rely on the DBMS_CLOUD.DROP_CREDENTIAL procedure. To list the existing Credential objects in a given schema, you can use the following SQL query as the schema owner:

```
SELECT * FROM all_credentials;
```

Loading data from a file to ADB can be summarized in three steps. We will be following them a bit later.

1. Upload the source file in a supported format such as .csv to an object storage bucket.

2. Create a new database table for the imported data if the table does not exist yet.

3. Execute DBMS_CLOUD.COPY_DATA to populate the table.

This process is conceptually illustrated in Figure 7-16.

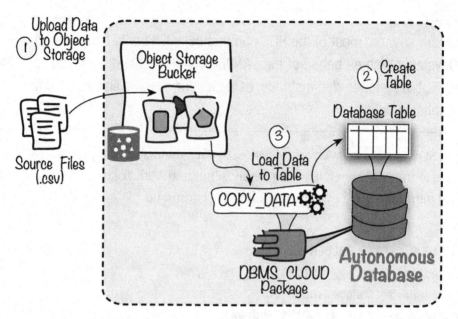

Figure 7-16. *Loading data from object storage to ADW*

Earlier, we created a Credential database object that will let the ADW instance access OCI object storage on behalf of a named IAM user. We still need to create an object storage bucket. In Chapter 5, you learned that to set up a new bucket you can rely on the following OCI CLI command and execute it on behalf of the sandbox-admin user via the SANDBOX-ADMIN profile. Do it now and create a new bucket called roadadw-load.

```
$ oci os bucket create --name roadadw-load --profile SANDBOX-ADMIN
```

Based on the IAM policy set in Chapter 5, the sandbox-user is allowed to upload data to only to the object storage bucket called blueprints. Let's extend this access scope by adding the new IAM policy statements shown in Listing 7-2. Now, we are going to let sandbox-users upload objects to the roadadw-load bucket.

Listing 7-2. sandbox-users.policies.adwstorage.json

```
[
"allow group sandbox-users to read buckets in compartment Sandbox where
target.bucket.name='roadadw-load'",
"allow group sandbox-users to manage objects in compartment Sandbox where
target.bucket.name='roadadw-load'"
]
```

We can create a new policy in the Sandbox compartment using the `oci iam policy` create CLI command in the same way we added new policies in the previous chapters. The policy should be added to the Sandbox compartment. As long as you are still using the `oci_cli_rc` file configured as described in the previous chapters, these commands should do the work:

```
$ cd ~/git/oci-book/chapter07/1-setup/
$ oci iam policy create --name sandbox-users-adw-storage-policy
--statements file://sandbox-users.policies.adwstorage.json --description
"ADW-Storage-related policy for regular Sandbox users" --profile SANDBOX-
ADMIN
```

With the new policy in place, we are ready to upload the files that hold various input data for new ADW tables to the `roadadw-load` object storage bucket. At this stage, it may be worth mentioning what these files are and how we are going to use them.

Star Schema

I have already said that we are going to simulate a simple data warehousing use case. A *star schema* is a typical constellation of relational database tables that makes it easier to perform typical business intelligence operations such as pivoting, selection, slice, and dice as well as drill-down and roll-up. At the beginning of this chapter, I introduced you to the concept of relationships between tables and their importance in relational databases. At the heart of a star schema, there is a *fact table* that contains partially aggregated, numeric data such as sales results expressed in currency, various measurements expressed in measured units, production volumes expressed in quantities, or observed events quantified using gathered statistics. The exercises in this chapter are built around data that resembles accidents and incidents reported on Polish roads. These events are quantified using the following measures:

- The number of these events (occurrence)

- People injured

- People killed

To be able to analyze data, numbers alone are insufficient. We need to know the context of each record stored in the fact table. These contexts are addressed as dimensions. A road event can take place on a given day (Time dimension) and on a given road segment (Road dimension) and have a particular type such as rear-end car collision, speeding, or unlicensed driving (Event Type dimension). You may want to group specific types of road events into a hierarchy of categories. A rear-end car collision and side collision may both belong to the "collision" category. Next, multiple categories can be grouped into road event classes such as "accidents" or "incidents." As a result, the Event Type dimension would have a hierarchy of three levels: topmost road event classes, middle-level road event categories, and finally low-level road event types. If you consider the Time dimension hierarchy, the most common levels of granularity are day, month, and year. In the case of the Road dimension hierarchy, you may differentiate road segment and road. Dimensions provide each individual fact table entry with a diverse context, as illustrated in Figure 7-17.

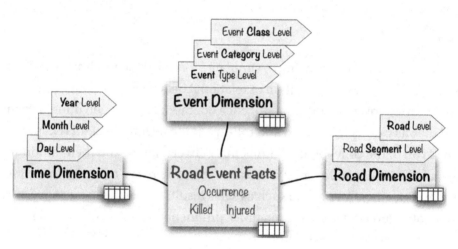

Figure 7-17. *Star schema*

For example, one of the observations included in the Road Events fact table could indicate that on March 7, 2017, there were seven run-off-road accidents on the expressway DK5 road segment in the Kuyavian-Pomeranian voivodeship (area). Further numeric data included in this particular fact table record could inform us that these seven accidents involved two injured and six killed in total.

With this chapter in mind, I have already prepared all the data required to perform the upcoming exercises. You will load the three dimensions and the entire fact table from the comma-separated-value (CSV) files that are available in the Git repository of this book.

Dimensions

We have already said that without proper context, your fact data is virtually useless. Dimensions provide the context for your facts and let you gain valuable insights into what the data means. You can find the dimension data files in the `chapter07/2-dimensions` directory.

```
$ cd ~/git/oci-book/chapter07/2-dimensions/
$ ls -1 *_dim.csv
event_dim.csv
road_dim.csv
time_dim.csv
```

The filenames indicate what kind of data records are stored in each of these files. The `event_dim.csv` file contains Event Type dimension entries, the `road_dim.csv` contains the Road dimension entries, and the `time_dim.csv` contains the Time dimension entries. The files use a well-known CSV human-readable text format. Values are separated using the comma (,) character. Each row resembles one record of data. The first row contains a header with column names. Figure 7-18 shows how the `.csv` file contents map to the database table we are about to create and feed.

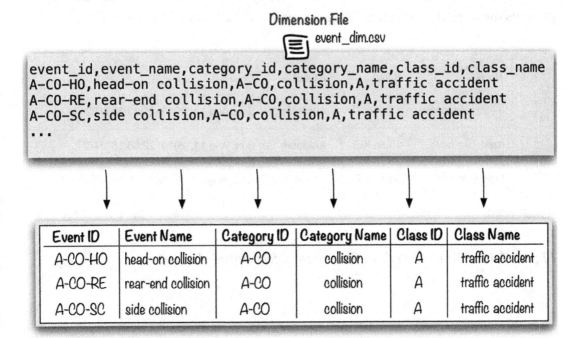

Figure 7-18. *Dimension files*

I am assuming you have already created the `roadadw-load` bucket as instructed a few moments ago. Let's upload the dimension files to this bucket. We are going to use the `os object put` OCI CLI command. You learned how to do this in Chapter 5. Remember to choose the SANDBOX-USER CLI profile, which you created in Chapter 4. The profile will eventually execute the API call on behalf of `sandbox-user`.

```
$ oci os object put -bn roadadw-load --file time_dim.csv --profile SANDBOX-USER
Uploading object  [#################################]  100%
$ oci os object put -bn roadadw-load --file road_dim.csv --profile SANDBOX-USER
Uploading object  [#################################]  100%
$ oci os object put -bn roadadw-load --file event_dim.csv --profile
SANDBOX-USER
Uploading object  [#################################]  100%
```

You can view the newly uploaded files in the Bucket Details view of the object storage dashboard in the OCI Console. To do so in the OCI Console, perform the following steps:

1.   Go to Menu ➤ Object Storage ➤ Object Storage.

2.   Click the bucket name.

In the Objects table of the Bucket Details view, you should see the objects. Figure 7-19 presents the three files as object storage objects in the `roadadw-load` bucket.

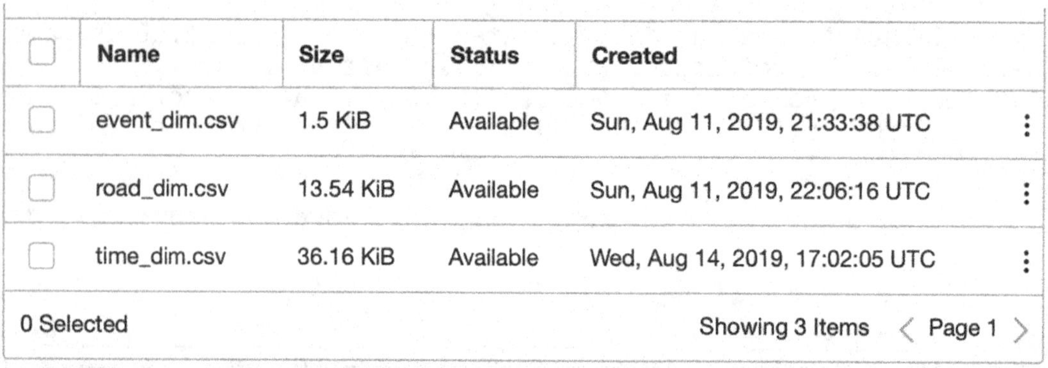

	Name	Size	Status	Created	
☐	event_dim.csv	1.5 KiB	Available	Sun, Aug 11, 2019, 21:33:38 UTC	⋮
☐	road_dim.csv	13.54 KiB	Available	Sun, Aug 11, 2019, 22:06:16 UTC	⋮
☐	time_dim.csv	36.16 KiB	Available	Wed, Aug 14, 2019, 17:02:05 UTC	⋮

0 Selected   Showing 3 Items   ‹ Page 1 ›

Figure 7-19. *Dimension data files in an object storage bucket*

The Time dimension includes 731 records. Each record represents one calendar day between January 1, 2016, and December 31, 2017. If you wondered why there are 731 days instead of 730 days (2 × 365 days), the answer is simple. The year 2016 is a leap year and has 366 days in total. The Time dimension has three hierarchy levels, as shown in Figure 7-20. Each dimension attribute eventually maps to a database table column and belongs to one particular level. Furthermore, there is one attribute for each level that uniquely identifies the given level. These attributes (day_id, month_id, and year_id) are typically suffixed with the _id in their name.

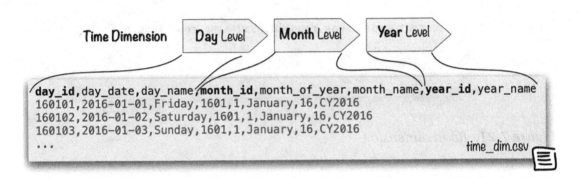

Figure 7-20. *Time dimension*

The Road dimension includes 263 records and has two hierarchy levels, namely, Road Segment and Road. A single segment represents all road parts in one particular voivodeship and of a given type such as regular road (G), main road (GP), expressway (S), and highway (A). If you look at Figure 7-21, the segment R01S01 represents all roads of highway type that, from an organizational point of view, belong to the road DK1 and are located in the Pomeranian voivodeship.

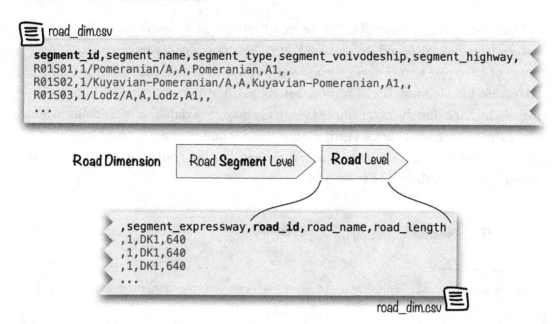

Figure 7-21. *Road dimension*

The Event dimension includes 24 records and has three hierarchy levels. We already discussed them a bit earlier, but to recap, the most granular Road Event Types are the middle-level Road Event Category and the topmost Road Event Class, as shown in Figure 7-22.

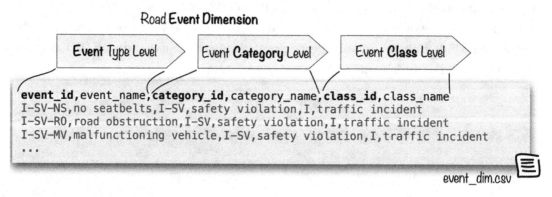

Figure 7-22. *Road Event dimension*

All in all, the dimension data has been successfully uploaded to the object storage in Oracle Cloud. We still need to create the dimension database tables in our Autonomous Data Warehouse instance before we attempt to feed these tables. Open SQL Developer Web for the SANDBOX_USER user, and execute the first SQL Data Definition Language (DDL) statement.

```
create table EVENT_DIM (
   event_id         char(7) not null,
   event_name       varchar2(50) not null,
   category_id      char(4) not null,
   category_name    varchar2(50) not null,
   class_id         char(1) not null,
   class_name       varchar2(50) not null,
   constraint pk_event_dim primary key (event_id)
);
```

As a result, the first dimension table for the Event Type dimension will be created.

Autonomous Database is basically a cloud-based Oracle database; therefore, we are using Oracle Database data types such as VARCHAR2. We create a table with six columns, one for each dimension attribute. The primary key of the table is set to the identifier of the most granular dimension hierarchy level. You should observe the message that the table has been successfully created.

```
Table EVENT_DIM created
```

It is time to feed the newly created database table and load the data from the corresponding object that encapsulates the comma-separated-value file for the Event Type dimension. Still, in SQL Developer Web, prepare the DBMS_CLOUD.COPY_DATA procedure. You will have to amend the file_uri_list input parameter and set it to the URI of the object that represents the event_dim.csv file. Basically, you have to use your region code (in my case, it is eu-frankfurt-1) and your object storage namespace (in my case, it is jakobczyk). You can find the precise value for each object in the Object Details pop-up of this object in the OCI Console. When ready, execute the following procedure:

```
BEGIN
  DBMS_CLOUD.COPY_DATA(
    table_name => 'EVENT_DIM',
    credential_name => 'OCI_SANDBOX_USER',
    file_uri_list => 'https://objectstorage.eu-frankfurt-1.oraclecloud.
    com/n/jakobczyk/b/roadadw-load/o/event_dim.csv',
    format => json_object('type' value 'CSV', 'skipheaders' value '1')
  );
END;
```

The DBMS_CLOUD.COPY_DATA procedure uses a Credential database object referenced by name that you provide as the value to the credential_name parameter. The procedure processes all files mentioned with the file_uri_list parameter, taking into consideration any specific format-related settings that you provide with the format parameter. Finally, data is inserted into the target table with the name you set with the table_name parameter. In our case, it will be the EVENT_DIM table we created just a while ago. We instruct the procedure that the files are in the CSV format, and they include headers we want to skip. The procedure should result in a brief message that says that everything went fine.

```
PL/SQL procedure successfully completed.
```

We won't practice error handling here, but it is good to know, briefly, how the procedure handles any unexpected load issues. First, you have to know the rejectlimit attribute you can add to the format field. The rejectlimit attribute defines the maximum number of any encountered invalid rows that will be ignored without forcing the procedure to error out. This value is set by default to 0, which means that the entire data load will be rolled back if there is even one row that violates column data type, referential integrity, or any other constraints. In such a case, you will be notified in the output message where you can find the detailed procedure log. It is usually stored in a dynamically created table whose name looks something like COPY$1_LOG.

Let's take a glance at the Event Type dimension data in the EVENT_DIM database table. In the same SQL Developer Web worksheet, run the following query to select all records from the EVENT_DIM table:

```
select * from event_dim;
```

The results are shown in Figure 7-23. Feel free to compare what you see in your Query Results pane to the contents of the event_dim.csv file.

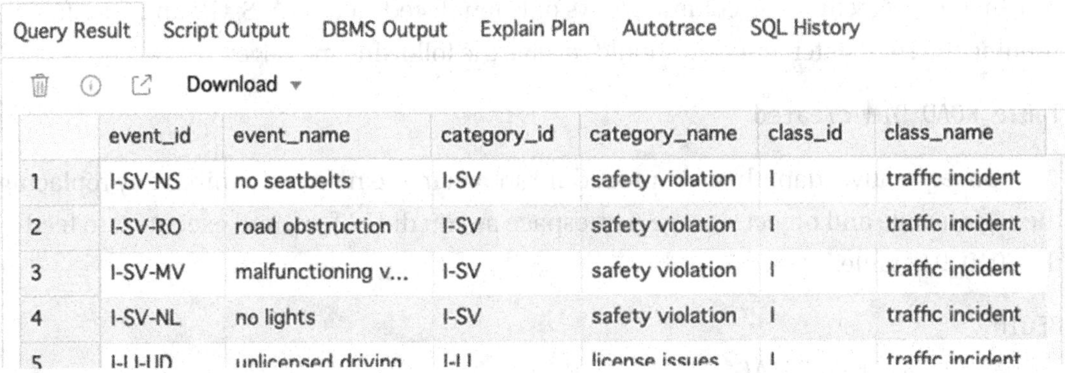

	event_id	event_name	category_id	category_name	class_id	class_name
1	I-SV-NS	no seatbelts	I-SV	safety violation	I	traffic incident
2	I-SV-RO	road obstruction	I-SV	safety violation	I	traffic incident
3	I-SV-MV	malfunctioning v...	I-SV	safety violation	I	traffic incident
4	I-SV-NL	no lights	I-SV	safety violation	I	traffic incident
5	I-LI-UD	unlicensed driving	I-LI	license issues	I	traffic incident

Query Result   Script Output   DBMS Output   Explain Plan   Autotrace   SQL History

Download ▾

Figure 7-23. *Event dimension data in SQL Developer Web*

Now, we are going to repeat what we did for the Event Type dimension and apply the same steps to load the remaining two dimensions. Create the new database table for the Road dimension using the following SQL DDL statement:

```
create table ROAD_DIM (
  segment_id          char(6) not null,
  segment_name        varchar2(50) not null,
  segment_type        char(2) not null,
  segment_voivodeship varchar2(50) not null,
  segment_highway     varchar2(50),
  segment_expressway  varchar2(50),
  road_id             varchar2(10) not null,
  road_name           varchar2(10) not null,
  road_lenght         number(5),
  constraint pk_road_dim primary key (segment_id),
  constraint chk_segment_type
    check ( segment_type in ('A','S','GP','G'))
);
```

The ROAD_DIM database table includes two columns that allow NULL values. In the database world and not only there, NULL is understood as "no value" and is used to differ from an "empty value." Furthermore, the table uses an additional CHECK constraint to make sure that the segment_type column allows only four listed values (A, S, GP, and G). After running the DDL statement, you should receive the following message:

```
Table ROAD_DIM created
```

Consequently, adapt the next procedure shown in the next code snippet by replacing the region code and object storage namespace as you did before, and execute it to feed the ROAD_DIM table.

```
BEGIN
  DBMS_CLOUD.COPY_DATA(
    table_name => 'ROAD_DIM',
    credential_name => 'OCI_SANDBOX_USER',
    file_uri_list => 'https://objectstorage.eu-frankfurt-1.oraclecloud.
    com/n/jakobczyk/b/roadadw-load/o/road_dim.csv',
    format => json_object('type' value 'CSV', 'skipheaders' value '1',
    'blankasnull' value 'true')
  );
END;
```

This time, we added a new format attribute called blankasnull. As a result, all empty fields in the source file will be represented as NULL in their corresponding database fields. We do not expect any surprises.

```
PL/SQL procedure successfully completed.
```

Again, use SQL Developer Web to display what has just been copied to the ROAD_DIM table.

```
select * from road_dim;
```

The results are shown in Figure 7-24.

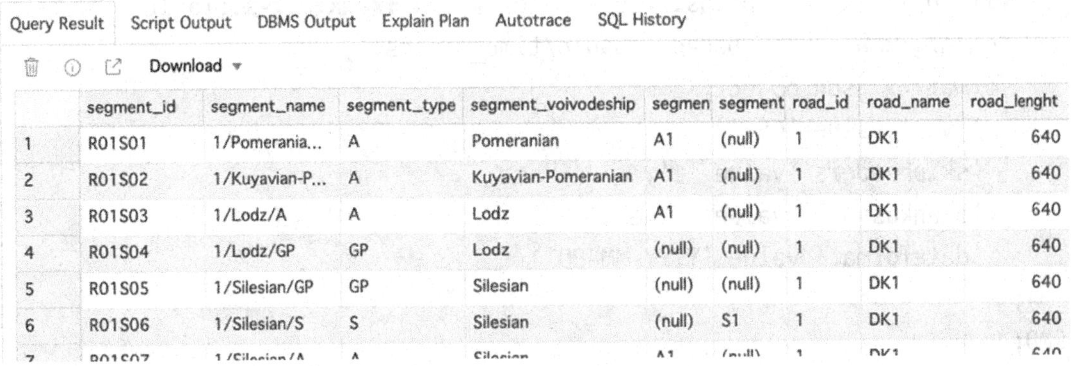

Query Result   Script Output   DBMS Output   Explain Plan   Autotrace   SQL History

🗑 ⓘ ⌷   Download ▾

	segment_id	segment_name	segment_type	segment_voivodeship	segmen	segment	road_id	road_name	road_lenght
1	R01S01	1/Pomerania...	A	Pomeranian	A1	(null)	1	DK1	640
2	R01S02	1/Kuyavian-P...	A	Kuyavian-Pomeranian	A1	(null)	1	DK1	640
3	R01S03	1/Lodz/A	A	Lodz	A1	(null)	1	DK1	640
4	R01S04	1/Lodz/GP	GP	Lodz	(null)	(null)	1	DK1	640
5	R01S05	1/Silesian/GP	GP	Silesian	(null)	(null)	1	DK1	640
6	R01S06	1/Silesian/S	S	Silesian	(null)	S1	1	DK1	640
7	R01S07	1/Silesian/A	A	Silesian	A1	(null)	1	DK1	640

Figure 7-24. *Road dimension in SQL Developer Web*

The only remaining dimension is the Time dimension. Create the following table:

```
create table TIME_DIM (
    day_id          char(6) not null,
    day_date        DATE not null,
    day_name        varchar2(20) not null,
    month_id        char(4) not null,
    month_of_year   number(2) not null,
    month_name      varchar2(20) not null,
    year_id         char(2) not null,
    year_name       char(6) not null,
    constraint pk_time_dim primary key (day_id)
);
```

At this stage as well, everything should go fine.

```
Table TIME_DIM created
```

Similar to before, adapt and execute the COPY_DATA procedure to load data from the time_dim.csv file stored in the object storage to the TIME_DIM database table.

```
BEGIN
  DBMS_CLOUD.COPY_DATA(
    table_name => 'TIME_DIM',
    credential_name => 'OCI_SANDBOX_USER',
```

```
    file_uri_list => 'https://objectstorage.eu-frankfurt-1.oraclecloud.
    com/n/jakobczyk/b/roadadw-load/o/time_dim.csv',
    format => json_object(
       'type' value 'CSV',
       'skipheaders' value '1',
       'blankasnull' value 'true',
       'dateformat' value 'YYYY-MM-DD')
   );
END;
```

The TIME_DIM table specifies the DATE data type for the day_date column. Usually, we need to be a bit careful with this kind of data type and make sure the database precisely understands the date encoding used in the source data. This is because it is generally possible to write down a date in multiple ways. For example, the most common date format in the United States is "month/day/year," for example "8/16/19." In Europe, you use "year month day," for example, "20190816." If you look into the time_dim.csv file, you will see that I applied another date format, namely, year-month-day. August 16, 2019, would be thus written as "2019-08-16." You use the dateformat attribute provided to the format field to instruct the procedure how to translate what it finds in the source data to the DATE data type if inserting the data field into a DATE-type column. Even though this dimension contains a few more records than the two previous, the procedure should inform on its success relatively fast.

```
PL/SQL procedure successfully completed.
```

You can use this query to see the newly loaded records:

```
select * from time_dim;
```

The results are shown in Figure 7-25.

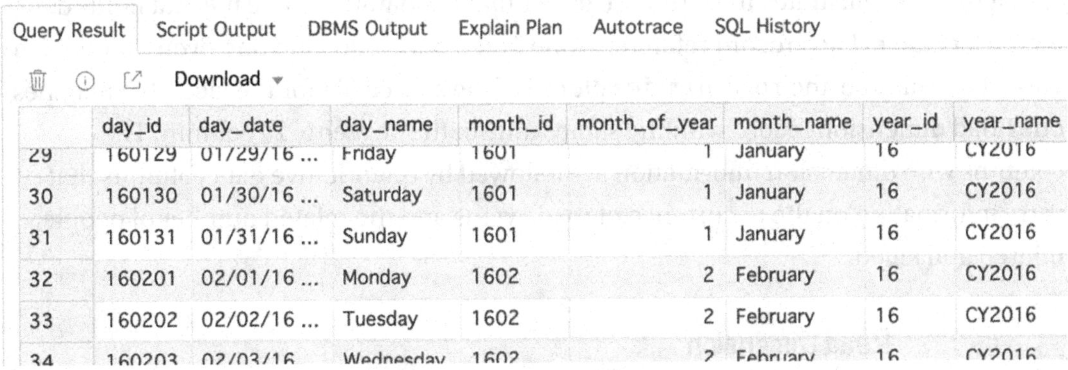

	day_id	day_date	day_name	month_id	month_of_year	month_name	year_id	year_name
29	160129	01/29/16 ...	Friday	1601	1	January	16	CY2016
30	160130	01/30/16 ...	Saturday	1601	1	January	16	CY2016
31	160131	01/31/16 ...	Sunday	1601	1	January	16	CY2016
32	160201	02/01/16 ...	Monday	1602	2	February	16	CY2016
33	160202	02/02/16 ...	Tuesday	1602	2	February	16	CY2016
34	160203	02/03/16	Wednesday	1602	2	February	16	CY2016

Figure 7-25. *Time dimensions in SQL Developer Web*

To sum up this part, the data of all three dimensions is currently present in the database. It is time to add the facts.

Facts

Dimensions set the context for the facts. The facts, however, carry the most valuable information, namely, diverse numeric data that can later be subjected to various analytical operations. Unlike dimensions, fact tables can indeed be very large and contain a vast collection of records. On many occasions, the collection of records is so big that it must be split into multiple source data files. To simulate this, I have prepared not one but four comma-separated-value files that include the source data for the fact table. Each file contains facts collected from a period of time that spans half a year. In this way, altogether, the four files contain data for the period of two calendar years. You can find the fact data files in the chapter07/3-facts directory.

```
$ cd ~/git/oci-book/chapter07/3-facts/
$ ls -1 *.csv
facts.16H1.csv
facts.16H2.csv
facts.17H1.csv
facts.17H2.csv
```

Figure 7-26 illustrates the structure of a comma-separated-value file that holds data for the fact table. Each record references one Time, one Road, and one Event dimension entry. For example, the road_dim_id column of the source file for the fact table matches one Road dimension record with the same value in the segment_id column. The columns with dimension information are followed by quantitative data columns that carry information on the occurrence of road events and the related number of people injured and killed.

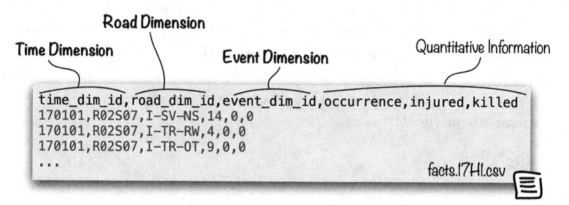

Figure 7-26. *Road Event facts*

Use the os object put CLI command to upload all four fact files to the object storage bucket. Remember to apply the SANDBOX-USER profile like before. You can use it in a Bash shell for loop in this way:

```
$ for fact in `ls facts.*.csv`; do echo $fact; oci os object put -bn
roadadw-load --file $fact --profile SANDBOX-USER; done
facts.16H1.csv
Uploading object  [################################]   100%
facts.16H2.csv
Uploading object  [################################]   100%
facts.17H1.csv
Uploading object  [################################]   100%
facts.17H2.csv
Uploading object  [################################]   100%
```

You should now see these files as objects in the roadadw-load bucket, as shown in Figure 7-27.

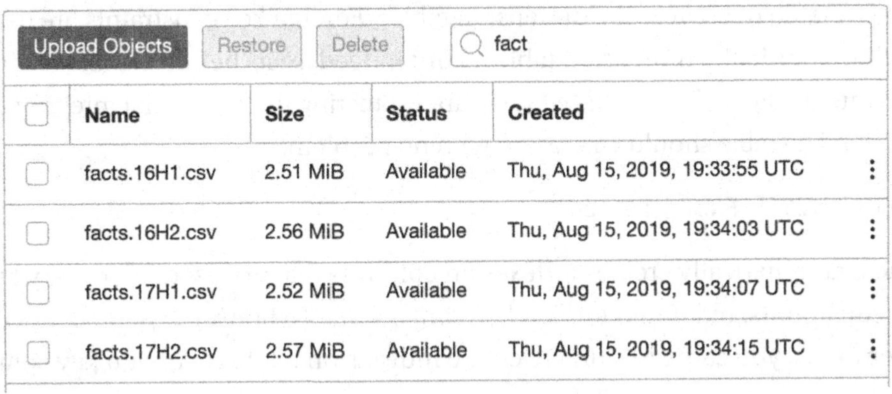
Upload Objects
Restore
Delete
fact
Name
Size
Status
Created
facts.16H1.csv
2.51 MiB
Available
Thu, Aug 15, 2019, 19:33:55 UTC
facts.16H2.csv
2.56 MiB
Available
Thu, Aug 15, 2019, 19:34:03 UTC
facts.17H1.csv
2.52 MiB
Available
Thu, Aug 15, 2019, 19:34:07 UTC
facts.17H2.csv
2.57 MiB
Available
Thu, Aug 15, 2019, 19:34:15 UTC

***Figure 7-27.** Facts data files in the object storage bucket*

Back in SQL Developer Web, still logged in as the SANDBOX_USER user, execute the SQL DDL statement that will create your database fact table.

```
create table ROADEVENTS_FACT (
  time_dim_id      char(6) not null,
  road_dim_id      char(6) not null,
  event_dim_id     char(7) not null,
  occurrence       number(10) not null,
  injured          number(10) not null,
  killed           number(10) not null,
  constraint pk_roadevents_fact
    primary key (time_dim_id, road_dim_id, event_dim_id),
  constraint fk_road_dim
    foreign key (road_dim_id)
      references ROAD_DIM(segment_id),
  constraint fk_event_dim
    foreign key (event_dim_id)
      references EVENT_DIM(event_id),
  constraint fk_time_dim
    foreign key (time_dim_id)
      references TIME_DIM(day_id)
);
```

The fact table references the dimension tables. Foreign key constraints are used to ensure that a particular dimension table record indeed exists before the fact record is inserted into the fact table. In this way, we are protecting the referential integrity of our data model. The table should be created with no problem.

```
Table ROADEVENTS_FACT created
```

Oracle automatically creates indexes on columns that are used in primary key and unique constraints, but not in foreign key constraints. To boost the performance of the join operations, you can additionally create indexes on all three foreign key columns like this:

```
CREATE INDEX roadevents_fact_time_ix
  ON roadevents_fact (time_dim_id);
CREATE INDEX roadevents_fact_road_ix
  ON roadevents_fact (road_dim_id);
CREATE INDEX roadevents_fact_event_ix
  ON roadevents_fact (event_dim_id);
```

You are now ready to execute the COPY_DATA procedure. Like always, adapt the region code and the object storage namespace, and execute the following code:

```
BEGIN
  DBMS_CLOUD.COPY_DATA(
    table_name => 'ROADEVENTS_FACT',
    credential_name => 'OCI_SANDBOX_USER',
    file_uri_list => 'https://objectstorage.eu-frankfurt-1.oraclecloud.
    com/n/jakobczyk/b/roadadw-load/o/facts.*.csv',
    format => json_object('type' value 'CSV', 'skipheaders' value '1',
    'blankasnull' value 'true')
  );
END;
```

You are already familiar with all the parameters. Please note the wildcard used in the value of the file_uri_list parameter. In this way, we can specify multiple source files with a similar name in a convenient way. The procedure should succeed after a short time.

```
PL/SQL procedure successfully completed.
```

To get an initial impression of how many fact records were actually inserted, we can run the select count(*) query.

```
select count(*) from ROADEVENTS_FACT;
```

The result tells us that there are 377,808 rows in total. Let's see some of them by executing a standard select SQL query.

```
select * from ROADEVENTS_FACT;
```

Unless you want to export the results, SQL Developer Web will load data gradually in batches, loading more only if you continue scrolling down. This prevents us from having to wait too long if not necessary. The results are shown in Figure 7-28.

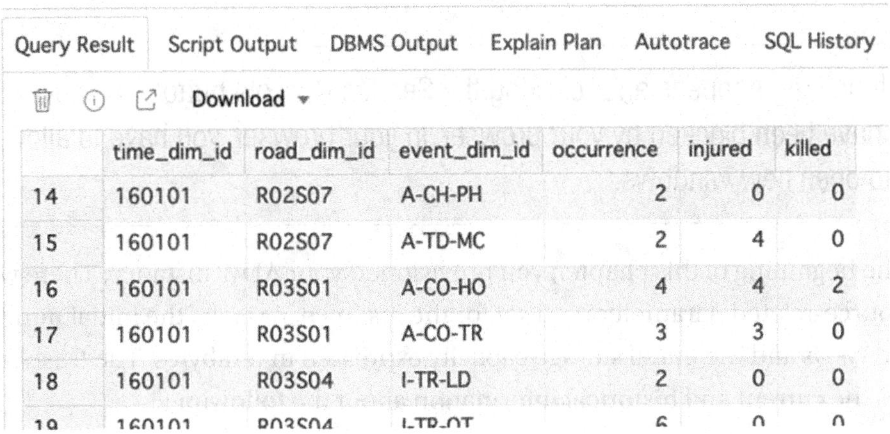

Query Result	Script Output	DBMS Output	Explain Plan	Autotrace	SQL History

🗑 ⓘ ☑   Download ▾

	time_dim_id	road_dim_id	event_dim_id	occurrence	injured	killed
14	160101	R02S07	A-CH-PH	2	0	0
15	160101	R02S07	A-TD-MC	2	4	0
16	160101	R03S01	A-CO-HO	4	4	2
17	160101	R03S01	A-CO-TR	3	3	0
18	160101	R03S04	I-TR-LD	2	0	0
19	160101	R03S04	I-TR-OT	6	0	0

Figure 7-28. Fact table in SQL Developer Web

You have completed the data loading part of the exercise. As a part of it, we executed a couple of SQL DDL statements and stored procedures and a few SQL select statements. The ADB instance gives you some insights into the details of your database. Let's take a look at some monitoring features included with ADW.

Database Monitoring

An Autonomous Database instance is equipped with a dedicated Service Console that can be used to monitor the performance of the instance. The ADB Service Console Dashboard was already shown in Figure 7-7. To access the Service Console, you can use its direct link, if you saved it earlier. Alternatively, you can always open the OCI Console and take the following steps:

1. Go to Menu ➤ Database ➤ Autonomous Data Warehouse.

2. Make sure that the Sandbox compartment is selected.

3. Click the name of your ADW instance.

4. Click the Service Console button.

Tip   If nothing happens after clicking the Service Console button, the new window might have been blocked by your browser. In your browser, you have to allow this page to open new windows.

At the beginning of this chapter, you provisioned your ADW instance. There were two resource-related parameters you set for the instance, namely, the initial number of assigned CPUs and the initial storage capacity expressed in terabytes. The Dashboard provides the current and historical information about the following:

*   The CPU allocation and utilization

*   The storage capacity used by all database tablespaces

*   The average number of executed SQL statements

*   The average SQL statement response time

The Activity view presented in Figure 7-29 delivers a bit more granular information on the service consumption and lets you inspect detailed SQL execution information.

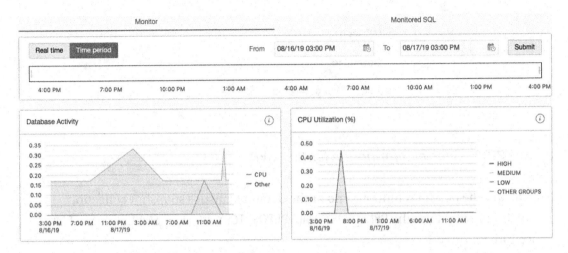

Figure 7-29. *ADW database Activity view*

The Activity view lets you adapt the time interval you would like to display statistics for. By default, ADW persists the historical information for service consumption for eight days and does it in one-hour intervals. You can increase the retention time to a value larger than these eight days and change the performance statistics collection interval. Autonomous Database, just like the traditional Oracle Database, relies on Automatic Workload Repository (AWR) tables to persist historical performance statistics. The AWR tables are stored in the SYSAUX tablespace and belong to the SYS schema. Open SQL Developer Web as ADMIN, and run the following query to display the current AWR settings:

```
select
  extract( hour from snap_interval) interval_hours,
  snap_interval,
  extract( day from retention) retention_days,
  retention
from SYS.DBA_HIST_WR_CONTROL
where dbid=(select con_dbid from v$database);
```

The results are shown in Figure 7-30. The snap_interval and retention columns are of the INTERVAL type so you can leverage the EXTRACT() function to print only the part (days, hours, minutes, seconds) you are interested in.

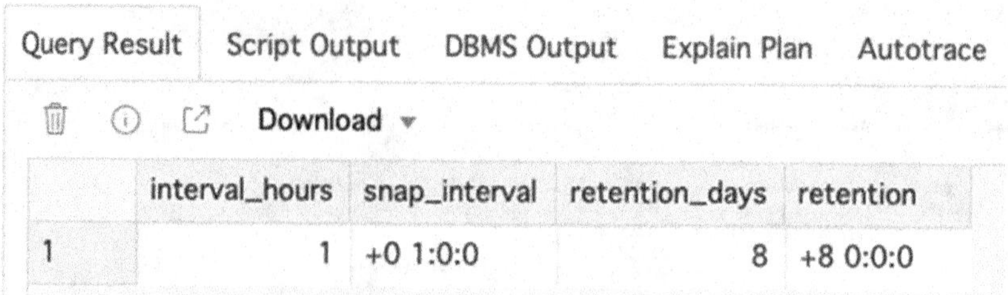

	interval_hours	snap_interval	retention_days	retention
1	1	+0 1:0:0	8	+8 0:0:0

Figure 7-30. *Control information for the AWR*

To alter the default retention time or the default statistics snapshot collection interval, you would use the `DBMS_WORKLOAD_REPOSITORY.MODIFY_SNAPSHOT_SETTINGS` procedure like this:

```
BEGIN
  DBMS_WORKLOAD_REPOSITORY.MODIFY_SNAPSHOT_SETTINGS(
    retention => 20160,
    interval => 60
    );
END;
```

In this example, we increase the retention period to two weeks (14 days is equal to the 20,160 minutes we use as the input to the `retention` parameter). Tune this parameter wisely because the more you increase the retention period, the more storage will be consumed in the SYSAUX tablespace for the AWR tables.

Accessing the Monitored SQL tab in the Activity view of the ADB Service Console provides you with a list of actively executed and past SQL statements, as shown in Figure 7-31.

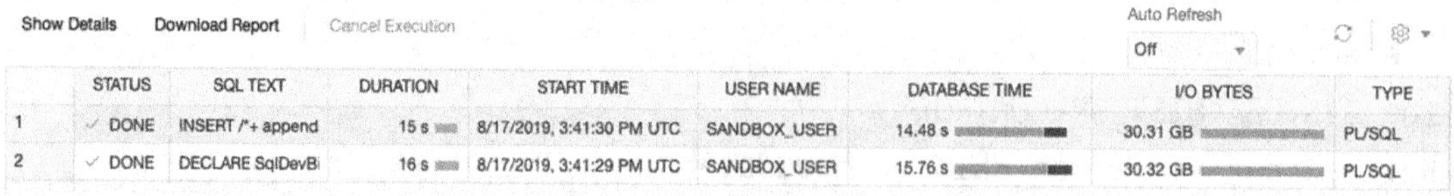

	STATUS	SQL TEXT	DURATION	START TIME	USER NAME	DATABASE TIME	I/O BYTES	TYPE
1	DONE	INSERT /*+ append	15 s	8/17/2019, 3:41:30 PM UTC	SANDBOX_USER	14.48 s	30.31 GB	PL/SQL
2	DONE	DECLARE SqlDevBi	16 s	8/17/2019, 3:41:29 PM UTC	SANDBOX_USER	15.76 s	30.32 GB	PL/SQL

Figure 7-31. *ADW SQL monitoring*

You can inspect each individual SQL statement and learn about its Wait statistics, I/O statistics, execution plan performance, and, if it applies, parallelism. To do so, on the Monitored SQL tab, right-click a query you are interested in and choose the Show Details option. There will be a new pop-up area displayed to you, as shown in Figure 7-32.

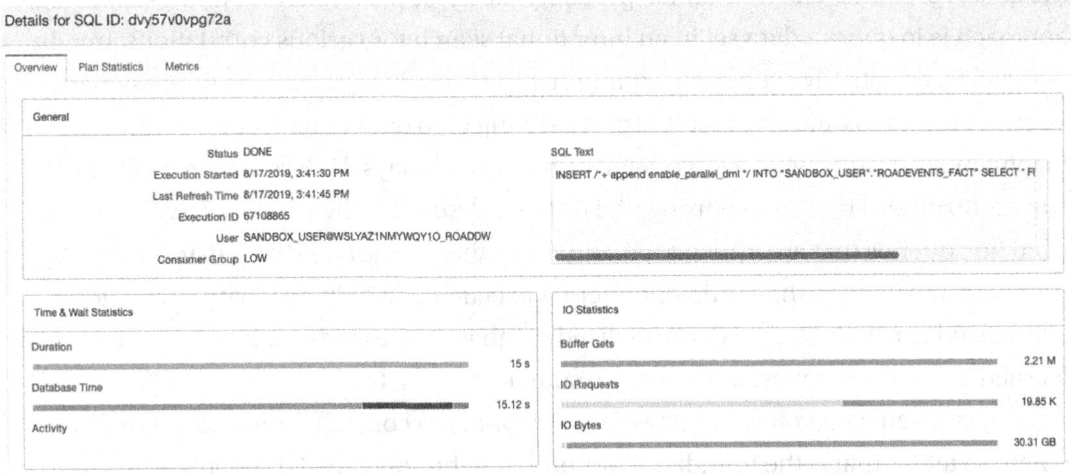

Details for SQL ID: dvy57v0vpg72a

| Overview | Plan Statistics | Metrics |

General

Status DONE	SQL Text
Execution Started 8/17/2019, 3:41:30 PM	INSERT /*+ append enable_parallel_dml */ INTO "SANDBOX_USER"."ROADEVENTS_FACT" SELECT * FI
Last Refresh Time 8/17/2019, 3:41:45 PM	
Execution ID 67108865	
User SANDBOX_USER@WSLYAZ1NMYWQY1O_ROADDW	
Consumer Group LOW	

Time & Wait Statistics

		IO Statistics	
Duration		Buffer Gets	
	15 s		2.21 M
Database Time		IO Requests	
	15.12 s		19.85 K
Activity		IO Bytes	
			30.31 GB

Figure 7-32. SQL execution details

You have learned how to monitor your database instance. It is time to bring our attention back to the dimensions and fact data we loaded earlier into database tables. It's time to get in touch with the information stored in these database tables. Let's execute some interesting queries.

Data Analytics

Collecting data is just one side of the story. It is more important to understand why we actually do it. The data can tell you different information, sometimes expected and sometimes surprising, about the business situation, objects, measurements, or events the data represents. The traditional, probably the most-prevalent and well-established, approach is to query a data set in an intentional search for various correlations, trends, anomalies, or, actually even more common, report-ready aggregations such as quarterly sales per business unit. The results are often subject to data visualizations, which are helpful in illustrating what a large set of numbers truly says. Unless we are dealing with standardized and routine reporting, the *data analysis* typically entails a large number of ad hoc queries that are understood as queries that are not predefined and cannot be determined before the particular query is executed. To help deal with such queries, specialized constellations of denormalized database tables are employed. You've already learned about the simplest and yet often sufficient star schema.

A star schema, as you are already familiar with, is a constellation of denormalized database tables that is the foundation for building the so-called OLAP cubes. What is an OLAP cube? We could say that it is a multidimensional structure that combines dimensional attribute hierarchies with quantitative facts. Well, this may sound a bit too sophisticated. From a practical point of view, it is convenient to say that an OLAP cube is a higher-level construct, typically built on top of a star schema, that provides a more abstract way of looking at data beyond the tabular structure underneath. We are no longer thinking about dimension tables but talking about dimension attribute hierarchies. In the context of this chapter, the corresponding OLAP cube is illustrated in Figure 7-33. I have deliberately chosen to use three dimensions for the sample data in this chapter because it makes it really easy to imagine the corresponding OLAP cube as a three-dimensional coordinate system. Each dimension is a base for an axis line. Each point in this coordinate system can be seen as a single fact entry that carries various quantitative data.

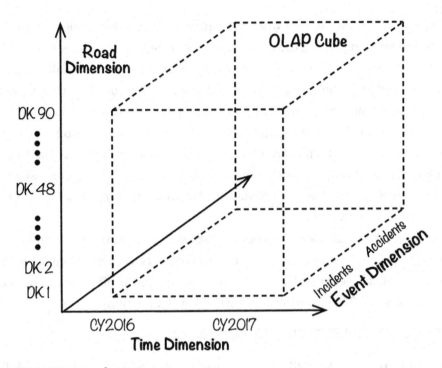

Figure 7-33. *OLAP cube*

OLAP cubes are not limited to a logical concept, but a database or data processing platform can include an OLAP cube engine module that takes some burden of handling selected aspects related to dimension hierarchy levels and lets you focus on more business-oriented queries. The implementation of OLAP cubes can range from database extensions such as Oracle Analytic Views, which rely on advanced SQL language features, to a middleware-based business intelligence solutions, such as Oracle Business Intelligence Suite, which supports a dedicated query language such as MDX. The OLAP cube will help us understand some of the basic queries we are going to execute against a star schema. First, however, we need to materialize a star schema.

The easiest way to produce a star schema is to run a SQL select query that basically joins all dimension tables with the fact table like this:

```
SELECT  FROM ROADEVENTS_FACT    F
JOIN TIME_DIM  T ON T.DAY_ID = F.TIME_DIM_ID
JOIN ROAD_DIM  R ON R.SEGMENT_ID = F.ROAD_DIM_ID
JOIN EVENT_DIM E ON E.EVENT_ID = F.EVENT_DIM_ID
```

To simplify future queries that will use more complex selection and filtering conditions and avoid repeating the entire star schema SQL select query, it may be convenient to incorporate the star schema query in a database object called a *view*. A view is just a saved SQL query against a set of database tables or other views. It does not store data physically but provides a predefined perspective on physical database tables. Still, the use of views may sometimes mean the costly calculation of query results dynamically. Knowing that typical ADW workloads are usually built on scheduled batch data loading of a large footprint, after the data loads have been completed, we could precompute the view and store data physically. For that purpose, we will use database objects called *materialized views*.

As you recall, the database user SANDBOX_USER was granted the predefined dwrole database role. This role, however, does not allow the users to create materialized views. Let's open SQL Developer Web, this time using the link for the ADMIN user, and add a new privilege for the SANDBOX_USER by executing the GRANT statement.

```
GRANT CREATE MATERIALIZED VIEW TO SANDBOX_USER;
```

If you want, you can optionally verify the roles and privileges held by the SANDBOX_ USER by running these queries as the ADMIN user.

```
SELECT * FROM DBA_ROLE_PRIVS where grantee='SANDBOX_USER';
SELECT * FROM DBA_SYS_PRIVS where grantee='SANDBOX_USER';
```

We are ready to switch to the SQL Developer Web window for SANDBOX_USER and execute the CREATE MATERIALIZED VIEW SQL DDL statement. Again, remember to execute this query in the SANDBOX_USER SQL Developer Web window.

```
CREATE MATERIALIZED VIEW ROADEVENTS_STAR AS
SELECT * FROM ROADEVENTS_FACT    F
JOIN TIME_DIM  T ON T.DAY_ID = F.TIME_DIM_ID
JOIN ROAD_DIM  R ON R.SEGMENT_ID = F.ROAD_DIM_ID
JOIN EVENT_DIM E ON E.EVENT_ID = F.EVENT_DIM_ID
```

You should receive the following message:

```
Materialized view ROADEVENTS_STAR created.
```

For the sake of this chapter, we have just created the materialized view over the entire fact table. It is good to know that materialized views, in contrast to views, do consume physical storage. For production use cases that involve large data sets, it may be rather undesired to persist the entire star schema query as a materialized view. The same applies to situations in which the data loads are incremental and of a high frequency, because materialized views usually have to be refreshed immediately after the underlying database tables change. In this context, best practice suggests that materialized views are built after applying dimension filters and only for these aggregations that are often used by the reporting engine.

We can query a materialized view just as an ordinary database table. Let's issue a SQL select statement that sums up all road event occurrences as well as the number of people injured and killed and groups the results by the calendar year and the road event class. Both the calendar year and the road event class are the topmost levels in their dimensions. The query is shown here:

```
SELECT
  year_name, class_name,
  SUM(occurrence) total_occurrence,
  SUM(injured) sum_injured,
  SUM(killed) sum_killed
FROM ROADEVENTS_STAR
GROUP BY year_name, class_name
ORDER BY year_name, class_name;
```

The results are shown in Figure 7-34. We can immediately draw some initial conclusions. For example, we can see that the numbers of accidents and accident victims decreased in 2017 when compared to 2016. At the same time, the number of reported traffic incidents increased a bit. This could lead us to the hypothesis that increased police activity could lead to detecting more incidents, improving the safety on the roads, and resulting in a lower number of accidents in 2017.

	year_name	class_name	total_occurrence	sum_injured	sum_killed
1	CY2016	traffic accident	43493	60493	6038
2	CY2016	traffic incident	1062379	0	0
3	CY2017	traffic accident	42394	59782	5844
4	CY2017	traffic incident	1065602	0	0

Query Result   Script Output   DBMS Output   Explain Plan   Autotrace   SQL History

Download ▾

Figure 7-34. *Aggregate query over a star schema*

The query result consists of four rows that can be illustrated on the corresponding OLAP cube, as shown in Figure 7-35. The query practically divides the original cube into four subcubes that were divided based on the topmost dimension hierarchy levels for the Time and Event dimensions. If we knew we were interested in analyzing traffic incidents that took place in 2017 only, we would focus on this one particular subcube. That kind of operation would be called *dicing*. The dicing operation produces a subcube by filtering the results based on a range of values typically applied on a few dimensions.

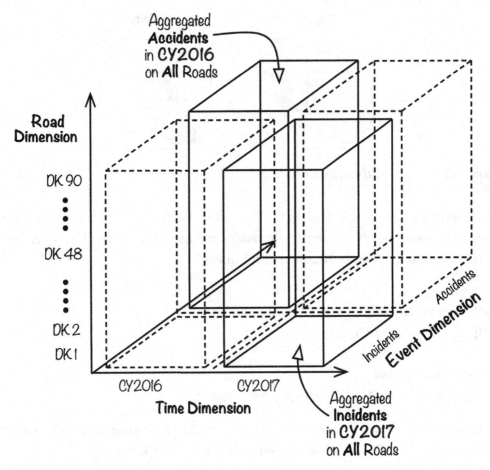

Figure 7-35. *OLAP cube perspective on the query*

Dicing is just one of a few types of OLAP cube operations you will encounter in the world of business intelligence (BI). These are the most common types of BI operations:

- Slice and dice

- Drill-down and roll-up

- Pivot

While dicing uses range filters on one or more dimensions to create a subcube, the *slicing* operation reduces the number of analyzed dimensions. You typically choose one fixed value for a particular dimension and use it as a filter over the data set. Both slicing and dicing are conceptually illustrated in Figure 7-36.

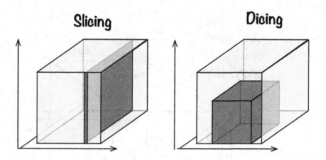

Figure 7-36. *OLAP cube slice and dice*

Let's slice the cube by eliminating the Time dimension. For example, we could be interested in displaying the aggregation totals for the very precise date, let it be August 12, 2017. To do so, execute the second `select` query.

```
SELECT
  SUM(occurrence) total_occurrence,
  SUM(injured) sum_injured,
  SUM(killed) sum_killed
FROM ROADEVENTS_STAR
WHERE day_date=TO_DATE('20170812','YYYYMMDD');
```

The results are shown in Figure 7-37. There were 2,777 occurrences of accidents and incidents altogether. The accidents caused 175 injured and 9 killed.

	Query Result	Script Output	DBMS Output	Explain Plan
	🗑 ⓘ ☐ Download ▾			
		total_occurrence	sum_injured	sum_killed
1		2777	175	9

Figure 7-37. *Slice operation*

The third select query performed over the star schema materialized view is an example of a *drill-down* operation. We are still using the previous slice of the cube. We add to it the GROUP BY clause, which effectively presents a more granular aggregate split. The ordering is aligned with the Event dimension hierarchy. The event class (the class_name column) splits into event categories (the category_name column) that subsequently split into event types (the event_name column). The intention is to make the results clearer and easier to understand. Now, issue the third query.

```
SELECT class_name, category_name, event_name,
  SUM(occurrence) total_occurrence,
  SUM(injured) sum_injured,
  SUM(killed) sum_killed
FROM ROADEVENTS_STAR
WHERE day_date=TO_DATE('20170812','YYYYMMDD')
GROUP BY class_name, category_name, event_name
ORDER BY class_name, category_name, event_name;
```

A more detailed split that is the result of the query you've just issued is displayed in Figure 7-38. Although we present the totals for each fact measurement, nothing is stopping you from making additional ad hoc calculations such as the averages or injured-to-killed ratio for each event type. Remember that we have worked on a slice of a cube, and the results are given for a single day only.

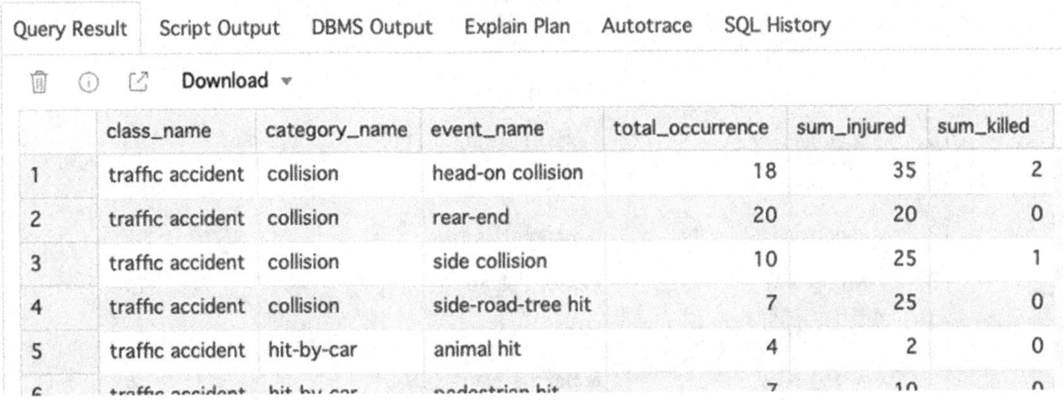

	Query Result	Script Output	DBMS Output	Explain Plan	Autotrace	SQL History		
	class_name	category_name	event_name		total_occurrence	sum_injured	sum_killed	
1	traffic accident	collision	head-on collision		18	35	2	
2	traffic accident	collision	rear-end		20	20	0	
3	traffic accident	collision	side collision		10	25	1	
4	traffic accident	collision	side-road-tree hit		7	25	0	
5	traffic accident	hit-by-car	animal hit		4	2	0	
6	traffic accident	hit by car	pedestrian hit		7	10	0

Figure 7-38. Drill-down operation

The fourth SQL statement is an example of a *dicing* operation. We are applying filters on each dimension to create a subcube. The Time dimension is limited to August 2017, Event dimension to the "traffic rules" Category, and the Road dimension only to these road segments that are located in three listed voivodeships. Execute the following select query:

```
SELECT event_name, segment_voivodeship,
  SUM(occurrence) occurrence_in_201708
FROM ROADEVENTS_STAR
WHERE
  month_of_year=8 and year_name='CY2017' and
  category_name='traffic rules' and
  segment_voivodeship
    in ('Masovian','Subcarpathian','Lesser Poland')
GROUP BY event_name, segment_voivodeship
ORDER BY event_name, segment_voivodeship;
```

Figure 7-39 presents the sum of various traffic rules road incidents additionally split based on their location. We can see, for instance, that there were 2,835 speeding traffic incidents reported on roads in the Masovian voivodeship in August 2017.

	event_name	segment_voivodeship	occurrence_in_201708
7	overtaking	Lesser Poland	902
8	overtaking	Masovian	1374
9	overtaking	Subcarpathian	538
10	speeding	Lesser Poland	1997
11	speeding	Masovian	2835
12	speeding	Subcarpathian	965
13	wrong-way	Lesser Poland	114
14	wrong-way	Masovian	209
15	wrong-way	Subcarpathian	89

Figure 7-39. *Dice operation*

What we are doing is creating ad hoc queries to explore and detect various characteristics of this particular data set. In the case of ad hoc queries, as long as we can read and understand the results, the formatting is not so important. This will drastically change when we are tasked with preparing the results for reporting. The aggregates presented in Figure 7-39 are based on a two-dimensional subdice. The Time dimension is no longer considered. Having two dimensions, we could imagine a report that relies on each remaining dimension for its two-dimensional structure. The x-axis could be based on the Road dimension while the y-axis on the Event dimension. Looking at the results of the previous query, the only thing remaining is to apply the *pivot* operation. The pivot operation basically rotates rows into columns, applying additional aggregation if required. Values that were stored in the row fields of a particular column can become a new set of columns. Oracle Database features a specialized PIVOT clause to perform pivoting. This is the fifth query to be executed:

```
SELECT
    *
FROM
(
  SELECT
    event_name,
    segment_voivodeship,
    SUM(occurrence) occurrence_in_201708
  FROM
    ROADEVENTS_STAR
  WHERE
    month_of_year = 8 AND year_name = 'CY2017'
    AND category_name = 'traffic rules'
    AND segment_voivodeship
        IN ( 'Masovian', 'Subcarpathian', 'Lesser Poland' )
  GROUP BY event_name, segment_voivodeship
  ORDER BY event_name, segment_voivodeship
) PIVOT (
    SUM ( occurrence_in_201708 )
    FOR ( segment_voivodeship )
    IN (
      'Masovian' as masovian,
```

```
      'Subcarpathian' as subcarpathian,
      'Lesser Poland' as lesser_poland
   )
)
```

Figure 7-40 shows the report-ready results of the pivot operation applied on the subcube. The values presented as row fields in the previous `segment_voivodeship` column became new columns. The previous `occurrence_in_201708` column was removed, and the values were distributed accordingly to the new layout. In this case, because of the well-grained grouping levels, no additional aggregation took place.

	event_name	masovian	subcarpathian	lesser_poland
1	forcing the right of way	530	195	382
2	lane departure	351	152	204
3	overtaking	1374	538	902
4	wrong-way	209	89	114
5	speeding	2835	965	1997

Figure 7-40. *Pivot operation*

The operations presented are just the tip of the iceberg. Oracle Autonomous Database supports many specialized clauses that let you properly structure, distribute, aggregate, and rank the results, but this is beyond the scope of this book. Oracle Database analytical views can be used to perform more advanced dimensional queries in a hierarchy-aware way and include embedded calculations over aggregates available in the underlying fact table.

Every Autonomous Data Warehouse instance comes with a feature called *Oracle Machine Learning* (OML), which is a web-based, interactive, notebook-oriented data visualization and data analytics tool based on the open source Apache Zeppelin project. For simple visualization use cases, you can easily use SQL to issue queries and, using a few clicks, prepare various charts. For example, Figure 7-41 shows how to display a line chart that illustrates the sum of car accident victims in Poland in 2017 grouped by the traffic accident category. As a reminder, the data you see is purely artificial and generated by me solely for the purpose of this book.

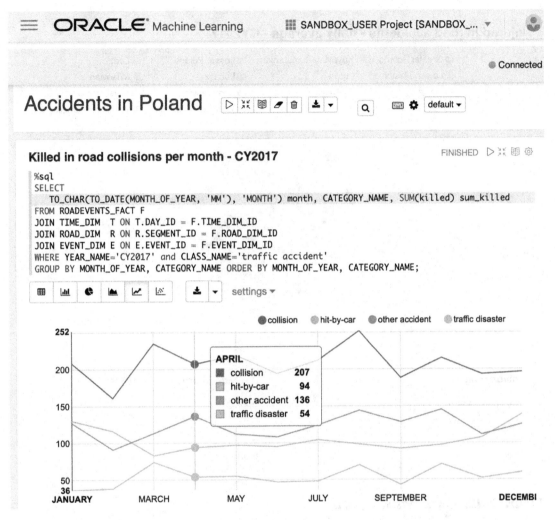

Figure 7-41. *Oracle Machine Learning Zeppelin-based visualizations*

Notebooks can be arranged in a way that resembles multi paragraph reports, like the one shown in Figure 7-42 that combines both a pie chart and a corresponding data table. Both views illustrate the daily average of people injured in 2017 in a voivodeship-based split.

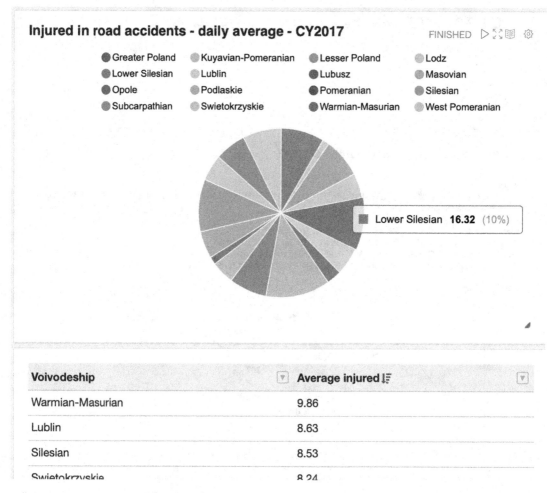

Figure 7-42. *OML-based reports*

You can access the OML Administration page from the Autonomous Data Warehouse Service Console on the Administration page. Here, you are able to allow the existing database users to work with OML notebooks. To find out more, please refer to the documentation.

The Autonomous Data Warehouse instance can be easily registered as a data source for Oracle Analytics Cloud that features with a much richer set of available charts. Figure 7-43 presents a Radar Area chart of people injured in 2017 on the roads of GP type. Each different angle corresponds to one particular voivodeship. The lower is the number of injured people on GP roads in a given voivodeship; the smaller is the blue area on this particular angle. There are plenty of things you can build using Analytics Cloud, and you perform interactive analysis and dynamically adapt the charts to come to an ideal dashboard in the context of your particular reporting scenario.

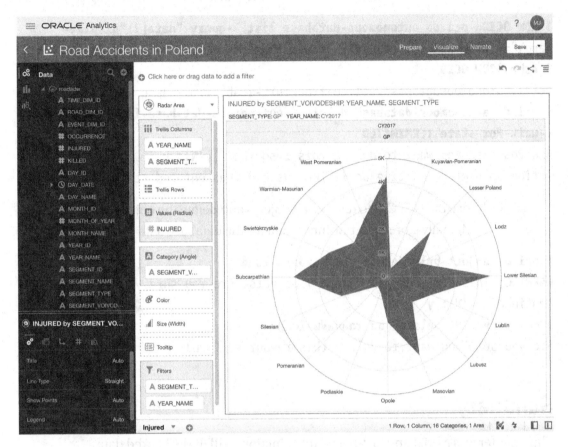

Figure 7-43. *Oracle Analytics Cloud*

Discussing business intelligence operations, data mining algorithms, and different visualization techniques like these supported by Zeppelin-based ADB extensions as well as Oracle Analytics Cloud is beyond the scope of this book. There is a broad range of materials available on the Internet, so feel free to explore.

Cleanup

We can now terminate the database instance because we won't need it beyond this point. To shut down and terminate the ADW instance, you can execute the following command:

```
$ ADW_OCID=`oci db autonomous-database list --query "data[?\"display-
name\"=='road-adw'] | [0].id" --raw-output`
$ echo $ADW_OCID
ocid1.autonomousdatabase.oc1.eu-frankfurt-1.ab......763psq
$ oci db autonomous-database delete --autonomous-database-id "$ADW_OCID"
--wait-for-state TERMINATED
Are you sure you want to delete this resource? [y/N]: y
Action completed. Waiting until the resource has entered state: TERMINATED
```

Similarly, use the OCI CLI to remove all objects and delete the object storage bucket in which we originally stored the raw input data for the database data load.

```
$ oci os object bulk-delete -bn roadadw-load
WARNING: This command will delete 7 objects. Are you sure you want to
continue? [y/N]: y
$ oci os bucket delete -bn roadadw-load
Are you sure you want to delete this resource? [y/N]: y
```

Summary

This chapter was a brief and fast-paced introduction to RDBMS-backed data warehousing and dimension-oriented data analytics. In the age of the fully managed cloud-based Autonomous Database, we were able to rapidly launch a data warehouse instance and, after some basic setup, move straight to building data-oriented solutions. This is what managed cloud platforms are all about: focusing on solving problems with minimal management effort by delegating these housekeeping tasks to the cloud platform. In the course of subsequent sections, you learned how to provision an instance of an autonomous database, access SQL Developer Web as ADMIN, create regular database users, load data from object storage to database tables, and understand the star schema and its role in business intelligence operations. Next, you familiarized yourself with database monitoring. Finally, you queried data in a number of ways and were introduced to data visualization options available in Oracle Cloud.

CHAPTER 8

Oracle Container Engine for Kubernetes

In this chapter, we are going to deal with *application containers*, which have revolutionized the contemporary software world. Containers have impacted the way we build, ship, and run applications and therefore have largely changed the process of software development. They empowered the new architectural style oriented around systems composed of a large number of highly specialized, autonomous, and usually small-in-size applications called *microservices*. It is no exaggeration to say that, on top of application containers, there has emerged a new *ecosystem* of standards, platforms, components, tools, libraries, protocols, and services. The ecosystem is truly immense in scope, powered by a broad open source community and provided with rich corporate sponsorship.

The first section in this chapter briefly explains what containers are and guides you through the most important tasks related to containerizing an application and storing container images in the Oracle Container Image Registry (OCIR). The second section discusses the need for container orchestration and introduces you to Oracle Kubernetes Engine (OKE), a managed Kubernetes service available on Oracle Cloud Infrastructure.

Containers

A *container* is a portable and shippable unit of software packaged with all its dependencies. Let's explore this definition by looking closer at the three core characteristics of containers.

- Self-contained
- Isolated
- Shippable

© Michał Tomasz Jakóbczyk 2020
M. T. Jakóbczyk, *Practical Oracle Cloud Infrastructure*, https://doi.org/10.1007/978-1-4842-5506-3_8

Each container is in principle *self-contained*. A service or an application wrapped inside a container is provided with all its dependencies such as software binaries, configuration files, libraries, environment variables, and, no matter how weird it may sound at first glance, the entire operating system. Even though there might be hundreds of containers running on the same bare-metal or virtual machine, each of them provides an impression of a fully *isolated* and exclusive environment to an application it encapsulates. In other words, an application inside any given container thinks it is running within a dedicated machine, no matter how many other containers coexist on the same host machine. Containers are considered easily *shippable* across different host machines that may even use varying host operating systems as long as they are all supporting the same container runtime. Figure 8-1 illustrates these three characteristics conceptually.

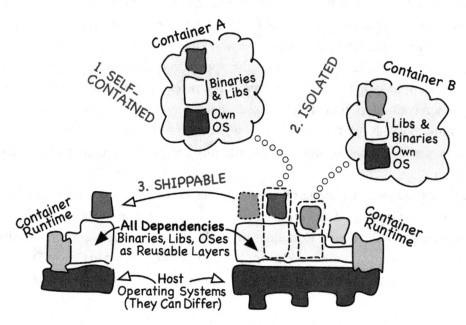

Figure 8-1. *Core container characteristics*

If you've never heard about containers and are new to the topic, you will probably wonder how it is all possible from a technical point of view. Furthermore, how do containers actually differ from virtual machines? Contemporary container runtimes originated from within the Linux ecosystem and leverage Linux kernel features such as namespaces, control groups, or `chroot` commands to implement filesystem, process, network, and resource *isolation*. No matter which container engine you eventually choose, whether be `Docker`, `rkt`, or `cri-o`, you can be sure they all use the same aforementioned Linux kernel features. In this context, it becomes clear that all containers running on the same host, even though fully isolated, use the host's Linux kernel. In terms of reusability, there is something even more impactful, namely, layers. Containers use *filesystem layers* that are stacked on top of other layers. The base layers "at the bottom" ship the entire operating system. It may sound heavy, but in the world of containers, you will often encounter very lightweight Linux distributions such as CoreOS Container Linux or Alpine Linux. On top of that, additional layers usually bring application runtimes, for example, Java Virtual Machine, Python, or Node.js. Earlier, further layers can ship required libraries like Python Flask. Finally, the topmost layers contain application binaries often supplemented with injected configuration files. All these layers are read-only, which allows multiple containers to share them. Every container comes with a dedicated writable layer to hold all changes done across the lifetime by the application of any other components within the container. Read-only layers are logically grouped into *container images* that can be shared across many machines. Each image is a self-contained entity that can serve as a base for multiple running containers. You can have hundreds of containers based on the same image effectively consuming just as much storage as if you were running only a single container.

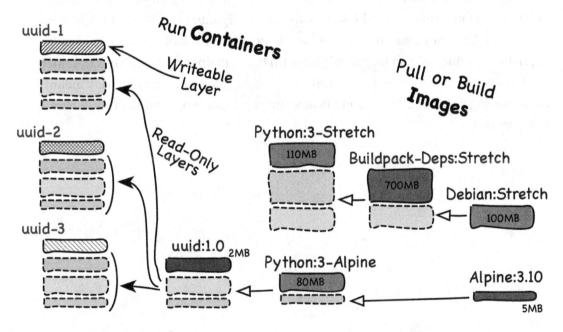

Figure 8-2. *Container layers*

Figure 8-2 illustrates the relation between individual images and containers. There are three containers called uuid-1, uuid-2, and uuid-3, all built using the same uuid:1.0 image. The uuid:1.0 image is a custom-built image that basically ships some application code and configuration files. The image is built on top of a downloaded python:3-alpine image that installs Python 3 on top of a base operating system image called alpine:3.10. Applications within each of the three containers think that they are running on separate hosts. Yet, they all share the host machine Linux kernel and read-only layers. There have been some voices across the community saying that not all Python applications are capable of running on Alpine Linux because of some missing distribution-specific dependencies. To address these concerns, you could, for instance, consider running more demanding Python apps using images that rely not on python:3-alpine but on a Debian-based python:3-stretch image.

Both kernel-level isolation combined with the reuse of kernel and various filesystem layers make containers considerably lighter in use when compared to virtual machines. Similarly, it is much easier to ship a container to another machine than to migrate the entire virtual machine. But what does it physically mean to ship a container? You have learned that any particular container requires an image that consists of read-only filesystem layers. In the case of stateless applications, shipping a container means nothing more than stopping an existing container and running another one, based on the same image and using the same runtime configuration, this time on another machine. It becomes clear that images have to be made available in some kind of *image registry* accessible from all host machines with the container runtime. The container platform would then pull an image from the image registry, which effectively means downloading all required filesystem layers and corresponding metadata, as illustrated in Figure 8-3.

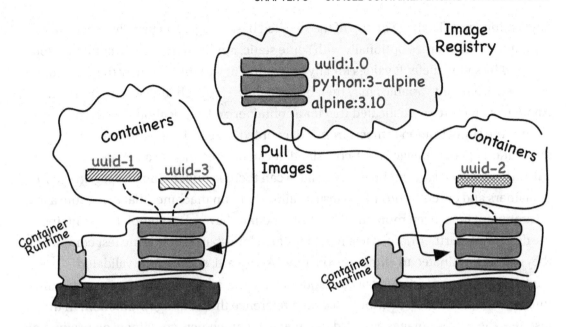

Figure 8-3. *Pulling an image from an image registry*

Applications always evolve during their life span. To track this, evolution application releases are versioned. The same applies to container images. If you look closer at the previous figures, you will see the version suffixes such as 1.0, 3-alpine, or 3:10. We call them *tags*. Container images are tagged mainly to denote different variants or the release chronology of a particular image. For example, let's assume you are publishing a new minor version of an image that encapsulates updated binaries of an UUID service. If the previous image version was tagged as uuid:1.0, the updated image version could be tagged with uuid:1.1. If it happened that a Python-based application was not fast enough, you could additionally implement a Golang-based alternative and publish it as a uuid:1.0-golang variant.

Knowing all the basic components, we are ready to outline the development process for a containerized application. Depending on the situation, you will either have to containerize an existing application or incorporate containerization already from the beginning as an automated process while developing a new application. To *containerize an application*, you need to carefully identify all dependencies and make choices on the entire execution environment including the operating system an application would think it is running on. Based on these decisions, you pick an existing image or, if it doesn't exist, start building it on your own. This will be the base image for your application-specific image. As soon as the base image is ready, you can finally start building an application-specific image on top of the selected base image. You usually do it by adding the application binaries optionally with some static, application-specific configuration files and by setting default values for any environment variables used by the application. These environment variables may then be overridden for each individual container. Another, a bit more sophisticated way for a containerized application is to fetch its runtime configuration artifacts from a decoupled, external config source. The application-specific image is self-contained. It can be uploaded to an image registry. We call this activity *pushing* an image. An image can then be pulled from the registry to run containers and execute automated tests against them on machines that constitute a test environment for a given moment. After test pipelines have been completed, containers are destroyed. Furthermore, if test machines are cloud-based, following test completion, they can be terminated to eliminate idle time. Afterward, successfully validated container images are properly tagged and pushed into another image registry, this time intended for production distribution. Some reference this as *image promotion*. In the last step, the newest images are used to replace or launch new containers on production machines. The entire process is conceptually shown in Figure 8-4.

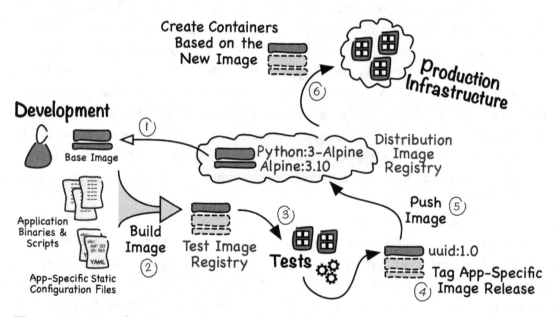

Figure 8-4. *Developing containerized applications*

The entire development process is usually fully automated. Developers check their code into version control systems such as Git, which triggers the test image build, deployment, and testing. If the image validates successfully, it is automatically tagged and pushed to the distribution image registry. Another set of automation rules can replace older containers in the production environment with the newer containers that are based on the newest image.

This section has equipped you with some base knowledge in the field of containers. We are ready now to apply these concepts in practice. To do so, we are going to containerize the UUID service that was covered in Chapter 2.

Containerize an Application

There are a few container runtimes on the market. Just to name a few, we could list `containerd` or `rkt` or `cri-o`. As a matter of fact, this is quite a dynamic scene, and things are rapidly changing nearly every month. Luckily, there have been some joint standardization efforts put in place by the community to bring some structure to this chaos of creativity and reuse some common components across various runtimes. One of the most popular container runtimes is `containerd`. It was taken from the previously monolithic Docker Engine and was donated to the community as an open source project governed by the Cloud Native Computing Foundation (CNCF). Docker alone actually pioneered the use of Linux containers, first using an existing set of Linux containers tool (LXC) and then switching to a custom-built, in-house platform. Docker is probably the most popular container engine technology at the moment and the leading provider of tools used to containerize applications. In this section, we are going to use Docker tools to containerize the existing UUID service application we worked on earlier as part of the Chapter 2 exercise. Back then we ran it as a Linux systemd service on two compute instance running in Oracle Cloud Infrastructure. That time, we hosted just one application instance on each compute instance. Now, we are going to build a container image that can be run by any number of containers, in this way providing multiple UUID API instances on a single machine, as shown in Figure 8-5. Each application will still think it is running alone on a dedicated host, even though, in reality, it is sharing the underlying image layers and the Linux kernel with all other containers based on the same image and running on the same machine. By containerizing the application, you will unlock the possibility to scale the entire UUID API horizontally out by adding more containers and hosts with the container runtime.

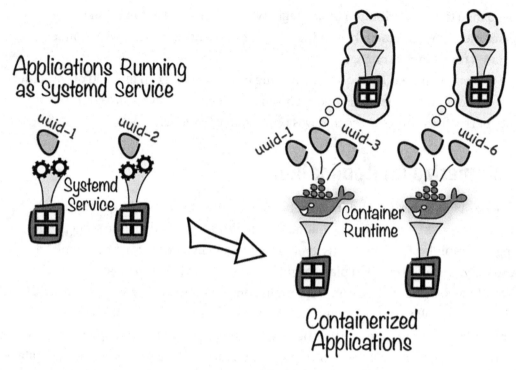

Figure 8-5. Containerized application scalability

Note   The code snippets from this book have been tested on macOS and Windows Subsystem for Linux. Moreover, all commands should work on major Linux distributions. If you are using Windows and do not want to use Windows Subsystem for Linux, you can always run Linux on a VM. Furthermore, the majority of code snippets may also work in Git Bash on Windows.

To build an image, you will need a developer machine with Docker tools. In the course of this chapter, we are going to provision and use a temporary development compute instance with all the required tools installed. I recommend that you follow these steps because that will make it easier to use the code snippets and avoid platform-specific discrepancies.

Development Instance in the Cloud

Let's provision a single compute instance based on the newest CentOS 7 platform image. I have already prepared the infrastructure code. You will find it in the chapter08/1-devmachine directory. The code structure is compliant with what we've already discussed in all previous chapters. There is one module called devmachine where the instance is defined with corresponding subnet-level cloud networking resources. The VCN alone is traditionally defined outside of the module in the top-level vcn.tf file.

```
$ cd ~/git
$ cd oci-book/chapter08/1-devmachine
$ find . \( -name "*.tf" -o -name "*.yaml" \) | sort
./devmachine/cloud-init/devvm.config.yaml
./devmachine/compute.tf
./devmachine/vars.tf
./devmachine/vcn.tf
./modules.tf
./provider.tf
./vars.tf
./vcn.tf
```

To perform the initial instance setup and provide you with all the required development tools, we use the cloud-config file, as shown in Listing 8-1.

Listing 8-1. 1-devmachine/cloud-init/devvm.config.yaml

```
#cloud-config
yum_repos:
    docker-ce-stable:
        name: Docker CE Stable - $basearch
        baseurl: https://download.docker.com/linux/centos/7/$basearch/stable
        enabled: true

        ...

    kubernetes:
        name: Kubernetes
        baseurl: https://packages.cloud.google.com/yum/repos/kubernetes-
        el7-x86_64
        enabled: true

        ...
```

packages:
```
  - git
  - docker-ce
  - docker-ce-cli
  - containerd.io
  - kubectl
```
runcmd:
```
  - [ systemctl, enable, docker ]
  - [ systemctl, start, docker ]
  - [ usermod, -aG, docker, opc ]
  - [ mkdir, "/home/opc/.kube" ]
  - [ chown, "opc:opc", "/home/opc/.kube" ]
  - [ firewall-offline-cmd, "--add-port=5010-5019/tcp" ]
  - [ systemctl, restart, firewalld ]
```
final_message: "DEV machine is running, after $UPTIME seconds"

Based on this cloud-config file, the cloud-init will add two external Yum repositories and install a Git client, the Docker Community Edition (CE) toolkit, and the kubectl command-line management tool for Kubernetes. You will learn about kubectl and Kubernetes in the second part of this chapter.

It is time to provision the development instance. On your local machine where you have installed and configured Terraform, please make sure you have sourced the relevant environment variables, which begin with TF_VAR_, required by your OCI provider. If they are not set, you might need to run the following:

```
$ source ~/tfvars.env.sh
```

Now, execute the following commands:

```
$ terraform init
Initializing modules...
- devmachine in devmachine

Initializing the backend...

Initializing provider plugins...
- Checking for available provider plugins...
- Downloading plugin for provider "oci" (terraform-providers/oci) 3.30.0...
```

```
* provider.oci: version = "~> 3.30"

Terraform has been successfully initialized!
$ terraform apply
data.oci_identity_availability_domains.ads: Refreshing state...
data.oci_core_images.centos_image: Refreshing state...

Terraform will perform the following actions:

  # oci_core_internet_gateway.igw will be created
  # oci_core_virtual_network.vcn will be created
  # module.devmachine.oci_core_instance.dev_vm will be created
  # module.devmachine.oci_core_route_table.dev_rt will be created
  # module.devmachine.oci_core_security_list.dev_sl will be created
  # module.devmachine.oci_core_subnet.dev_net will be created

Plan: 6 to add, 0 to change, 0 to destroy.

Do you want to perform these actions?
  Terraform will perform the actions described earlier.
  Only 'yes' will be accepted to approve.

  Enter a value: yes

  ...
  Apply complete! Resources: 6 added, 0 changed, 0 destroyed.

Outputs:

dev_machine_image_name = CentOS-7-2019.06.19-0
dev_machine_public_ip = 130.61.84.182

$ DEV_VM_PUBLIC_IP=`terraform output dev_machine_public_ip`
```

In my case, the instance has been provisioned in the third fault domain of the third availability domain in the Frankfurt region, as shown in Figure 8-5.

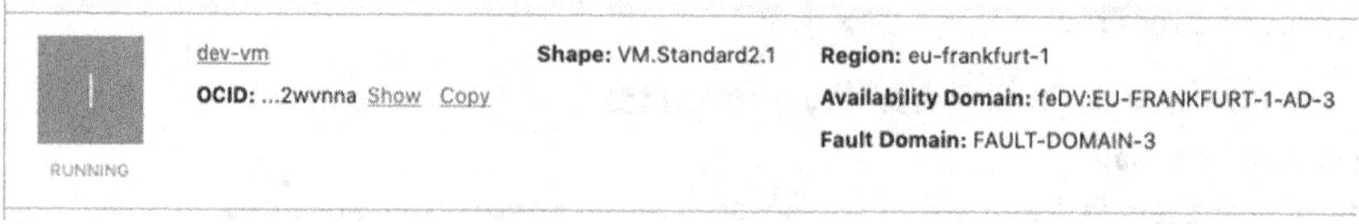

	dev-vm	**Shape:** VM.Standard2.1	**Region:** eu-frankfurt-1
	OCID: ...2wvnna Show Copy		**Availability Domain:** feDV:EU-FRANKFURT-1-AD-3
RUNNING			**Fault Domain:** FAULT-DOMAIN-3

Figure 8-6. *Viewing the developer VM in the OCI Console*

Wait a few seconds after the developer instance has been reported as Running to allow the sshd daemon to start and connect to the machine. Next, as always, you may need to wait one or two minutes until cloud-init has completed all the tasks defined in the cloud-config file. You can inspect cloud-init.log from time to time to verify whether cloud-init has finished.

```
$ ssh -i ~/.ssh/oci_id_rsa opc@$DEV_VM_PUBLIC_IP
[opc@dev-vm]$ sudo cat /var/log/cloud-init.log | grep "DEV machine is
running"
2019-06-22 12:46:49,899 - util.py[DEBUG]: DEV machine is running, after
116.90 seconds
[opc@dev-vm]$ exit
```

From now on, whenever you see the [opc@dev-vm]$ command prompt in any of the subsequent code snippets, it will be assumed that you are on the developer instance.

Note   The Oracle Cloud Infrastructure marketplace comes with a more comprehensive prebuilt Oracle Cloud Developer image where there are many other tools installed out of the box. Yet, in this chapter, we are using a more lightweight and tailored custom-built developer instance that you launched using the supplied infrastructure code.

To be able to run Docker as a regular user, the cloud-init has added the opc user to the docker group. Reconnect to the developer machine to get the group assignment in place.

```
$ ssh -i ~/.ssh/oci_id_rsa opc@$DEV_VM_PUBLIC_IP
```

We are going to continue working on this in the next section.

Docker Runtime

Let's explore a bit the Docker tools installed on the developer instance. At the beginning of this chapter, you learned about containers and container images. To list the images on a given machine, issue the docker images command. To list the running containers, issue the docker ps command, like this:

```
[opc@dev-vm]$ docker images
REPOSITORY     TAG     IMAGE ID     CREATED     SIZE
[opc@dev-vm]$ docker ps
CONTAINER ID   IMAGE   COMMAND    CREATED    STATUS    PORTS    NAMES
```

Perfect. At this moment, there are no images and no containers on this machine. What about learning something more about the Docker engine and the underlying container runtime? Issue the docker info command.

```
[opc@dev-vm]$ docker info
...
Server Version: 18.09.6
Storage Driver: overlay2
 Backing Filesystem: xfs
 Supports d_type: true
 Native Overlay Diff: true
...
Runtimes: runc
Default Runtime: runc
...
Kernel Version: 3.10.0-957.21.3.el7.x86_64
...
Docker Root Dir: /var/lib/docker
...
```

Earlier, I spoke briefly about the fact that all containers use the kernel of their host machine. This is why the kernel is still important for Docker Engine, and you can find its precise version listed as the *Kernel Version* entry in the output of the docker info command. Among various information entries, you will also see the *Runtimes* entry. Docker uses the container runtime called containerd. Here, however, we can see something called runc as the Runtimes entry. Nothing is wrong. The runc is a

421

component responsible for running containers based on the standardized Open Container Initiative (OCI) specification. The `containerd` container runtime uses the `runc` under the hood and adds more features around it. Another interesting entry refers to the way Docker works with the filesystem layers that are combined to serve as the filesystem seen by your containerized application. Stacked on top of the read-only layers, there is a writable container layer. If an application makes any changes to the filesystem, these will be resembled in the writable layer only. It is the job of the *storage driver* to manage these layers, taking into consideration the characteristics of the underlying physical filesystem that backs the *Docker root directory* on the host. There are a few storage drivers available, each with different strengths and weaknesses. We are using the currently preferred storage driver called overlay2 backed by the xfs filesystem. The filesystem layers hierarchy is located in the `/var/lib/docker/overlay2` subdirectory. While containers are running, you should be able to find how the layers are stacked on top of each other using the `mount` command. If this looks a bit complex at first glance, there is no need to worry. We are not going to work with these settings. I just wanted you to get some practical overview of what had been conceptually discussed about layers at the beginning of this chapter.

Docker Images

Our goal is to build an image that encapsulates the UUID service application, including application dependencies (Python 3 and the Flask microframework) and default values for the required environment variables (e.g., `FLASK_APP`). First, we have to choose the appropriate *base image* for the application-specific image that we are about to build. Luckily, there are official base images for Python on Docker Hub, which is probably the largest library for container images. Both community-driven open source projects and independent software vendors publish their ready-for-distribution images to Docker Hub. You can find a large set of images that bundle different Python versions on various platforms at `https://hub.docker.com/_/python`, as shown in Figure 8-7.

Figure 8-7. *Official Python images on Docker Hub*

For demonstrational purpose, we will choose Python 3 on Alpine Linux, the variant available under the python:3-alpine tag. How would our Docker engine, which is running on an instance in the Frankfurt region of Oracle Cloud Infrastructure, actually know how to fetch this image? If you run the docker info command again, you should see the *Registry* entry at the bottom of the output.

```
[opc@dev-vm]$ docker info
...
Registry: https://index.docker.io/v1
...
```

Docker CE comes with a preconfigured link to the Docker Hub container image registry by default. Based on the security rules used by the VCN subnet to which the compute instance is attached, the instance does have free outbound connectivity to the Internet that effectively allows the instance to download container images from Docker Hub.

So far so good. We know the name of the base image. Now, it is time to create the custom image that adds the Flask microframework, sets a few default environment variables, and tells the container runtime to execute the app.py file, which is the implementation of the UUID API. To instruct Docker how to build a new image, you use a *Dockerfile*, which basically consists of the sequence of commands that are used to build the given image.

First, we are going to clone the Git repository with the code for this book again, this time on the developer instance.

```
[opc@dev-vm]$ git clone https://github.com/mtjakobczyk/oci-book.git
[opc@dev-vm]$ cd oci-book/chapter08/2-docker/
[opc@dev-vm]$ cd uuid-service/
[opc@dev-vm]$ ls -1
app.py
Dockerfile
requirements.txt
```

The chapter08/2-docker/uuid-service directory contains three files.

- app.py

- Dockerfile

- requirements.txt

The app.py file is identical to the one we used in Chapter 2. This is basically the implementation of the UUID API. As per Python conventions, the requirements.txt file holds a list of Python packages that are required by our application and will be installed using the pip tool. As I mentioned a moment ago, the Dockerfile is used to build an image. Listing 8-2 shows the Dockerfile for our image.

Listing 8-2. Dockerfile

```
FROM python:3-alpine
ENV FLASK_APP /usr/src/app/app.py
ENV FLASK_ENV development
ENV FLASK_DEBUG 0
EXPOSE 5000
WORKDIR /usr/src/app
COPY requirements.txt ./
RUN pip install --no-cache-dir -r requirements.txt
COPY . .
CMD [ "flask", "run", "--host=0.0.0.0" ]
```

The Dockerfile contains a list of instructions that are executed in a declared sequence. The first instruction is always the FROM instruction and defines the base image we want to use for the newly built image. As discussed earlier, we are going to leverage one of the offical Python images available in the Docker Hub image registry called python:3-alpine. The three subsequent ENV instructions set three environment variables used by the Flask microframework development web server. FLASK_APP points to the path of the API implementation, while FLASK_ENV and FLASK_DEBUG tune the output of the server. The EXPOSE instruction denotes port 5000, which is the default port used by the Flask server to listen for incoming requests. The role of this instruction is mainly informational because the port exposure is set only when you run containers. The WORKDIR instruction sets the working directory within the virtual container filesystem for the upcoming COPY, RUN, and CMD instructions. The first occurrence of the COPY instruction creates an image filesystem layer with the requirements.txt file copied from the developer machine. The RUN command executes the pip install command, which effectively installs the Flask microframework. The results are persisted as another filesystem layer. The second occurrence of the COPY command brings the app.py script to the container image as yet another filesystem layer. All in all, each instruction produces a filesystem layer. Some of these layers are temporary, while the others are included in the final container image. The very last instruction, namely, the CMD instruction, in contrast to the previous RUN instruction, is not executed and, in this way, does not produce any additional image layer that would be based on the results of the given command. The role of the CMD instruction is to tell the Docker engine what command to execute for each newly created container that will be launched using this image. In our case, every newly created container will basically execute the Flask microframework development web server using the flask run command. Consequently, the Flask server will expose the API implemented in the app.py file whose path is set in the FLASK_APP environment variable.

To trigger the image build process, use the docker build command. The -t
parameter sets the tag for the newly built image. Do not forget to include the dot sign
at the end to instruct the docker build command to search for the Dockerfile in the
current working directory.

```
[opc@dev-vm]$ docker build -t uuid:1.0 .
Sending build context to Docker daemon  4.608kB
Step 1/10 : FROM python:3-alpine
3-alpine: Pulling from library/python
e7c96db7181b: Pull complete
799a5534f213: Pull complete
913b50bbe755: Pull complete
11154abc6081: Pull complete
c805e63f69fe: Pull complete
...
Status: Downloaded newer image for python:3-alpine
...
Step 2/10 : ENV FLASK_APP /usr/src/app/app.py
...
Step 3/10 : ENV FLASK_ENV development
...
Step 4/10 : ENV FLASK_DEBUG 0
...
Step 5/10 : EXPOSE 5000
...
Step 6/10 : WORKDIR /usr/src/app
...
Step 7/10 : COPY requirements.txt ./
...
Step 8/10 : RUN pip install --no-cache-dir -r requirements.txt
...
Successfully installed Flask-1.0.2 Jinja2-2.10.1 MarkupSafe-1.1.1
Werkzeug-0.15.4 click-7.0 itsdangerous-1.1.0
...
Step 9/10 : COPY . .
...
```

```
Step 10/10 : CMD [ "flask", "run", "--host=0.0.0.0" ]
...
Successfully built b16f04d1bb7f
Successfully tagged uuid:1.0
```

You can now use the docker images command, optionally with the --format parameter to filter the output, to list the images.

```
[opc@dev-vm]$ docker images --format "table {{.Repository}}\t{{.Tag}}\t{{.
ID}}\t{{.Size}}"
REPOSITORY  TAG        IMAGE ID        SIZE
uuid        1.0        b16f04d1bb7f    96.7MB
python      3-alpine   fe3ef29c73f3    87MB
```

You should see two top-level images.

- uuid:1.0

- python:3-alpine

We mentioned python:3-alpine a few times before. This is the base image. It was downloaded from the Docker Hub image registry. It is 87MB and consists of some intermediary layers that are not shown by default. uuid:1.0 is the image we have just built on top of the base image. It adds the Flask microframework, sets three environment variables, and adds the app.py application. The size you see (96.7MB) is slightly misleading. This is the total size that includes the size of the base image. The layers we added take just 9.7MB (96.7MB – 87MB).

To display the history of how the image was built and, thus, all layers including transient intermediate layers, you can issue the docker history command, as shown in Figure 8-8.

```
[opc@dev-vm ~]$ docker images
REPOSITORY            TAG                 IMAGE ID          CREATED           SIZE
uuid                  1.0                 b16f04d1bb7f      8 minutes ago     96.7MB
python                3-alpine            fe3ef29c73f3      6 weeks ago       87MB
[opc@dev-vm ~]$ docker history b16f04d1bb7f
IMAGE                 CREATED             CREATED BY                                              SIZE
b16f04d1bb7f          8 minutes ago      /bin/sh -c #(nop)  CMD ["flask" "run" "--hos…          0B
9d58d9013e50          8 minutes ago      /bin/sh -c #(nop) COPY dir:e9e2b67315f6bc0d7…          1.17kB
8b74fc033521          8 minutes ago      /bin/sh -c pip install --no-cache-dir -r req…         9.76MB
e969ef1f2dc8          8 minutes ago      /bin/sh -c #(nop) COPY file:d9f8bdf66eea14ac…          31B
a92961639881          8 minutes ago      /bin/sh -c #(nop) WORKDIR /usr/src/app                 0B
3ef6ef80d4b3          8 minutes ago      /bin/sh -c #(nop)  EXPOSE 5000                         0B
9e4be5194fe2          8 minutes ago      /bin/sh -c #(nop)  ENV FLASK_DEBUG=0                   0B
8a1c13a829c7          8 minutes ago      /bin/sh -c #(nop)  ENV FLASK_ENV=development           0B
cb3c6bf083e1          8 minutes ago      /bin/sh -c #(nop)  ENV FLASK_APP=/usr/src/ap…         0B
fe3ef29c73f3          6 weeks ago        /bin/sh -c #(nop)  CMD ["python3"]                     0B
<missing>             6 weeks ago        /bin/sh -c set -ex;   wget -O get-pip.py 'ht…         6.06MB
<missing>             6 weeks ago        /bin/sh -c #(nop)  ENV PYTHON_PIP_VERSION=19…         0B
<missing>             6 weeks ago        /bin/sh -c cd /usr/local/bin  && ln -s idle3…         32B
<missing>             6 weeks ago        /bin/sh -c set -ex  && apk add --no-cache --…         74.8MB
<missing>             6 weeks ago        /bin/sh -c #(nop)  ENV PYTHON_VERSION=3.7.3            0B
<missing>             6 weeks ago        /bin/sh -c #(nop)  ENV GPG_KEY=0D96DF4D4110E…         0B
<missing>             6 weeks ago        /bin/sh -c apk add --no-cache ca-certificates         551kB
<missing>             6 weeks ago        /bin/sh -c #(nop)  ENV LANG=C.UTF-8                    0B
<missing>             6 weeks ago        /bin/sh -c #(nop)  ENV PATH=/usr/local/bin:/…         0B
<missing>             6 weeks ago        /bin/sh -c #(nop)  CMD ["/bin/sh"]                    0B
<missing>             6 weeks ago        /bin/sh -c #(nop) ADD file:a86aea1f3a7d68f6a…         5.53MB
```

Figure 8-8. *Docker image top-level and intermediate images*

With a new image in place, we can proceed and run containers.

Running Containers

Images alone can be simply seen as logically associated read-only filesystem layers. To be able to use containerized applications, you have to launch one or more containers based on a particular image. You do this using the docker run command. The -d parameter runs the container as a detached process in the background and effectively does not block the terminal. Even though the Dockerfile declares port 5000 as the one exposed by the image, you still need to map a chosen host port to that port for each created container. You do this using the -p parameter. We are free to override or set additional environment variables using one or more -e parameters. You may remember that the UUID API returns the UUID_GENERATOR_NAME environment variable value as the generator field in the response. For each container we are about to launch, we will use a different value that is identical to the name of the container that is set with the --name parameter.

The exercises in Chapter 2 helped you to run a single instance of the UUID API as a systemd service on each of the two hosts. This time, we will run a few instances of the same application, binding them to different ports on the development instance like this:

```
[opc@dev-vm]$ docker run -d -p 5011:5000 -e "UUID_GENERATOR_NAME=uuid-1"
--name uuid-1 uuid:1.0
d6e9112b0950.........40adc3
[opc@dev-vm]$ docker run -d -p 5012:5000 -e "UUID_GENERATOR_NAME=uuid-2"
--name uuid-2 uuid:1.0
224256288f19.........d63b8c
[opc@dev-vm]$ docker run -d -p 5013:5000 -e "UUID_GENERATOR_NAME=uuid-3"
--name uuid-3 uuid:1.0
b15d1d26614c.........45b8dd
```

To list running containers, you can use the docker ps command.

```
[opc@dev-vm]$ docker ps --format "table {{.ID}}\t{{.Image}}\t{{.
Names}}\t{{.Status}}\t{{.Ports}}"
CONTAINER ID   IMAGE      NAMES    STATUS     PORTS
b15d1d26614c   uuid:1.0   uuid-3   Up 3 min   0.0.0.0:5013->5000/tcp
224256288f19   uuid:1.0   uuid-2   Up 3 min   0.0.0.0:5012->5000/tcp
d6e9112b0950   uuid:1.0   uuid-1   Up 3 min   0.0.0.0:5011->5000/tcp
```

Now, let's test the UUID API on each of the containers.

```
[opc@dev-vm]$ curl 127.0.0.1:5011/identifiers
{
  "generator":"uuid-1",
  "uuid":"d89d68bf-c093-4774-ab0e-0089674c184e"
}
[opc@dev-vm]$ curl 127.0.0.1:5012/identifiers
{
  "generator":"uuid-2",
  "uuid":"e141eef7-e578-4272-934b-68b48b6e146c"
}
[opc@dev-vm]$ curl 127.0.0.1:5013/identifiers
{
  "generator":"uuid-3",
  "uuid":"52ea3c08-adf2-452b-bd28-ef7b26aa2fc2"
}
```

Because we are running the dev-vm compute instance on Oracle Cloud Infrastructure, you may want to test containerized UUID APIs by making calls from your local machine using the instance's public IP. To do so, you have to add an ingress security rule that allows the inbound traffic on ports 5011–5013. The infrastructure related to dev-vm was provisioned using Terraform. To add new ingress security rules, you would need to do it in the dev_sl resource in the devmachine/vcn.tf infrastructure code file. We discussed security rules in Chapters 2 and 6.

We have successfully validated the newly built image by instantiating three containers and testing their APIs. You can now exit from the developer instance console.

```
[opc@dev-vm]$ exit
```

The uuid:1.0 image is currently stored in our local image registry on the development instance. This kind of local registry is perfectly fine for the tests we've just conducted but cannot serve as a distribution registry.

Container Registry

In theory, you could push the newly built image from your local image registry on the developer instance to one of the public registries in the Internet such as Docker Hub. Yet, you will often prefer to keep all custom images in some kind of a private registry, invisible by the general public, that is additionally geographically close to your target infrastructure in which the containers run. Every Oracle Cloud Infrastructure tenancy comes with an image registry that is capable of storing both private and public repositories. *Oracle Cloud Infrastructure Registry* (OCIR) is fully integrated with identity and access management. As a consequence, the access to OCIR is granted to IAM users and managed using the IAM polices you are already familiar with. In the background, the container images are redundantly stored in the OCI object storage that backs the OCIR. *Repositories* are used to group related images. A single *repository* can be thought of as a set of related, tagged Docker image versions for a single service or application. In the context of OCIR, carefully assigned *tags* are used not only to denote particular versions or variants of containerized applications but also to indicate the tenancy namespace, destination region, and repository name. To push an image to your tenancy OCIR, you have to tag the image using a strictly defined notation, as presented in Figure 8-9.

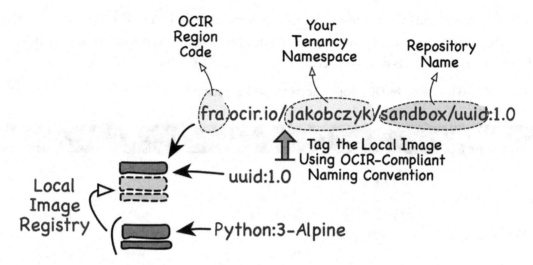

Figure 8-9. *Image tags and OCIR*

OCIR uses different region codes than the ones you've encountered up to now.
Table 8-1 presents a few of them. An updated list can be found here: `https://docs.`
`cloud.oracle.com/iaas/Content/General/Concepts/regions.htm`.

Table 8-1. *OCIR region codes*

Region Name	Region Identifier	OCIR Key
Australia East (Sydney)	ap-sydney-1	syd
Brazil East (Sao Paulo)	sa-saopaulo-1	gru
Canada Southeast (Toronto)	ca-toronto-1	yyz
Germany Central (Frankfurt)	eu-frankfurt-1	fra
India West (Mumbai)	ap-mumbai-1	bom
Japan East (Tokyo)	ap-tokyo-1	nrt
London (UK)	uk-london-1	lhr
South Korea Central (Seoul)	ap-seoul-1	icn
Switzerland North (Zurich)	eu-zurich-1	zrh
UK South (London)	uk-london-1	lhr
US East (Ashburn)	us-ashburn-1	iad
US West (Phoenix)	us-phoenix-1	phx

You can find the *tenancy namespace* in the Registry view in the OCI Console. If logged in as the tenancy superuser, you do not need any particular IAM policies to see OCIR in the OCI Console. This is how you access the relevant view using the OCI Console:

1.   Go to Menu ➤ Developer Services ➤ Registry.

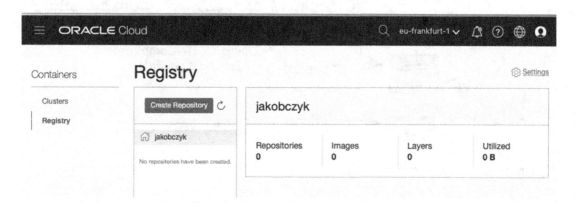

Figure 8-10. *Viewing an Oracle container Image registry in the OCI Console*

The *tenancy namespace* is visible as a root node of the repository list. You will find it next to an icon of a house. In my case, the namespace name is the same as my tenancy name (jakobczyk), but this might no longer be the case for newer tenancies. You will probably find a random string.

To allow other IAM users to interact with OCIR, you have to create the appropriate IAM policies that explicitly grant particular access to the chosen IAM groups. In the course of this book, we have been dealing with two groups: sandbox-admins and sandbox-users. Let's assume we would like to grant the sandbox-admins group members a permission to list all Docker repositories in the tenancy. Furthermore, both groups should be able to push, pull, and delete images in repositories whose names begin with the sandbox prefix such as sandbox/uuid or sandbox-cicd/uuid. On your local host with the OCI CLI, open the chapter08/2-docker/policies directory.

```
$ cd ~/git
$ cd oci-book/chapter08/2-docker
$ cd policies
$ ls -1
tenancy.ocir.policies.json
```

The JSON file contains three policy statements, as shown in Listing 8-3. The manage repos gives full access to all Registry-related OCI APIs over the repositories whose names match the where target.repo.name filter. The third rule gives the sandbox-admins group members inspect repos access over all repositories. The inspect-level access refers to just two APIs, ListDockerRepositories and ListDockerRepositoryManifests.

Listing 8-3. tenancy.ocir.policies.json

```
[
  "allow group sandbox-users to manage repos in tenancy where target.repo.
  name = /sandbox*/",
  "allow group sandbox-admins to manage repos in tenancy where target.repo.
  name = /sandbox*/",
  "allow group sandbox-admins to inspect repos in tenancy where request.
  operation='ListDockerRepositories'"
]
```

Because the OCIR scope is the tenancy level, we have to create the policy in the root compartment by pointing to it with the -c parameter of the iam policy create CLI command. As you probably remember, we maintain three profiles in the CLI config. The default profile calls the API on behalf of the tenancy admin and will be used when the --profile parameter is unset. Back on our local machine, let's execute the OCI CLI as the tenancy admin.

```
$ TENANCY_OCID=`cat ~/.oci/config | grep tenancy | sed 's/tenancy=//'`
$ echo $TENANCY_OCID
tenancy=ocid1.tenancy.oc1..aa..........3yymfa
$ oci iam policy create -c $TENANCY_OCID --name tenancy-ocir-policy
--description "OCIR Polices"  --statements "file://tenancy.ocir.policies.
json"
{
  "data": {
...
    "lifecycle-state": "ACTIVE",
    "name": "tenancy-ocir-policy",
```

```
    "statements": [
      "allow group sandbox-users to manage repos in tenancy where target.
      repo.name = /sandbox*/",
      "allow group sandbox-admins to manage repos in tenancy where target.
      repo.name = /sandbox*/",
      "allow group sandbox-admins to inspect repos in tenancy where
      request.operation='ListDockerRepositories'"
    ],
...
  },
  "etag": "d705d10ec093dbaf7c116054709951d38d3f7651"
}
```

You can verify the presence of the newly created IAM policy in the OCI Console. Remember to switch the scope to the root compartment, as shown in Figure 8-11.

Figure 8-11. *OCIR policy*

Having said that OCIR is fully integrated with IAM, it is clear that only authenticated and authorized IAM users are allowed to pull or push images in private repositories. You already worked with authentication tokens in the previous chapter. As a quick recap, let me mention a couple of facts. Users are authenticated based on the authentication tokens. A token is a relatively short Oracle-generated string. Any IAM user can have up to two authentication tokens at a time. Tokens can be created by the users themselves or arbitrarily by administrators either using the OCI Console or by leveraging API-based automation such as the OCI CLI.

This is how you generate an authentication token as a sandbox-user in the OCI Console:

1. Log in to the OCI Console as the sandbox-user.

2. Go to the user profile by clicking the user name, as shown in Figure 8-12.

3. On the Resources tab, click Auth Tokens.

4. Click Generate Token.

5. Provide a description for your token, and click Generate Token.

6. Write down your token. You will see it only once.

Figure 8-12. *Accessing the user profile in the OCI Console*

It is crucial to remember that you see a newly generated authentication token only once, as shown in Figure 8-13. If you lose it, you will have to delete the old token and generate a new one.

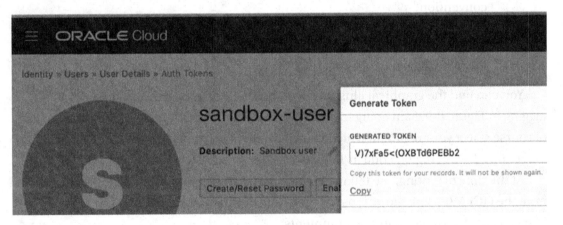

Figure 8-13. *Seeing a generated token*

To programmatically generate an authentication token for a selected user, you can execute the following CLI commands on behalf of the tenancy admin using the default CLI profile (just omit the `--profile` parameter). First, you query for the OCID of a particular user, and then you use the `iam auth-token create` CLI command for that user.

```
$ IAM_USER_OCID=`oci iam user list -c $TENANCY_OCID --query
"data[?name=='sandbox-user'] | [0].id" --raw-output --all`
$ echo IAM_USER_OCID
ocid1.user.oc1..aa..........dzqpxa
$ oci iam auth-token create --user-id $IAM_USER_OCID --description token-
ocir --query 'data.token' --raw-output
B8.E_Ry7o0tN1KFOdo9x
```

No matter which way you choose, please make sure you have an authentication token for the `sandbox-user` IAM user.

We are about to push the `uuid:1.0` image we built a few moments ago. To push a local container image in OCIR, you have to do the following:

1. Choose the OCIR region.

2. Properly tag the local image according to the OCIR naming convention.

3. Log in to the region-specific OCIR as a named IAM user.

4. Push the tagged image.

You can find the graphical illustration of the OCIR naming convention for image tagging in Figure 8-9. I am going to push the image to the OCIR in Frankfurt, but you can of course select your region in which you've worked until now. In such case, you will find the required OCIR region code in Table 8-1.

At the time of writing, the tenancy namespace can be programmatically read from the OCI API using the `oci os ns get` CLI command. Let's identify our tenancy namespace. We will use it in a few moments.

```
$ oci os ns get --query data --raw-output
jakobczyk
```

As you can see, my tenancy namespace has the same value as my tenancy name. This is because I am using a relatively old cloud account. For newer cloud accounts, probably including yours, the tenancy namespace and tenancy name nearly always differ.

> **Caution**   While working with OCIR, be careful not to confuse the *tenancy name* with the *tenancy namespace*. Make sure you use the tenancy namespace to tag the image and log in to OCIR.

Connect to the developer instance now.

```
$ ssh -i ~/.ssh/oci_id_rsa opc@$DEV_VM_PUBLIC_IP
[opc@dev-vm] $
```

Here's how I am tagging the local uuid:1.0 image as **fra**.ocir.io/**jakobczyk**/ sandbox/uuid:1.0 using the docker tag command:

```
[opc@dev-vm] $ OCI_PROJECT_CODE=sandbox
[opc@dev-vm] $ OCI_TENANCY_NAMESPACE=jakobczyk
[opc@dev-vm] $ OCIR_REGION=fra
[opc@dev-vm] $ OCI_USER=sandbox-user
[opc@dev-vm] $ IMAGE_NAME=uuid
[opc@dev-vm] $ IMAGE_TAG=1.0
[opc@dev-vm] $ docker tag $IMAGE_NAME:$IMAGE_TAG $OCIR_REGION.ocir.io/$OCI_
             TENANCY_NAMESPACE /$OCI_PROJECT_CODE/$IMAGE_NAME:$IMAGE_TAG
[opc@dev-vm] $ docker images --format "table {{.Repository}}\t{{.Tag}}\t{{.ID}}"
REPOSITORY                          TAG        IMAGE ID
uuid                                1.0        b16f04d1bb7f
fra.ocir.io/jakobczyk/sandbox/uuid  1.0        b16f04d1bb7f
python                              3-alpine   fe3ef29c73f3
```

As you can see, both the uuid:1.0 and fra.ocir.io/jakobczyk/sandbox/uuid:1.0 tags refer to the same b16f04d1bb7f image. This was our goal. Now, log in to the OCIR and push the image like this. You will be prompted for the Auth Token.

```
[opc@dev-vm] $ docker login -u $OCI_TENANCY_NAMESPACE/$OCI_USER $OCIR_
             REGION.ocir.io
Password: B8.E_Ry7oOtN1KFOdo9x

Login Succeeded
[opc@dev-vm]$ docker push $OCIR_REGION.ocir.io/$OCI_TENANCY_NAMESPACE/
             $OCI_PROJECT_CODE/$IMAGE_NAME:$IMAGE_TAG
```

```
The push refers to repository [fra.ocir.io/jakobczyk/sandbox/uuid]
4954d6a23347: Pushed
7337b89d95ab: Pushed
1821dd20f0ac: Pushed
640ae8435b21: Pushed
5191bfc553a0: Pushed
0db5724f9017: Pushed
7f61afcc4a4d: Pushed
8cec11e3dff0: Pushed
f1b5933fe4b5: Pushed
1.0: digest: sha256:33645f08e7eed90afde92b7331254a6d24a6480b12f01e13148be3b
ae81fc180 size: 2200
[opc@dev-vm]$ docker logout $OCIR_REGION.ocir.io
Removing login credentials for fra.ocir.io
[opc@dev-vm]$ exit
```

Tip   If you receive a docker login error stating that a tenant with a given namespace was not found, you probably used the tenancy name instead of the tenancy namespace. Please use the tenancy namespace to tag the image and log in to OCIR. You can use the oci os ns get command to find out your tenancy namespace.

Now, you can verify that the image has been successfully pushed into OCIR as a new private Docker repository. This time, I am logging into the OCI Console as sandbox-admin. If you logged in as sandbox-user, you wouldn't be able to list the Docker repositories because the policy we had set lets only sandbox-admins group members do this. Figure 8-14 presents the newly created repository that represents the newly pushed uuid:1.0 image. The Access field indicates that we are dealing with a private repository, which is visible for successfully authenticated and authorized IAM users. In the User field, you can see the OCID of the user who created the repository. Figure 8-15 presents the details of a concrete image version.

Figure 8-14. *Viewing an OCIR repository*

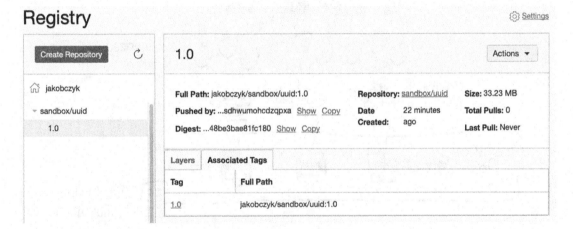

Figure 8-15. *Viewing an OCIR repository image*

The image is present in OCIR.

Container Management

Think about provisioning an instance pool fronted by a load balancer. In an instance pool, each compute instance uses Docker and pulls an image on startup to run multiple, let's say three, containers based on the uuid:1.0 image. In this way, a large number of UUID API instances would be capable of serving a truly demanding stream of requests incoming over the load balancer. This is conceptually presented in Figure 8-16.

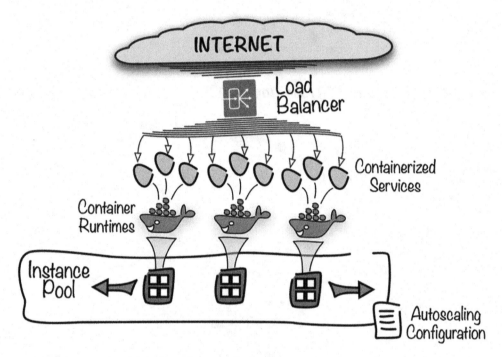

Figure 8-16. *Many instances of a containerized application on many VMs*

This could work well, and you would have the opportunity to horizontally scale out the number of compute instances as demand grows or scale them in as the demand decreases, either manually or by employing the autoscaling mechanism.

Take a moment to consider a few challenges, though.

- Upgrading all running containers by introducing a newer image version

- Adding other containers based on different images

- Changing the number of containers per compute instance

At first glance, you just need to push the relevant images to OCIR and adapt the cloud-config files, Terraform providers, or Ansible Playbook depending on the instance initialization style you follow. Yet, if you look closer at the challenge, you will start asking yourself the following questions:

- How do I securely manage the Auth Tokens on these instances?

- How would I avoid downtime?

- What should I do if I have to handle dependencies between different containerized applications?

- How would I actually manage virtual networking between various containerized applications on many compute instances if they have to interact with each other?

- How would one container discover and talk to other containers?

As you can see, sometimes, or I dare say often, it is not enough just to launch an instance pool with a container runtime on each instance that runs containerized applications that are all fronted by a load balancer. The questions I listed prove that you need a more sophisticated and more powerful mechanism to manage the containers and support the full lifecycle of containerized applications. This is where the container orchestration comes into play.

Container Orchestration

Contemporary backend systems are composed of many interacting applications and application modules that belong to more specialized systems. This approach was intensified with the arrival of service-oriented architecture (SOA) years ago. SOA has been broadly adapted ever since. Service orientation is a design paradigm in which preferably stateless software components are considered as *services* that offer their functionality through well-described APIs. This approach results in a more granular split of capabilities between individual software components and entails an increased demand for various types of interactions between individual services.

Running each service as a stand-alone process in the context of the operating system would be a pretty cumbersome task. This is why services have been traditionally deployed to *application servers* that fulfilled many crucial nonfunctional tasks such as managing dependencies, offering resource injection, providing security, persisting state,

441

delivering monitoring capabilities, and implementing APIs. Service developers benefited from delegating these support tasks to application servers simply because they were able to focus on functional goals in their service code. Application servers could be then combined into clusters to enable load distribution and high availability. Furthermore, the dependencies were installed and registered on the level of application servers and therefore decoupled from the service code. At first glance, it sounds absolutely wonderful, like an ultimate solution for enterprise software. Yet, it could lead and often led to problems during the migration of particular services from one environment to another. In the world of application servers, developers usually handed their deployment artifacts together with the list of required dependencies to the operations team whose role was to install the services in various environments and plug them into the messaging bus if needed. Sometimes, it happened that the configuration of different environments differed so much that unexpected problems occurred due to incorrect properties or incompliant versions of libraries. To deploy a service to a given application server, the service code had to adhere to standards supported and interfaces implemented by a particular application server. For example, you deployed Java EE applications to JEE-compliant servers, Python applications to WSGI-compliant web servers, and .NET applications to Microsoft IIS.

One thing that distinguishes services deployed to an application server from containerized applications is the fact that all dependencies, in the case of the latter, are bundled with the application in the form of an image. Thanks to the filesystem layers shared by many images, this doesn't cause any major storage capacity problems. No application server, however, means that the containers have to handle all *nonfunctional tasks* themselves. To address this challenge, you might create a set of dedicated containers, which handle these nonfunctional tasks, for each container that implements a service or part of a business process. As a matter of fact, this is a well-known pattern called the *sidecar pattern*. This creates a need to logically combine the main container with its sidecar containers and govern their lifecycle jointly as a single logical deployment unit. Containerization often results in even more granular applications, each focused on a narrow and specialized task, whether it is data transformation, the implementation of a single REST resource that belongs to a standardized API, or the interaction with various software-as-a-service business solutions. Some tend to call these highly specialized services as *microservices*. A number of microservices have to interact in order to accomplish one or more business processes. Therefore, containerized applications need some kind of service discovery mechanism and connectivity. To achieve fault tolerance and enable highly availably application deployments, multiple hosts with container runtimes are grouped together to form clusters. These clusters must provide some kind of overlay network to let all containerized applications smoothly interact with each other when needed. All in all, we come back, to some extent, to the problems that had been already solved for services deployed to application servers. What we need for containerized applications is some kind of an *infrastructure-agnostic platform* that will support clustering, built-in scaling, lifecycle management, and flat overlay network for related groups of containers, as illustrated in Figure 8-17.

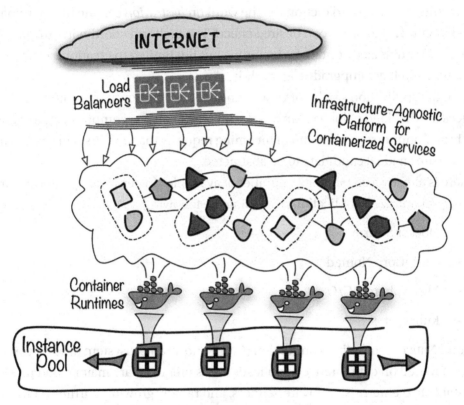

Figure 8-17. *Platform for containerized applications*

The goals for that kind of *container platform* are as follows:

- Orchestrating containerized applications
- Abstracting underlying infrastructure

- Providing applications with the following:

  - A flat overlay network

  - Scalable computing capacity

  - Persistent storage

  - An integrated service discovery for applications

  - Health checks functionality

- And more

According to the Oxford dictionary, the word *orchestration* can mean "coordination of the elements (...) to produce a desired effect." The platform coordinates the lifecycle of individual and related containers including but not limited to creation, scaling, termination, intelligent upgrades, and self-healing.

From the application's point of view, it does not matter how many compute instances or what kind of load balancers are involved. It is the computing power and a steady and uninterrupted stream of incoming requests that matters. This makes the infrastructure an ideal candidate to be abstracted.

There is already a considerable number of available cluster-aware platforms for running containerized applications including the following:

- Docker Swarm

- HashiCorp Nomad

- Mesosphere DC/OS

- Kubernetes

Cloud Native Computing Foundation (CNCF) hosts an ecosystem of open source software focused on containerized applications. Its members are major cloud providers, well-established enterprise software vendors, and rapidly growing startups. At the time of writing, Kubernetes is the only graduated project in the area of container orchestration, has more than 2,100 direct contributors on GitHub, and has been adopted by a number of cloud providers as the engine for their managed container platforms.

Kubernetes

Kubernetes is a truly immense topic that could fill a separate book. The platform and a diverse ecosystem of related tools provide a broad range of container-oriented functionalities, mentioned in the previous section. Kubernetes comes with an extendable and pluggable control plane. Kubernetes, being a rich-feature container platform built around container orchestration, provides containerized applications with an infrastructure-agnostic, scalable deployment canvas equipped with a pluggable, flat-space networking.

Containerized applications are organized into *pods*. A *pod* is a logical construct that groups closely related containers, usually one main and a few sidecar containers. Even though still somehow isolated, containers in the same pod do share some elements such as the hostname, network interfaces, and the IPC namespace. What remains separate are the filesystem layers each individual container is built from, unless they share the same or similar images. Containers can communicate with other containers in the same pod using localhost because they share the loopback interface. How do you group containers into pods? First, think about scaling. Pods can be replicated to increase the processing throughput or simply provide high availability to respond to a failure. If you feel that it is more appropriate to scale two particular containers separately, put them into two separate pods. Second, think about the sidecar pattern. Having a particular main container, you would often put the dedicated support containers into the same pod to let them communicate freely with the main container, for example, over the loopback interface.

A pod is an example of a core Kubernetes object type. There are a few other types of Kubernetes objects. I mentioned before that pods can be replicated. The replication is handled by a *ReplicaSet* object. One of the fundamental Kubernetes concepts is the presence of controller control loops. A ReplicaSet defines the expected count of pods that have a particular label attached. The corresponding control loop ensures the number of pods is correct according to the expected state. If there are too few pod replicas running in a given moment in time, the control loop will make sure that the instance count is increased to what is expected in a particular ReplicaSet definition.

With a set of pod replicas that provides an implementation of a particular API, you may be asking how to expose this API. Another type of Kubernetes object, a *Service* object, is used to provide a static point of entry to the group of pod replicas that implement a particular service. Kubernetes knows where to dispatch the incoming requests based on selectors. As you define a Service object, you provide a label selector.

445

All pods with the given label will be considered addressees of the service. The default type of a Service object is called a *ClusterIP*. It provides a service with an internal IP address reachable from within the cluster only. This is perfectly fine for containers with services called by other containers within the cluster. To let a service be reachable from the outside of a cluster, you can choose a *LoadBalancer* type, provided that your underlying cloud infrastructure supports this type. Oracle Cloud Infrastructure does offer public load balancers that are attached to a public IP and reachable from the Internet. I will show this in action in a few moments.

If you think about upgrade strategies, you could probably name a few. First, if you accept a short period of downtime, the easiest approach is to simply kill all pods whose containers use a deprecated image and let the ReplicaSet re-create them automatically in the background, this time using the newest image. Alternatively, you could apply the blue-green deployment strategy in which you create the new pods, which are based on the new image version, in parallel to the actively running pods, which are based on the previous image version, and switch the service to point to these new pods in a single moment. Finally, you could perform a rolling upgrade by replacing pods, one by one, with newer image versions. The rolling upgrade strategy would require you to employ two ReplicaSet resources and perform changes step-by-step in a procedural manner. ReplicaSet is rather a low-level object. To enhance the upgrading experience, a higher-level object called *Deployment* has been made available. A Deployment object controls pods through a ReplicaSet in a way that makes it much easier to handle the upgrade process based on purely declarative changes. We are not going to explore upgrade strategies in this book, but we are going to use the Deployment object, and this is the reason why I am briefly describing it.

To wrap up this fast-paced introduction to the main types of Kubernetes objects, let's take a look at Figure 8-18. There are two deployments defined. The one shown on the left side defines a single-container pod, tagged with Tag A, and sets the expected count to two replicas. The second one, shown in the right side, defines a two-container pod, tagged with Tag B, and sets the expected count to three replicas. Furthermore, there are two LoadBalancer-type services created. One is forwarding traffic to the pods with the tag Tag A attached, while the second one is forwarding traffic to the pods with Tag B.

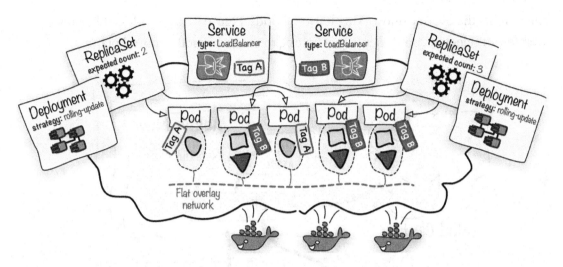

Figure 8-18. *Kubernetes objects*

There are a couple of other types of Kubernetes objects such as StatefulSets, DaemonSets, Jobs, Ingresses, PersistentVolumes, StorageClasses, and others. If I tried to cover all of them here, the book would grow to an enormous size. This is why we are focusing only on the objects that are used to demonstrate Oracle Kubernetes Engine in the incoming sections of this chapter. Do not worry if this all seems too theoretical. You will see these objects in action in a few moments from now. Just read on.

Building a production-ready cluster with various additional features can be a challenge on its own. Even if you are not tasked with designing and launching a Kubernetes cluster, it is still good to understand its high-level architecture.

The Kubernetes control plane is built from various software components replicated and distributed across an uneven number of *master nodes*. These components are the API server, scheduler, and controller manager. The Kubernetes object definitions are stored in a distributed, persistent key-value store called *etcd*. The etcd cluster has a lifecycle separate from Kubernetes that increases the planning effort when launching production-ready clusters. Only the API server accesses etcd directly. Pods are scheduled to the other types of nodes called *worker nodes*. On each node, there is a *kubelet* daemon usually running as a systemd host service manager. You could think of the kubelet as the node agent. It takes care of pod-specific containers on a given node by talking to the local container runtime. From a networking point of view, the Kubernetes Service proxy is responsible for controlling the traffic routing between services and pods, while another pluggable component called the Container Network Interface plugin implements the overlay networking between pods. Figure 8-19 provides a high-level overview of selected components that belong to the Kubernetes control plane.

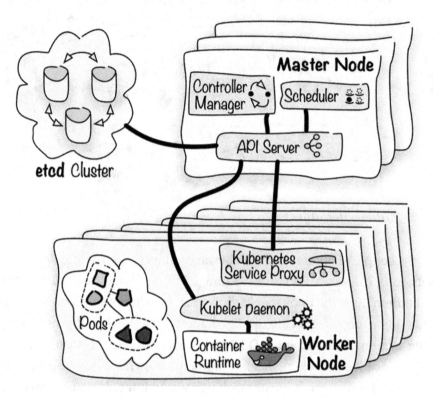

Figure 8-19. *Kubernetes, underlying infrastructure*

This book is not devoted to Kubernetes administration, and you need to be aware that there are plenty of various caveats to be considered when planning a custom installation of a Kubernetes cluster. Luckily, we won't need to bother about these aspects because of the presence of a managed Kubernetes engine.

Managed Cluster

Oracle Cloud Infrastructure comes with Oracle Kubernetes Engine (OKE), a managed Kubernetes platform-as-a-service cloud offering validated against the CNCF Certified Kubernetes Conformance Program. The certification ensures that the required Kubernetes APIs are fully supported and in line with the open source distribution. A managed service means that within a few minutes you get a fully operational cluster managed in an intelligent way by the platform. You do not need to bother about the etcd cluster or master node configuration. All control plane components are installed automatically. Your role is to choose the worker node shapes and point to the VCN subnets in which the worker nodes and load balancers are to be created. The cluster will be fully integrated with IAM and run on Oracle Cloud Infrastructure compute instances.

Creating a cluster in the OCI Console is pretty straightforward. First things first, however. If you have never launched any OKE cluster in your tenancy, you have to explicitly enable the OKE service. You do this by adding a simple IAM policy within the root compartment. The required statement is presented in Listing 8-4 and allows the OKE service to manage all the resources in the entire tenancy. The OKE service must be able to provision instances and dynamically change some networking resources such as security lists.

Listing 8-4. tenancy.oke.policy.json

```
[ "allow service OKE to manage all-resources in tenancy" ]
```

Make sure you are on your local machine. Let's create the required policy. We are not using the --profile parameter; therefore, the command will be executed as the tenancy admin because this user is defined in the DEFAULT profile of our CLI configuration file.

```
$ TENANCY_OCID=`cat ~/.oci/config | grep tenancy | sed 's/tenancy=//'`
$ echo TENANCY_OCID
ocid1.tenancy.oc1..aa.........3yymfa
$ cd ~/git
$ cd oci-book/chapter08/3-kubernetes
$ cd policies
$ oci iam policy create -c $TENANCY_OCID --name tenancy-oke --description
"OKE Policy"  --statements "file://tenancy.oke.policy.json"
```

```
{
  "data": {
    ...
    "lifecycle-state": "ACTIVE",
    "name": "tenancy-oke",
    "statements": [
      "allow service OKE to manage all-resources in tenancy"
    ],
    ...
  },
}
```

Nowadays, with more and more end-to-end automation in place, we are used to a "one-click" approach that assumes no complex actions are needed to complete a task such as cluster provisioning. As I said earlier, launching a cluster in the OCI Console (or using CLI) is pretty straightforward. To provision a cluster using the OCI Console, you need to go to Developer Services, choose Container Clusters, click Create Cluster, and provide a few details such as the Kubernetes version, worker node shape, and initial quantity per worker node subnet. This book, however, is oriented on code-driven automation; therefore, I will show how to use the Terraform-powered infrastructure code to provision a cluster on top of a custom virtual networking layout.

We want sandbox-admin to be recognized by the OKE cluster as its initial administrator. This is why it is absolutely crucial that you provision the cluster as the sandbox-admin user. Until now, Terraform created all resources on behalf of the tenancy admin. To make Terraform use another set of credentials and interact with the OCI API this time as sandbox-admin, you have to prepare a new variable definition file, as shown in Listing 8-5.

Listing 8-5. sandbox-admin.tfvars

```
tenancy_ocid = "<put-here-tenancy-ocid>"
region = "<put-here-region-identifier>"
user_ocid = "<put-here-sandbox-admin-ocid>"
private_key_path = "<put-here-path-to-sandbox-admin-auth-key>"
private_key_password = "<put-here-sandbox-admin-auth-key-pass>"
fingerprint = "<put-here-sandbox-admin-auth-key-fingerprint>"
compartment_ocid = "<put-here-sandbox-compartment-ocid>"
```

We will use the `--var-file` parameter to pass the new file to `terraform` and in this way set the values for the `oci` provider to execute all the API calls on behalf of the sandbox-admin user. All required details are already present in the SANDBOX-ADMIN profile in the `.oci/config` file. I have prepared a helper script to generate the `sandbox-admin.tfvars` file out of the values stored in the `.oci/config` file.

```
$ SANDBOX_COMPARTMENT_OCID=`oci iam compartment get --query data.id --raw-
output --profile SANDBOX-ADMIN`
$ cd ~/git/oci-book/chapter08/3-kubernetes
$ chmod a+x oci_config_to_tfvars.sh
$ ./oci_config_to_tfvars.sh ~/.oci/config ~/sandbox-admin.tfvars $SANDBOX_
COMPARTMENT_OCID
```

Make sure the newly created `tfvars` file is indeed present at the `~/sandbox-admin.tfvars` path and continue.

We are going to use Terraform to provision VCN-related resources such as subnets, security lists, and gateways with the Kubernetes cluster cloud resource and an instance pool of worker nodes. OKE requires various resources such as compute instances, load balancers, and virtual networking. The `sandbox-admins` group members and tenancy administrators already have all permissions in place to manage the required cloud resource types in the Sandbox compartment. In the `chapter08/3-kubernetes` directory, you will find the infrastructure code. Let's provision it.

```
$ cd ~/git
$ cd oci-book/chapter08/3-kubernetes
$ cd infrastructure
$ find . | sort
./kube
./kube/cluster.tf
./kube/vars.tf
./kube/vcn-lb.tf
./kube/vcn-workers.tf
./modules.tf
./provider.tf
./vars.tf
./vcn.tf
$ terraform init
```

```
Initializing modules...
- kubernetes in kube

Initializing the backend...

Initializing provider plugins...
- Checking for available provider plugins...
- Downloading plugin for provider "oci" (terraform-providers/oci) 3.30.0...

Terraform has been successfully initialized!
```
$ **terraform apply -var-file="~/sandbox-admin.tfvars" -auto-approve**
...

Tip   If you have received an 401 error, you are most probably using a relative path to your private key. Please open the `sandbox-admin.tfvars` file and replace the ~ character or the $HOME variable with an absolute path to your home directory such as `/home/thomas/`or `/Users/thomas/`.

Provisioning the infrastructure and subsequent cluster control plane components' installation on the master and worker nodes will take a couple of minutes, usually less than eight minutes. Terraform will be displaying the `Still creating` message. You can also access the OCI Console and observe the new cluster in the Creating state, as shown in Figure 8-20. To do so, do the following:

1.   Go to Menu ➤ Developer Services ➤ Clusters.

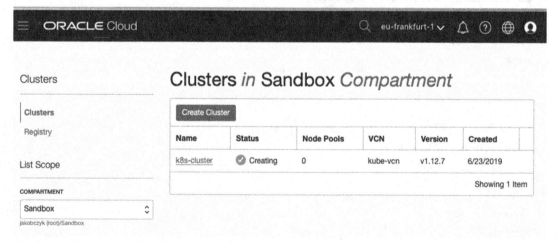

Figure 8-20. *OKE cluster provisioning*

At some point in time, the cluster will transfer to the Active state. This announces the readiness of the control plane. You still need to wait a few moments for the worker nodes until the node pool instance enters the running state. In the meantime, please take a look at the cluster and networking information, as shown in Figure 8-21. The infrastructure code provisions a Kubernetes cluster with a single-worker node pool. We can clearly see who has created the cluster.

Caution   In the Created By field, you should see the name or the OCID of the sandbox-admin user, as shown in Figure 8-21. If you see another user such as the tenancy admin, it means you have either skipped the --var-file parameter when executing terraform apply or somehow have invalid user data in the ~/sandbox-admin.tfvars file. Please use terraform destroy to delete the current cluster, make sure the new Terraform properties file for the sandbox-admin user is correct, and re-create the infrastructure.

All cloud resources have been provisioned in the Sandbox compartment. There are two load balancer subnets. They will be used to host highly available, floating-IP-based, public load balancers that will appear when you start creating LoadBalancer-type Service Kubernetes objects. The Pods CIDR field shows the private IP address range that will be used by dynamically created pods, while the Services CIDR field shows the same for the addresses exposed by Kubernetes services. Both pods and service address ranges are chosen in such a way that they do not overlap with the address range used by the kube-vcn VCN to which the worker nodes are attached.

Cluster Information

Cluster Status: ✅ Active

Node Pools: 1

Cluster Id: ...c4wmntdg42w Show Copy

Compartment: jakobczyk (root)/Sandbox

Kubernetes Version: v1.12.7

Kubernetes Address: ...com:6443 Show Copy

Launched: Sun, 23 Jun 2019 03:18:55 GMT

Created By: sandbox-admin

Network Information

VCN Name: kube-vcn

VCN Id: ...qzms3uiq Show Copy

Compartment: jakobczyk (root)/Sandbox

Pods CIDR: 10.244.0.0/16

Services CIDR: 10.96.0.0/16

Service LB Subnet 1: oke-lb-ad1-net Show Copy

Service LB Subnet 2: oke-lb-ad2-net Show Copy

Figure 8-21. Viewing an active OKE cluster summary in the OCI Console

If you look at the final output in Terraform, you will see not only cluster resources but also a node pool mentioned.

```
...
module.kubernetes.oci_containerengine_cluster.k8s_cluster: Creation
complete after 6m6s module.kubernetes.oci_containerengine_node_pool.k8s_
nodepool: Creating...
module.kubernetes.oci_containerengine_node_pool.k8s_nodepool: Creation
complete after 2s
Apply complete! Resources: 13 added, 0 changed, 0 destroyed.
```

The node pool is managed by OKE, and you can see it in the OCI Console at the bottom of the Cluster details view, as shown in Figure 8-22. The pool controls the compute instances that serve as worker nodes. If you click one of the names of any of these instances, you will be transferred to the Instance Details view of the corresponding instance. All worker nodes that belong to an OKE cluster node pool are visible just like any ordinary compute instance, as presented in Figure 8-23. You can watch their metrics and inspect other instance-specific information. You can also spot that instance display names contain a small part of the cluster OCID. If you wondered where the instances for the master nodes and etcd hosts are, the answer is that the entire OKE cluster control plane is fully managed by OKE and never exposed in any part in the API. You won't see them in the OCI Console, and you won't be able to list them using API. These compute resources are invisible.

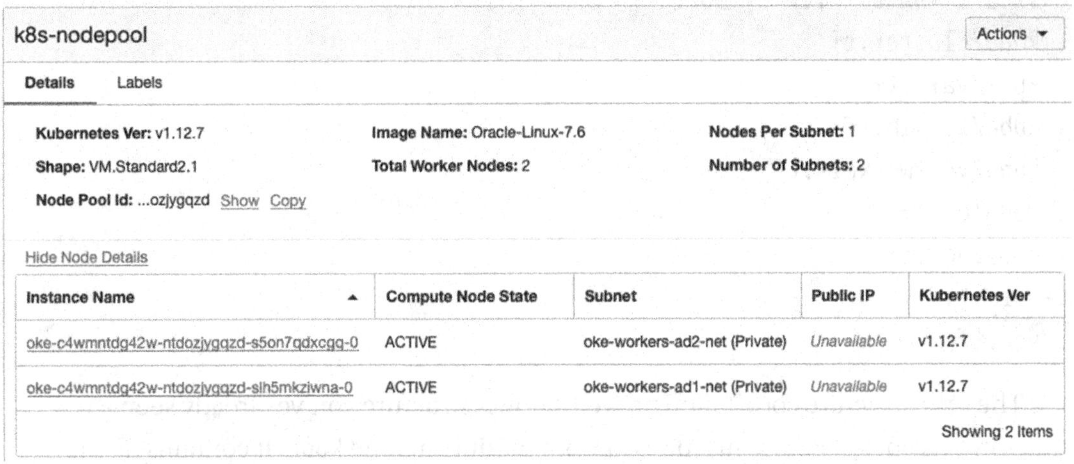

Figure 8-22. *OKE cluster node pool in the OCI Console*

Figure 8-23. *OKE cluster instances in the OCI Console*

The infrastructure code declares one compute instance in each worker node subnet that we chose to be private subnets. You have two options for the worker nodes. They can be attached to public subnets and hold public IPs or be isolated from the outside world in private subnets that inhibit the instances from having public IPs. In our case, we chose the second option. This is why you see Unavailable in the Public IP column of the Node Pool table. The instances were deployed in two different ADs. They are of the VM.Standard2.1 shape and based on the Oracle Linux 7.6 image. Where do these choices actually come from? Let's take a look at selected elements in the infrastructure code:

```
$ find . -name "*.tf" | sort
./kube/cluster.tf
./kube/vars.tf
./kube/vcn-lb.tf
./kube/vcn-workers.tf
./modules.tf
./provider.tf
./vars.tf
./vcn.tf
```

The infrastructure code follows a well-known structure you've already seen a few times in this book. There is just one nonroot module named kube. It contains all the infrastructure cloud resources used by the OKE cluster excluding VCN and gateways. The VCN, the NAT gateway, and the Internet gateway are declared in the vcn.tf file. The modules.tf file provides the OCIDs of the aforementioned networking resources as input parameters to the kube module. The code from the root module is similar to what you've seen in the previous exercises; therefore, I am not going to list the root module files here. You can check them directly in the infrastructure code. Listing 8-6 shows the vars.tf file from the kube module.

Listing 8-6. vars.tf (kube Module)

```
# kube module - vars.tf
...
variable "oke_cluster" {
  type = map
  default = {
    cidr = "10.0.2.0/24"
    version = "v1.12.7"
    worker_image = "Oracle-Linux-7.6"
    worker_shape = "VM.Standard2.1"
    worker_nodes_in_subnet = 1
```

```
    pods_cidr = "10.244.0.0/16"
    services_cidr = "10.96.0.0/16"
  }
}

variable "oke_wn_subnet_cidr" {
  type = list(string)
  default = [ "10.0.2.0/27", "10.0.2.32/27" ]
}
variable "oke_lb_subnet_cidr" {
  type = list(string)
  default = [ "10.0.2.128/28", "10.0.2.144/28" ]
}
variable "oke_engine_cidr" {
  type = list(string)
  default = [ "130.35.0.0/16", "138.1.0.0/17"]
}
```

You may be overwhelmed by the number of various IP address ranges defined for different subnets in the vars.tf file of the kube module. It is not as complicated as it may seem. Take a look at Figure 8-24. Kubernetes alone requires two nonoverlapping private IP address ranges for pods and services. These are set in the oke_cluster Terraform variable map and later passed to the oci_container_engine_cluster Terraform resource that represents the OKE cluster we have just provisioned. The underlying infrastructure such as compute instances or OCI load balancers will be distributed across four subnets that belong to the same VCN. The subnets for worker nodes are set in the oke_wn_subnet_cidr list variable, while the subnets for load balancers are set in the oke_lb_subnet_cidr list variable.

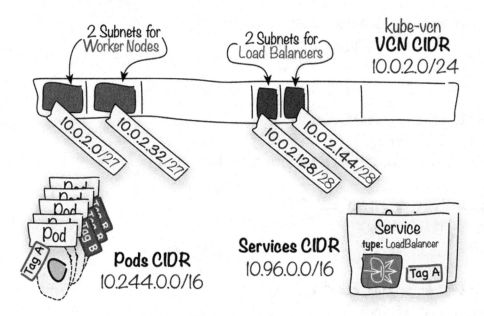

Figure 8-24. *OKE cluster-related subnets*

Listing 8-7 presents the `vcn-workers.tf` file that contains declarations for VCN resources related to the subnets for worker nodes. There are two private subnets defined, each in a different availability domain.

Listing 8-7. vcn-workers.tf (kube Module)

```
resource "oci_core_route_table" "oke_workers_rt" {
  compartment_id = var.compartment_ocid
  vcn_id = var.vcn_ocid
  display_name = "oke-workers-rt"
  route_rules {
    destination = "0.0.0.0/0"
    network_entity_id = var.vcn_nat_ocid
  }
}

resource "oci_core_security_list" "oke_workers_sl" {
  compartment_id = var.compartment_ocid
  vcn_id = var.vcn_ocid
  display_name = "oke-workers-sl"
```

```
  # Allow all traffic within the VCN
  egress_security_rules {
    stateless = true
    destination = var.oke_cluster["cidr"]
    protocol = "all"
  }
  ingress_security_rules {
    stateless=true
    source = var.oke_cluster["cidr"]
    protocol="all"
  }
  # Allow all outbound traffic
  egress_security_rules {
    destination = "0.0.0.0/0"
    protocol = "all"
  }
}

resource "oci_core_subnet" "oke_workers_ad1_net" {
  compartment_id = var.compartment_ocid
  vcn_id = var.vcn_ocid
  display_name = "oke-workers-ad1-net"
  availability_domain = var.ads[0]
  cidr_block = var.oke_wn_subnet_cidr[0]
  route_table_id = oci_core_route_table.oke_workers_rt.id
  security_list_ids = [ oci_core_security_list.oke_workers_sl.id ]
  prohibit_public_ip_on_vnic = true
  dns_label = "work1"
}

resource "oci_core_subnet" "oke_workers_ad2_net" {
  compartment_id = var.compartment_ocid
  vcn_id = var.vcn_ocid
  display_name = "oke-workers-ad2-net"
  availability_domain = var.ads[1]
  cidr_block = var.oke_wn_subnet_cidr[1]
```

```
  route_table_id = oci_core_route_table.oke_workers_rt.id
  security_list_ids = [ oci_core_security_list.oke_workers_sl.id ]
  prohibit_public_ip_on_vnic = true
  dns_label = "work2"
}
```

Similarly, the VCN resources dedicated to the subnets for load balancers are declared in an analogous file called vcn-lb.tf and presented in Listing 8-8. Again, there are two subnets defined, each in a different availability domain. The two subnets are public so that OKE is able to create OCI public load balancers for any LoadBalancer-type Kubernetes services.

Listing 8-8. vcn-lb.tf (kube Module)

```
resource "oci_core_route_table" "oke_lb_rt" {
  compartment_id = var.compartment_ocid
  vcn_id = var.vcn_ocid
  display_name = "oke-lb-rt"
  route_rules {
    destination = "0.0.0.0/0"
    network_entity_id = var.vcn_igw_ocid
  }
}

resource "oci_core_security_list" "oke_lb_sl" {
  compartment_id = var.compartment_ocid
  vcn_id = var.vcn_ocid
  display_name = "oke-lb-sl"
  # Allow all traffic within the VCN
  egress_security_rules {
    stateless = true
    destination = var.oke_cluster["cidr"]
    protocol = "all"
  }
```

```
  ingress_security_rules {
    stateless=true
    source = var.oke_cluster["cidr"]
    protocol="all"
  }
  # Allow all inbound traffic on ports 30000-32767
  egress_security_rules {
    stateless = true
    destination = "0.0.0.0/0"
    protocol = "all"
  }
  ingress_security_rules {
    stateless=true
    source = "0.0.0.0/0"
    protocol="6"
    tcp_options {
      min = 30000
      max = 32767
    }
  }
}

resource "oci_core_subnet" "oke_lb_ad1_net" {
  compartment_id = var.compartment_ocid
  vcn_id = var.vcn_ocid
  display_name = "oke-lb-ad1-net"
  availability_domain = var.ads[0]
  cidr_block = var.oke_lb_subnet_cidr[0]
  route_table_id = oci_core_route_table.oke_lb_rt.id
  security_list_ids = [ oci_core_security_list.oke_lb_sl.id ]
  dns_label = "lb1"
}
```

```
resource "oci_core_subnet" "oke_lb_ad2_net" {
  compartment_id = var.compartment_ocid
  vcn_id = var.vcn_ocid
  display_name = "oke-lb-ad2-net"
  availability_domain = var.ads[1]
  cidr_block = var.oke_lb_subnet_cidr[1]
  route_table_id = oci_core_route_table.oke_lb_rt.id
  security_list_ids = [ oci_core_security_list.oke_lb_sl.id ]
  dns_label = "lb2"
}
```

Finally, the OKE cluster and its corresponding node pool for compute instances that serve as Kubernetes worker nodes are declared in the cluster.tf infrastructure file. The code is shown in Listing 8-9.

Listing 8-9. cluster.tf (kube Module)

```
resource "oci_containerengine_cluster" "k8s_cluster" {
  compartment_id = var.compartment_ocid
  kubernetes_version = var.oke_cluster["version"]
  name = "k8s-cluster"
  vcn_id = var.vcn_ocid
  options {
    kubernetes_network_config {
      pods_cidr = var.oke_cluster["pods_cidr"]
      services_cidr = var.oke_cluster["services_cidr"]
    }
    service_lb_subnet_ids = [
      oci_core_subnet.oke_lb_ad1_net.id,
      oci_core_subnet.oke_lb_ad2_net.id
    ]
  }
}

resource "oci_containerengine_node_pool" "k8s_nodepool" {
  compartment_id = var.compartment_ocid
  cluster_id = oci_containerengine_cluster.k8s_cluster.id
  kubernetes_version = var.oke_cluster["version"]
```

```
name = "k8s-nodepool"
node_image_name = var.oke_cluster["worker_image"]
node_shape = var.oke_cluster["worker_shape"]
subnet_ids = [
  oci_core_subnet.oke_workers_ad1_net.id,
  oci_core_subnet.oke_workers_ad2_net.id
]
quantity_per_subnet = var.oke_cluster["worker_nodes_in_subnet"]
ssh_public_key = file("~/.ssh/oci_id_rsa.pub")
}
```

Figure 8-25 illustrates the provisioned OCI infrastructure components that serve for the k8s-cluster OKE cluster instance. Kubernetes control plane elements such as master nodes and etcd hosts are fully managed, inaccessible, and therefore invisible from the API or OCI Console. What you can inspect, monitor, and to some extent govern are compute instances that serve as worker nodes, load balancers, and other virtual networking components.

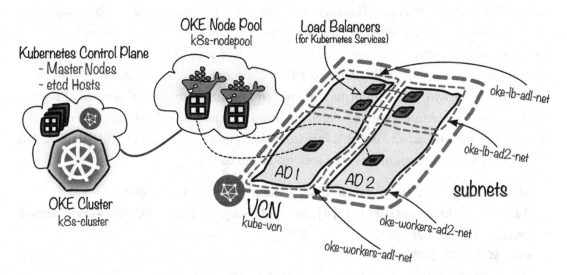

Figure 8-25. *Provisioned OKE cluster*

With a managed Kubernetes cluster in place, it is time to connect to the Kubernetes API.

Connecting As Superuser

Kubernetes assumes that users are fully managed externally to Kubernetes. If you are working with an unmanaged Kubernetes cluster that is installed, for example, in your data center or on some IaaS, you would usually set up certificate-based authentication for clients or employ OpenID Connect that leverages ID tokens signed by an identity trusted by the Kubernetes API. The latter would allow more production-oriented user management strategies in the context of Kubernetes API authentication and, later, authorization.

It is all much easier with a managed service such as Oracle Kubernetes Engine. For OKE clusters, all IAM users are recognized and successfully authenticated, out of the box, provided that they are members of groups with the proper IAM policies. What comes next, though, is the authorization. IAM users who are members of a group that has been assigned `manage clusters` in a given compartment where the cluster exists are automatically considered cluster administrators by the Kubernetes OCI Authorizer and have the full access to the entire Kubernetes API for that particular cluster. The rest of the IAM users must be explicitly bound to either predefined or custom RBAC roles. You will learn about this later. The `sandbox-admin` user belongs to the `sandbox-admins` group, which has been granted full manage-level access over all the resources in the Sandbox compartment. In this way, the Kubernetes API should recognize this user as a cluster admin. First, you will need a so-called *kubeconfig* file, which is nothing more than a YAML file with all the information needed to connect to the Kubernetes API as a named user. To generate a kubeconfig file tailored to a particular IAM user, you can use the OCI Console or OCI CLI like this (please note that we use `--profile SANDBOX-ADMIN` to execute the CLI commands as the `sandbox-admin` user):

```
$ CLUSTER_OCID=`oci ce cluster list --name k8s-cluster --query
"data[?name=='k8s-cluster'] | [0].id" --lifecycle-state ACTIVE --raw-output
--profile SANDBOX-ADMIN`
$ echo $CLUSTER_OCID
ocid1.cluster.oc1.eu-frankfurt-1.aa.........tdg42w
$ REGION=eu-frankfurt-1
$ mkdir ~/.kube
$ oci ce cluster create-kubeconfig --cluster-id $CLUSTER_OCID --file
~/.kube/sandbox-admin.config --region $REGION --profile SANDBOX-ADMIN
New config written to the file /Users/mjk/.kube/sandbox-admin.config
```

```
$ chmod 600 ~/.kube/sandbox-admin.config
$ ls -l ~/.kube | awk '{print $1, $9}'
-rw------- sandbox-admin.config
```

Based on the convention, the kubeconfig file is placed in the newly created directory ~/.kube. The ~/.kube/config path is considered by the kubectl tool we are about to use as the default path for the kubeconfig file. We have deliberately used a custom name to be able to use this configuration only intentionally. Listing 8-10 presents the kubeconfig file generated for the sandbox-admin user.

Listing 8-10. .kube/sandbox-admin.config

```
apiVersion: v1
clusters:
- cluster:
    certificate-authority-data:
      ::: Base64-encoded cluster certificate :::
    server: https://c4wmntdg42w.eu-frankfurt-1.clusters.oci.oraclecloud.
            com:6443
  name: cluster-c4wmntdg42w
contexts:
- context:
    cluster: cluster-c4wmntdg42w
    user: user-c4wmntdg42w
  name: context-c4wmntdg42w
current-context: context-c4wmntdg42w
kind: ""
users:
- name: user-c4wmntdg42w
  user:
    exec:
      apiVersion: client.authentication.k8s.io/v1beta1
      args:
      - ce
      - cluster
      - generate-token
      - --cluster-id
```

```
    - ::: Cluster OCID :::
    - --region
    - eu-frankfurt-1
    command: oci
    env: []
```

The clusters:cluster:certificate-authority-data field is a Base64-encoded certificate of the cluster, while the users:user:exec field is an instruction to use a custom command to dynamically fetch the credentials and to authenticate as a particular IAM user. If you want to authenticate, it is not enough just to hold this file. The command used to fetch the credentials relies on the OCI CLI and a user-specific CLI configuration file. You will see it in action in a few moments.

Do not forget that we are using a particular CLI profile for sandbox-admin. We have to take it into consideration and amend the kube/sandbox-admin.config file accordingly. Edit the .kube/sandbox-admin.config file and add two new lines (in bold), as shown here:

```
...
users:
- name: user-c2gmyzqguzt
  user:
    exec:
      apiVersion: client.authentication.k8s.io/v1beta1
      args:
      - ce
      - cluster
      - generate-token
      - --profile
      - SANDBOX-ADMIN
      - --cluster-id
...
```

You will use a tool called kubectl to connect to the Kubernetes API. The tool will read the kubeconfig file to do the following:

1. Find out what the Kubernetes API public endpoint is

2. Securely connect to the Kubernetes API

3. Use the OCI CLI to fetch the token and authenticate us as a named IAM user

The kubectl tool has been already preinstalled on the developer instance by the cloud-init based on the supplied cloud-config file, so you should be able to use the tool out of the box. We still need to install the OCI CLI on the developer instance. Now, connect to the developer instance and execute the following command:

```
[opc@dev-vm ~]$ bash -c "$(curl -L https://raw.githubusercontent.com/
oracle/oci-cli/master/scripts/install/install.sh)"
...
-- Installation successful.
-- Run the CLI with /home/opc/bin/oci --help
[opc@dev-vm ~]$ oci --version
2.6.14
[opc@dev-vm ~]$ mkdir ~/.oci
[opc@dev-vm ~]$ mkdir ~/.apikeys
[opc@dev-vm ~]$ exit
```

Now, we need to prepare and upload the CLI configuration for sandbox-admin.

```
$ cat ~/.oci/config | grep -A 4 "\[SANDBOX-ADMIN\]" > ~/.oci/devvm.config
$ cat ~/.oci/config | grep tenancy >> ~/.oci/devvm.config
$ cat ~/.oci/config | grep region >> ~/.oci/devvm.config
$ scp -i ~/.ssh/oci_id_rsa ~/.oci/devvm.config opc@$DEV_VM_PUBLIC_IP:/home/
opc/.oci/config
devvm.config    100%   329   5.5KB/s
```

The CLI configuration references the API signing key. Let's upload it as well.

```
$ scp -i ~/.ssh/oci_id_rsa ~/.apikeys/api.sandbox-admin.pem opc@$DEV_VM_
PUBLIC_IP:/home/opc/.apikeys/api.sandbox-admin.pem
api.sandbox-admin.pem   100% 1766      10.0KB/s
```

The only thing missing is the kubeconfig file on the developer instance. We are therefore going to securely copy the kubeconfig file to the developer instance like this:

```
$ scp -i ~/.ssh/oci_id_rsa ~/.kube/sandbox-admin.config opc@$DEV_VM_PUBLIC_
IP:/home/opc/.kube/config
sandbox-admin.config            100% 3669    117.0KB/s   00:00
```

Tip   To find out how the developer instance has been initialized, you can read the cloud-config file available at `chapter08/1-devmachine/devmachine/cloud-init/devvm.config.yaml`.

Now, please connect to the developer instance.

```
$ ssh -i ~/.ssh/oci_id_rsa opc@$DEV_VM_PUBLIC_IP
```

Shortly before we start interacting with the Kubernetes API, we will adjust the file permissions for the newly uploaded configuration files.

```
[opc@dev-vm ~]$ chmod 600 .kube/config
[opc@dev-vm ~]$ chmod 600 .oci/config
```

We are going to issue a few `kubectl` commands to test the connectivity with the Kubernetes API and inspect the basic Kubernetes objects in our cluster. While still on the developer instance, issue the following commands:

```
[opc@dev-vm ~]$ kubectl get nodes
NAME         STATUS    ROLES    AGE     VERSION
10.0.2.2     Ready     node     14h     v1.12.7
10.0.2.34    Ready     node     14h     v1.12.7
[opc@dev-vm ~]$ kubectl get namespaces
NAME           STATUS    AGE
default        Active    14h
kube-public    Active    14h
kube-system    Active    14h
[opc@dev-vm ~]$ kubectl get pods -n kube-system
NAME                                      READY    STATUS
kube-dns-7db5546bc6-4gvqq                 3/3      Running
kube-dns-7db5546bc6-gq6fq                 3/3      Running
kube-dns-autoscaler-7fcbdf46bd-5sdnx      1/1      Running
kube-flannel-ds-gvkxn                     1/1      Running
kube-flannel-ds-vlsgk                     1/1      Running
kube-proxy-blzxf                          1/1      Running
kube-proxy-sdv4m                          1/1      Running
kubernetes-dashboard-7b96874d59-w5tfj     1/1      Running
```

```
proxymux-client-10.0.2.2                    1/1       Running
proxymux-client-10.0.2.34                   1/1       Running
tiller-deploy-7c4c4bfbc4-nsscm              1/1       Running
```

Tip   If you encountered errors, please double-check if all files (`.oci/config`, `.kube/config`, `.apikeys/api.sandbox-admin.pem`) are set as required, the CLI is installed, and you have added the `SANDBOX-ADMIN` profile to the Kubeconfig file as described a few paragraphs earlier.

The `kubectl get nodes` command lists the worker node. The master nodes are not listed in the OKE cluster. The `kubectl get namespaces` command lists the Kubernetes namespaces that can be thought of as a convenient way to isolate different environments within the same physical cluster. Various Kubernetes objects such as pods or services exist in the scope of a particular namespace. The `kube-system` namespace is used to host the Kubernetes network proxy (`kube-proxy-`) and the cluster feature add-ons such as the Container Networking Interface plugin pods (`kube-flannel-`) or cluster DNS pods (`kube-dns-`). You can list these pods using the `kubectl get pods` command with the namespace parameter `-n` set to the `kube-system` value.

The output of these three commands actually proves that you were successfully authenticated by the Kubernetes OCI Authorizer. But how powerful is the given user in terms of the Kubernetes APIs? Is there any way to inspect that? Yes, there is. A straightforward one is the `auth can-i` Kubernetes API call. You can make this call using `kubectl` like this:

```
[opc@dev-vm ~]$ kubectl auth can-i create namespace --all-namespaces
Yes
[opc@dev-vm ~]$ kubectl auth can-i '*' '*' --namespace=default
yes
```

The first execution of the command asks the Kubernetes API whether the user on whose behalf the `kubectl` calls are made is entitled to create a Kubernetes namespace. The answer is self-explanatory, isn't it? The second command uses the * wildcard to inspect whether all kinds of actions are allowed for the given user in the `default` namespace.

As a matter of fact, as I mentioned, the `sandbox-admin` user should be able to perform all kinds of operations on the Kubernetes API for this cluster because he belongs to the Sandbox compartment administrators IAM group and, based on this, is considered by the Kubernetes OCI Authorizer as a cluster admin for that cluster. Let's verify it.

```
[opc@dev-vm ~]$ kubectl auth can-i '*' '*' --all-namespaces
Yes
```

This is all correct. The sandbox-admin user is authorized to perform all operations on all Kubernetes objects no matter in which Kubernetes namespace they reside.

Sandbox Namespace

Kubernetes namespaces can be used to isolate different environments within the same physical cluster. Most Kubernetes resources are namespace-scoped, and you are required to specify the namespace while creating a particular resource such as a pod or service. Namespaces are also useful during Kubernetes service name resolution with Kubernetes DNS because the FQDN of a Kubernetes services does include its namespace. We would like sandbox-user to be able to perform actions such as creating Kubernetes objects such as pods, services, and deployments, but only in the scope of a dedicated Kubernetes namespace. Last but not least, there are various quotas you can set to impose consumption limits by Kubernetes resources in a particular namespace.

Let's create a new Kubernetes namespace called the dev-sandbox namespace.

```
[opc@dev-vm ~]$ cd oci-book/chapter08/3-kubernetes/platform
[opc@dev-vm ~]$ kubectl create -f dev-sandbox-namespace.yaml
namespace/dev-sandbox created
```

We have used the kubectl create command to create a new Kubernetes namespace resource as defined in a YAML Kubernetes object descriptor. We passed the relative path to the file using the -f parameter. Listing 8-11 shows the YAML file.

Listing 8-11. dev-sandbox-namespace.yaml

```
apiVersion: v1
kind: Namespace
metadata:
  name: dev-sandbox
  labels:
    environment: dev
```

The new Kubernetes object is of a `Namespace` kind, uses `dev-sandbox` as its name, and is labeled with a custom `environment` label with the value set to `dev`. Because of the pluggable and extendable nature of the Kubernetes platform, labels are often a primary means to associate various objects. In this case, we are not going to use this particular label, but I took the opportunity to show you how to tag a Kubernetes object. You can now use `kubectl` to list and describe the newly created namespace.

```
[opc@dev-vm ~]$ kubectl get namespaces
NAME            STATUS    AGE
default         Active    15h
dev-sandbox     Active    41m
kube-public     Active    15h
kube-system     Active    15h
[opc@dev-vm ~]$ kubectl describe namespace dev-sandbox
Name:           dev-sandbox
Labels:         environment=dev
Annotations:    <none>
Status:         Active

No resource quota.

No resource limits.
[opc@dev-vm ~]$ exit
```

Now, with the new namespace set, we can prepare the `sandbox-user` user to connect to the Kubernetes API.

Connecting As Developer

We have already learned that to talk to the Kubernetes API using `kubectl`, we have to possess a kubeconfig file. Furthermore, you've also seen that the OKE client authentication mechanism assumes that tokens are dynamically generated using the OCI CLI in the background. Based on that fact, we uploaded the CLI configuration and API signing key for the `sandbox-admin` user. Earlier in this chapter, we employed the `ce cluster create-kubeconfig` CLI to generate the kubeconfig for the `sandbox-admin` user. The command was issued on behalf of the `sandbox-admin` user, thanks to the presence of the `SANDBOX-ADMIN` profile in the CLI configuration file. In this section, we are going to let the sandbox-user generate a personal kubeconfig file. It is rather clear that not every IAM user should be allowed to generate personal kubeconfig files. To generate a kubeconfig file, the OCI API requires the GetClusterKubeconfig permission set for the IAM user on whose behalf the API is called. This permission is included with the use clusters IAM policy verb. Let's create a new policy that allows sandbox-users to use all OKE clusters in the Sandbox compartment. Even though the policy is intended for the members of the sandbox-users group, we are executing the CLI command as sandbox-admin using the SANDBOX-ADMIN profile like this:

```
$ TENANCY_OCID=`cat ~/.oci/config | grep tenancy | sed 's/tenancy=//'`
$ echo $TENANCY_OCID
ocid1.tenancy.oc1..aa.........3yymfa
$ cd ~/git
$ cd oci-book/chapter08/3-kubernetes
$ cd policies
$ oci iam policy create --name sandbox-users-containers-policy
--description "Containers-related policy for regular Sandbox
users"  --statements "file://sandbox-users.containers.policy.json"
--profile SANDBOX-ADMIN
{
  "data": {
    ...
    "lifecycle-state": "ACTIVE",
    "name": "sandbox-users-containers-policy",
    "statements": [
      "allow group sandbox-users to use clusters in compartment Sandbox"
    ],
    ...
}
```

Listing 8-12 presents the contents of the JSON file we used to create the new IAM policy. As I said before, we are giving the right to use all OKE clusters in the Sandbox compartment to the members of the sandbox-users group. This set of permissions includes the right to generate a personal kubeconfig file as well.

Listing 8-12. sandbox-users.containers.policy.json

```
[
  "allow group sandbox-users to use clusters in compartment Sandbox"
]
```

We are now ready to execute the ce cluster create-kubeconfig CLI command on behalf of the sandbox-user user by applying the SANDBOX-USER CLI profile like this:

```
$ oci ce cluster create-kubeconfig --cluster-id $CLUSTER_OCID --file
~/.kube/sandbox-user.config --region $REGION --profile SANDBOX-USER
New config written to the file /Users/mjk/.kube/sandbox-user.config
$ chmod 600 ~/.kube/sandbox-user.config
```

We have to amend the newly generated kubeconfig file by setting the correct OCI CLI profile. Please edit the sandbox-user.config file and add the SANDBOX-USER profile like this:

```
...
users:
- name: user-c2gmyzqguzt
  user:
    exec:
      apiVersion: client.authentication.k8s.io/v1beta1
      args:
      - ce
      - cluster
      - generate-token
      - --profile
      - SANDBOX-USER
      - --cluster-id
...
```

All in all, at this stage, we have two configuration files.

```
$ ls -l ~/.kube | awk '{print $1, $9}'
-rw------- sandbox-admin.config
-rw------- sandbox-user.config
```

Now, upload the newest kubeconfig file to the developer instance.

```
$ scp -i ~/.ssh/oci_id_rsa ~/.kube/sandbox-user.config opc@$DEV_VM_PUBLIC_
IP:/home/opc/.kube
sandbox-user-config                 100% 3669     262.9KB/s    00:00
```

We have to extend the OCI CLI configuration on the dev-vm by adding the
SANDBOX-USER profile. Let's do it locally and upload it again to replace the previous
version.

```
$ cat ~/.oci/config | grep -A 4 "\[SANDBOX-USER\]" >> ~/.oci/devvm.config
$ cat ~/.oci/config | grep tenancy >> ~/.oci/devvm.config
$ cat ~/.oci/config | grep region >> ~/.oci/devvm.config

$ scp -i ~/.ssh/oci_id_rsa ~/.oci/devvm.config opc@$DEV_VM_PUBLIC_IP:/home/
opc/.oci/config
devvm.config    100%   656    5.2KB/s
```

Last but not least, we need to upload the API signing key for the sandbox-user.

```
$ scp -i ~/.ssh/oci_id_rsa ~/.apikeys/api.sandbox-user.pem opc@$DEV_VM_
PUBLIC_IP:/home/opc/.apikeys/api.sandbox-user.pem
api.sandbox-user.pem    100% 1766     13.7KB/s
```

Let's connect to the developer machine.

```
$ ssh -i ~/.ssh/oci_id_rsa opc@$DEV_VM_PUBLIC_IP
```

At this moment, there should be two kubeconfig files in the ~/.kube directory on the
developer machine:

```
[opc@dev-vm ~]$ chmod 600 ~/.kube/sandbox-user.config
[opc@dev-vm ~]$ ls -l ~/.kube | grep config | awk '{print $1, $9}'
-rw-------. config
-rw-------. sandbox-user.config
```

You are going to use the --kubeconfig parameter to instruct the kubectl tool which
file it should use, as illustrated in Figure 8-26. If you leave the parameter unset, the
~/.kube/config file will be selected by default.

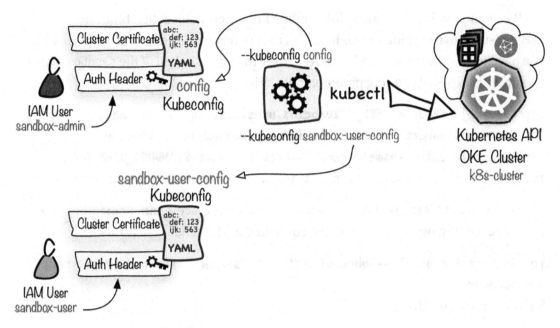

Figure 8-26. *Kubeconfig files*

Let's try to list the pods in the dev-sandbox namespace, this time on behalf of the sandbox-user. Remember to choose the appropriate kubeconfig file by setting the --kubeconfig parameter like this:

```
[opc@dev-vm]$ kubectl --kubeconfig ~/.kube/sandbox-user-config get pods -n
dev-sandbox
Error from server (Forbidden): pods is forbidden: User "ocid1.user.oc1..
aa.........dzqpxa" cannot list resource "pods" in API group "" in the
namespace "dev-sandbox"
```

The response you received clearly states that the given user is not entitled to perform this kind of operation. The sandbox-user user belongs to a group that does not have the manage clusters policy assigned. As a result, this particular user has no predefined role set in the k8s-cluster OKE cluster. We have to explicitly bind the user to a role. We are going to create a *role binding* that binds the sandbox-user to the edit role, solely in the scope of the dev-sandbox namespace. The edit role is a predefined Kubernetes role that gives write-read access over most types of Kubernetes objects in a particular namespace but does not allow the user to create role bindings.

We are now going to create a Rolebinding Kubernetes object that binds the sandbox-user to the predefined edit role in the context of the dev-sandbox namespace. You have to execute the kubectl create rolebinding on behalf of the sandbox-admin by skipping the --kubeconfig parameter like this:

```
[opc@dev-vm]$ SANDBOX_USER_OCID=ocid1.user.oc1..aa.........dzqpxa
[opc@dev-vm]$ kubectl create rolebinding sandbox-users-binding
--clusterrole=edit --namespace=dev-sandbox --user=$SANDBOX_USER_OCID
rolebinding.rbac.authorization.k8s.io/sandbox-users-binding created
```

We can try to list the pods in the dev-sandbox namespace again. Remember to set the --kubeconfig parameter to run the command as the sandbox-user user.

```
[opc@dev-vm]$ kubectl --kubeconfig ~/.kube/sandbox-user-config get pods -n
dev-sandbox
No resources found.
```

The No resources found message proves that we were able to call Kubernetes API as sandbox-user.

For the sandbox-user user, we expect to execute all kubectl commands only within the scope of the dev-sandbox namespace. Instead of using the -n parameter explicitly, you can add the default namespace to your config file like this:

```
[opc@dev-vm]$ cat ~/.kube/sandbox-user.config
...
contexts:
- context:
    cluster: cluster-...
    namespace: dev-sandbox
    user: user-...
  name: context-...
...
```

Finally, we are ready to deploy some pods to our OKE cluster.

Pods

As you remember, earlier in this chapter, you containerized the UUID API and pushed the uuid:1.0 Docker image to the OCI Registry. We are now going to create a Kubernetes pod based on this image. We will do it by issuing a YAML descriptor that defines a new single-container pod and its container image. We need to remember that we used a private OCIR repository for the uuid:1.0 image. From the OCIR perspective, an OKE cluster is just another client, and, to successfully pull an image, it has to authenticate using an Auth Token. You can store the token in a Kubernetes object of a *secret* type. This lets you reference this secret while creating Kubernetes pods, which are supposed to pull images from one or more container repositories in a given registry. In our case, the secret will encapsulate the regional OCIR endpoint, IAM user name, and the Auth Token for that user. Consequently, Kubernetes will be able to pull images only from the repositories that can be accessed by the particular IAM user. To create a single-container pod, we are going to use kubectl create with a simple YAML descriptor that defines the pod. The process is conceptually illustrated in Figure 8-27.

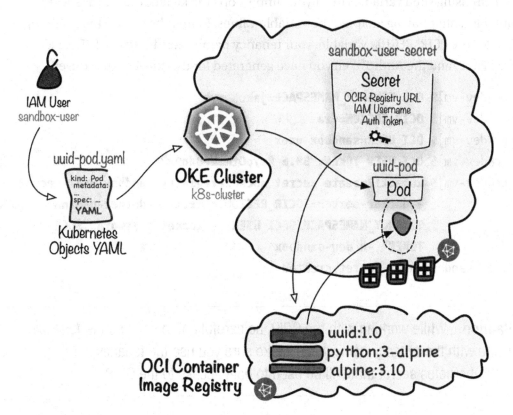

Figure 8-27. *Token and secret*

In this section, all `kubectl` calls will be done on behalf of the `sandbox-user` user. To save us from unnecessary typing, we can override the default kubeconfig path by setting the `KUBECONFIG` environment variable. Set and export the variable to point to the kubeconfig file that belongs to the `sandbox-user` user like this:

`[opc@dev-vm]$ export KUBECONFIG=~/.kube/sandbox-user.config`

You will use the `kubectl create secret` command to create a new Secret object within the `dev-sandbox` namespace. The Secret object will be called `sandbox-user-secret`, be of the `docker-registry` type, and contain all the information that Kubernetes needs to access the OCIR private repositories that stores the `uuid:1.0` container image, namely:

- Regional OCIR registry URL

- IAM User

- Auth Token for the IAM user

I am using shell variables to let you simply copy the `kubectl create secret` command after having adapted the variable values. Remember to use the OCIR region code for the `OCIR_REGION` variable, your tenancy namespace for the `OCI_TENANCY_NAMESPACE`, and the Auth Token you have generated for the `sandbox-user` user.

```
[opc@dev-vm]$ OCI_TENANCY_NAMESPACE=jakobczyk
[opc@dev-vm]$ OCIR_REGION=fra
[opc@dev-vm]$ OCI_USER=sandbox-user
[opc@dev-vm]$ OCI_USER_TOKEN="B8.E_Ry7o0tN1KF0do9x"
[opc@dev-vm]$ kubectl create secret docker-registry sandbox-user-secret
            --docker-server=$OCIR_REGION.ocir.io --docker-username="$OCI_
            TENANCY_NAMESPACE/$OCI_USER" --docker-password="$OCI_USER_
            TOKEN" -n dev-sandbox
secret/sandbox-user-secret created
```

Caution   While working with the OCIR, be careful not to confuse the *tenancy name* with the *tenancy namespace*. Make sure you use the tenancy namespace for the Kubernetes secret that will be used to gain access to the OCIR.

We can display the secrets that exist in a particular namespace like this:

```
[opc@dev-vm]$ kubectl get secrets -n dev-sandbox
NAME                     TYPE                                  DATA  AGE
default-token-wg574      kubernetes.io/service-account-token 3     3d1h
sandbox-user-secret      kubernetes.io/dockerconfigjson        1     51s
```

The newly created sandbox-user-secret of the kubernetes.io/dockerconfigjson type stores all the data required to access OCIR as the sandbox-user user.

We are now going to create a single-container pod based on the uuid:1.0 container image. All you need to do is to execute the kubectl create command using the uuid-pod.yaml file that defines the new pod. A few moments ago, you overrode the default kubeconfig path using the environment variable. This means all kubectl commands are invoked as the sandbox-user user. You have to create the pod in the dev-sandbox namespace; otherwise, the operation fails. Create the pod like this:

```
[opc@dev-vm]$ cd oci-book/chapter08/3-kubernetes/platform
[opc@dev-vm]$ sed -i "s/OCIR_REGION/$OCIR_REGION/; s/OCI_TENANCY_
             NAMESPACE/$OCI_TENANCY_NAMESPACE/" uuid-pod.yaml
[opc@dev-vm]$ kubectl create -f uuid-pod.yaml -n dev-sandbox
pod/uuid-pod created
[opc@dev-vm]$ kubectl get pods -n dev-sandbox
NAME       READY    STATUS    RESTARTS    AGE
uuid-pod   1/1      Running   0           8s
```

Tip   If you see the ErrorImagePull status or the ImagePullBackOff status instead of the Running status, there is probably something wrong with the token. Make sure you put the token in quotes while setting the OCI_USER_TOKEN variable.

Listing 8-13 presents the YAML file used to create the new pod. The metadata section is used to place the object in a particular namespace and set the name of the object. The spec section contains the container definition and the name of the Secret object to be used when pulling the image. The image name references a properly tagged uuid:1.0 container image. We used the sed command to replace two placeholders denoted in capitalized letters inside the YAML file with your OCIR region and tenancy namespace.

Listing 8-13. uuid-pod.yaml

```
apiVersion: v1
kind: Pod
metadata:
  name: uuid-pod
  namespace: dev-sandbox
spec:
  containers:
  - image: OCIR_REGION.ocir.io/OCI_TENANCY_NAMESPACE/sandbox/uuid:1.0
    name: uuid-container
    ports:
    - containerPort: 5000
      protocol: TCP
  imagePullSecrets:
  - name: sandbox-user-secret
```

Honestly speaking, a pod alone does not give us any value-added. We know it runs an UUID API, but we cannot reach its endpoint in a straightforward way. Let's delete this pod.

```
[opc@dev-vm]$ kubectl delete pod uuid-pod -n dev-sandbox
pod "uuid-pod" deleted
```

Deployments and Services

A containerized application is nearly always more than just a lonely single-container pod. Most containerized applications, especially those that are stateless, are expected to be able to scale horizontally and expose service endpoints to service consumers. A service consumer can be thought of as other containerized applications running in other pods within the same cluster or external systems or clients coming from the public Internet. To control and conveniently manage the service side of a set of pod clones, you will use the *Service* Kubernetes object. The Service object decouples somewhat the static side that represents a web service from the service implementation provided by a set of pods. One of the reasons for this is that pods can be scaled in and out dynamically. At the same time, the service side is supposed to remain unaltered to ease service discovery. Furthermore, the Service object is responsible for properly load balancing the incoming traffic. To manage operations on a set of pods such as the upgrade strategy and maintaining the number of healthy pods as expected, you will use the *Deployment* Kubernetes object. The *Deployment* object creates a *ReplicaSet* that keeps a steady number of identical pods and replaces these pods that enter the unhealthy state. Moreover, it is careful about the way containers are updated to the newer images by using various upgrade strategies. Figure 8-28 illustrates a simple collaboration between these Kubernetes objects.

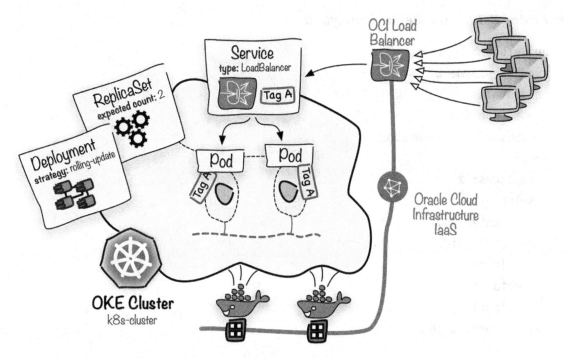

Figure 8-28. *Stateless service on Kubernetes*

Assuming that you are still on development instance, the KUBECONFIG variable is set as earlier, and you are still in the 3-kubernetes/platform directory and create a set of Kubernetes objects using the kubectl create command with uuid-deployment.yaml like this:

```
[opc@dev-vm] $ sed -i "s/OCIR_REGION/$OCIR_REGION/; s/OCI_TENANCY_
            NAMESPACE/$OCI_TENANCY_NAMESPACE/" uuid-deployment.yaml
[opc@dev-vm] $ kubectl create -f uuid-deployment.yaml -n dev-sandbox
deployment.apps/uuid-dpm created
service/uuid-srv created
```

Listing 8-14 presents the file `uuid-deployment.yaml` file that creates the associated Kubernetes objects, namely, Service, Deployment, ReplicaSet, and Pods that host containers based on the `uuid:1.0` container image pulled from the tenancy's OCIR. All pods are tagged with the `app=uuid` label. The Service object uses the tag-based selector `app:uuid` to learn where to route and distribute the traffic incoming from its dedicated Oracle Cloud Infrastructure load balancer. The load balancer is created dynamically if the type of the Service object is set to `LoadBalancer`.

Listing 8-14. uuid-deployment.yaml

```
apiVersion: apps/v1
kind: Deployment
metadata:
  name: uuid-dpm
  namespace: dev-sandbox
spec:
  replicas: 2
  selector:
    matchLabels:
      app: uuid
  template:
    metadata:
      labels:
        app: uuid
    spec:
      imagePullSecrets:
      - name: sandbox-user-secret
      containers:
      - name: uuid-container
        image: OCIR_REGION.ocir.io/OCI_TENANCY_NAMESPACE/sandbox/uuid:1.0
        ports:
        - containerPort: 5000
          protocol: TCP
---
```

```
apiVersion: v1
kind: Service
metadata:
  name: uuid-srv
  namespace: dev-sandbox
spec:
  type: LoadBalancer
  selector:
    app: uuid
  ports:
  - port: 80
    targetPort: 5000
```

You can use kubectl get commands to display the newly created objects.

```
[opc@dev-vm]$ kubectl get pods -n dev-sandbox -o wide
NAME                         READY STATUS    IP          NODE
uuid-dpm-78cf484f96-rj4br    1/1   Running   10.244.1.7  10.0.2.2
uuid-dpm-78cf484f96-wg2zw    1/1   Running   10.244.0.7  10.0.2.34
[opc@dev-vm]$ kubectl get replicasets -n dev-sandbox
NAME                  DESIRED    CURRENT    READY
uuid-dpm-78cf484f96   2          2          2
[opc@dev-vm]$ kubectl get services -n dev-sandbox
NAME      TYPE          CLUSTER-IP    EXTERNAL-IP    PORT(S)
uuid-srv  LoadBalancer  10.96.26.62   130.61.195.20  80:31475/TCP
```

The newly created Service object is of the LoadBalancer type. This results in the
provisioning of a new highly available public OCI load balancer that spans the two
subnets you have set for cluster load balancers. The EXTERNAL-IP column shows the
public IP address of the load balancer. If you see *Pending*, just wait a few moments. Your
load balancer is being launched. In my case, the public IP address of the load balancer
is 130.61.195.20, and your address probably will be different. Write it down. We will need
it in a few moments. In the meantime, you can observe the load balancer in the OCI
Console, as shown in Figure 8-29. You may have to wait a few moments to see Overall
Health set to OK. Sometimes, this flag is initially set to Unknown for a slightly longer
period of time, even though the load balancer is fully operational. Figure 8-30 shows the

detailed view of the load balancer, including its shape, public IP address, VCN, and two public subnets you've chosen for load balancers, while launching your OKE cluster.

Name	State	OCID	IP Address	Overall Health
b0ea17e4-9921-11e9-b6ba-0a580aed32ec	● Active	...xl4tna Show Copy	130.61.195.20 (Public)	✓ OK

Figure 8-29. *Kubernetes service load balancer*

Load Balancer Information

OCID: ...xl4tna Show Copy

Created: Thu, 27 Jun 2019 21:22:39 GMT

Shape: 100Mbps

IP Address: 130.61.195.20 (Public)

Virtual Cloud Network: kube-vcn

Subnet (1 of 2): oke-lb-ad1-net

Subnet (2 of 2): oke-lb-ad2-net

Overall Health

✓ OK

Backend Sets Health

0	Critical
0	Warning
0	Unknown
1	OK

Figure 8-30. *Kubernetes service load balancer details*

If you are still on the developer instance, disconnect.

```
[opc@dev-vm]$ exit
```

Let's send a series of identical requests to the external IP address of the service. You will have to replace the LB_PUBLIC_IP value with the IP address that has been assigned to your load balancer before running these commands:

```
$ LB_PUBLIC_IP=130.61.195.20
$ for i in {1..10}; do curl $LB_PUBLIC_IP:80/identifiers; done
{"generator":"uuid-dpm-78cf484f96-wg2zw","uuid":"a5bf.......d471"}
{"generator":"uuid-dpm-78cf484f96-wg2zw","uuid":"f2a4.......b902"}
{"generator":"uuid-dpm-78cf484f96-rj4br","uuid":"564c.......1496"}
{"generator":"uuid-dpm-78cf484f96-rj4br","uuid":"2473.......f7f9"}
{"generator":"uuid-dpm-78cf484f96-rj4br","uuid":"9709.......bc47"}
{"generator":"uuid-dpm-78cf484f96-wg2zw","uuid":"cffd.......22d9"}
{"generator":"uuid-dpm-78cf484f96-wg2zw","uuid":"6bb3.......5285"}
```

{"generator":"uuid-dpm-78cf484f96-rj4br","uuid":"6b02.......cafc"}
{"generator":"uuid-dpm-78cf484f96-rj4br","uuid":"fdb5.......dcf7"}
{"generator":"uuid-dpm-78cf484f96-wg2zw","uuid":"ee94.......b038"}

The generator field is populated based on the name of the pod that received the request. Looking at the results, you should see a rather equal split between the two pods that back our service. If you want, you could scale out the number of containerized application instances to dozens and even hundreds in a few seconds.

What we have done with Oracle Kubernetes Engine in this chapter only scratches the surface of what can be done using the cloud-based managed Kubernetes. Feel free to experiment, and when you are ready to proceed to the next chapter, do not forget to terminate the cluster and developer instance to spare your resource consumption.

Cleanup

There are three groups of resources we need to terminate in the proper order.

- Kubernetes objects and their related OCI resources

- OKE cluster and the related resources

- The dev-vm compute instance and related resources

First, we have a Kubernetes service that was created with the provisioning of a load balancer. We need to delete this service to remove the corresponding load balancer. Let's connect to the developer instance again and use kubectl to delete the Kubernetes objects we've just successfully tested.

```
$ ssh -i ~/.ssh/oci_id_rsa opc@$DEV_VM_PUBLIC_IP
[opc@dev-vm]$ export KUBECONFIG=~/.kube//sandbox-user.config
[opc@dev-vm]$ kubectl delete all --all -n dev-sandbox
pod "uuid-deployment-78cf484f96-rj4br" deleted
pod "uuid-deployment-78cf484f96-wg2zw" deleted
service "uuid-service" deleted
deployment.apps "uuid-deployment" deleted
[opc@dev-vm]$ exit
```

The second step involves terminating the cluster. Enter the infrastructure code directory, and issue the `terraform destroy` command, properly referencing the `sandbox-admin.tfvars` file to perform this operation on behalf of the `sandbox-admin` user.

```
$ cd ~/git
$ cd oci-book/chapter08/3-kubernetes/infrastructure
$ terraform destroy -var-file="$HOME/sandbox-admin.tfvars" -auto-approve
```

Finally, you can move to the last cleanup step for this chapter and terminate the dev-vm compute instance.

```
$ source ~/tfvars.env.sh
$ cd ~/git
$ cd oci-book/chapter08/1-devmachine
$ terraform destroy -auto-approve
```

Summary

In this chapter, you experienced the end-to-end process of containerizing an application. First, we built a multilayered container image based on the UUID API that was originally built and deployed on compute instances as an operating system service in Chapter 2. We tested containers based on this image locally and pushed them to the OCIR private repository. Next, we discussed the need for container orchestration based on the most popular open source container platform called Kubernetes. Then, we prepared and provisioned a managed Kubernetes cluster with the use of Oracle Kubernetes Engine. Following that, you learned how to work with the Kubernetes API and manage granular access for IAM users. Finally, you created a complete set of Kubernetes objects to properly manage a stateless containerized application based on the container image you prepared at the beginning of this chapter.

In the next chapter, we will discuss what does cloud-native architecture actually means nowadays.

CHAPTER 9

Cloud-Native Architecture

In the recent years, the degree and pace of changes on the software scene have accelerated like never before. The *open source* movement ignited a large number of scattered and often independent teams racing to bring new software components, tools, platforms, protocols, and services to market at an incredible pace. *Cloud computing* removed many hardware-related entry barriers by allowing teams to self-provision virtualized hardware resources in a matter of seconds. With cloud-provider-managed hardware capabilities, both virtualized and even bare-metal, available at one's fingertips, nearly anyone can launch and develop a small software project. *Containerization*, briefly covered in the previous chapter, often enables new approaches in designing applications and requires the presence of new supplementary tools to make the solutions production-ready. There are old questions to be answered such as how to solve storage, networking, messaging, and service discovery challenges, this time in the age of containers. There are new waters to explore—service mesh, container registries, and schedulers, to name a few. Let's list the three information age turning points that considerably impact the way we architect new-generation software solutions. These are as follows:

- Open source
- Cloud computing
- Containerization

The growing number of open source contributors and the ease of launching cloud-based software projects sparked software development on an unprecedented scale. The arrival of containerization brought demand for new types of software components and the need to adapt some of the existing tools. To roll out a production-ready software solution, you usually have to carefully pick the existing components of various types, add your in-house application codebase, and properly integrate everything. A large number of actively developed, usually not-yet-mature, and often competing container-oriented,

© Michał Tomasz Jakóbczyk 2020
M. T. Jakóbczyk, *Practical Oracle Cloud Infrastructure*, https://doi.org/10.1007/978-1-4842-5506-3_9

components, utilities, platforms, protocols, and services are making it more and more difficult for companies to choose what they need, as illustrated in Figure 9-1.

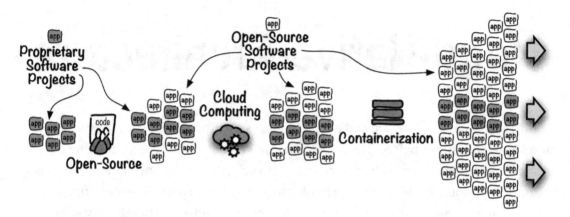

Figure 9-1. *Information age turning points*

Having too many approaches for solving the same kind of problems and a plethora of competing and often immature open source software projects can lead to some degree of chaos. To avoid running into troubles, there arises the need for *standardization*. This is similar to having design patterns that address common software development challenges. There are a few types of standards to consider. Some standards are crucial to get software components that need to interact to speak the same language. For example, the OpenAPI specification provides a standard for defining REST APIs using YAML or JSON documents that are readable both by humans and by machines. The CloudEvents specification is aimed at defining a common event structure so that a broad range of applications are able to seamlessly understand others' events. Other standards such as Container Network Interface (CNI) and Container Storage Interface (CSI) focus on defining interfaces that will let vendor-specific plugins communicate with various container runtimes in a unified way. One of the biggest challenges that arises especially for tech leads and technical architects is to deal with the flood of open source projects. People who hold these roles are confronted with questions on what open source projects to rely on when designing and building their cloud-based solutions. Because the majority of these projects are relatively new and still immature, there is a risk that, as the time goes by, some projects are abandoned or lose ground to their open source competition. In other words, it would be good to have some kind of reference architecture agreed on by the industry, in other words, a collection of graduated projects that meet reasonable requirements and are safe choice to include, while designing cloud-oriented solutions. To address this need, the leading cloud providers, independent software vendors, tech-driven companies, and academic and nonprofit organizations gathered together and created *Cloud Native Computing Foundation* (CNCF). CNCF hosts the entire ecosystem of cloud- and container-oriented open source projects and supports them during their evolution. Projects that are accepted to join the CNCF project portfolio are graded based on their maturity and adoption. There are three levels of grades: sandbox, incubation, and graduation. For tech leads and architects, CNCF provides a convenient landscape of projects to consider while choosing the components for the architected solutions, as illustrated in Figure 9-2. Furthermore, CNCF coordinates global events such as KubeCon + CloudNativeCon and supports a broad network of cloud-native Meetups around the world.

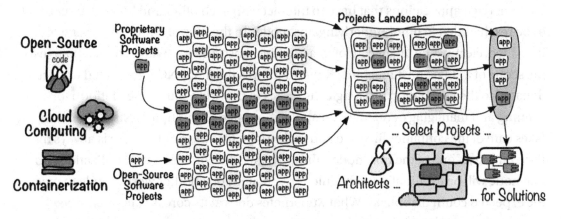

Figure 9-2. *Choosing cloud-native projects while architecting a cloud solution*

Cloud Native

What is cloud native? Looking at the word *native,* we could assume that a cloud-native tool or a component is deliberately designed for and built to fit the cloud-oriented industry-agreed reference architecture. We need examples to better understand this term and the various types of tools, applications, and components that represent the cloud-native ecosystem. If we refer to the CNCF definition of *cloud native*, we will learn the following:

> *Cloud native technologies empower organizations to build and run scal-*
> *able applications in modern, dynamic environments such as public, pri-*
> *vate, and hybrid clouds. Containers, service meshes, microservices,*
> *immutable infrastructure, and declarative APIs exemplify this approach.*

The most up-to-date definition is available on GitHub at `https://github.com/cncf/toc/blob/master/DEFINITION.md`.

The list that exemplifies cloud-native technologies starts with containers. As you know, containers are meant to work in the same way regardless of the underlying host platform. To run, containers require a *container runtime*. One of the graduated CNCF projects is *containerd*. As discussed in Chapter 8, containerd is the industry-standard container runtime that supervises the lifecycle of containers, taking care of container execution, image management, and host-system-related tasks such as the underlying storage or network attachments. Even if you've never heard of containerd, you have already worked with it, actually indirectly, because it is used, under the hood, by Docker. A modern-architecture solution is usually composed of a large number of containerized applications that have to interact with each other and be easy to scale out or be rescheduled to other underlying host nodes in the case of failure. In other words, their lifecycle must be taken care of in a broader sense and in a wider context than just the scope of a single host machine. Kubernetes was the first CNCF-graduated project donated to the foundation by Google. Its task is to provide a pluggable platform for running and managing containerized applications across multiple hosts. Kubernetes takes care of the container lifecycle and makes sure that the desired state is always met. For example, if one of the host nodes abruptly fails, the containerized applications on that node will be eventually rescheduled (re-created) on another worker node to meet the expected count of replicas. What Kubernetes does at its core is called *container orchestration and scheduling*. From a developer point of view, it comes with other crucial features such as API-driven declarative Kubernetes objects that encapsulate or abstract application components such as grouping containers called *pods, services, volumes, jobs, deployments*, and many more. You worked with a few of these types in the previous chapter. Containerized applications are based on multilayered container images. The images have their own lifecycle and are stored in *container image registries*. Container platforms such as Kubernetes dynamically fetch images from the image registries to create containers as defined by the expected state declared by developers. CNCF hosts image registry projects such as Docker Registry, JFrog Artifactory, Quay, and Harbor, to name a few. Various nonfunctional aspects of the interactions between containerized services such as security or observability can be handled using lightweight proxies installed as sidecar containers within each Kubernetes pod. These proxies form another layer called a *service mesh*. A service mesh simplifies communication between containerized services and provides out-of-the-box features such as service discovery, retries, load balancing, or circuit-breaking. Using a service mesh removes the burden of implementing these nonfunctional interservice communication tasks from the developer. Linkerd is a CNCF-incubating service mesh project. You may also have heard about Istio, which is another service mesh project hosted by CNCF. A new trending model of running applications with no server management at all is called *serverless* and belongs to the cloud-native ecosystem as well. Fn Project is an exemplification of a serverless platform built from scratch for containers. Container runtimes, orchestration platforms, image registries, service mesh, or serverless frameworks are just the tip of the iceberg. To bring a complete cloud-based solution into existence, there are many other types of cloud-native components to be included such as service discovery, key management, streaming, messaging, continuous delivery, API gateways, monitoring, logging, tracing, and others.

CNCF groups the open source projects it hosts together with selected proprietary, but still ecosystem-related, solutions using a convenient map called CNCF Cloud Native Landscape available at `https://landscape.cncf.io`. This map is supposed to help tech leads and architects follow a rapidly changing and evolving cloud-native stack. To give you the initial impression of how broad and diverse this ecosystem is, take a look at Figure 9-3.

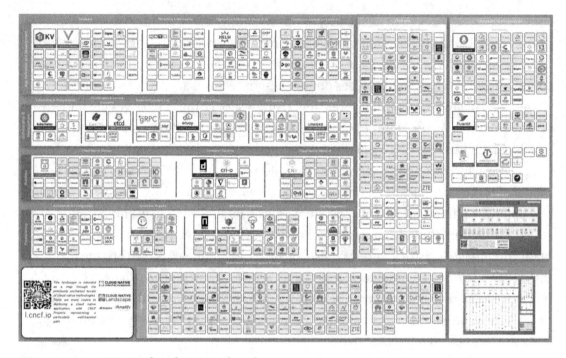

Figure 9-3. *CNCF cloud-native landscape*

This book is about Oracle Cloud. You learned about containers in the previous chapter. Now, it is time to experience the impact of cloud-native open source projects on Oracle Cloud.

Oracle is a CNCF platinum member. It has contributed a container-based serverless open source project called the Fn Project to the CNCF cloud-native ecosystem. Oracle Cloud features Oracle Kubernetes Engine, a fully managed, hosted Kubernetes engine certified by CNCF. You worked with OKE in the previous chapter. Oracle Linux comes with a certified Kubernetes distribution available as part of Oracle Container Services for use with Kubernetes. Last but not least, two leading relational databases, the open source MySQL and the proprietary Oracle Database, are referenced in the CNCF landscape. Furthermore, Oracle Cloud uses to some extent other CNCF open source projects. For example, Oracle Cloud Infrastructure events are compliant with an event structure as defined by the industry-standard CNCF project called CloudEvents.

It is time to do some hands-on exercises. We are about to delve into Oracle Functions, which is a function as a service (FaaS) based on the open source Fn Project. In other words, let's take a look at serverless computing.

Serverless

The term *serverless* is becoming another cloud computing buzzword. You might think that the name implies that executing a serverless application does not involve any servers. Well, this is a bit misleading. There are servers in the backend. As always. What this term really emphasizes is that operating a serverless application allows you to neglect the backend-related aspects. The runtime and application's lifecycle are completely managed by a particular serverless framework or managed serverless service. The latter is commonly associated with the term *function as a service* (FaaS). "Function" because serverless applications are usually considered as loose packages of stateless functions. A function like that should be designed to focus on a single, rather short-running, stateless task. A serverless framework or a managed cloud-based serverless service typically instantiates a particular function instance only when there is a request incoming or some function trigger activated. The instance is usually terminated as soon as the idle time interval has elapsed to free the computing resources. In other words, serverless function instances are not supposed to be idle. Another important aspect to mention is that serverless functions are expected to be scalable. Therefore, a serverless framework or a cloud-based FaaS may create many instances of the same serverless function in order to be able to serve many parallel requests. From a developer's point of view, serverless implies simplicity. A serverless function is typically implemented as a simple handler function that returns a result. Depending on the trigger, a function may consume input or read some information on its own. For example, an HTTP-based serverless function could process an image passed as a binary stream, apply some relatively simple filters, and either return the result or persist it in an object storage bucket. Another example could be a function that gets executed as soon as some kind of cloud event is captured. A new object uploaded to a particular bucket could generate such a cloud event, eventually triggering the function. You could come up with many ideas for serverless functions. Just remember two key characteristics. Serverless functions are supposed to be *stateless* and *short-lasting*. Serverless frameworks often limit the allowed maximum function execution time. Nowadays, serverless frameworks are expected to support multiple programming languages. This allows developers to choose the best language for a given task or simply the one they are good at. Figure 9-4 illustrates a conceptual use of a sample serverless function. The function is triggered by the incoming HTTP requests, and their payload data is processed and written to a particular database table.

493

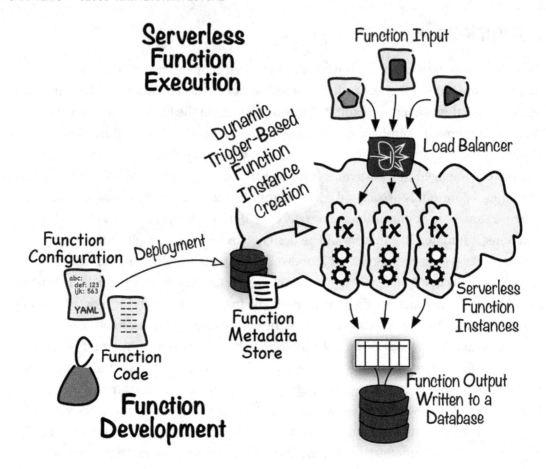

Figure 9-4. *Serverless*

Serverless is not limited to cloud computing. As a matter of fact, there are frameworks that let you operate a serverless platform on your local server or development machine. The same framework can be then used by a managed cloud-based serverless platform. In this way, you can implement and test a function locally, before pushing it to the compliant serverless platform in the cloud. This is exactly how we are going to work in this chapter. First, you need to set up a client machine for serverless development.

Developer VM

I have prepared infrastructure code to provision a new Ubuntu-based compute instance and a subnet required later for Oracle Functions. Please navigate to the chapter09/1-infrastructure directory, as shown in the following:

```
$ cd ~/git/oci-book/chapter09/1-infrastructure
$ find . \( -name "*.tf" -o -name "*.yaml" \) | sort
./devmachine/cloud-init/ubuntu.config.yaml
./devmachine/compute.tf
./devmachine/vars.tf
./devmachine/vcn.tf
./functions/vars.tf
./functions/vcn.tf
./modules.tf
./provider.tf
./vars.tf
./vcn.tf
```

The devmachine module contains the cloud resource definitions required by the compute instance that will be used for function development. The functions module is much simpler and is basically used to create one private subnet with a dedicated security list as well as routing table. This subnet will let us control the networking context in which Oracle Functions will be executed. We will discuss it later, but let's save some time and get it provisioned together with the compute instance for function development. I am not going to discuss each of these files because we covered analogous infrastructure code files in earlier chapters. Like always, please set the relevant environment variables expected by Terraform.

```
$ source ~/tfvars.env.sh
```

Next, initialize and provision the infrastructure.

```
$ terraform init
...
Terraform has been successfully initialized!
$ terraform apply
...
```

```
Plan: 10 to add, 0 to change, 0 to destroy.

Do you want to perform these actions?
  Enter a value: yes
...
Apply complete! Resources: 10 added, 0 changed, 0 destroyed.
Outputs:
dev_machine_image_name = Canonical-Ubuntu-18.04-2019.08.14-0
dev_machine_public_ip = 130.61.88.227
functions_subnet_ocid = ocid1.subnet.oc1....
```

From now on, in the course of this chapter, we are going to work mainly on this compute instance. You will be executing a lot of commands on the cloud-based instance. These commands will be prefixed with the [ubuntu@dev-vm] command prompt. You can verify the instance is running in the OCI Console, as shown in Figure 9-5.

	dev-vm		**Shape:** VM.Standard2.1	**Region:** eu-frankfurt-1
	OCID: ...nra33a Show Copy			**Availability Domain:** feDV:EU-FRANKFURT-1-AD-1
RUNNING				**Fault Domain:** FAULT-DOMAIN-1

Figure 9-5. *Compute instance for function development*

Let's go back to the terminal. Terraform outputs three values. We will need two of them throughout this chapter, namely, the public IP of the compute instance for functions development and the OCID of the subnet. You do not have to note the output values. We will be using the terraform output command to read them on the fly from the state file. The compute instance is based on an operating system image with Ubuntu. The infrastructure code uses cloud-init to install some additional packages required for the exercises including Docker CE as the most notable one.

Note   As you recall, cloud-init executes asynchronously. You may need to wait a minute or two before the machine is really ready. If you connect before cloud-init has completed, you will have to reconnect afterward to get the docker commands to work for the ubuntu user without the preceding sudo.

Please connect to the instance and execute the `cat` command, as shown in the following, until you see the `DEV machine is running` entry in the `/var/log/syslog` file.

```
$ DEV_MACHINE_IP=`terraform output dev_machine_public_ip`
$ ssh -i ~/.ssh/oci_id_rsa ubuntu@$DEV_MACHINE_IP
Welcome to Ubuntu 18.04.3 LTS (GNU/Linux 4.15.0-1021-oracle x86_64)

[ubuntu@dev-vm]$ sudo cat /var/log/syslog | grep "DEV machine"
Sep 14 12:30:53 dev-vm cloud-init[1799]: DEV machine is running, after
86.18 seconds
```

To validate that the instance has been provisioned as expected, please run one of the Docker commands such as `docker version`, `docker images`, or `docker ps`. There should be no errors. If you encounter errors because of insufficient privileges, you may need to exit and reconnect to the compute instance.

Note   There is nothing against using your local computer for function development instead of the newly provisioned cloud-based compute instance, but, depending on your system, you may need to adapt a bit of the commands I am using in this chapter.

As soon as the compute instance for function development is running as expected, we are ready to proceed.

Fn Project

Serverless functions execute on *serverless platforms* that isolate function developers from the underlying infrastructure and provide all the required function lifecycle services. CNCF lists a couple of serverless platforms as a part of its cloud-native landscape. One of them is Fn Project. Fn Project is a container-based serverless platform that supports multiple programming languages including Golang, Java, and Python. The project was open sourced in 2017 and can be found on GitHub at `https://github.com/fnproject`, as shown in Figure 9-6.

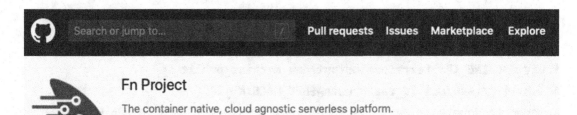

Figure 9-6. *Fn Project on GitHub*

We are going to implement two simple functions in Python and run them initially on a local Fn Project installation. Later, you will take one of them and deploy it with no code changes to Oracle Functions, which is a managed function-as-a-service platform on Oracle Cloud.

Installation and Configuration

First, make sure you are still connected to the newly provisioned compute instance. To install Fn Project, you just need to execute this neat one-liner:

```
[ubuntu@dev-vm]$ curl -LSs https://raw.githubusercontent.com/fnproject/cli/
                 master/install | sh
fn version 0.5.86
```

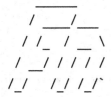

```
[ubuntu@dev-vm]$ fn version
Client version is latest version: 0.5.86
Server version:  ?
```

The Fn Project client binary fn has been installed, and the ~/.fn directory tree for client configuration files have been initialized. To proceed with local development and testing, we need to start a local Fn server. To do so, you will use the fn start command.

The local Fn server is implemented as a Docker container. The command will download the newest container image and start the Fn server container.

```
[ubuntu@dev-vm]$ fn start -d
[1] 4971
Unable to find image 'fnproject/fnserver:latest' locally
latest: Pulling from fnproject/fnserver
...
Status: Downloaded newer image for fnproject/fnserver:latest
```

We used the -d flag (the d stands for detached mode) to execute the local Fn server container in the background. This will allow us to continue working in the same Terminal session.

The container-based server architecture makes Fn Project an ideal candidate for building serverless platforms simply because it can run anywhere as a container. Let's see its image and the container.

```
[ubuntu@dev-vm]$ docker images
REPOSITORY            TAG      IMAGE ID       CREATED        SIZE
fnproject/fnserver   latest   e63938b4a8e1   12 days ago   161MB
[ubuntu@dev-vm]$ docker ps
IMAGE                      PORTS                      NAMES
fnproject/fnserver:latest  2375/tcp,*:8080->8080/tcp  fnserver
```

To see the Fn server logs at any time, you can apply the docker logs command.

```
[ubuntu@dev-vm]$ docker logs fnserver
time="2019-09-16T17:04:43Z" level=info msg="Registering data store provider 'sql'"
time="2019-09-16T17:04:43Z" level=info msg="Connecting to DB"
url="sqlite3:///app/data/fn.db"
...
time="2019-09-16T17:04:43Z" level=info msg="Fn serving on `:8080`"
type=full version=0.3.731
```

The fnserver container is created from the fnproject/fnserver image. The fnserver performs all the metadata as well as lifecycle management tasks for functions. Fn Project functions are deployed individually as separate container images. When triggered, the fnserver instantiates a function-specific container based on a particular function-specific image to handle the function call. If there are parallel function calls, the Fn server may decide to create more containers for the same function. Function metadata, on the other hand, in the case of a local Fn Project installation, is stored in the local filesystem using a file-based, embeddable relational database called SQLite. The default SQLite file location is .fn/data/fn.db. If you really are curious, you can access this function metadata database file using the sqlite3 client. This will make sense only after we have defined and deployed some functions. At the moment, our local SQLite-based function metadata database is still empty. Looking further, the connectivity-related client-side configuration is stored in the form of configuration files called *contexts*. The fn client will use dedicated contexts for each Fn Project platform you are working with, no matter if the platform is local, on-premise, or cloud-based. The context files will be stored in the .fn/contexts directory in the form of YAML files.

```
/home/ubuntu/.fn/
├── config.yaml
├── contexts
│    └── default.yaml
├── data
│    └── fn.db
└── iofs
```

Let's use the fn tool to list all the contexts.

```
[ubuntu@dev-vm]$ fn list contexts
CURRENT NAME.    PROVIDER  API URL.                    REGISTRY
        Default  default   http://localhost:8080
```

Because this is a new local Fn Project installation, there is only one, actually still incomplete and nonfunctional, context called the default context. Before we move on and add any missing configuration to allow local function development, I would like you to understand the three important pieces of information defined by an Fn client context. These are the following:

- Fn Project server API endpoint of the target platform

- Container registry to store function-specific images

- Provider that defines a set of properties for the target platform

The client is able to interact with multiple Fn Project platforms. At any given moment, however, the client works with a single platform, the one defined by the current context. To set the current context, you use the fn use context command.

```
[ubuntu@dev-vm]$ fn use context default
Now using context: default
```

As I mentioned a few moments ago, function instances are executed as containers that are based on function-specific images. You use the fn client to deploy a function. What does it mean to deploy a function in a container-based serverless environment? The *function deployment* involves building and pushing a new function-specific container image to a container image registry. The registry is defined by the current context. For local development, it is sufficient to store images on the local machine. To do so, we will use the --local option while executing the fn deploy command. Images will be prefixed with the name set for the registry in the current contexts. Let's use localdev as the name. To update the current context, please use the fn update context command like this:

```
[ubuntu@dev-vm]$ fn update context registry localdev
Current context updated registry with localdev
[ubuntu@dev-vm]$ fn list contexts
CURRENT NAME      PROVIDER    API URL               REGISTRY
    *   default   default     http://localhost:8080  localdev
```

We can move into developing and deploying a first function.

Your First Function

Serverless *functions* are meant to be stateless and perform one, relatively short task. Fn Project is able to run functions implemented in various programming languages. At the time of writing, these are Java, Golang, Python, JavaScript (with Node.js), Ruby, and C# (using .NET Core). You do not need to install any development tools for these languages. The code will execute within function-specific containers. In addition to using Terraform for the infrastructure code, this book is Python-oriented. To stay consistent with the rest of code examples, we will be using Python for function development. Later, after completing the exercises from this chapter, feel free to play with other languages. For now, let's use the fn init command to bootstrap a Python-based function stub like this:

```
[ubuntu@dev-vm]$ fn init --runtime python blankfn
Creating function at: ./blankfn
Function boilerplate generated.
func.yaml created.

[ubuntu@dev-vm]$ tree blankfn/
blankfn/
├── func.py
├── func.yaml
└── requirements.txt
```

The fn init command was executed with the --runtime python option. As a result, the func.py function stub has been created and uses Python as the programming language. In addition, the command creates the func.yaml function configuration file shown in Listing 9-1.

Listing 9-1. blankfn/func.yaml

```
schema_version: 20180708
name: blankfn
version: 0.0.1
runtime: python
entrypoint: /python/bin/fdk /function/func.py handler
memory: 256
```

The function configuration file can be used to fine-tune the function build process and execution characteristics such as allocated memory or maximum time the function is allowed to run. A couple of properties are used while building the function-specific container image. For example, it is possible to adjust the base image for the function.

In the previous chapters, we already worked with the requirements.txt file. This file is used to provide a list of Python packages your function is dependent on. You denote which Python packages your function requires, and the pip tool installs them as a new layer to the function-specific container image. Listing 9-2 presents the requirements. txt file created inside the function directory. Our function stub references only the fdk

Python package. The fdk package is the function developer kit for Python maintained by Fn Project. It is primarily needed to handle the input and output of the function. If you ever need any additional Python packages to implement a bit more sophisticated functions, this will be the file to add them.

Listing 9-2. blankfn/requirements.txt

```
fdk
```

The cloud-init configuration, which is processed on the first boot of our compute instance, fetches a trivial function code file called blankfn. The code is downloaded from the code repository associated with the book and placed in the ~/functions directory. Let's replace the function stub created by the fn init command with the blankfn.py file like this:

```
[ubuntu@dev-vm]$ cp ~/functions/blankfn.py ~/blankfn/func.py
```

Listing 9-3 presents the code for that function.

Listing 9-3. blankfn/func.py

```python
import io
import json

from fdk import response

def handler(ctx, data: io.BytesIO=None):
    res_str = json.dumps({"message": "blank message"})
    headers_dict={"Content-Type": "application/json"}
    rsp = response.Response(ctx, response_data=res_str, headers=headers_dict)
    return rsp
```

The blankfn function always returns a static text. I have created this function to provide you with the easiest Python-based Fn Project development experience. Generally speaking, your role as a function developer is to implement the function handler. If you look at the code presented in Listing 9-3, you will see that the function handler returns an fdk.response.Response object fed with the response_data string that holds a JSON objects with a meaningless test message. Additionally, the function handler code sets the headers dictionary set in the HTTP header. By default, if no trigger is explicitly stated in the function's configuration file, the HTTP trigger is applied, and we should treat the output as an HTTP response.

Before we build the function-specific container image, we have to create an application. An application is merely a logical construct. You use the fn create app command to register a new application in the Fn server pointed at with the current context, which is, in our case, the local Fn server running as the fnserver container. We will use blankapp for the new application and register it like this:

```
[ubuntu@dev-vm]$ fn create app blankapp
Successfully created app:  blankapp
[ubuntu@dev-vm]$ fn list apps
NAME.      ID
blankapp   01DMQZJPDDNG8G00GZJ0000006
```

The fn list apps command shows the newly registered application. We are ready to build and deploy the function. To do so, enter the blankfn function directory and run the fn deploy command like this:

```
[ubuntu@dev-vm]$ cd blankfn
[ubuntu@dev-vm]$ fn --verbose deploy --app blankapp --local
Deploying blankfn to app: blankapp
Bumped to version 0.0.2
Building image localdev/blankfn:0.0.2
FN_REGISTRY:  localdev
Current Context:  default
...
Successfully built 29e36845273a
Successfully tagged localdev/blankfn:0.0.2

Updating function blankfn using image localdev/blankfn:0.0.2...
Successfully created function: blankfn with localdev/blankfn:0.0.2
```

The fn deploy command reads the func.yaml function configuration file it finds in the current directory to create the function-specific container image. The file that stores the function code and the corresponding requirements.txt file are added to the container image. Using the --local option stores the image on the client machine. If you had left it out, the fn client would have attempted to push the image to the localdev repository on Docker Hub, which is not our intention here. The --verbose option lets us see the output from the image build. This is an ordinary docker build output enriched with some side operations from the fn client. All in all, the function is ready. Let's inspect the function metadata to confirm that everything went fine. To do so, use the fn list functions command.

```
[ubuntu@dev-vm]$ fn list functions blankapp
NAME     IMAGE                  ID
blankfn  localdev/blankfn:0.0.2  01DMQZNA73NG8G00GZJ0000007
```

At the moment, the blankapp application references one function called blankfn. Function instances will be created as containers based on the localdev/blankfn:0.0.2 container image. You can see the image like this:

```
[ubuntu@dev-vm]$ docker images | grep blank
localdev/blankfn   0.0.2   e3cdfd6089b4   2 minutes ago   344MB
```

At the moment, there is only the local fnserver container running, as shown by the following docker ps command:

```
[ubuntu@dev-vm]$ docker ps --format '{{.Names}} [{{.Image}}] {{.Status}}'
fnserver [fnproject/fnserver:latest] Up 4 minutes
```

Let me repeat: function instances will be created as separate containers. The local fnserver coordinates function containers, which are created on the fly when functions are triggered. Equipped with that knowledge, you should know what to expect. This is how you make your first serverless function call using the fn invoke command:

```
[ubuntu@dev-vm]$ fn invoke blankapp blankfn
{"message": "blank message"}
```

That is it. Just like that. You could say the response came from nowhere. If you are fast enough and execute the docker ps command again, you will spot a new container that is based on the local/blankfn:0.0.2 image.

```
[ubuntu@dev-vm]$ docker ps --format '{{.Names}} [{{.Image}}] {{.Status}}'
01D...00C  [local/blankfn:0.0.2]        Up 2 seconds (Paused)
fnserver   [fnproject/fnserver:latest]  Up 22 hours
```

This function-specific container instance was created to serve the function call. If no further function calls arrive, the container will disappear after 30 seconds. You can use the watch docker ps command to observe that behavior. This interval can be extended in the function configuration file.

Another interesting experiment is to send two function calls at once.

```
[ubuntu@dev-vm]$ fn invoke blankapp blankfn &
[1] 2903
[ubuntu@dev-vm]$ fn invoke blankapp blankfn &
[2] 2972
```

Listing the containers will show that this time there were two function-specific containers created.

```
[ubuntu@dev-vm]$ docker ps --format '{{.Names}} [{{.Image}}] {{.Status}}'
01D...00H [local/blankfn:0.0.2] Up Less than a second (Paused)
01D...00F [local/blankfn:0.0.2] Up 1 second (Paused)
fnserver [fnproject/fnserver:latest] Up 22 hours
```

This was a simple way to prove that the serverless platform is natively scalable.

If we were to briefly summarize the serverless function development process for Fn Project functions, these would be the steps to follow:

1.   Create a project stub.

2.   Implement the function handler.

3.   Adjust and optionally extend the function configuration file.

4.   Deploy the function.

The function deployment leads to two state changes in the Fn platform backend:

1.   The function metadata is placed on the Fn server.

2.   The function-specific container image is pushed to the container image registry.

Every time the function trigger is fired, the Fn server creates or unpauses an existing function-specific container to handle the request. The entire process from development to execution is conceptually illustrated in Figure 9-7.

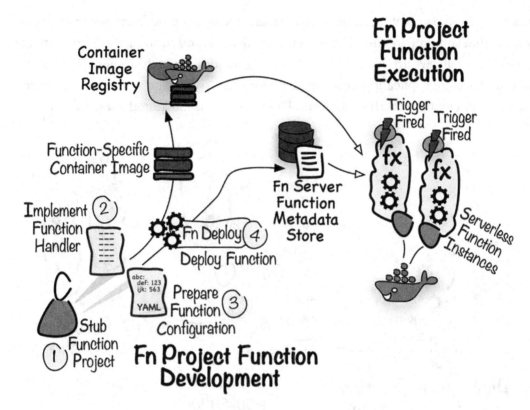

Figure 9-7. *Fn Project function development and execution*

Now, we are going to create a bit more meaningful function than the blankfn that had no applicable purpose at all.

UUID Function

After reading the previous chapters, you are now familiar with the UUID generation function. First, you deployed it as a systemd service on a Linux-based compute instance. This was the exercise included in the second chapter. Next, you containerized this application and deployed it inside a Kubernetes pod on a cluster instance of Oracle Kubernetes Engine. This was the exercise in Chapter 8. Now, we are going to use the most lightweight deployment model for the UUID generation logic and run it as a serverless function. As stateless, short-lasting, and specialized logic, this is a perfect candidate to become a serverless function. At this point, it is worth mentioning that what I've just described is an excellent example of the way software evolves nowadays. At the beginning, we dealt with a dedicated compute instance where the application lifecycle was bound to the operating system service managed by systemd. Next, we were able to remove that coupling by containerizing the application and running it on the container platform. Finally, we arrive at the most lightweight mode for such simple, specialized, and short-lasting application logic and use serverless to delegate all function lifecycle management to the serverless platform. This evolution is illustrated in Figure 9-8.

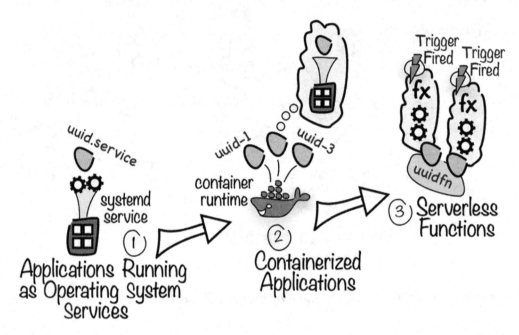

Figure 9-8. UUID function deployment model evolution

Let's create a new function stub in a similar way as we did it before. This time, we are using uuidfn for the function name.

```
[ubuntu@dev-vm]$ cd
[ubuntu@dev-vm]$ fn init --runtime python uuidfn
Creating function at: ./uuidfn
Function boilerplate generated.
func.yaml created.
```

Again, issue the following command to replace the function stub with the function code I already prepared for you while writing this book:

```
[ubuntu@dev-vm]$ cp ~/functions/uuidfn.py ~/uuidfn/func.py
```

Listing 9-4 shows the UUID generation function code.

Listing 9-4. uuidfn/func.py

```python
import io
import json
import uuid

from fdk import response

def handler(ctx, data: io.BytesIO=None):
    res_dict = {}
    try:
        # Generate UUID
        res_dict["generator_uuid"] = str(uuid.uuid4())
        # Intercept input and prepare optional response part
        if data is not None:
            data_bytes = data.getvalue()
            if len(data_bytes)>0:
                data_json = json.loads(data_bytes)
                res_dict["generator_client"] = data_json.get("client_name")
    except (Exception, ValueError) as ex:
        res_dict["message"] = str(ex)

    headers_dict={"Content-Type": "application/json"}
    res_str = json.dumps(res_dict)
    rsp = response.Response(ctx, response_data=res_str, headers=headers_dict)
    return rsp
```

Contrary to the blankfn function, uuidfn does parse the input provided in the form of the data object of the io.ByteIO type. In addition to generating the UUID using the uuid.uuid4() method, we are processing the input. If there is no input, we return just the newly generated UUID string in JSON format as the generator_uuid object. If there is input, we expect it to be in JSON format and parse it to extract the client_name object to return it as the generator_client object in the JSON response. Providing an invalid input will throw an error, which we eventually capture, and return an error message in the response.

Please create a new application called uuidapp.

```
[ubuntu@dev-vm]$ fn create app uuidapp
Successfully created app:   uuidapp
```

At this stage, we should see two applications.

```
[ubuntu@dev-vm]$ fn list apps
NAME        ID
blankapp    01DMQZJPDDNG8G00GZJ0000006
uuidapp     01DMR30A3TNG8G00GZJ000000P
```

To build the function-specific container image, we need to enter the function directory and invoke the fn deploy command.

```
[ubuntu@dev-vm]$ cd ~/uuidfn
```

```
[ubuntu@dev-vm]$ fn --verbose deploy --app uuidapp --local
Deploying uuidfn to app: uuidapp
Bumped to version 0.0.2
Building image localdev/uuidfn:0.0.2
FN_REGISTRY:   localdev
Current Context:   default
...
Successfully built 569fa6a25ec1
Successfully tagged localdev/uuidfn:0.0.2

Updating function uuidfn using image localdev/uuidfn:0.0.2...
Successfully created function: uuidfn with localdev/uuidfn:0.0.2
```

To test the function, use the fn invoke command with the proper application and function names as arguments.

```
[ubuntu@dev-vm]$ fn invoke uuidapp uuidfn
{"generator_uuid": "f03abce5-3615-4994-9680-157b057198d3"}
```

The function returns JSON with a newly generated UUID.

You can provide the input to the function like this:

```
[ubuntu@dev-vm]$ echo -n '{ "client_name": "some_app"  }' | fn invoke
uuidapp uuidfn --content-type application/json
{"generator_uuid": "3298bb2e-9cd5-476b-83b6-f4343d7c8522", "generator_
client": "some_app"}
```

As you can see, this time, there are two JSON objects in the response. The generator_client object in the response stores the client_name value that was passed as the input.

The function is implicitly defined to be launched on an HTTP trigger. This means that there must be an HTTP endpoint associated with the function. As a matter of fact, an HTTP endpoint is something that we need to make the majority of our serverless functions useful in production. You can see the function-specific endpoint using the fn inspect function command.

```
[ubuntu@dev-vm]$ fn inspect function uuidapp uuidfn
{
        "annotations": {
                "fnproject.io/fn/invokeEndpoint": "http://localhost:8080/
                invoke/01DMR7VTNHNG8GO0GZJ0000009"
        },
        "app_id": "01DMR7TZRFNG8GO0GZJ0000008",
        "created_at": "2019-09-14T15:57:01.489Z",
        "id": "01DMR7VTNHNG8GO0GZJ0000009",
        "idle_timeout": 30,
        "image": "localdev/uuidfn:0.0.2",
        "memory": 256,
        "name": "uuidfn",
        "timeout": 30,
        "updated_at": "2019-09-14T15:57:01.489Z"
}
```

In addition add the endpoint, the command reveals other information such as the maximum function execution time, the idle timeout, and the container image the function uses. The proper combination of the `fn inspect function` command and the jq command will let you extract the endpoint and save it in the shell variable.

```
[ubuntu@dev-vm]$ FN_INVOKE_ENDPOINT=`fn inspect function uuidapp uuidfn |
                 jq -r '.annotations."fnproject.io/fn/invokeEndpoint"'`
```

Next, we can use the well-known `curl` tool to send an HTTP request to the endpoint.

```
[ubuntu@dev-vm]$ curl -X "POST" -H "Content-Type: application/json"
                 $FN_INVOKE_ENDPOINT
{"generator_uuid": "84eb8921-663f-4469-ad3b-fa34813da319"}
```

This section gave you a brief introduction to Fn Project and locally executed serverless functions in practice. There are many other aspects I have not covered such as packaging a number of functions in a single application, unit testing, and pushing the function image to other registries. More importantly, serverless does give a no-infrastructure impression for serverless function developers only. If you want to operate a serverless platform, especially in production, there are various crucial tasks to plan for and carry out. These tasks refer to security, load balancing, and worker node pool management. Fn Project documents these instructions on its web page. All these things are beyond the scope of this book.

Instead of operating a serverless platform on your own, you can rely on a managed cloud-based serverless platform. In the next section, we will be working with Oracle Functions, which is a managed serverless platform built with Fn Project on Oracle Cloud Infrastructure.

Oracle Functions

Fn Project serves as a foundation for *Oracle Functions*, a function-as-a-service platform available on Oracle Cloud. In the previous section, you worked with a local Fn server. Now, you can take the same function code and deploy it to Oracle Functions. By doing that, you will let your function run in an Oracle Cloud region of your choice. There is no need to configure any compute instances or container orchestration clusters like we did in the previous chapters to run applications. The underlying compute resources are fully managed by Oracle Functions in the background. Function instances are dynamically created in response to the function *triggers*. As you would probably expect, the most basic trigger type is an HTTP request. Every Fn Project function that gets deployed to Oracle Functions will be given a dedicated HTTP-based *function endpoint*. Requests sent to that endpoint must be properly signed to pass through the authentication and authorization done with OCI Identity and Access Management. When they succeed, Oracle Functions reads function metadata and, based on that information, creates a function-specific container to process the request. Other types of triggers are various *events* that take place within Oracle Cloud. For instance, a newly created object in a particular object storage bucket may generate an event that is propagated by the Oracle Events service to a selected function in the Oracle Functions service. You will learn about that in the second part of this chapter. Both triggers, HTTP-based and event-based, and the general way Oracle Functions work are illustrated in Figure 9-9.

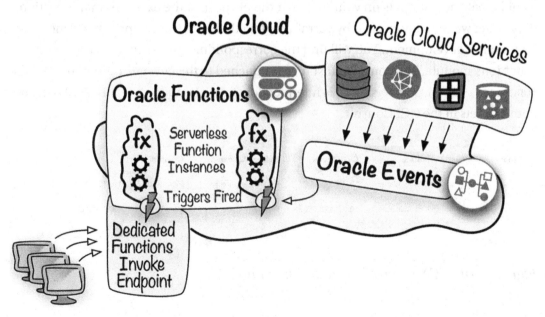

Figure 9-9. *Oracle Functions*

It is recommended that function-specific container images are stored in Oracle Container Image Registry (OCIR) in the same region as the Oracle Functions endpoint you want your serverless function to run on. You already worked with OCIR in the previous chapter. At that time, Oracle Kubernetes Engine was pulling images from OCIR to create containers in Kubernetes pods. This time, the images will be dynamically pulled by Oracle Functions to create short-living function containers that handle function calls as they arrive.

OCI Networking and Policies

Before you start using Oracle Functions, there are two additional infrastructure-related, initial-setup selections to be made.

- Choose virtual cloud network subnets for serverless functions.

- Create the required IAM policy statements for the FaaS service.

Why do we even talk about virtual networks if there should be no infrastructure management needed for Oracle Functions? When you define an Fn application, which groups serverless functions, and intend this application to run on Oracle Functions, you have to denote the VCN subnet. The VCN subnet must contain at least 32 available IP addresses in its IP range and should rely on stateless security rules. It is absolutely fine to use various VCNs for running serverless functions. You will learn how to specify the VCN for an Oracle Functions application in one of the sections ahead. Normally, you would create new subnets on your own. For the purpose of the exercises in this section, the subnet was already created by Terraform, together with the compute machine for function development. You will find the corresponding infrastructure code in the `functions` module. The compute instance is attached to the `dev-net` public subnet. The `functions-subnet` private subnet is intended for Oracle Functions. Figure 9-10 presents both subnets in the OCI Console.

Name	State	CIDR Block	Subnet Access	Created	▾
dev-net	● Available	10.0.9.0/27	Public (Regional)	Mon, Sep 16, 2019, 3:51:18 PM UTC	⋮
functions-subnet	● Available	10.0.9.128/25	Private (Regional)	Mon, Sep 16, 2019, 3:51:18 PM UTC	⋮
				Showing 2 Items ‹ Page 1 ›	

Figure 9-10. *VCN subnet for Oracle Functions*

Oracle Functions is fully integrated with IAM. This fact impacts both sides of the service. Not only must Oracle Functions be granted the required access, but also function developers and function consumers must belong to the IAM groups that are referenced by the relevant IAM policy statements. Let's discuss this in a bit more structured way. First, the FaaS service, which represents Oracle Functions in IAM, must be allowed to do the following:

- To use virtual networks in the tenancy or selected compartments

- To read container image registry repositories in OCIR

These privileges are granted with the policy statements shown in Listing 9-5.

Listing 9-5. tenancy.functions.policy.json

```
[
  "allow service FaaS to use virtual-network-family in compartment
  Sandbox",
  "allow service FaaS to read repos in tenancy"
]
```

Second, to deploy and monitor their serverless functions, function owners have to belong to IAM groups that are allowed.

- To interact with the manage-level OCI APIs for the functions family

- To read the metrics

- To use the virtual networks

- To manage selected repositories in OCIR

The statements can be narrowed to selected compartments. In our case, we will let the members of the sandbox-users group deploy and monitor the functions in the Sandbox compartment only. Three of the required privileges are granted with the policy statements shown in Listing 9-6.

Listing 9-6. sandbox-users.functions.policy.json

```
[
  "allow group sandbox-users to manage functions-family in compartment
  Sandbox",
  "allow group sandbox-users to read metrics in compartment Sandbox",
  "allow group sandbox-users to use virtual-network-family in compartment
  Sandbox"
]
```

If you completed exercises from Chapter 8, the fourth remaining policy statement is already defined. It should be defined in the root compartment (on the tenancy level) in the policy called `tenancy-ocir-policy` and looks like this:

```
allow group sandbox-users to manage repos in tenancy where target.repo.name =
 /sandbox*/
```

Let's create the two new policies shown in Listings 9-5 and 9-6. To do so, go back to our local machine with the OCI CLI and execute the following commands:

```
$ cd ~/git/oci-book/chapter09/3-functions/policies
$ TENANCY_OCID=`cat ~/.oci/config | grep tenancy | sed 's/tenancy=//'`
$ echo $TENANCY_OCID
ocid1.tenancy.oc1..aa...3yymfa
$ oci iam policy create -c $TENANCY_OCID --name functions-policy
--description "FaaS Policy" --statements "file://tenancy.functions.policy.
json"
{
  "data": {
    ...
    "lifecycle-state": "ACTIVE",
    "name": "functions-policy",
    ...
}

$ oci iam policy create --name sandbox-users-functions-policy --description
"Functions-related policy for regular Sandbox users" --statements "file://
sandbox-users.functions.policy.json" --profile SANDBOX-ADMIN
```

```
{
  "data": {
      ...
    "lifecycle-state": "ACTIVE",
    "name": "sandbox-users-functions-policy",
      ...
}
```

We have prepared our tenancy for Oracle Functions. Now, let's move to the fn client and create a new context.

Client Setup

From a function developer's point of view, in terms of fn client configuration, we need to add a new Fn client context first. The Fn client context

- Uses the oracle provider

- Points to an Oracle Functions API endpoint

- Pushes function-specific container images to OCIR

Second, the Fn client context that uses the oracle provider must reference a profile stored in the existing OCI CLI configuration file. This is needed because Oracle Functions functions are integrated with IAM in Oracle Cloud. Function developers must have an identity of an existing Oracle Cloud user, for example, the sandbox-user user, to perform operations such as creating new applications or functions in Oracle Functions. As an analogy, you can recall the use of the OCI CLI. All CLI commands, or the underlying API calls to be more precise, are executed on behalf of an IAM user defined under a named profile in the OCI CLI configuration file.

To ease the development process, you can work with the local Fn server and Oracle Functions interchangeably. In this way, you will be able to develop and unit test your newly created functions locally and only then deploy them to Oracle Functions. To work like that, it is enough to switch between the contexts illustrated in Figure 9-11.

```
[ubuntu@dev-vm:~$ fn list contexts
CURRENT NAME                PROVIDER   API URL                                            REGISTRY
*       default             default    http://localhost:8080                              localdev
        sandbox-user-fra-oci oracle    https://functions.eu-frankfurt-1.oraclecloud.com   fra.ocir.io/jakobczyk/fn
```

Figure 9-11. *Fn Project contexts*

517

You know the theory now. It's time to make it real. Connect to the compute instance, and create a new context using the fn create context command with the --provider option set to oracle like this:

```
[ubuntu@dev-vm]$ fn create context sandbox-user-fra-oci --provider oracle
Successfully created context: sandbox-user-fra-oci
```

In the fn client configuration directory, there should be a new YAML file created.

```
/home/ubuntu/.fn/contexts/
├── default.yaml
└── sandbox-user-fra-oci.yaml
```

For the time being, this new context file is practically empty and definitely unusable. You have to add the following details to let the fn client properly work with Oracle Functions:

- Regional Oracle Functions API endpoint

- Regional Oracle Container Image Registry (OCIR) repository endpoint

- Fn Project oracle-provider-specific information:

  - Compartment OCID

  - Name of the OCI CLI configuration profile

The Oracle Functions API endpoint should be set in the following format:

```
https://functions.<region-name>.oraclecloud.com
```

The OCIR repository endpoint uses a format like this:

```
<region-code>.ocir.io/<tenancy-namespace>/<repository-name>
```

For example, if you are working in the Frankfurt region, you will use eu-frankfurt-1 as the region name and simply fra as the region code. You can find the list of other region names and their codes in the OCI documentation. To identify your *tenancy namespace*, you can use the following command:

```
$ oci os ns get --query 'data' --raw-output
jakobczyk
```

Now, reconnect to the compute instance, and add the aforementioned information by editing the context file.

```
$ ssh -i ~/.ssh/oci_id_rsa ubuntu@$DEV_MACHINE_IP

[ubuntu@dev-vm]$ vi ~/.fn/contexts/sandbox-user-fra-oci.yaml
```

You can start with the chapter09/3-functions/configuration/sandbox-user-fra-oci.yaml template file and edit it in a similar way, as shown in Listing 9-7.

Listing 9-7. ~/.fn/contexts/sandbox-user-fra-oci.yaml

```
api-url: https://functions.eu-frankfurt-1.oraclecloud.com
registry: fra.ocir.io/jakobczyk/sandbox-fn
provider: oracle
oracle.compartment-id: ocid1.compartment.oc1..aa...gzwhsa
oracle.profile: SANDBOX-USER
```

Do not forget to use the OCID of the Sandbox compartment as the value to the oracle.compartment-id field. The context file mentions an OCI CLI configuration profile name as a value of the oracle.profile property. Until now, you have used the OCI CLI on your local development machine. This chapter assumes you are using a cloud-based compute instance for function development. The new fn client context that is supposed to let the fn client work with Oracle Functions references a particular OCI CLI configuration profile. Because of that, we need to create the config file on the compute instance as well. There is no need to install the CLI, however. It is all about the configuration in this case. Let's create the config in the default path. In this way, the fn client will be able to pick it up.

```
[ubuntu@dev-vm]$ mkdir ~/.oci
[ubuntu@dev-vm]$ vi ~/.oci/config
```

Copy only the SANDBOX-USER profile from the OCI CLI config file you are using on your original development machine. Do not forget to add the tenancy OCID and the region name, as shown in Listing 9-8.

Listing 9-8. ~/.oci/config (on Compute Instance for Function Development)

[SANDBOX-USER]
```
tenancy=ocid1.tenancy.oc1..aa...3yymfa
region=eu-frankfurt-1
user=ocid1.user.oc1..aa...dzqpxa
fingerprint=ad:82:99:bf:93:27:63:7b:35:75:f5:27:d4:95:78:86
key_file=~/.apikeys/api.sandbox-user.pem
pass_phrase=secret
```

The IAM identity for the fn client is derived from the information stored in the configuration file. More precisely, the fn client reads only the information under the referenced profile. To interact with Oracle Functions, the oracle provider used by the fn client will eventually translate the fn client commands to OCI API requests, as illustrated in Figure 9-12. This information is required to properly sign these requests; otherwise, the OCI API would reject them.

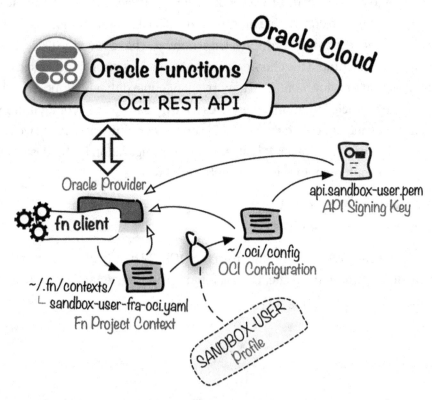

Figure 9-12. *Fn client configuration for Oracle Functions*

The last missing element in the client configuration is the private key used to sign API requests. To simplify the exercise, we are going to reuse the same API signing key that we use for standard OCI CLI calls. Back on your original development machine with the OCI CLI, you can use the scp tool to upload the API signing key to the compute instance for function development like this:

```
$ cd ~/git/oci-book/chapter09/1-infrastructure
$ DEV_MACHINE_IP=`terraform output dev_machine_public_ip`
$ scp -i ~/.ssh/oci_id_rsa ~/.apikeys/api.sandbox-user.pem ubuntu@$DEV_
MACHINE_IP:/home/ubuntu
api.sandbox-user.pem          100% 1766     57.2KB/s   00:00
```

Next, connect to the compute instance and move the API signing key to the directory that is declared in the configuration file.

```
[ubuntu@dev-vm]$ mkdir ~/.apikeys
[ubuntu@dev-vm]$ mv ~/api.sandbox-user.pem ~/.apikeys/api.sandbox-user.pem
[ubuntu@dev-vm]$ chmod go-rwx ~/.apikeys/api.sandbox-user.pem
```

All in all, the three files required by the fn client to work with Oracle Functions are on our dev-vm compute instance.

```
/home/ubuntu
├── .apikeys
│     └── api.sandbox-user.pem
...
├── .fn
│     ├── config.yaml
│     ├── contexts
│     │     ├── default.yaml
│     │     └── sandbox-user-fra-oci.yaml
...
├── .oci
│     └── config
```

Now, set the new context to be the current one by using the fn use context command, and, in the subsequent step, issue the fn list apps command to test the connectivity to Oracle Functions.

```
[ubuntu@dev-vm]$ fn use context sandbox-user-fra-oci
Now using context: sandbox-user-fra-oci
[ubuntu@dev-vm]$ fn list apps
No apps found
```

This time, there are no Fn applications shown, but this is exactly what we were expecting. At the moment, there are no functions deployed to the cloud yet. The old applications, namely, blankapp and uuidapp, did not disappear but are still registered on our local Fn server. They are not listed in the fn list app output at the moment simply because, this time, we are interacting with Oracle Functions and not with the local Fn server. If you change the context back to the local one, you should see these two apps again. Anyway, let's continue using the new context that makes our fn client commands work with Oracle Functions.

Deploying the UUID Function

We are ready to deploy the same uuidfn function code, which we tested locally on our machine, to Oracle Functions. First, we will register a new application for Oracle Functions. As part of this activity, you must denote the VCN subnet, which will be used by Oracle Functions to dynamically plug transient function-specific containers for that particular function into OCI networking. As you recall, the infrastructure code described at the beginning of this chapter has created a subnet that can be referenced by the application we are about to register.

Tip   It is absolutely fine to use different VCN subnets for your Oracle Functions applications. Just make sure they fulfill the recommendations such as the number of available private IP addresses or the use of stateless security rules.

Back on your local developer machine, use the terraform output command to get the OCID of this subnet.

```
$ cd ~/git/oci-book/chapter09/1-infrastructure
$ terraform output functions_subnet_ocid
ocid1.subnet.oc1.eu-frankfurt-1.aa...sp2ufa
```

Next, connect to the dev-vm compute instance, store the subnet OCID in a shell variable, and issue the fn create app command with the oracle.com/oci/subnetIds annotation set to the value of the variable. The commands you execute will look similar to these:

```
[ubuntu@dev-vm]$ FN_SUBNET_ID=ocid1.subnet.oc1.eu-frankfurt-1.aa...sp2ufa
[ubuntu@dev-vm]$ fn create app uuidcloudapp --annotation oracle.com/oci/
                subnetIds="[\"$FN_SUBNET_ID\"]"
Successfully created app:  uuidcloudapp
```

At this stage, if you want, you can verify in the OCI Console that the application has been indeed created. To do so, do the following:

1. Go to Menu ➤ Developer Services ➤ Functions.

2. Make sure that the Sandbox compartment is selected.

You should be able to see an entry in the list of applications, as shown in Figure 9-13.

Figure 9-13. *Viewing functions in the OCI Console*

An application alone does not provide us with any kind of services. It is just a logical grouping of functions. It is recommended to store function-specific container images in the Oracle Container Image Registry (OCIR) in the same region in which we want the function instances to serve trigger-based function calls. Before we deploy a function, we need to log in to the OCIR. I have already covered this task in the previous chapter, so let me assume you are already familiar with this task. Just remember to use the tenancy namespace and not the OCID. Similarly, use the region code such as fra instead of a region name. Just make sure you find the authentication token for the sandbox-user you used in the previous chapter or create a new one. You will need it as a password to sign in to the OCIR. As soon as you are ready, please adjust the values of the OCI_TENANCY_ NAMESPACE variable and the OCIR_REGION variable in the following code snippet and execute the docker login command:

```
[ubuntu@dev-vm]$ OCI_TENANCY_NAMESPACE=jakobczyk
[ubuntu@dev-vm]$ OCIR_REGION=fra
[ubuntu@dev-vm]$ OCI_USER=sandbox-user
[ubuntu@dev-vm]$ docker login -u $OCI_TENANCY_NAMESPACE/$OCI_USER $OCIR_
                 REGION.ocir.io
Password: <PUT-HERE-AUTH-TOKEN>
Login Succeeded
```

To deploy the uuidfn function, you can use the fn deploy command. You will be required to reference the application that you created in Oracle Functions only a few moments ago. Furthermore, we have not changed anything in the function code; therefore, the --no-bump parameter will disable the default behavior of incrementing the image version. All in all, these are the commands to execute:

```
[ubuntu@dev-vm]$ cd ~/uuidfn
[ubuntu@dev-vm]$ fn -v deploy --app uuidcloudapp --no-bump
Deploying uuidfn to app: uuidcloudapp
Building image fra.ocir.io/jakobczyk/sandbox-fn/uuidfn:0.0.2
FN_REGISTRY:  fra.ocir.io/jakobczyk/sandbox-fn
Current Context:  sandbox-user-fra-oci
...
Successfully built 258fbf5d0629
Successfully tagged fra.ocir.io/jakobczyk/sandbox-fn/uuidfn:0.0.2

Parts:  [fra.ocir.io jakobczyk sandbox-fn uuidfn:0.0.2]
Pushing fra.ocir.io/jakobczyk/sandbox-fn/uuidfn:0.0.2 to docker registry...
The push refers to repository [fra.ocir.io/jakobczyk/sandbox-fn/uuidfn]
...
Updating function uuidfn using image fra.ocir.io/jakobczyk/sandbox-fn/
uuidfn:0.0.2...
Successfully created function: uuidfn with fra.ocir.io/jakobczyk/sandbox-
fn/uuidfn:0.0.2
```

As you can see in the build output, the image was properly tagged and pushed to the OCIR in the region of our choice. Finally, the function creation was reported to be successful.

Back in the OCI Console, if you click the `uuidcloudapp` application name, you will be taken to the more detailed view and should see the newly created function in the list, as presented in Figure 9-14.

Resources

Functions

Functions	Create Function			
Metrics				
Network	Name	Image	Image Digest	OCID
Configuration	uuidfn	fra.ocir.io/jakobczyk/sandbox-fn/uuidfn:0.0.2	...90cdad87 Show Copy	...sggsoxsq Sh

Figure 9-14. *Viewing functions in the OCI Console*

Similarly, the function-specific container image will be listed in the OCIR view in the OCI Console, as shown in Figure 9-15. If you completed the exercises from the previous chapter, you may also see another image in the `sandbox/uuid` repository.

Figure 9-15. *Viewing the function-specific container image in the OCI Console*

Function testing can be done in the same way as before. We will use the `fn invoke` command that takes the application name and the function name as parameters. For a simple smoke test, let's issue a single-function call.

```
[ubuntu@dev-vm]$ fn invoke uuidcloudapp uuidfn
{"generator_uuid": "921d63a9-f20c-44c0-97e6-5ff875fb1b39"}
```

As you recall, the uuidfn function parses the input in a search for a top-level client_name JSON object that is used to set the value for the generator_client object in the JSON response. To test the input data processing, issue the following command:

```
[ubuntu@dev-vm]$ echo -n '{ "client_name": "some_app"  }' | fn invoke
                    uuidcloudapp uuidfn --content-type application/json
{"generator_uuid": "7685e3b8-5db7-49e1-8f1b-1561e16e9103", "generator_client": "some_app"}
```

Let's trigger the function two more times.

```
[ubuntu@dev-vm]$ fn invoke uuidcloudapp uuidfn
{"generator_uuid": "9b4ad9bb-7d20-47d9-a53c-b3eb61854e4d"}
[ubuntu@dev-vm]$ fn invoke uuidcloudapp uuidfn
{"generator_uuid": "b60fa2f0-3778-4a6a-9932-90d852a78ab1"}
```

Now, in the OCI Console, you can go to the Metrics tab in the Resources menu and inspect various metrics for this particular function. For example, one of the simplest but still very interesting metrics is the number of function invocations. It looks like what is shown in Figure 9-16.

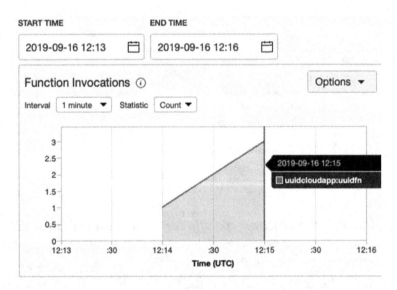

Figure 9-16. *Viewing function invocations in the OCI Console*

A moment ago, to conduct function tests, we employed the fn invoke command. Normally, function consumers such as regular client applications or other systems will use the function's HTTP *invoke endpoint* instead, either directly or, in the case of more sophisticated solutions, hidden behind an enterprise-grade API management platform. You can discover the endpoint in the OCI Console as well as by using the fn inspect function command like this:

```
[ubuntu@dev-vm]$ fn inspect function uuidcloudapp uuidfn | jq -r
             '.annotations."fnproject.io/fn/invokeEndpoint"'
https://wup2t5yjlba.eu-frankfurt-1.functions.oci.oraclecloud.com/20181201/
functions/ocid1.fnfunc.oc1.eu-frankfurt-1.aa...gsoxsq/actions/invoke
```

Function calls in the form of HTTP requests are sent to the invoke endpoints and must be signed using the correct Oracle Cloud Infrastructure signature. In other words, Oracle Functions accepts external requests only when they are sent by known tenancy users no matter if they are human or system users. If you send an unsigned request to a function invoke endpoint, you will receive the following response:

```
{"code":"NotAuthenticated","message":"Not authenticated"}
```

To send signed requests, you will need to map your function consumers to existing Oracle Cloud users, which would require some careful planning. Furthermore, to expose more user-friendly REST APIs to the function consumers, you would probably deploy some kind of a gateway or even employ an aforementioned fully fledged API management platform. Let me skip this topic here because it relates to aspects that are beyond the scope of this book. In the meantime, let's move on to discuss the second type of function triggers, namely, events.

Events

What is an *event*? Usually, we use this word to refer to an occurrence of a particular situation of some kind. Let me take a business process as an example. An incoming e-mail to a particular inbound e-mail address could be treated as an event and effectively trigger a new business process case in the system. Similarly, a new file uploaded to the object storage bucket could also be treated as an event and trigger a serverless function instance to process the newly uploaded data. In both cases, events need to carry some additional, but preferably limited and lightweight, context information. In the latter example, an event would carry at least the name of the new object as well as the name of the bucket. In this way, the corresponding serverless function would be able to recognize the object whose creation caused the event. Events are crucial in contemporary software architectures and provide the foundation for different application integration patterns such as fire-and-forget, publish-subscribe, or store-and-forward. Event-driven application architectures, where components communicate by exchanging events, benefit from loose coupling, the key enabler for independent component development and lifecycle management that eventually boosts productivity.

As an exercise, we are going to deploy and test a serverless function that processes newly created objects that appear in a particular object storage bucket. Function instances will be triggered by object creation events in that particular bucket. When a new object is uploaded to the `reports` bucket, an instance of the `reportingfn` serverless function will be created and provided with the event context information that carries the object name. Next, the function will verify whether the name of the object uses the `.raw.csv` suffix. If yes, the function will read the contents of the object, perform a simple data aggregation in memory, and create a new object to store the results of the operation. The new object will be suffixed with the `.processed.csv` suffix. Figure 9-17 illustrates the data processing logic stated earlier.

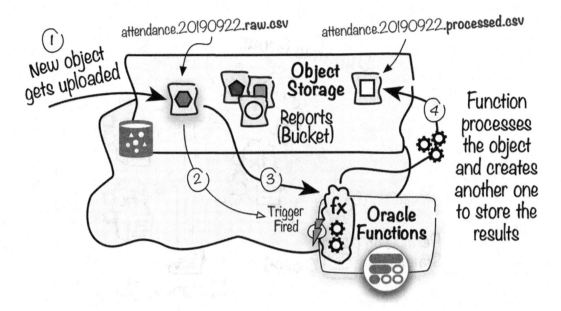

Figure 9-17. *Event-based function calls*

Functions and Object Storage

Functions running on the Oracle Functions platform access object storage in a similar way as traditional applications running on compute instances do. Just like with compute instances, the OCI API calls originating from functions are done on behalf of the instance principals you got familiar with in Chapter 5. As you recall, instance principals can be included in dynamic groups. To include all dynamically created function instances of a particular function in a dynamic group, you can design the dynamic group matching rule simply to include all functions with a specific tag key. Finally, you create IAM policy statements to allow dynamic group members to access particular APIs and interact with OCI resources such as object storage buckets and objects. Figure 9-18 illustrates these access-related aspects.

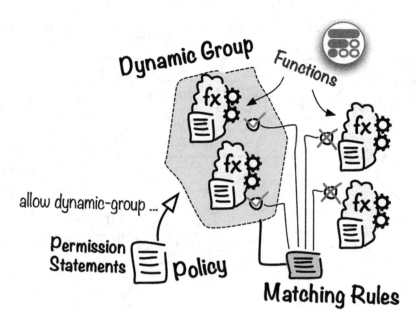

Figure 9-18. *Dynamic groups and functions*

Now, you should understand the goal for this section as well as the mechanisms we are about to employ to allow function instances to interact with object storage APIs and effectively process objects.

Preparing Infrastructure

As a first step, we have to prepare a new object storage bucket. Disconnect from the compute instance for function development, and execute the `oci os bucket create` command on your development machine with the OCI CLI.

```
$ oci os bucket create --name reports --profile SANDBOX-ADMIN
{
  "data": {
    ...
    "name": "reports",
    "public-access-type": "NoPublicAccess",
    "storage-tier": "Standard",
    ...
  }
}
```

Next, we are going to let the sandbox-user manage all the objects in the newly created reports bucket. To do so, use oci iam policy create to create the new policy, as shown in the following:

```
$ cd ~/git/oci-book/chapter09/4-events/policies
$ oci iam policy create --name sandbox-users-storage-reports-policy
--statements file://sandbox-users.policies.storage-reports.json
--description "Storage-related (reports) policy for regular Sandbox users"
--profile SANDBOX-ADMIN
{
  "data": {
    ...
    "name": "sandbox-users-storage-reports-policy",
    "description": "Storage-related (reports) policy for regular Sandbox
    users",
    "lifecycle-state": "ACTIVE",
    ...
  }
}
```

You should be already familiar with the read buckets and manage objects policy verbs. You applied them for another bucket, back in Chapter 5. Listing 9-9 shows the statements for the reports bucket.

Listing 9-9. sandbox-users.policies.storage-reports.json

```
[
"allow group sandbox-users to read buckets in compartment Sandbox where
target.bucket.name='reports'",
"allow group sandbox-users to manage objects in compartment Sandbox where
target.bucket.name='reports'"
]
```

Now, upload the first test file:

```
$ cd ~/git/oci-book/chapter09/4-events/reports
$ oci os object put -bn blueprints --file customer_attendance.20190922.raw.
csv --profile SANDBOX-USER
Uploading object  [#################################]  100%
```

As a part of the Chapter 5 exercise, we created the `test-projects` tag namespace. Within this already existing tag namespace, let's prepare a new tag key called `reports`. We will use this key later to tag the object-processing function. Now, use `oci iam tag-namespace list` with the following query to read the OCID of the tag namespace. Next, use this OCID in the `oci iam tag create` command that creates the new tag key.

```
$ TAG_NAMESPACE_OCID=`oci iam tag-namespace list --query
"data[?name=='test-projects'] | [0].id" --raw-output`
$ echo $TAG_NAMESPACE_OCID
ocid1.tagnamespace.oc1..
aaaaaaaac7doek63tcdgt3xqtjfx5is3twcpdsszaqsmxlurkwx7pu6qu2eq
$ oci iam tag create --tag-namespace-id $TAG_NAMESPACE_OCID --name reports
--description "Reports project" --profile SANDBOX-ADMIN
{
   "data": {
     ...
     "tag-namespace-name": "test-projects",
     "name": "reports",
     "description": "Reports project",
     "is-cost-tracking": false,
     "lifecycle-state": "ACTIVE",
     ...
   }
}
```

We are going to use the following dynamic group matching rule that includes all functions tagged with the `test-projects.reports` tag key:

```
ALL {resource.type = 'fnfunc', tag.test-projects.reports.value}
```

Now, use `oci iam dynamic-group create` to create the dynamic group.

```
$ echo $TENANCY_OCID
ocid1.tenancy.oc1..aa...3yymfa
$ MATCHING_RULE="ALL { resource.type = 'fnfunc', tag.test-projects.reports.
value = 'r1' }"
$ oci iam dynamic-group create --name reporting-functions --description
"Functions related to the reporting project" --matching-rule "$MATCHING_
RULE" -c $TENANCY_OCID
```

```
{
  "data": {
    ...
    "name": "reporting-functions",
    "description": "Functions related to the reporting project",
    "matching-rule": "tag.test-projects.reports.value",
    "lifecycle-state": "ACTIVE",
    ...
  }
}
```

The last step is to add a new IAM policy statement to permit the members of that dynamic group to manage objects stored in the reports bucket in the Sandbox compartment. Listing 9-10 shows this IAM policy statement.

Listing 9-10. functions.policies.storage-reports.json

```
[
"allow dynamic-group reporting-functions to manage objects in compartment
Sandbox where target.bucket.name='reports'"
]
```

These commands will get the new IAM policy in place:

```
$ cd ~/git/oci-book/chapter09/4-events/policies
$ oci iam policy create --name functions-storage-reports-policy --statements
file://functions.policies.storage-reports.json --description "Storage-
related (reports) policy for tagged functions" --profile SANDBOX-ADMIN
{
  "data": {
    ...
    "name": "functions-storage-reports-policy",
    "description": "Storage-related (reports) policy for tagged functions",
    "lifecycle-state": "ACTIVE",
    ...
  }
}
```

In a few steps, we prepared the object storage access control configuration for the function instances attached to the test-projects.reports defined tag.

Deploying Function

The new function will be called reportingfn and use a Python-based implementation. Now, connect to the compute instance for function development, and use the fn init command to create the function stub.

```
[ubuntu@dev-vm]$ cd ~
[ubuntu@dev-vm]$ fn init --runtime python reportingfn
Creating function at: ./reportingfn
Function boilerplate generated.
func.yaml created.
```

Like before, cloud-init has already downloaded the function code and placed it in the functions directory. Copy the code to the function stub.

```
[ubuntu@dev-vm]$ cp ~/functions/reportingfn.py ~/reportingfn/func.py
```

The function uses the OCI SDK for Python to interact with OCI object storage. This implies a dependency to the oci module and forces us to amend the requirements.txt file. Only in this way will the function-specific image ship with the oci module. You can use a simple echo command to append the oci name to the requirements.txt file.

```
[ubuntu@dev-vm]$ echo -ne "\noci" >> ~/reportingfn/requirements.txt
[ubuntu@dev-vm]$ cat ~/reportingfn/requirements.txt
fdk
oci
```

The reportingfn.py code is slightly larger than two functions we worked before. Listing 9-11 shows the most important parts of the handler function.

Listing 9-11. reportingfn.py Function

```
...
def handler(ctx, data: io.BytesIO=None):
...
  bucket_name = "reports"
  object_name = extract_object_name(data)
```

```
...
  signer = oci.auth.signers.get_resource_principals_signer()
  client = oci.object_storage.ObjectStorageClient(
    config={},
    signer=signer)
  storage_namespace = client.get_namespace().data

  object_content_str = load_object_content(
    client, storage_namespace,
    bucket_name, object_name)
  city_attendance_str = process_city_attendance_data(
    object_content_str)

  processed_object_name = object_name.replace(
    '.raw.csv','.processed.csv')
  put_response = put_city_attendance_object(
    client, storage_namespace, bucket_name,
    processed_object_name, city_attendance_str)
...
```

The function is implemented to interact solely with the reports bucket. It reads the newly created object name from the input data. This logic is provided in the extract_object_name function we will cover in a few moments. Next, the OCI SDK functions are called to obtain an ObjectStorageClient object and get the object storage namespace to work with. In subsequent steps, the function loads the contents (load_object_content function) of the newly created object, processes that data (process_city_attendance function), and finally persists the results of the processing in another new object (put_city_attendance_data function) with the same name as the original object but a different suffix (.processed.csv). You will find these functions in the same reportingfn.py file. As long as you know the basics of Python, the code should be relatively easy to understand.

Based on the current Fn client context, deploying a function to Oracle Functions will push the image to OCIR. Although we already executed the docker login command, you may need to repeat this operation. If this is the case, these are the commands to execute:

```
[ubuntu@dev-vm]$ OCI_TENANCY_NAMESPACE=jakobczyk
[ubuntu@dev-vm]$ OCIR_REGION=fra
[ubuntu@dev-vm]$ OCI_USER=sandbox-user
[ubuntu@dev-vm]$ docker login -u $OCI_TENANCY_NAMESPACE/$OCI_USER $OCIR_
                REGION.ocir.io
Password: <PUT-HERE-AUTH-TOKEN>
Login Succeeded
```

Now, make sure FN_SUBNET_ID is properly defined and use fn create app to create the application.

```
[ubuntu@dev-vm]$ FN_SUBNET_ID=ocid1.subnet.oc1.eu-frankfurt-1.aa...sp2ufa
[ubuntu@dev-vm]$ fn create app reportingapp --annotation oracle.com/oci/
                subnetIds="[\"$FN_SUBNET_ID\"]"
Successfully created app:  reportingapp
```

We are ready to deploy the function.

```
[ubuntu@dev-vm]$ cd reportingfn/
[ubuntu@dev-vm]$ fn -v deploy --app reportingapp
...
Updating function reportingfn using image fra.ocir.io/jakobczyk/sandbox-fn/
reportingfn:0.0.2...
Successfully created function: reportingfn with fra.ocir.io/jakobczyk/
sandbox-fn/reportingfn:0.0.2
```

Figure 9-19 shows the newly deployed function in the OCI Console. Similarly, Figure 9-20 presents the function-specific container image in OCIR.

Functions

Name	Image	Image Digest	OCID	Invoke endpoint
Create Function				
reportingfn	fra.ocir.io/jakobczyk/sandbox-fn/reportingfn:0.0.2	...24dcfda8 Show Copy	...qdj3lfqa Show Copy	...loud.com Show Copy

Figure 9-19. *Viewing the function in the OCI Console*

Figure 9-20. *Viewing a function-specific container image in the OCI Console*

We mustn't forget about the tag we need to attach to the function. This can be done with the OCI CLI. First, you use the `oci fn application list` command with a tailored JMESPath query to obtain the OCID of the Oracle Functions application. Next, you use the `oci fn function list` command to fetch the OCID of the function. Finally, you can use the `oci fn function update` command to attach the test-projects.reports-defined tag to the function.

```
$ FN_APP_OCID=`oci fn application list --query "data[?\"display-name\" ==
  'reportingapp'] | [0].id" --raw-output`
$ echo $FN_APP_OCID
ocid1.fnapp.oc1.eu-frankfurt-1.aa...spf2rq
$ FN_FUN_OCID=`oci fn function list --application-id $FN_APP_OCID --query
  "data[?\"display-name\" == 'reportingfn'] | [0].id" --raw-output`
$ echo $FN_FUN_OCID
ocid1.fnfunc.oc1.eu-frankfurt-1.aa...j3lfqa
$ oci fn function update --function-id $FN_FUN_OCID --defined-tags '{
  "test-projects": {"reports": "r1"} }'
WARNING: Updates to config and freeform-tags and defined-tags will replace
any existing values. Are you sure you want to continue? [y/N]: y
{
  "data": {
    ...
    "defined-tags": {
      "test-projects": {
        "reports": "r1"
      }
```

```
    },
    "display-name": "reportingfn",
    "freeform-tags": {},
    ...
    "lifecycle-state": "ACTIVE",
    ...
  }
}
```

If you want, follow these steps in the OCI Console to visually confirm that the tag has been properly attached to the function:

1. Go to Menu ➤ Developer Services ➤ Functions.

2. Make sure that the Sandbox compartment is selected.

3. Click the name of the reportingapp application.

4. Click the name of the reportingfn function.

5. Click the Tag tab.

You should see the new defined tag that exists in the test-projects tag namespaces and uses the reports key, as presented in Figure 9-21.

Figure 9-21. *Viewing a defined tag key attached to the function*

The function has been deployed to Oracle Functions. Before we test it, let's discuss the way it is triggered.

Events As Function Triggers

The reportingfn function will be triggered by the creation of a new object in the reports bucket. The event must carry some basic information about the context. A function instance must be informed about the name of the object to process. Let's come up with a simple example for the event payload. You could imagine that the event context information is stored in a JSON format that looks like the sample shown in Listing 9-12.

Listing 9-12. event.mock.json

```json
{
  "eventType": "createobject",
  "source": "ObjectStorage",
  "eventTime": "2019-09-23T10:49:00.195Z",
  "data": {
    "resourceName": "customer_attendance.20190922.raw.csv",
  }
}
```

The function code would then parse the incoming event payload and extract the resourceName element that carries the name of the newly created object. The reportingfn function uses the aforementioned extract_object_name function, which is presented in Listing 9-13.

Listing 9-13. reportingfn.py: extract_object_name Function

```python
...
def extract_object_name(data: io.BytesIO):
    data_bytes = data.getvalue()
    data_json = json.loads(data_bytes)
    object_name = data_json['data']['resourceName']
    return object_name
...
```

Coming back to the test object we uploaded a few moments ago, let's check its name in the OCI Console. The object uses the `customer_attendance.20190922.raw.csv` name, as shown in Figure 9-22.

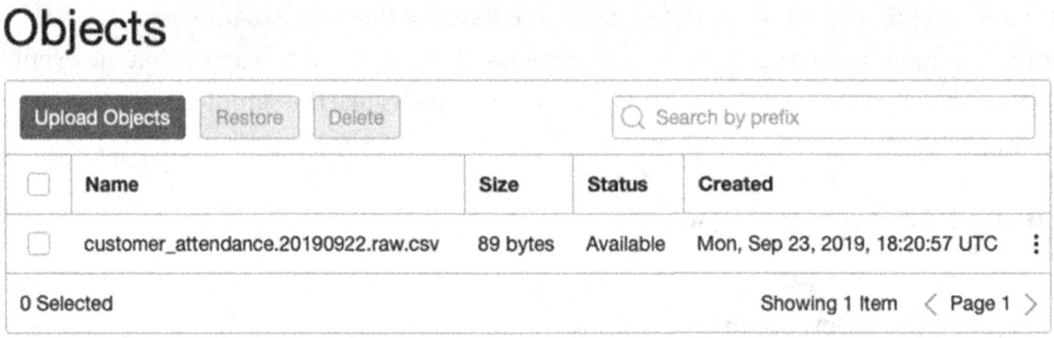

Objects

	Name	Size	Status	Created	
☐	customer_attendance.20190922.raw.csv	89 bytes	Available	Mon, Sep 23, 2019, 18:20:57 UTC	⋮

Upload Objects Restore Delete 🔍 Search by prefix

0 Selected   Showing 1 Item   ‹ Page 1 ›

Figure 9-22. Viewing the raw data object in the OCI Console

In the home directory for the ubuntu user, on the compute instance for functions development, you can find the `~/event.mock.json` file. The file contains the event payload, as shown in Listing 9-13. The file was downloaded during the initial boot by cloud-init, in the same way as the files with function code for the three functions you deployed. To test the function, we will provide the contents of the file as the input stream to the function.

```
[ubuntu@dev-vm]$ cat ~/event.mock.json | fn invoke reportingapp reportingfn
                --content-type application/json
{"object_name": "customer_attendance.20190922.raw.csv", "processed_object_
name": "customer_attendance.20190922.processed.csv",
"result": "success"}
```

Now, if you look at the list of objects in the reports bucket in the OCI Console, you should soon see the new object, as shown in Figure 9-23. This new object was created by a dynamically generated function instance running on the Oracle Functions platform.

	Name	Size	Status	Created	
☐	customer_attendance.20190922.processed.csv	50 bytes	Available	Mon, Sep 23, 2019, 18:57:38 UTC	⋮
☐	customer_attendance.20190922.raw.csv	89 bytes	Available	Mon, Sep 23, 2019, 18:20:57 UTC	⋮

Figure 9-23. *Viewing the processed data object in the OCI Console*

All right, so far so good, but this is still not what we originally intended. Our goal is to get function instances triggered automatically, as soon as a new object appears in the bucket. It is time to cover another open source project that belongs to the CNCF project ecosystem.

CloudEvents

The CloudEvents project is one of the relatively new initiatives that operates under the umbrella of CNCF. The project's main goal is to provide the community with a unified specification that describes event data. Event-driven applications are not new, and there have been plenty of various structures used for events by different software components. When an event publisher emits events in a different format than the one expected by event consumers, this usually leads to a sometimes costly and in other cases just annoying need for an additional application integration effort. To alleviate that kind of pain, it has become clear that something as simple and rather limited in scope as event context information should be agreed on by the industry in the form of a joint effort. CloudEvents delivers a specification that describes event data. Furthermore, it is accompanied with reference implementations in various programming languages. You can find all of that on GitHub, as shown in Figure 9-24.

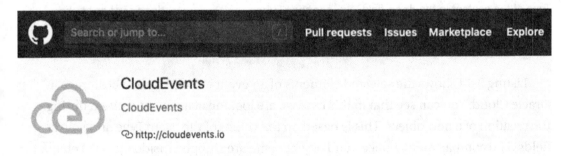

Figure 9-24. *CloudEvents project on GitHub*

The CloudEvents specification is lightweight in content and relatively quick to read. At the time of writing, there are three stable versions of the specification. It is highly probable that when you are reading this book, there are already newer versions available. Do not worry about that. To briefly discuss the specification, we will focus on version 0.1. The details will change in time, but the general rules remain. I have picked version 0.1 because it is still the current standard for Oracle Events you will learn about in the next sections.

At the heart of the CloudEvents specification (version 0.1), there are three sections.

- Terminology

- Type system

- Context attributes

The most interesting part are the *context attributes* that effectively define the event envelope or, in other words, basically the payload that carries the event context information. These are mainly metadata such as the type, source, and time of the event as well as event-specific data and their content-type. These attributes are listed in Table 9-1.

Table 9-1. *CloudEvents Context Attributes*

CloudEvents Version	0.1	0.3 / 1.0-rc1
Specification version in use	cloudEventsVersion	specversion
Type of the event	eventType	type
Version of the event type	eventTypeVersion	-
Event emitter	source	source
Unique event identifier	eventID	id
Event occurrence timestamp	eventTime	time
Type of the content in the data field	contentType	datacontenttype
Domain-specific data for an event	data	data

Listing 9-14 shows the selected elements of an event emitted by object storage in Oracle Cloud. You can see that in this case we are looking at an event emitted during the creation of a new object. This is based on the values of the eventType and source fields. The compartment, bucket, and object name are shipped inside the data element. The listing shows only the object name stored in the resourceName field. Many of other domain-specific event data were omitted for the brevity of the listing.

Listing 9-14. CloudEvent (Version 1)

```
{
  "eventType": "com.oraclecloud.objectstorage.createobject",
  "cloudEventsVersion": "0.1",
  "eventTypeVersion": "2.0",
  "source": "ObjectStorage",
  "eventTime": "2019-09-23T10:49:00.195Z",
  "contentType": "application/json",
  "data": {
    ...
    "resourceName": "customer_attendance.20190923.csv",
    ...
  },
  "eventID": "b163df45-de9c-9f01-2928-b0906cd8a3e4"
}
```

With this brief understanding of CloudEvents specification, we can move to the final section of this chapter.

Oracle Events

Selected services on Oracle Cloud can be configured to emit events. These events are compliant with the open source CloudEvents specification. At the time of writing, we are talking about version 0.1 of the specification. Oracle Events is used to connect the emitted events with other Oracle Cloud services that perform actions when particular events occur. For example, you could register a function that takes some action; as soon as the launch of a new compute instance completes, a database backup is created, a notification is received, or a new object is created in a particular bucket. You connect event emitters with services that take actions by defining the appropriate OracleEvents rules. A rule defines conditions and actions for the implemented event processing chain, as illustrated in Figure 9-25.

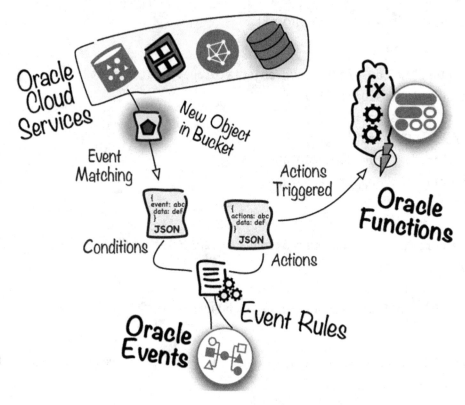

Figure 9-25. *Oracle Events*

Coming back to our exercises, first of all, we have to allow the Oracle Events service to call Oracle Functions so that we can trigger serverless functions defined in the Sandbox compartment when an event of a particular type occurs. Listing 9-15 presents the only IAM policy statement we need for that purpose.

Listing 9-15. cloudevents.policies.json

```
[
  "allow service cloudEvents to use functions-family in compartment
  Sandbox"
]
```

Now, use `oci iam policy create` to get this statement added.

```
$ cd ~/git/oci-book/chapter09/4-events/policies
$ oci iam policy create --name cloudevents-policy --statements file://
cloudevents.policies.json --description "Functions-related policy for
CloudEvents" --profile SANDBOX-ADMIN
{
  "data": {
    ...
    "name": "cloudevents-policy",
    "description": "Functions-related policy for CloudEvents",
    "lifecycle-state": "ACTIVE",
    ...
  }
}
```

We are about to create an Oracle Events rule that combines a condition that defines the kind of event to react to with an action. Listing 9-16 presents the condition we are going to use.

Listing 9-16. oracleevents.conditions.json

```
{
  "eventType": [ "com.oraclecloud.objectstorage.createobject" ],
  "data": {
    "compartmentName": ["Sandbox"],
    "additionalDetails": {
      "bucketName": ["reports"]
    }
  }
}
```

To put it simply, when a new object is created in the `reports` bucket inside the Sandbox compartment, the rule will perform the action defined, as shown in Listing 9-17.

Listing 9-17. oracleevents.actions.template.json

```
{
  "actions": [
      {
        "actionType": "FAAS",
        "description": "string",
        "functionId": "PUT_HERE_FUNCTION_ID",
        "isEnabled": true
      }
  ]
}
```

We will reference these files in a moment. In the meantime, there is still one important thing to be done. Some types of event emitters must be explicitly enabled. This is the case for events related to object storage objects. We need to enable emitting object events for the reports bucket. In the OCI Console, you can perform this task in the following way:

1. Go to Menu ➤ Object Storage ➤ Object Storage.

2. Make sure that the Sandbox compartment is selected.

3. Click the name of the reports bucket.

4. Click Edit next to Emit Object Events.

5. Check the Emit Object Events box, as shown in Figure 9-26.

6. Click Save Changes.

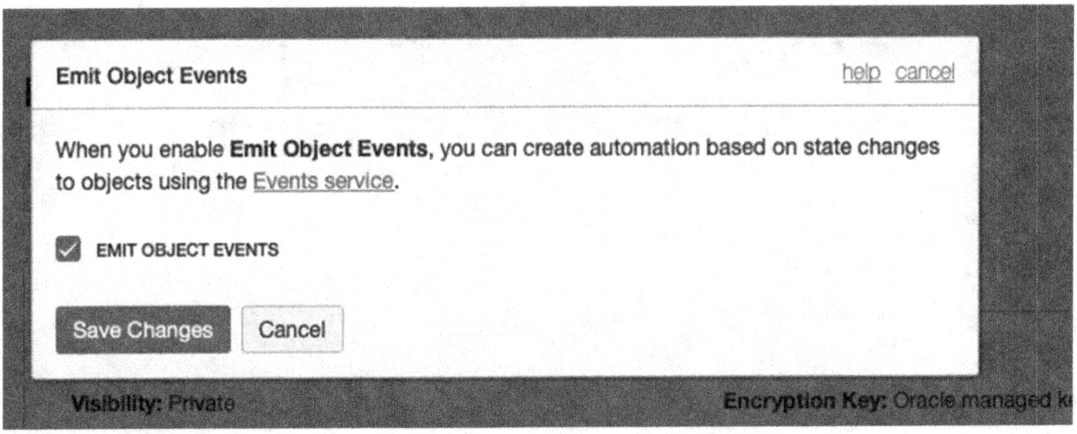

Figure 9-26. *Enabling event generation for the object in a bucket*

At this stage, we are ready to create a new Oracle Events rule that takes the conditions and action files you saw a moment ago. As shown in the following code snippet, you will serialize the contents of the conditions file and use the `sed` program to create the JSON file that includes the final action. We do it to prepare the input to the `oci events rule create` command. Be careful, the `FN_FUN_OCID` variable is still expected to be set. This is the code to execute:

```
$ cd ~/git/oci-book/chapter09/4-events/events
$ echo $FN_FUN_OCID
ocid1.fnfunc.oc1.eu-frankfurt-1.aa...j3lfqa
$ cat oracleevents.actions.template.json | sed -e "s/PUT_HERE_FUNCTION_
ID/$FN_FUN_OCID/g" > oracleevents.actions.json
$ SERIALIZED_CONDITIONS=`cat oracleevents.conditions.json | sed 's/"/\\"/g'
| sed 's/[[:space:]]//g' | tr -d '\n'`
$ echo $SERIALIZED_CONDITIONS
{"eventType":["com.oraclecloud.objectstorage.createobject"],"data":{"compar
tmentName":["Sandbox"],"additionalDetails":{"bucketName":["reports"]}}}
$ oci events rule create --display-name new-reports --is-enabled true
--condition $SERIALIZED_CONDITIONS --actions file://oracleevents.actions.
json
```

The rule has been created. If you want, you can always go to the OCI Console to view or optionally amend the Oracle Events rule, as shown in Figure 9-27.

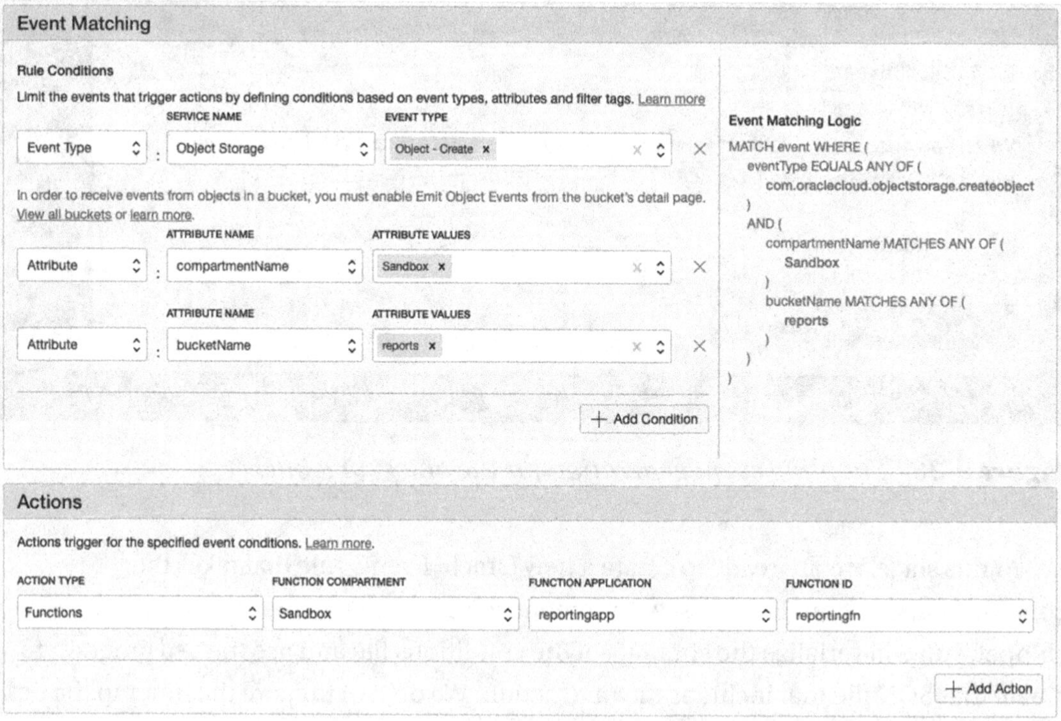

Event Matching

Rule Conditions

Limit the events that trigger actions by defining conditions based on event types, attributes and filter tags. Learn more

	SERVICE NAME	EVENT TYPE			Event Matching Logic
Event Type ⌄ :	Object Storage ⌄	Object - Create ✕	✕ ⌄	✕	MATCH event WHERE (

In order to receive events from objects in a bucket, you must enable Emit Object Events from the bucket's detail page. View all buckets or learn more.

```
MATCH event WHERE (
    eventType EQUALS ANY OF (
        com.oraclecloud.objectstorage.createobject
    )
    AND (
        compartmentName MATCHES ANY OF (
            Sandbox
        )
        bucketName MATCHES ANY OF (
            reports
        )
    )
)
```

	ATTRIBUTE NAME	ATTRIBUTE VALUES		
Attribute ⌄ :	compartmentName ⌄	Sandbox ✕	✕ ⌄	✕

	ATTRIBUTE NAME	ATTRIBUTE VALUES		
Attribute ⌄ :	bucketName ⌄	reports ✕	✕ ⌄	✕

＋ Add Condition

Actions

Actions trigger for the specified event conditions. Learn more.

ACTION TYPE	FUNCTION COMPARTMENT	FUNCTION APPLICATION	FUNCTION ID
Functions ⌄	Sandbox ⌄	reportingapp ⌄	reportingfn ⌄

＋ Add Action

Figure 9-27. *Viewing Oracle Events rule in the OCI Console*

To test whether the events emitted by object storage really trigger the reportingfn function deployed to Oracle Functions, put the two remaining test files in the reports bucket. You can do it with the oci os object put command like this:

```
$ cd ~/git/oci-book/chapter09/4-events/reports
$ oci os object put -bn reports --file customer_attendance.20190923.raw.csv
--profile SANDBOX-USER
Uploading object  [####################################]   100%
$ oci os object put -bn reports --file customer_attendance.20190924.raw.csv
--profile SANDBOX-USER
Uploading object  [####################################]   100%
```

After a while, you should see two more files appear in the same bucket, this time with the .processed.csv suffix, as shown in Figure 9-28.

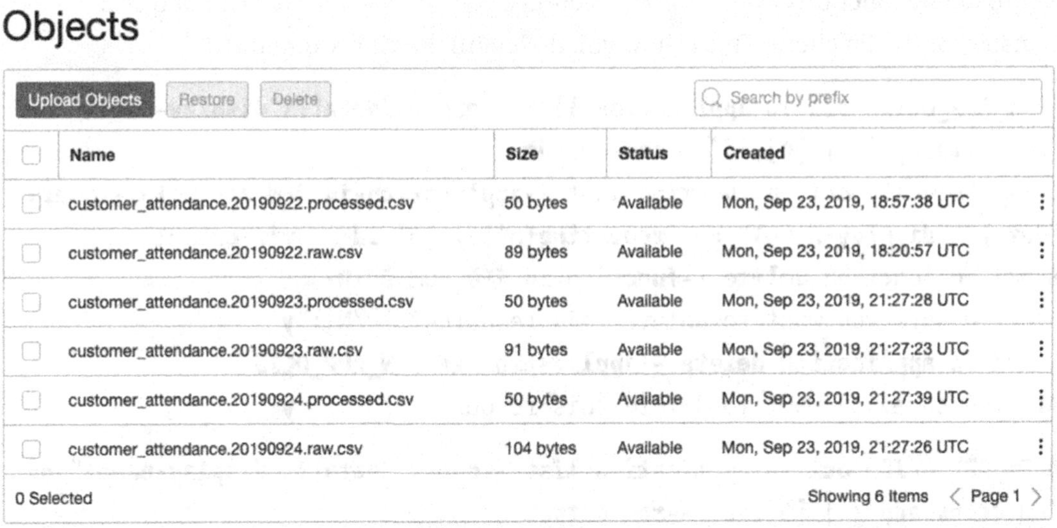

Objects

	Name	Size	Status	Created	
☐	customer_attendance.20190922.processed.csv	50 bytes	Available	Mon, Sep 23, 2019, 18:57:38 UTC	⋮
☐	customer_attendance.20190922.raw.csv	89 bytes	Available	Mon, Sep 23, 2019, 18:20:57 UTC	⋮
☐	customer_attendance.20190923.processed.csv	50 bytes	Available	Mon, Sep 23, 2019, 21:27:28 UTC	⋮
☐	customer_attendance.20190923.raw.csv	91 bytes	Available	Mon, Sep 23, 2019, 21:27:23 UTC	⋮
☐	customer_attendance.20190924.processed.csv	50 bytes	Available	Mon, Sep 23, 2019, 21:27:39 UTC	⋮
☐	customer_attendance.20190924.raw.csv	104 bytes	Available	Mon, Sep 23, 2019, 21:27:26 UTC	⋮

Upload Objects | Restore | Delete   Search by prefix

0 Selected   Showing 6 Items   ‹ Page 1 ›

Figure 9-28. *Viewing processed files in the OCI Console*

Feel free to explore the contents of these files, compare `.raw.csv` to `.processed.csv`, and see the Python code that was used to implement the function.

> **Tip** If nothing happens and there are no `.processed.csv` files, you probably skipped the step in which you enable emitting events on the bucket. Delete the two `.raw.csv` files, enable emitting events on the `reports` bucket, and reupload the `.raw.csv` files.

Cleanup

After having completed the exercises, you can terminate the cloud resources created in this chapter. First, let's remove the bucket with its contents.

```
$ oci os object bulk-delete -bn reports
There are 6 object in the bucket. Are you sure you want to delete them?
[y/N]: y
$ oci os bucket delete -bn reports
Are you sure you want to delete this resource? [y/N]: y
```

To delete functions from Oracle Functions, you can use the OCI CLI, the OCI Console, or the Fn client. This is how you do it with the CLI commands:

```
$ FN_APP_OCID=`oci fn application list --query "data[?\"display-name\" ==
'reportingapp'] | [0].id" --raw-output`
$ FN_FUN_OCID=`oci fn function list --application-id $FN_APP_OCID --query
"data[?\"display-name\" == 'reportingfn'] | [0].id" --raw-output`
$ oci fn function delete --function-id $FN_FUN_OCID
Are you sure you want to delete this resource? [y/N]: y
$ oci fn application delete --application-id $FN_APP_OCID
Are you sure you want to delete this resource? [y/N]: y

$ FN_APP_OCID=`oci fn application list --query "data[?\"display-name\" ==
'uuidcloudapp'] | [0].id" --raw-output`
$ FN_FUN_OCID=`oci fn function list --application-id $FN_APP_OCID --query
"data[?\"display-name\" == 'uuidfn'] | [0].id" --raw-output`
$ oci fn function delete --function-id $FN_FUN_OCID
Are you sure you want to delete this resource? [y/N]: y
$ oci fn application delete --application-id $FN_APP_OCID
Are you sure you want to delete this resource? [y/N]: y
```

To delete the Oracle Events rule, use the oci events rule delete CLI command like this:

```
$ EVENTRULE_OCID=`oci events rule list --query "data[?\"display-name\" ==
'new-reports'] | [0].id" --raw-output`
$ oci events rule delete --rule-id $EVENTRULE_OCID
Are you sure you want to delete this resource? [y/N]: y
```

To terminate dev-vm and any related networking resources, you have to issue the terraform destroy command in the infrastructure project directory like this:

```
$ source ~/tfvars.env.sh
$ cd ~/git
$ cd oci-book/chapter09/1-infrastructure
$ terraform destroy -auto-approve
```

This is the last chapter of this book. In the course of the book, we created a number of supplementary tenancy-level cloud resources such as users, groups, IAM policies, dynamic groups, and the Sandbox compartment. These resources do not incur costs, at least at the time of writing. Feel free to remove them, unless you want to use them to explore further the Oracle Cloud Infrastructure features on your own. To find all the cloud resources that exist at a given time in your tenancy or in a particular compartment, you can use the Search function covered in Chapter 4 or the Compartment Explorer available in the OCI Console under Menu ➤ Governance ➤ Compartment Explorer.

Summary

Cloud-native architecture, even though still immature, is slowly becoming a reality. In this chapter, you learned about the emerging CNCF ecosystem and its origins that are based on open source, cloud computing, and containerization. Next, you got familiar with the concepts of serverless functions and applied this knowledge with the open source, container-based serverless framework called Fn Project. Then, you worked with Oracle Functions, which is a managed platform on Oracle Cloud that allows you to execute Fn Project functions. Going further, you understood how functions deployed to Oracle Functions can interact with other Oracle Cloud services. As an example, you learned how to read and write to object storage. Finally, you were introduced to the CNCF-hosted CloudEvents project, which is working on defining an industry-wide event specification, and saw how to leverage event-based function triggers by configuring Oracle Events rules.

This chapter concludes *Practical Oracle Cloud Infrastructure*. I am happy that I could be your guide. Good luck in the future!

Index

A

ACID properties, 351

ADW instance,
 terminate, 408

ADW, load data
 database credential
  Auth Token, 369, 370
  CLI command, 370
  DBMS_CLOUD.COPY_DATA
   procedure, 370
  DBMS_CLOUD.DROP_
   CREDENTIAL procedure, 371
  roadadw-load, 372, 373
  SANDBOX_USER, 370
 DBMS_CLOUD.COPY_DATA
  procedure, 368
 Star schema (*see* Star schema)

American National Institute of
 Standards and
 Technology (NIST), 3

Ansible, 345

Application design
 API response, 53
 components sketch, 53
 JSON format, 56
 round robin policy, 53
 service implementation, 55
 UUID, 52
 WSGI, 54

Application Programming
 Interface (API), 10
 REST, 11–14
 SOAP, 10, 11

Architectural patterns, 279

AttachVnic API, 282

Auditing
 event search, 223, 224
 OCI Console, 222

Automatic Workload
 Repository (AWR), 391

Autonomous Database (ADB), 35,
 347–408

Autonomous Data Warehouse (ADW), 32
 ADMIN, 358
 backups, 362, 363
 CLI command, 359, 360
 database creation, 358
 geographical region, 356
 instances, OCI Console, 361, 362
 OCI Console, 357
 OLAP systems, 356
 SANDBOX-ADMIN CLI, 358
 schema, 363
 Service Console, 360, 361

Autonomous Transaction
 Processing (ATP), 32, 355

Autoscale, 92, 320

Availability domain (AD), 34, 41, 53

© Michał Tomasz Jakóbczyk 2020
M. T. Jakóbczyk, *Practical Oracle Cloud Infrastructure*, https://doi.org/10.1007/978-1-4842-5506-3

V

VCN peering
  cross-tenancy, 307
  dedicated networking
    compartment, 306, 307
  local, 304
  LPG, 304, 305
  point-to-point, 306
  remote, 307
  route rules, 305
--verbose option, 504
Vertical scaling, 8, 20, 308
Virtual cloud network (VCN), 15, 22, 35,
    56, 66–67, 135, 145
  AD-specific subnets, 280
  subnet types, 280
Virtual hardware resources, 2

Virtual machines (VM), 2, 8, 14, 16, 27, 28,
    36, 39, 41, 44, 58, 59, 118, 410, 412
Virtual networking, 22, 117, 279–280

W, X

Warm backup, 20
Web Application Description Language
    (WADL), 12
Web Application Firewall (WAF), 22, 24, 38
Web Services Description Language
    (WSDL), 10
WORKDIR instruction, 425

Y, Z

your pay as you go (PAYG), 44

Printed in the United States
By Bookmasters